Unsung Heroes Of Rock Guitar

Unsung Heroes Of Rock Guitar

Sterling C. Whitaker

2003

Unsung Heroes Of Rock Guitar

ACKNOWLEDGEMENTS

The author wishes to thank the following people for their assistance with *Unsung Heroes of Rock Guitar:* All of my interview subjects, without whom there could be no book. Bob Laul/Viceroy Music Group, Dave Mac/Guitar Recordings, Premier Talent Agency, Higher Octave Music, Shirley Greer and Laura Engel/Engel Entertainment, Gary Perel/GSRecords, Melinda Skinner, Paul Strathdee/Random Entertainment, Larry Mazer/Entertainment Services Unlimited, David Armas/Occasional Gentle Giant Newsletter, Ginger Greagor/Mercury Publicity, Lisa Janzen/Borman Entertainment, Tiffany/East End Management, Wendy Weisburg/IRS Records, Lynne DeVernardis/Hit & Run (US), Ann Lawler and John Arnison/Hit & Run (UK), Ray Daniels/SRO Management, Phil Ehart and Greg Roberts/Kansas, Jeff Davis/Intersound.

Thank$ for the money: Mark A$ton and Richard Lacy, Financier$ Extraordinaire

Special Thanks to: My family for their love and support (at times financial as well as emotional); Mom, Dad and Paula, Russell, Shantel, Donna, and my entire extended family as well. I wouldn't have made it this far without you. Stephen Frey, the only person in the world who could ever have been the other half of Beggarz Opera. Lisa Rose. Hammill B. Anderson (RIP) for his inspiration and years of friendship. The Neuwirth family. Nicholas Steinbach. Farmer Will. Roots of Consciousness members Bill Schuessler, Robert Stallings, Matt Miller, Jay Taylor and Geoff Logsdon. Greg Spiro, Jim Bowser and Chris Tsuboi for sparking my interest in the guitar in the first place. Piers Anthony and Stephen R. Donaldson for their inspiration and words of encouragement. Jim Vose for his early belief in me. Dustin and Julie, as well as Hailey, Zoe and Kylee Dowling (collectively known as "The Grandmunchkins"). Deidrah and Steve Edwards, Glenda and John Greer. Tom Strickert for listening to me blather on and on and on and on about a topic in which I suspect he has absolutely no real interest. Dwight and Delores Lynch for their exceptional kindness.

Extra Special Thanks to: Carla Ann Neet, the love of my life, whose love and support means more to me than any words could ever say.

And finally, last but not least: Thanks and praise to God, without Whom there would be nothing to write about, nor any reason to write about it. In my own humble way, may I always strive to be worthy of the many gifts You have given me. It's going to take me a lifetime to figure out what to do with them. I must admit, You're still a mystery to me most of the time.

PHOTO CREDITS

The author wishes to acknowledge the following photographers and sources for the photos which appear in *Unsung Heroes of Rock Guitar:* Mick Abrahams photo courtesy of SquirrelMusic.com. Randy Bachman photo by Wayne Hoecherol, courtesy of Bachman Headquarters. Martin Barre photo cropped from group photo courtesy of JTull.com. Craig Chaquico photo courtesy of Engel Entertainment. Larry Crane photo courtesy of Gary Perel/GSRecords. Rik Emmett photo by Ian Brown, courtesy of RikEmmet.com. Peter Frampton photo by Pam Springsteen, courtesy of El Dorado Records. Gary Green photo by Patrick Degallaix, used by permission. Bruce Kulick photo by Glen LaFerman, courtesy of Bruce Kulick. Howard Leese photo courtesy of Capitol Records. Doug Marks photo courtesy of Doug Marks/MetalMethod.com. Trevor Rabin photo by Lisa Powers, courtesy of East End Management. Steve Rothery photo by Dana Sherman/The Web USA. A special nod of thanks to Marillion's old management for the lovely photo of Steve *Hogarth* they sent to me. (Thanks anyway…right band, wrong Steve!) Ty Tabor photo courtesy of Metal Blade Records. Richard Williams photo courtesy of Intersound Records.

No rock stars or photographers were harmed in the production of this book.

*In memory of Brian Wesley Neuwirth
(September 12, 1969—May 23, 1995)
The most unsung hero of them all*

*Last regrets, so profound
You're still around*

This Book Is Dedicated To All Unsung Heroes Of Rock Guitar, Everywhere.

INTRODUCTION

The first thing we do is, let's kill all the lawyers.
-William Shakespeare-

While I did not originate the above sentiment, I can certainly relate to it most heartily. In the time that I have been working on this book, I have had one subject drop out of the project altogether on the advice of his attorney, and several more have expressed deep-seated concerns ranging from the petty to the absolutely ridiculous over various comments they made in the course of their interviews. The reason for their overblown caution is quite simple. They're afraid of getting sued.

While most rock and roll fans imagine their rock heroes as defiant bad boys who do exactly as they please, the more mundane truth is that the life of a typical "rock star" is fairly regimented, with much of their time scheduled in advance for recording sessions, tours, interviews, photo shoots, and dozens of other day-to-day business concerns. Every decision receives input from a manager, an A&R man, a tour manager, a publicist, an accountant, and, of course, an attorney.

Oh yes, an attorney! Let's not forget that most prevalent of music industry parasites. The business is bursting with them, their services invaluable in negotiating contracts, making deals, suing wayward managers, breaking contracts and, in some cases, threatening well-intentioned writers. (But that's another story). Without them, the music industry would simply grind to a halt. Their expertise greases the gears and smoothes the way for the hottest new bands to be sprung onto an unsuspecting public, either burning their names into the history books, or ending up another sad footnote in the Rock And Roll Hall Of Shame. All for a hefty fee, of course. As one well-known guitarist ruefully commented, "I should go back to school and become a lawyer. At least that way I could keep some of my money, 'cause that's where it all goes!"

Let's just say that writing this book was not the easy ride I initially envisioned. The strange thing about the life of a writer—or any artist for that matter—is that while you spend weeks, months or years wrapped up in the creation of whatever artistic fantasy it is that you're pursuing, reality has an unfortunate way of continuing unabated. It's a tightrope that all artists walk, and I'm no exception.

During the years that I have spent on this project, I have experienced some of the highest highs and the lowest lows of my life. The excitement of being able to interview a number of guitarists whose work I have always admired, as well as the imminent prospect of having my first book in print, produced some of the proudest moments I have ever known.

In that same time I have suffered a series of personal and professional setbacks over which I have no control. Deaths in my family and circle of friends, delays on this project, near-crippling depression, and legal problems on a biography I have been working on for years, to name a few.

I suspect like most writers, I tend to get a feeling of power from writing that I do not find in any other part of my life. Words are something over which I feel confident that I have total control; I can bend them and shape them into any form I choose, at will. It's an intoxicating feeling, and no small wonder that it's something I find totally addictive. It feels incredible to create something from nothing, like you're the king of your own literary realm.

Then the real world bursts in and quickly reminds you what an insignificant fool you really are, and you come crashing back down to earth in the blazing comet trail of your own shattered ego. One of the most painful experiences of my life took place during the early stages of this book, the death of my best friend, Roots of Consciousness guitarist Brian Neuwirth. We had been best friends and musical collaborators for seven years, as close as brothers. Brian was an exceptionally talented musician whose natural abilities often amazed me. He is partly responsible for my interest in British progressive rock, which influenced this book heavily.

During the early stages of this book, Brian was at home trying to recuperate from chemotherapy, and we spoke almost daily. His insight and support helped me to formulate a lot of my ideas, and he in turn seemed to really get a kick out of the fact that I was interviewing people like Martin Barre and Gary Green, two of his all-time favorites. He'd say, "Hey, when you talk to Martin, you've gotta ask him about the time..."

Brian passed away on May 23, 1995. It's a tragedy whenever a musician dies and leaves behind an unfinished legacy. It's even more painful when that musician is just twenty-five years old. Brian never really got the chance to be heard that we all felt he deserved, and I think that's one of the most difficult things for me. Even now I'll hear a new, young band on the radio and think of Brian, how proud he was the first time he heard one of his songs on the radio, and I can't help but think about what would, could or *should* have been. It should have been Brian, and now it never will be, and that just doesn't seem fair.

Sometimes I'll hear something funny and reach for the phone, knowing that Brian would see the humor in it, only to realize that he's not there to take my call. It's still hard to believe that he's not in his house, sitting by the phone with his guitar in hand, waiting to pick up in the middle of my message and greet me with the familiar, "What's up, Action Jackson?" (Where he got that nickname for me remains a mystery). It used to irritate me when we would talk on the phone and I could hear him playing his guitar in the background, only half paying attention to what we were saying. Now I'd give anything to hear that sound again.

When I started writing this book, I had two motivations; first, I saw it as a way to legitimately call up a bunch of guitar players I liked and ask them a bunch of questions without having them call the police and get a restraining order against me. And second, it was my ticket to finally getting a full-length book published after years of struggling and paying my dues writing articles and reviews for smaller-market magazines and music papers.

Brian's death made me re-think my motivations. Somehow, personal enjoyment, money and public acclaim don't seem like good enough reasons anymore. That's not to say I don't still want those things to come from this book. Obviously, I do. But even more than that, I want to be the kind of writer who connects with people and makes them feel that they are not alone in their struggles in this world. Life is often difficult and painful for us all, and it is one of my most deeply held beliefs that art can help ease those burdens.

Consequently, I altered the focus of the book to orient more on in-depth portrayals of each subject as the human beings they really are, rather than the public figures we often celebrate. There is a unique story in each and every one of these musicians' lives, a story filled with times of hope and despair, triumph and tragedy. There is also often a strong element of unintentional comedy in the course of a professional musician's career, which I hope comes across in what I've written. The various ways in which my subjects have dealt with these circumstances have made them into the artists—and the people—they are today. People just like you and me. People just like Brian.

Not terribly long after Brian died, Kurt Cobain took his own life. At the time it made me angry; Brian had wanted his shot and never gotten it, and now this guy who *had* gotten his shot and made it big deliberately threw it all away. Sometimes it seems to me that rock and roll breeds a strange set of heroes; damaged personalities are set up on pedestals and praised, as if somehow their personal demons set them apart and mark them as true artists. There have been enough articles and books written about these empty icons to last until the end of time.

I think it's time to say enough. Enough praise for the poor lost souls who sacrifice their sanity and their very lives to feed the public's craving for tortured artists. Enough idolatry heaped upon those who don't need it, don't want it, and can ultimately never live up to it. Let us at last praise those whose only aim is to serve their musical vision as truly as they are able, whose only desire is to simply create the best music they can, and in so doing, maybe in some small way make the world a little more bearable for themselves and the rest of us.

This book is for them.

STERLING C. WHITAKER

PLAYING THE BLUES

Mick Abrahams was a founding member of Jethro Tull. His playing is recognizable from Tull's first record, 'This Was', as well as two classic albums, 'Getting To This' and 'Ahead Rings Out' from his own group Blodwyn Pig. He also recorded two solo albums under the name Mick Abrahams Band in the mid-seventies before leaving the music industry altogether, disgusted by the politics of the business. In the early Nineties he returned with a re-formed Blodwyn Pig.

I spoke with Mick Abrahams on November 4th, 1994 by phone from his home in England, within a few days of the release of Blodwyn Pig's latest album, 'All Tore Down Live'. Abrahams was remarkably blunt in an industry that does not reward bluntness; it's not hard to imagine why he has often been at odds with the powers that be in the music business. He doesn't hesitate to say what he thinks about a person or situation, regardless of the consequences.

*One funny side note to this interview is that Mick Abrahams curses perhaps more than any other person I have ever interviewed. When I transcribed this and ran it through spell check, which does not recognize curse words, the program stopped every few words to let me verify that yes, in fact, that is the correct spelling of "f***ing a**hole". The interview that follows has been edited so that it retains the flavor of Abrahams' speech, without including so much swearing that it's distracting.*

If it bothers Abrahams that he has never achieved the kind of stardom that has been conferred upon Jethro Tull, a band which he helped start, he didn't let on. He impressed me as a hard-working musician whose primary goal is simply to have enough success that it will allow him to continue to pursue his first love—playing the blues.

SW: What age did you start playing the guitar?

MA: Ten.

SW: How did you decide you wanted to start playing guitar?

MA: Oh, Christ, that was easy. I remember seeing a few of the old rock and roll heroes on TV, like Little Richard—well, not on TV, it was radio in those days—but hearing the odd thing like Bill Haley's "Rock Around The Clock" and Little Richard's "Rip It Up", and Elvis Presley and things like that, and I think even Frankie Lane, the guy with "Cool Water". What was the other one, Guy Mitchell, "Singing The Blues". All that sort of stuff I really liked.

I can remember actually standing in front of a massive great old Victorian ornate mirror at home, sort of hiding in the front room where my mom couldn't see me, standing there with a broomstick and aping all the bits and pieces, as we do. *(Laughs)*. It was a very early sort of nearly-Edwardian air guitar, if you like. *(Laughter)*. So that was my first introduction to it as a sort of prop, I guess, and then of course I got so interested my mom bought me a real one for about seven

I

quid that was advertised in the local paper, and I took it home and immediately learned, I think it was "Baby, You're So Square", opening the E string and pressing on the F *(hums the guitar part from the song)*, and I thought, 'Gosh, come on mirror!' *(Laughter)*. So I was in front of the mirror giving it all a big one with "You're So Square"!

My next recollection was, there was a big band over here called Ted MacIntosh's Orchestra who did a number called "Raunchy", which was quite easy to play, it just sort of went *(hums the guitar line)*. I thought, 'Fuck, I'm in with a chance!' *(Laughter)*. So there you go. What with the mirror and me, and the guitar, and Ted MacIntosh and Little Richard and other people, that's really how it all got started.

See, when I got started, the skiffle thing was the big thing, and what we used to do was when I'd actually learned a few chords, we used to go down to the shed at the bottom of the garden with a couple of guys, and one would play a bass with a broomstick and a length of chord attached to it to form a bass. Kind of Cajun shit, I guess, but we called it skiffle over here, and somebody nicked my old lady's washing board and all that. God, I really got a vicious caning one day when we broke it. But the road to rock and roll, I'm led to believe, is supposed to be hard, so I accepted the flogging with the virtue that I've adhered to for the rest of my later life! *(Laughter)*. They're still doing it, mate, they're still doing it, you know what I fucking mean?

SW: How did that lead you to become a professional?

MA: I guess my mind started expanding a little bit, and I'd taken on board people like Chuck Berry, and there was B.B. King around at that time, and I went that route more. In fact, I was more kind of steeped in, or listening to, kind of jazz/blues guitar.

Herb Ellis was and still is one of my favorite jazz players, because he's a real kind of blues player too, and I very recently had the great privilege of actually sitting in with the man. You know, it took my fucking breath away, man. I was scared shitless. He's great. Seventy-two years old and still doing it like he did it twenty years ago. It was something else.

So I'm listening to guys like that, and obviously, with the rock and roll thing so big over here…I'm fifty-one now, so at the time that I started, American imports had just started coming over in a big way. So I started taking on board everybody, really. I mean country players especially, like Jerry Reed, Chet Atkins, and Merle Travis; I still listen to them now, and they're great. I listen to Ricky Skaggs and Albert Lee and Steve Morse and those people now as well, too, but some of the old guys can really still hack it, you know.

SW: Definitely. What was the first band you recorded in?

MA: I remember shaking like a leaf turning up to an audition at sort of a demo studio, which was probably only a two-track in those days. We were in a local band called The Hustlers which we'd formed. The reason for the name was, we played a lot of American air bases, and the Hustler bomber was big on deck at the time, so we used the name. It sounded quite heavy.

We did a gig at Finsbury Park Empire; we actually ended up getting a residency there, which was quite a big thing in those days. We only had to play about half an hour a night, to support the big band. It was quite strange, because the band leader said there was a particular song that we did that he really liked, and that he'd like to do a demo of it. So having no experience apart from just playing in a Shadows-cum-pop-cum-R&B band, R&B being the last thing with this particular band, now we were due to go out into the great big world of London and do a demo in a recording studio, my God! *(Laughter)*.

And I can remember, man, it was so funny, because we all turned up in our fucking uniforms, you know, we all turned up in our band uniforms, because of course my mom said, "You've got to dress properly, Michael, if you're going to one of these things. It's a big moment for you." It was quite freaky. The minute we were down there it was cool, we were good to go, you know. That's the first real recording I ever made. Whatever happened to it I have no idea, but I remember going away from the place completely freaking out, "We've cracked it—we've been in a *recording studio!*" There you go, early days. *(Laughs)*.

SW: What was the first band you were in that actually got a deal?

MA: The band that got a deal was Jethro Tull. I'd recorded with other people. I'd recorded with Neil Christian and I'd done a couple of sessions with other people; nobody of any great quality, hardly memorable. But as a deal, that's the first time we'd ever been in a real big situation. Mind you, fifteen quid a week back then went a long way, because that's all we ever got fucking paid.

SW: *(Laughs)*. Oh, yeah?

MA: Oh, yeah.

SW: How did you get together with Tull?

MA: That was a kind of accident, really. I was in a band, and I'd just come back from living in Manchester, because my hometown was in Luton at the time. I came back from Manchester sort of destitute and starving, so I went back to Mum for a few weeks to get some good old-fashioned cooking, and actually get fed and get a few calories inside me; now it's the opposite, I wish I could go back to Manchester to get rid of the fucking things! *(Laughter)*.

I remember that I came home and I think Clive Bunker was free, and Andy Pyle was playing in another band, and we just formed this little three-piece band. It was a four-piece originally; we had a guy called Pete Fensome in the band, and he left after a little while. He was initially just a vocalist, so we ended up as a three-piece, and purely coincidentally we played this place called the Beachcomber Discotheque. It had two stages, with a band at each end, and the band would change over immediately so there wasn't a break, and the band playing the opposite end to us was the John Evans Smash, I believe it was called at the time, or the John Evan Band or whatever, and that of course contained the infamous blatherer otherwise known as Ian Anderson, who talked as much then as he does today *(laughs)*, and Glen Cornick and a few of the other guys, and they approached me and said, "We're looking for like a blues-rock guitar player. We've got a possible deal with an agency down in London. Our guitar player's leaving and we've heard you. We like it. Do you fancy the job?" So I sort of thought for a minute and I said, "Can I come back to you on it?"

And the weirdest thing happened; when we went to the dressing room, Andy quit. He was given to doing things like that. I mean, he had no idea of what these other guys had just asked me, he just sort of said, "I'm leaving next week." And me and Clive said, "Well, we've still got a few gigs to do." He said, "Well, it's not my fault, mate, I'm going." I think he went out to Gibraltar for a while. So I thought, okay, fine. I said, "Clive, what are you doing?" Clive said, "Well, there's nothing really I can do; I don't fancy doing it without Andy and yourself." So that was it.

Anyway, strange enough, to cut a long story short, the John Evans Band came down and lived in Luton, and within about a week all of them were gone with the exception of Ian and Glen. *(Laughs)*. I think they all missed their mum's cooking, too. So I immediately called Clive and asked him if he wanted the gig, and he said yes. So he came down and we rehearsed as a four-piece, and went out under various guises and names, and did all the John Evans Band gigs under the Chris Wright and Terry Ellis Agency, which was then in Regency Street, which was later to become Chrysalis Records, or Chrysalis Empire, more like.

SW: How long was it before you made the first record, *This Was*?

MA: I think about five or six months, because we started getting a bit of a name for ourselves on the circuit. There was a good blues circuit then, and also at the Marquee we had a residency. We were there every, I can't remember if it was every other week or something like that, and we eventually got the top spot, which was great.

And then we got the Sunbury Festival, and it was at the time when we'd just made the album, and at the Sunbury Festival we tore the ass out of them. They just went potty for us, and that was kind of the beginning of the end, as far as I was concerned anyway. *(Laughs)*.

SW: You left the band after just one album...

MA: That's right. You see, there's been a lot of bone of contention about whether I actually left the band, or whether I was shoved or coerced or whatever. And the truth is I actually turned around to Ian one day, because I just couldn't hack being in Jethro Tull, because it was going in all the wrong direction musically for me, and I didn't particularly enjoy the politics, I suppose, and as a consequence, I ended up falling out with Ian.

I also fell out with a manager, whom I had no time for then and still don't now. I'm not being arrogant, it's just the guy does fucking stupid things that just don't agree with me personally. So we kind of fell out, and I went to Ian and I said, "Look, I've had enough. You're going in a completely different direction; you won't let me write songs with you anymore, so obviously I'm not contributing what you want to the band." And I admit, there was a certain amount of jealousy in there; there has to be, because that's just a normal human emotion, but I got a bit miffed with that, and I said, "That's not how I figured the band was going."

And there were certain things that I didn't want to do, and certain things he didn't want to do, and it ended up in a bit of a scrabble, but I mean, no big deal. I just said, "Look, I'll quit, and I'll give you notice now, but I'll stay in the band as long as it takes to work another guitar player in." Which they fortunately did with Martin Barre, who's great. And about a week later, after having said that, Terry Ellis called me into the office and fired me! *(Laughter)*. Because you don't leave Jethro Tull; well, not when you're under Terry Ellis', dare I say "guidance"? He got a bit pissed off with me, because I told him I thought he was a fucking asshole, and he always was and always would be!

SW: After you left the band, have you kept track of their career?

MA: No, not really. I mean, except to say that within the last two or three years I've been playing with them again. I get invited to all these Tull conventions and stuff that they do, and Ian and I are quite friendly. All that aggravation was died down after about a year of when it first started. A lot of other people made more of it than there really was, and Ian, unfortunately, being the bit of a blatherer that he is, never seems to explain it any other way than his selective memory allows him to. *(Laughs)*.

SW: How long was it before you got involved in Blodwyn Pig?

MA: Well, I went directly on to form Blodwyn Pig. I just had Christmas at home and formed Blodwyn Pig, and that was it.

SW: Is there any significance to the name?

MA: None whatsoever. There's simply a mate of ours, this guy that used to come out with great dry, witty remarks, and he actually happened to be in the area when we were rehearsing and just heard the noise from the studio and popped his head around the door, and we said, "Hey, Graham, how you doing, mate? Give us a name, man, give us a name!" And the guy just sort of looked whimsically amused for a moment and said, "Thou shalt forevermore be known as Blodwyn Pig. What a splendid band!" and walked off, and we were all just rolling about on the floor over the fact that it's Blodwyn Pig. There's no deep meanings, nothing. *(Laughs)*.

SW: You put out *Ahead Rings Out* in 1969, and then *Getting To This* in 1970. Did the band do a lot of touring at that time?

MA: We did about three tours of the States, and we did quite well, but you know, we had a lot of internal hassle in the band, and it was mainly caused by Andy Pyle, the bass player. He was constantly scheming to see how he could get pole position in the band and get the most money out of it, because he's a great bass player, but as a man he's rather a mercenary fellow.

So unfortunately, I genuinely believe that it was Andy's fault that the band split up as it did, because what he did was, he rang me on the end of an American tour, and there was a lot of shit flying about; I was going through a big thing about flying at the time, and I would have preferred, if I could do it, to travel another way. Obviously with going over to the States and coming back, it's rather impossible. And he didn't like it, because it didn't suit his pocket, so what he did was, effectively he turned Jack and Ron against me, and pointed me out as the bad guy in the band. He'd already contacted a couple of other people, and he kind of sacked me from my own band.

I said, "Hold on a minute, mate. Wait a minute, mate, you can't do that, it's my band!" And he said, "Well, we've all gotten together and we feel that…" and it was a real kind of counselor voice. I said, "Oh, you're full of fucking shit, go shove it up your ass anyway," And I don't mean to be nasty, but it proved a point; I mean, they lasted for five gigs after I left and then dissolved. And guess who called me five weeks later? (Imitates whiny voice). "Mick, have you ever reconsidered…" And I said, "Go fuck yourself, mate."

SW: That's a crazy situation.

MA: What do you do? Who do you get in touch with? Is this any way to run a ballroom, I ask you? (Laughter). So that's the sad story of Blodwyn Pig— fired from my own band, or at least they tried to, and fucked it up. I'm sure they'd have me blamed out of all of it, so there you go. At least I own up to my mistakes. Some people won't.

SW: You went and did a couple of solo albums after that. How were those experiences?

MA: I liked the first one, I liked the first Mick Abrahams Band album. I was quite happy with that, but the second one, with a couple of reservations, I'm not that keen on it, because it was a kind of time when Chris Thomas, the producer, had sort of become more…it's the story of my life, man, is other people becoming full of their ideas and their view of it rather than my own.

When you do something creative and you try to put forward your point of view, it's great if people come and help you, and they're constructive with their criticism. If it's based around you and it's what you do, and they can nurture it and expand on that, that's got to be the right way as far as I can see. That actually allows you the proper artistic freedom. And instead of that, I kind of got the reverse end: "We now think this band ought to do *this*, and ought to do *that*." Obviously these things are all in the past; you know, I still speak to plenty of people up at Chrysalis. They're a different ballgame altogether now.

SW: After that you quit the business altogether.

MA: I quit the business—well, what I did was, I did a lot of work. I had a year's sabbatical. I got really totally pissed off with the whole thing, and I don't know whether to prove it to myself, or whether I wanted to step back down into more of a normal, what I considered at the time to be on-the-level kind of situation. I actually went out and did a window cleaning round. I cut my hair, and nobody knew me anyway, so I didn't care. So I had a little window cleaning company which kind of expanded. After a couple of months I got bored with that, and then I went and worked as a lorry driver again, which I had done as a kid anyway, and ended up managing a swimming pool then, which was fun.

But I was playing all the while. I had a couple of guys that I'd work with locally, and we'd go out a couple of nights a week, just play some blues, get pissed, get stoned, vomit on the audience as one does. *(Laughs)*. But nothing of any great consequence; it was just a bit of a jam, a bit of a fuckabout. We never used to rehearse or nothing like that, and I'd be up for any charity gig that was going.

Then eventually I moved into trading cars and stuff like that, and eventually ended up selling life insurance, which was quite profitable. And then about six years ago I got so pissed off with all of it I thought, 'I really fancy playing music full time again.' So I did.

SW: You re-formed Blodwyn Pig in 1988, but it was a couple of years before you put a record out. Were you just touring around at that time and working up some new material?

MA: Just farting around in general, yeah.

SW: How has it been since you re-formed the band?

MA: It's been going great. Really good. The band we've got now as Blodwyn Pig is the longest Blodwyn Pig there ever has been in the whole history of Blodwyn Pig. I've got a real nice bunch of guys to work with. I'm kind of the boss of the band situation, but it is a band, and we work like a band. Everybody gets a share of what goes on. So nobody gets kind of stamped down in their own artistic freedom, because they all actually like what I do and they're in that direction anyway. So at last I seem to have found a kind of niche, which is great.

They're a good bunch of cats to work with, and I really like that, to be able to work with people I like. I'm not very keen on arty-farty people, people with their head stuck up their ass or on the planet Pluto. I like people that are just good players and good fun to be with, and don't get fucked up every day of the week.

SW: You put out *All Said And Done*, and then went on to put out *Lies*...

MA: And now we've got a new—well it's kind of an old one, actually, but put out as a new one. It's a string of tour dates from Germany in 1993 that got picked up and put out as a live album.

SW: Are you pleased with the album?

MA: It's good. I mean, there's a few of the vocals I wasn't truly happy with, but it was live, and live is live, isn't it? There's the odd twinge here and there and the odd croak in the voice. I think it was on about the nineteenth day on the ones they chose the vocals for, and my voice was just about gone. But it was good; it has the kind of ambiance the Blods get going. We work with the audience, try to play our best always, and try to be a good bunch of gentlemen.

You know, we occasionally fall from grace after the gig and get riotously pissed and stoned, but these days we don't do any bad things. We just fall asleep. *(Laughs)*. Because we need it, you know. Because we've got to be up at eight o'clock to get the three-wheeled cart batteries charged up. *(Laughter)*.

SW: When will you put out another studio album?

MA: I think we'll be recording some time around the start of January, so I would imagine it's going to be some time around March, but things change. Times are not pleasant at the moment in any country of the world, especially not here in England. I don't work much at all here, because there ain't no money in it. I tend to work a lot in Germany and Scandinavia and Switzerland and Austria.

SW: Do you have any plans to come and tour the States?

MA: I'm definitely going to come over there at some point in time, when the guys offer the right sensible money. I don't mean megabucks, because nobody's got megabucks, and I'm not conceited enough to think that I warrant ten grand a night or something like that. But the problem is that they offer you the opposite. It's such shit money that you couldn't even buy a fucking hamburger with it after you've paid for everything. And that's stupid, because I'm doing it for a living.

I'm very fortunate that I've got other projects as well as the Blods that keep me going; I'm about to start filming for a three part teaching video, and I do a few voice-overs for various commercials and stuff like that. It's okay, because it keeps the old wolf from the door, and it allows me to go and Blod it up every now and then. And ninety-nine percent of the time we win, when we get the right gigs and right people.

We played the Cropredy Festival a couple of months back, and there were about twenty thousand people there, and we just tore the living shit out of them, and they loved it, and we loved them. It was a real nice thing. We got on national TV, and I got an interview on TV, which is kind of good because it's getting the profile back.

SW: What are your future plans? Do you intend to stay in music?

MA: Oh, yeah, I'm back in music to stay. I don't really want to be involved in anything else. I think a lot of the thing with me is that now I'm a little bit more mature. *(Laughs wildly)*. I looked in the mirror when I said that and realized...now I'm a little bit more mature! It sounds so funny, doesn't it? I can handle more of the situation more easily. I can delegate when I need to. And I suppose to be brutally honest, I'm in charge of my own life; I don't have someone whose point of view I most genuinely disagree with telling me what to do. I've got a couple of good people who look to me and want to develop what I do. As a result, that's actually made me become a little bit better, and that's what I'm after. I'm never gonna get perfect, but I'm still striving, mate, and that's what it's all about.

For more information about Mick Abrahams, please visit
www.squirrelmusic.com

ANY ROAD WILL TAKE YOU THERE

Randy Bachman has been described as a Canadian national treasure. In a career which spans thirty years, he has headed up two of the most successful bands in Canadian rock music history, along the way penning some of rock music's most enduring songs.

*Beginning in his teens with stints in several local bands in Winnipeg, **Bachman** first came to international prominence in **The Guess Who**, with a string of hit singles from 1965 to 1970 that included "Shakin' All Over", "These Eyes", "No Sugar Tonight" and "American Woman". In 1970 **Bachman** left the band, unable to reconcile his Mormon beliefs with the drugs and high living which had infiltrated the group with its success.*

***Bachman** went on to record a solo album, 'Axe', before forming **Brave Belt**, which recorded two comparatively unsuccessful albums together. In 1973 **Bachman** re-emerged in **Bachman-Turner Overdrive**; after facing rejection from twenty-four record companies, the band went on to become one of the most successful rock acts of the Seventies whose string of hits included "Let It Ride", "Takin' Care Of Business", "You Ain't Seen Nothin' Yet", and "Hey You".*

***Bachman** left **BTO** in 1977, releasing a solo album, 'Survivor', and working with a band called **Ironhorse**, which had several minor chart successes. He spent the next few years in relative obscurity, working the club scene all over the world. **Bachman** also participated in various reunions of **The Guess Who** and **Bachman-Turner Overdrive**, neither of which yielded any new material.*

*I spoke to **Randy Bachman** on January 12th, 1995 by phone from his home in Canada. His recent album 'Any Road' had earned rave reviews the previous year in Canada, and **Bachman** was waiting to see if the album would catch on with the American record buying public. He wasn't exactly sitting around waiting for the phone to ring, though; he was touring in support of 'Any Road' and working up material for his next album between trips to Nashville to participate in songwriting conferences with some of country music's leading lights. A couple of months after we spoke, his name was announced as one of the guitarists on **Ringo Starr's All Starr Band** tour.*

***Bachman** struck me as a straight shooter, a plain-spoken, down-to-earth guy totally unimpressed by his own success. Through all the ups and downs of a life spent largely on the road, and all the fads that have come and gone in that time, he has remained focused on what he does best—playing good old-fashioned rock and roll.*

SW: How is the *Any Road* album doing here in America?

RB: It just got a really positive review in *Billboard* just before Christmas, so they've come out full guns now, the label and promo guys; they're servicing it to AAA and AOR radio and all that stuff, so we'll see what happens. I have a little tour planned in the middle of February, too, for about ten days in California.

We're calling there today to see if the guy is still in the mind frame to go through with the tour, because there's flood disasters there everywhere.

SW: I guess it makes it pretty hard to give a concert when the building's been washed away.

RB: Yeah, so we'll see what happens.

SW: You've already been on tour for a while with this record.

RB: Well, it came out in Canada two years ago, so we toured there two years ago, and then again last summer. And then it just came out in early October of last year in the States. So it looks like I'm going to be touring all this year with regards to the *Any Road* album. I'm also working on the next one. I have a home studio, so whenever I feel like it, I go up there. I'm working on about twenty tracks for the new one.

SW: And then out of those twenty will you pick and choose?

RB: Yes, I'll pick ten or twelve that are of a really good direction. I'm half through everything now, I'm just not sure how they're going to finish up. I like very similar rhythm tracks, and then how I finish them up, with light or heavy guitar, depends on what happens.

SW: What do you do with the songs that you demo that never make it onto a record?

RB: I compile them. I've got quite a few, and the odd time I'll get asked to contribute a track to a charity album, where everybody gives a track, I like to pull out one of those because it's not available on any other record. It's usually a little diversionary for me, because you know, it didn't fit on an album because it didn't have a certain sound. I like to put those on compilation albums. I think every artist is the same; they get to contribute something a little out of the ordinary, that's not on their last album, that was a good tune but just didn't fit the shape and sound of the whole album. And then I send them out for demos to other bands.

SW: To see if they want to record them for themselves.

RB: Right.

SW: I read somewhere that you have a big guitar collection. Do you remember the first one you ever owned?

RB: I started out cheaply with a thirty dollar Harmony f-hole acoustic from Sears, and then progressed to the electric section of the same catalog, the Sears catalog, and got a Silvertone, which in the States were Danelectros. I still have that. It's really still a great guitar. I had the neck all re-fretted and done, and it has got an incredible sound. In fact, on the *Any Road* album I used it on the solo on "Just One Night In Texas". The Silvertone guitar is kind of a clean distortion, it's really neat. And then from that point I got an Orange Gretsch, and that was it.

SW: How many guitars do you have in all?

RB: Well, I have a little over three hundred Gretsches…

SW: Really? That's unbelievable! *(Laughs)*.

RB: I'm pretty sure I have the world's largest Gretsch collection. I've been told that by Fred Gretsch and whoever else has seen it. I'll be doing a book on it very soon, a pictorial book on Gretsches from the beginnings—which some of mine go back to the late Twenties and early Thirties—right up to all the current models and prototypes. And then I've got about fifteen great Fenders, fifteen great Gibsons, fifteen great others, you know, Rickenbackers and Nationals and so on. I guess total it's probably three hundred and fifty. Between three-fifty and four hundred.

SW: Obviously with that many, you probably don't get around to playing them all.

RB: No. I used to. I used to have them on the walls in a room in the house, and I just got so many, I put them in the cases and tagged them and stored the cases.

I've got a photographer; I'm just waiting to get a few special models back. You get Gretsches in all different array of conditions, and some I would just buy because I knew that it was the only model that existed that I would be able to get my hands on, so you have to have them restored sometimes. I'm trying to have them all cosmetically restored, so when my book comes out, it'll be like a new catalog of every Gretsch from the late Twenties up to current.

SW: That's pretty amazing.

RB: I've got a photographer now, a really good one, and we decided that it's pretty much impossible to photograph them all at once, in one session. And we would take a whole year, but then I'd have to pay him too much.

I mean, you could do two or three guitars a day. You want to set them up, you want to do maybe six to twelve different shots of each guitar from different angles and lighting. You want each one to look interesting and different. I don't want them all on a blue background like some of those sterile books, yet I don't want the background to detract from the guitar. So you maybe put it up with a green slate background, or a black Indian blanket with a sheaf of wheat, you know, just something to add into the picture. And you can lay a strap beside it, or a flower, or I don't know, just something else to add into the picture that doesn't detract from the guitar. You don't want it to look sterile, like it's a catalog.

SW: Yeah, I guess if you shoot them all that carefully, it will take a long time to photograph that many guitars. Sounds like a great book. Good luck with it.

RB: I've already got photos of them all that I've sent out, so I have publishers interested in the book already. It's just a matter of when the photographer gets a hole in his schedule, if it matches mine, I will take ten days out and we'll go and try to do another thirty or forty guitars, and then those are put away.

But you know, I've got to go to each guitar before it's photographed and polish it, clean it, re-string it, make it look really spanking shiny new. So there's a certain amount of prep that goes into it to make sure they're all absolutely perfect; all the tuners, all the little screws, everything.

SW: Are there certain ones that you refuse to take on the road with you?

RB: I don't take any Gretsches at all. I've taken them and had them stolen, and it broke my heart. I think it's probably one of the cruelest things in the world anyone can do is to steal a musician's instrument, whether it's a trumpet or a violin or whatever...you don't hear about too many guys stealing sets of drums! But it's a thing that you hold close to you that someone can pick up and run away with. I've lost too many really good guitars on the road.

SW: What about in the studio; do you take out a large part of your collection and try various guitars on various tracks?

RB: On *Any Road* it was a lot of fun. I took ten or twelve amps that were all vintage, and worked with about forty different guitars. There's certain known combinations; you know ahead of time what a Strat is going to sound like through a blond piggyback Fender amp, or a Les Paul through a Bluesbreaker Marshall. There's certain sounds you know you're going to get real close to with a certain guitar and amp, so that's your starting point. If you want that texture in a song, you pull out that guitar, each guitar having its characteristic sound. So those were starting points for me, and then it's just a matter of micing it and getting it into a room.

Any Road was cut in Jim Vallance's studio in downtown Vancouver, with live drums, bass and guitar, and then I brought it home and started overdubbing guitar parts and doing better vocals. Now I just record in my home studio, so there's not much room to set up amplifiers and stuff. In this other studio I'd set up a wall of amplifiers, and just take the guitar from one to the other and plug them in and see how each one sounded. Now I've got these amps that each have a hundred and fifty presets in them, which is absolutely fantastic. You don't need to play around with amplifiers and mics and speaker cabinets anymore. But I find that just the right guitar through those things still gets you very close to the old combinations that you want.

SW: Have you been collecting since the very beginning of your career?

RB: Not really. I only ever had, since the very beginning, a Gretsch, a Stratocaster, and a '59 Les Paul. That's all I had through the Guess Who and all of BTO. But near the end of BTO, I think it was '76, the Orange Gretsch that I first played on a record, "Shakin' All Over" way back in 1964, was stolen from a Holiday Inn right after we were recording. In my quest to find that, I was contacting dealers all over Canada and the States, little music stores and pawn shops. And I started getting calls saying, "Well, I don't have your guitar, but I do have this other Gretsch that's very nice." And you could pick them up cheap back then, so a lot of the time I did.

Then video started to come in ten years later, and the Gretsches were really great in videos, because immediately it was like dangling a diamond in front of a camera. It sparkled, it glowed, it caught the eye. And when everyone started using them in videos, the value went up and everybody wanted them. Tom Petty uses a little Rancher on 'Saturday Night Live', and suddenly Ranchers double overnight. And then I saw my collection as having some value.

And then I had people calling me, saying that I was the Gretsch expert. And I didn't really feel that I was, but all I had to do was run down to my room and look at the guitar, if they were calling for a description of the guitar; what should it have, what should it look like. I was able to answer most of their questions, so through default in a way—not from studying any kind of book, because there was none *(laughs)*—I became kind of an expert on Gretsches, and now I think I have the world's largest collection.

SW: Did you ever wind up getting your original back?

RB: Never did. Still looking. But I've got two dozen like it. I've got two dozen Orange Gretsches. I've got two dozen White Falcons. As I went along, I ended up not just getting each model, I got each model in its transformation. Every few years, just like a car, the body style or something on a Gretsch would change. So I've got the early 6Is in the Fifties, and then they changed three years later, 1958 or '59, and then they changed in '62 or '63. And as they change every three to five years, I've got a really great, probably ten on a ten scale specimen of each change. I have the complete visual history of the White Falcon, the White Penguin…any Gretsch you can think of. I've got pretty much an evolution of each guitar; I've got the early ones, the prototypes, and the issued models.

When Fred Gretsch wanted to bring the Gretsches back about five or six years ago, all his templates had been destroyed by fire, so he and Duke Kramer called me, and basically would borrow one guitar out of my collection at a time. I'd send it to them, they would measure it with calipers and take photos. They made the new Gretsch line out of my collection. My deal was that I would get the prototypes. So they took one of my old ones, copied it as far as where the switches went, where the controls went, the size, depth, color, everything. They'd copy it, and then my deal with them was that I got mine back, plus I got the prototype of that model. Which was great, because the prototypes were flawed in certain ways; sometimes the f-holes would be at the wrong angle, tilted too much, or straight up and down. I'd get to say what should be corrected, but I'd get to keep the flawed one, which wasn't really ugly; it just wasn't as perfect as it was supposed to be. Even the new prototypes added greatly to the collection.

SW: So you've got quite a few one-of-a-kind pieces in there.

RB: A lot of the Gretsches I've got, maybe fifteen or twenty percent of my collection, are one-of-a-kind prototypes, old ones and new ones.

SW: That's amazing. Now, shifting focus here, in the early days of your career you came up in the rock scene in Canada. Was there a strong rock scene in Canada twenty-five or thirty years ago?

RB: Not really. Canada was such a young, under-developed country. Now to go back to when I started in the early Sixties in the early Guess Who, usually either myself or some other guys in the group were too young to get into the clubs. The drinking age was twenty-one, so we couldn't even get in. Clubs then had jazz guys, you know, Buddy Rich and Tony Bennett kinda guys. *(Laughs)*. Tony Bennett's still around! But that kind of music was in the clubs, so basically we played dances and high schools and things like that in the early Guess Who, and then as we grew to be of a certain age we had a hit record, and we didn't really have to play clubs.

SW: So you skipped that step up the rock and roll ladder.

RB: Well, I've since played thousands of them in BTO, because BTO was a real club band, rock and roll with a beat kind of thing.

SW: How did you come to be in the Guess Who—well, originally it was Chad Allan and the Reflections. How did you wind up in that band?

RB: I was just playing in a band on my side of town in Winnipeg, and it was basically two members of the band, myself and Gary Peterson, who was the drummer, with other guys always coming and going because of a girlfriend or a hockey team or whatever. *(Laughs)*. They weren't really interested in being in a band, and Gary and I were real true musicians, so we were always in the band, with other guys always in and out.

Now, on the other side of Winnipeg was a band called Allan and the Silvertones, and there was Neil Young and the Squires, and those were the two big bands that were getting all of the high school dances and everything. And one day I heard that Allan and the Silvertones—who evolved to be Chad Allan and the Reflections after Gary and I joined—needed a rhythm guitar player, so I went over and auditioned for rhythm just to get in the band. And two days later I was asked to play lead guitar, because I had also learned the leads to all the songs they wanted, which was pretty much the Shadows stuff from England. And the minute I got in the band and had a foothold in the band and felt secure, I vied to get Gary Peterson in, so he got in the following week. And that band went on to be Chad Allan and the Reflections.

We had to change our name because of a band called the Reflections from Baltimore, who had a hit record called "Romeo and Juliet". We got a letter from their lawyer saying to change our name, so we changed it from 'Reflections' to 'Expressions', and we recorded a song called "Shakin' All Over" and sent it to our record label, who said, "This sounds like a hit, but we don't like your name. We're just going to put 'Guess Who' on the label." So they did, and suddenly we were called The Guess Who! *(Laughs)*.

"Shakin' All Over" went on to become a hit in Canada in 1964, and in '65 it was released in the States and went to the Top Twenty in *Billboard*. That was pretty unusual for a band from Winnipeg; we were still in high school and college at the time, and had a record in the Top Twenty in *Billboard*. And then one day we had a call from a manager in New York; "Shakin' All Over" had been released on Scepter Records out of New York, and we got a call to go to New

York to go into the recording studio and to go on tour with the Kingsmen. The Kingsmen were on Wand Records, which was a sister label to Scepter.

So we went and did the Kingsmen tour, the Louie Louie Tour in 1965, which was a really great time to be on the road. We went out in two great big buses, and it was the Kingsmen, the Guess Who, Dion and the Belmonts, Barbara Mason, and Sam the Sham and the Pharaohs. It was really a fun time for us.

SW: You were one of the first really successful Canadian bands to break in the States.

RB: I think we were the first to really…there were some others that had one radio hit. We actually had the hit, and then we went down and we worked and toured and built a following and struggled for many years to have a follow-up, which took a long time, until we got a new lead singer. Chad Allan left the band, we got Burton Cummings, we evolved to be a four-piece Guess Who, and that's when we started that string of hits that began with "These Eyes" and went through "American Woman" and ended up with "Bus Rider" or "Share The Land". That was almost a twenty-year band on the American scene.

SW: Probably the most successful Canadian band in America that I can think of.

RB: Yeah, I think so.

SW: In all that time you remained based in Canada.

RB: We stayed based in Winnipeg, although we weren't there that much. We'd only get home two or three days a month, but it was always a place to come to that was our anchor, to just come home and see the family and friends and do the laundry and go back out on the road.

SW: Did you ever have business advisors and people like that tell you, "That's not the place to be. Why don't you come to New York or LA?"

RB: Yeah, they wanted us to be in New York, but New York was too frightening for us. Growing up in Winnipeg, we didn't get a whole lot of TV, and when you got TV, you had this thing called 'The Naked City'. Somebody got killed every week on that show! And it was about New York. *(Laughs)*. There was basically no crime growing up in Winnipeg in the Forties, Fifties and Sixties, like there was in New York. And it was magnified and amplified by this TV show. When we got there, we were afraid to go out in the street! It took us a long time just to get used to walking around. We were always looking over our shoulders. It was just too big of a city.

I think that happens to anyone who's from a smaller kind of town, when you go to New York or Chicago or one of those places; the only movies you see about those towns are gang killings and murders. You don't see too many stories about your typical family living in their little area that's just like the family you came from in your little town. So it was kind of scary.

SW: I guess it would be. If it were today, you'd be worried about drive-by crack shootings and all kinds of crazy things.

RB: We got asked to go to LA, but that was too far, and we decided it was best to remain in Winnipeg, which is almost the geographical center of North America. It made a lot of sense to be based there. You could go anywhere in either direction in a day. You could get to LA in a day, or New York in a day, and we drove a lot in those days, so the driving time was very important.

SW: That makes good sense. Now, you didn't sing lead in the Guess Who, but you've sung lead throughout the rest of your career.

RB: Purely by default, by accident. When I started BTO a couple of years after I left the Guess Who—I left the Guess Who in 1970, and BTO kind of evolved and came out in '72—Fred Turner, who has this incredible Harley Davidson kind of voice, a gruff, John Fogerty kind of voice; when we started, that's when we were really playing clubs, four or five sets a night, six nights a week, and he just couldn't keep up the vocal screaming. He asked me to sing a song or two in every set just to give him a breather, so I would do an instrumental or two, a couple of Santana kind of songs, with long, long solos, and I started to sing Bob Dylan and Neil Young songs, real easy songs like "Down By The River" and "Cinnamon Girl", things like that that people danced to that you didn't need to have a great voice. I had this real shaky, insecure kind of voice, which was very similar to a Neil Young or something! *(Laughs)*. It wasn't a fabulous voice, but it was distinctive, and I enunciated the words properly, so I got by singing these couple of songs.

One night Fred Turner lost his voice completely, and I had to sing the entire last set, which was on a Saturday night in a club. After I sang my Dylan and Neil Young and Dave Crosby songs, I ran out of cover songs. So I had an old song called "White Collar Worker" that I'd changed the title to "Takin' Care Of Business", and I turned around on stage live and said, "Follow me. Here's three chords; play them over and over. We're doing a brand-new song, and when I get to the hook, help me." And I started to play the song and I sang it, and when I got to the hook they sang it with me.

And then two weeks later we went to record *BTO II*, and I wrote up the lyrics and gave them to Fred Turner. And he asked me, "What are these for?" And I said, "So you don't make a mistake." And he said, "I'm not gonna sing this, you are. Then when you give me a break on stage you'll be legitimately doing one of our songs, and let's stop doing 'Cinnamon Girl' and 'O-H-I-O' and all those Neil Young things. Let's start to do our own songs with you singing." So I sang "Takin' Care Of Business" by default, and it turned out to be a pretty popular song, and has endured now for twenty years. So I was thrust into the position of…you know, I used to just love standing on stage like Eric Clapton, over to the side, just grooving and playing solos, and suddenly I was up front.

The next song I sang was a reject from the album called "You Ain't Seen

Nothin' Yet", which ended up being a number one song in many countries, and suddenly I was a vocalist! *(Laughs)*. I wouldn't say I was a vocalist; I was a singer, I sang songs, but I don't think of myself really as a vocalist.

But as time has gone by, I find that I write songs now to match my vocal range so that I have some freedom in vocals. I don't make them too acrobatic. Before I could write anything, and Burton Cummings or Fred Turner could sing it. So I write songs a little bit more controlled now, that are within my range. And if I do stuff that's out of my range, I get someone else to sing it and send it out to demo for another band.

SW: As you've gone along and found yourself more in the center stage, have you learned any tricks to try and strengthen your voice, or do you find that you just get better at it as you go along?

RB: I find that on the first two days you get a certain soreness. It's like going to work out; if you haven't worked out in a while, you get sore, stiff muscles. You've got to do two days and then lay off, and then when you start again you go real slow; your muscles hurt, because they aren't used to working that way. I don't know how to do anything to warm up my voice. I just try to get lots of sleep. I never smoke. I try to stay away from smoke because it just clogs my voice. That's about it; there's nothing else I do. I don't know any exercises or anything. I just go out and sing.

SW: So you don't view yourself primarily as a singer; do you view yourself more as a songwriter or a guitarist?

RB: Pretty much a songwriter. I started out a guitar player, and I used to teach guys guitar. I would teach somebody five or ten years younger than me, and they would pull off something that was way better than me. And I figured there's always going to be a younger, faster gun. I'll be happy to be a real good, competent guitarist, but I'll never be one of those great guys like Steve Vai or Joe Satriani, somebody who's just totally acrobatic and everything they play is amazing. I'll just be adequate and competent, but I think I can write really good songs.

I studied all the great songs of the Beatles and the Stones and Burt Bacharach and anybody else who wrote a good song of any style, I got it and listened to it. There were no books on it then; I just got records and collected them. I'm a real fan of music. When I listen to something on the radio, I don't just listen to what everybody else listens to; I'm listening to the format of a song—how long is the intro, when did they go to the hook, what kind of solo is it, and how they repeated each part. So I listen to it more clinically, and then I don't really copy it, but it goes into my mind as part of how a song should be, and if I write a song similar to it, I copy a similar format. Because it's got to be over in about four minutes, and it has to have a beginning and an end, just like a story.

I think my songwriting has improved; I think that on the *Any Road* album and on the next album that I'm working on now, it's the best songs that I've written. I've been invited to Nashville a couple of times and have done showcases there; the people are real song-oriented there, and the response to me there has been tremendous. I was really overwhelmed by how welcome I was in Nashville, and how the people there grew up with my songs in the Sixties and Seventies. I'm sure I'll have some recordings done in the next year by some pretty prominent, national country artists, who are pretty much like Seventies rock guys.

SW: A lot of those bands are bringing that kind of energy to country now because they grew up on rock music. Some of those bands are already doing live covers of some of your stuff.

RB: For the last four or five years I've heard that Alan Jackson has done "Takin' Care Of Business" as his encore. Alabama did it, too; it's on one of their live albums. Pirates of the Mississippi…Kentucky Headhunters always did "Let It Ride" or "Takin' Care Of Business" or one or two BTO tunes. At the end of the night you can see that the people by then are really into rockin'. I'm pretty sure I'm going to get a couple of really good cuts done of my songs in the next year or so out of Nashville, and that's kind of where I think I'm going to end up.

SW: That's interesting. It's definitely taking a turn; it's much more roots-oriented than most rock music these days.

RB: Well, it's like Seventies rock with a violin or pedal steel. And a lot of the guys in the bands, like in Blackhawk there's a couple of guys from the Bob Seger Band. Brooks and Dunn also have a Seger guy.

You know, rock music turned into pretty much of a dance-oriented thing in the Eighties, and the classic rock musicians of the Seventies had nowhere to go, and when the Nashville Network went twenty-four hours, which is now nine or ten years ago, they didn't have enough videos to play, so they started playing some classic rock in there too. And it's not that much different; you go see Hank Williams Jr. or Sawyer Brown live, or Garth Brooks, you're pretty much looking at a Seventies rock show. These guys are much different live than on radio. For radio, they have a certain mix that's more commercial; it's more snare, and less loud guitar, more acoustic, and a lot of vocal. But when these guys are on stage, there's no difference between them and a Seventies rock show. You might as well be seeing BTO and Bob Seger and Aerosmith and REO Speedwagon as seeing Sawyer Brown.

SW: That's true. It's funny how it turned out that way. When you look back over your own career, is there a period that you think represents your best playing?

RB: I think this last album, *Any Road*, has got some really good guitar playing. Songs like "It's Only Money"; not real fast playing, but real emotional and proper playing—playing the right notes in the right spots. And the first BTO album *Blue Collar* has some pretty incredible jazz playing, pretty much influenced by me spending several months with Lenny Breau when I first started playing guitar, and him teaching me certain movements, from rock guitar into jazz and country.

I don't know, I think I'm like anyone else; my playing gets really good, and then I get really bored with it and stop practicing and start doing other things. So you fall back, and then you go see some other band live and you say, "Wow, that guy's good. I gotta go home and practice." *(Laughs)*.

I set up a practice schedule of one or two hours a day for a full three or four weeks, which is a lot, because I've always got a guitar writing songs, so this is actually sitting down doing movements and looking at these videos, which are great, these home videos that you can put on and guys are showing you licks and stuff. Usually before a tour I'll go and do a week of crash course and study, just to get my fingers moving again. Because when you're writing songs, you're not playing solos and stretching for new stuff. You're just trying to create songs, and basically it's done with chords.

SW: Do you find when you're on tour that you play better toward the end of it?

RB: Oh, yeah. The last two or three days of any tour, the whole band is always saying, "Wow, we really want to go home, because we're tired and homesick, but we're playing *so good*." The first one is pretty shaky, and it doesn't matter how much you rehearse; you can rehearse for a whole week, but you've actually got to go and play in front of people. It doesn't matter if we rehearse for an hour, or every day for a whole week before we go on tour, it still starts out shaky. The second one's a bit better. The third one, you start looking around thinking, "Wow, this is really hot." And then the last three or four are just incredible nights, where everyone is oiled and greased and everything is running smoothly, and you're playing together and all the timing is right. By then you've got your voice and your chops back, so the last few days are always the best.

SW: Do you ever suffer from stage fright or nerves?

RB: No, never.

SW: That's pretty fortunate.

RB: See, I started playing when I was five; I started playing violin, and I used to go on stage and play with a pianist, and then with a little school symphony orchestra. So when I went to guitar, I never really had stage fright.

I do get anxious. I hate to get to a gig two hours ahead of time and wait. I like to get there, get the guitar and go on. There's an anxious kind of thing where I just want to get on with it. I just want to get on stage. It's not like I'm nervous that I'm not going to play right or do anything right, I just want to get on and get moving and get playing.

SW: You're sort of renowned throughout your career for endless touring, through BTO and through the past few years. Do you feel like you do your best playing live?

RB: That's a tough question. *(Long pause)*. I think most guys play better live, especially like we just discussed, toward the end of a tour. You get comfortable with your solos, and then you get a little bit bored with them, so you try to change them a little bit and you play a little bit extra. Then you find that you're playing really great stuff, amazing yourself and the rest of the band. And unless you're recording it live, it's gone in an instant. You come off stage saying, "That was a great night," and unless it's been recorded, it's gone, it's history. So it's really hard to compare, because when you're in the studio playing something great, it's there forever.

It's great to come right off the road and go straight into the studio, because you've got that edge. You've got the smoothness of your style back, and you're bored with what you've been playing on stage, so you go a little bit further and do a little bit extra in your solos. That's when it's great, to take that attitude in playing right into the studio. That's why I like to go on the road now. I've got an album half done, and when I come home with my chops after being on the road ten days, I've got the fluidity in playing and the ideas, and I maybe stretch a little bit more and do something better. Or I've seen and played with other guys on the road who reminded me of old licks that I've forgotten, since there really are no new licks. *(Laughs)*. I mean, you've heard everything. It's just how you play it and where you play it that's new.

We did some touring with Bloodline, and they have a really cool guitar player. Smokin' Joe's like a young protégé, an incredible guitar player. And to see some of the stuff that he was playing, I'd think, 'Gee, I used to play that,' and you come home and pull out the licks. They're just old Eric Clapton and Allmann Brothers licks, and you put them in a new song.

SW: BTO's album *Not Fragile* always struck me as kind of a strange title. Where did that come from?

RB: Well, in the early Seventies Yes had an album called *Fragile*, and I didn't like that album title. It seemed like it was gonna break! Our music seemed like you could drop it and kick it around and it wouldn't break. So just as a pun, we called our album *Not Fragile*, and then had a box full of gears that looked like it was unbreakable. I still have the box today; it's a big wooden box, a one-inch-thick pine box with rivets and great big bolts on it. We filled it with gears because that was our logo, an overdrive gear, and just kind of tongue-in-cheek called ours *Not Fragile*, whereas Yes were calling theirs *Fragile*.

I think the Yes album cover actually had a picture of the world breaking, which is true; I mean, the world is a fragile place as far as the ecology and things like that. So it's not us against the band Yes. We just thought that was kind of a strange title, so we thought we'd call ours *Not Fragile*.

SW: After you left BTO, you put out a solo album and a couple of albums with Ironhorse which were relatively successful, although not quite as successful. How did you enjoy that period?

RB: I've enjoyed every period, whether it's successful or non-successful. It all contributes to my next album, if you know what I mean. It's the learning experience. Everything you do right, you try to retain, and when you try to stretch out, you might get lucky, and sometimes you might get burned, but it's all part of developing. Some of my greatest failures, like some of those solo excursions and other bands, all added to what I think will be my next success coming up in the next year or two. It's all learning experience, and I've enjoyed every bit of it.

I knew at such an early age that I was going to play music; it's all I do, so I enjoy playing even in a dumpy little club that's a rat hole with twenty people in there. I still get some enjoyment out of that. It's not a downer for me. Just playing is a fun, great thing. It's the greatest life you can have, to be a musician and go out and play an instrument and make a few bucks. I've had a lot of straight jobs. (*Laughs*). They just don't compare.

SW: Over the past ten years ago, there have been a few Guess Who reunions and BTO reunions. How much of a part have you had in those?

RB: There was a big Guess Who reunion in 1983, the original Guess Who. We got together, the four of us, and I took part in that. But it was a window in time; somebody approached us a year earlier and said, "Can you make this window from May to August of 1983?" So we all agreed to do that and got together. We did some concerts in Canada, we did a live album and video, and then the window closed and it was over. That was fun.

And while I was doing that, a lot of people kept saying, "Well, this Guess Who reunion is great, the music is great. What about BTO? Are you gonna bring BTO back?" So about a year and a half after that, in '85 and '86, we got together the BTO guys and did some touring, and then got asked to tour with Van Halen on the 5150 tour in 1986, which was supposed to be a three week favor from me to Sammy Hagar, and ended up being ten and a half months. We opened for Van Halen for ten and a half months, most of 1986. It was really a great tour. It was great fun to hang out with Eddie and Sammy and the guys, and get to know them real well.

After that I continued with the BTO thing, but nobody wanted anything new. It's like classic rock was all they wanted. All the previously deleted albums came out on CD, and everybody just wanted to hear that. And I already said this to you—I am a songwriter. I was writing songs and demoing them, and wanted to get them out, and the rest of the guys in BTO weren't really interested in doing it. We tried it, and we didn't have the magic that Aerosmith had when they did it. They had magic and came back real strong. We did it, and we weren't able to find the chemistry again.

Then when I had submitted enough demos of my own, I had offers to release it. People were saying, "Gee, you've got a new voice here, you've got a new sound; it's grown up, and there's a maturity there. Why don't you release your own album?" I jumped at the chance and released *Any Road*.

SW: The title for *Any Road* came from Lewis Carroll...

RB: It's from *Alice In Wonderland*, which I've never read. *(Laughs)*. Growing up, you know, that was a girl's book. I never read *Alice In Wonderland*; I was reading the Hardy Boys and things like that. But I heard a guy on the radio—there's CBC Radio in Canada, and it's very BBC-ish, where they review books on the radio—and at the end of one of these book reviews, the guy was signing off the show, and he said, "Remember what Lewis Carroll said: 'If you don't know where you're going, any road will take you there'." And I thought, 'What a great sentence.' I pulled my car over to the side of the road and wrote that down on a McDonald's napkin, and came home and just wrote the whole song, inspired by that line.

I thought it was a great album title, because I really didn't know where I was going, but I wanted to go there. I wanted to release another album, and take a band on the road, and see if, at age fifty—the same vintage as Jagger and Richards and McCartney and those guys—I could go back out there and do it again. So when I had the offer from the record label, it was, "Do you want to travel down this road again?" And I said, "You bet; I'll take a shot. I still enjoy the ride, and I'm ready to go."

SW: That's great. You've mentioned Neil Young a couple of times; he guested on that album.

RB: Like I mentioned, we knew each other back in Winnipeg in the Sixties, and we'd always bump into each other, but never had the opportunity to play together. I was either in the Guess Who on the road, or when we'd be on a break I'd go to visit him in California and he'd just be leaving Buffalo Springfield and joining Crosby, Stills and Nash, or doing his own solo thing. All this time went by, and we were kind of distant friends who always stayed in touch, and I think we were always watching each other's career and what we were doing.

When I was cutting the *Any Road* album, I got a message from his guitar tech that he needed some Gretsch parts. I get those requests from everybody all over the world; they need a little tip for a switch, or they need a little strap thing to hold the strap on, and if I've got the extra part I just put it in an envelope and send it out to them. So I sent Neil Young's guitar roadie a couple of little Gretsch parts, and just for fun I sent him a fax copy of the lyrics to "Prarie Town". And then he showed the lyrics to Neil Young without me knowing it, and I got a fax back from Neil the next day saying, "I love the lyrics to this song. I want to play and sing on it. It really touches my heart; it makes me long for those great days of the Sixties growing up in Winnipeg."

And so I finished the album, and then as the timing was right, got invited down to Neil's studio. I took my tapes down there and he played and sang on both versions of "Prarie Town", and it was a great coming of full circle. Here were he and I playing together, and playing together on a song I had written that's pretty autobiographical about me and the early Guess Who and Neil Young and the Squires. So we played together on it, and have since done videos for both versions of the song.

SW: Great. I wanted to ask you about the Guitar Marathon that happened, what, last year?

RB: It was last May, I think. I had been invited to Nashville for Tin Pan South, which is a whole week of songwriters where they invite songwriters from all over North America, Canada and the world to come there and merge and co-write with Nashville writers. That's what I think is so great about country music; they invite all the pop and rock and jazz guys to come there and co-write, and I think it's very healthy for country music.

So here I was in Nashville, and my phone rang one morning, and somebody said, "We're from Music West, and we're promoting a big music festival in Vancouver in May, and we want to use the song 'Takin' Care Of Business.'" And I said, "For what? For a commercial, or what?" And they said, "No, we want to try to break the record that the Hard Rock Cafe set with 'Louie Louie', with four hundred guitar players playing it for forty-five minutes. We want to try to break that record." So I said, "That's fine, you can use my song." And they said, "No, we want you to lead the band." And I said, "What band?" And they said, "We're going to try to get more than four hundred and fifty guitar players." So I said, "Well, that's okay, but I'm in Nashville, and I'm leaving for England as soon as I get home from there."

So they asked me to delay my trip to England, and I delayed it for a day. They went on the radio and got together this big thing in Vancouver, and I basically had my band, guitar, bass, drums and keyboards, and we set up a stage. And then to make it legal, so it would be in the *Guinness Book Of World Records*, they had to register every guitar player who came; name, address, guitar, phone number, and give them a number. So we ended up with thirteen or fourteen hundred guitar players, which was incredible.

We played the song for seventy-five minutes, and the only reason we stopped playing was because I had to get into a car and drive to the airport and fly to England. I had delayed my trip for a day, and my family had gone ahead without me, or we probably could have played the song for two and a half or three hours. I changed the key, because "Takin' Care Of Business" is in C. If you try to play it in C for about an hour, you get hand cramps. I changed it to A, so you go back and forth between fifth position and open strings, so for everybody it was much easier in A.

So we just played it and played it and played it, and it was a beautiful sunny day, and it was shot on video. And near the end, probably the last forty-five minutes, we were facing out into the audience while they played along, and they came to the front of the stage one at a time. We'd pull them up on stage, and I'd unplug and plug them in; each guy would play a little solo and sing a verse, wave to his friends and jump off stage, and the next person came on. So it was really cool. The whole crowd was participating. And when it was all done, we had set a record, which is going to be in the *Guinness Book Of World Records*.

SW: That's pretty strange.

RB: Yeah, it is. I thought it was a weird idea, and I would have never had the idea myself, because the first thing you think is, 'What if nobody comes and it's a failure?' *(Laughs)*. But they had agreed to do the whole thing, and I didn't care; I was in between Nashville and England, and I thought, 'Well, I'll give it a shot.' I didn't want anybody else leading the band, because they were going to do the song anyway, so I might as well be there.

And it turned out to be really cool, because after that I went to England, and I saw a couple of guys in bands there; Motley Crue, and Cyndi Lauper and her band were there, and they'd all seen it on CNN, and they all got on the train and saw me and started singing "Takin' Care Of Business". Because when you tour Europe there's nothing to watch but CNN. TV goes off there, and MTV Europe is terrible; it's a three hour loop of Ace of Base and Roxette or something, which is okay, but I mean, every three hours! *(Laughs)*. So you end up watching CNN; that's your link back to the States and the world, because you can't understand the German or French that's on the other channels. So to have this "Takin' Care Of Business" thing on CNN for three days, every musician saw it.

SW: That's pretty funny. Now, you also donated a huge collection to a museum some time recently, is that right?

RB: Way, way back when I started in Chad Allan and the Reflections, I would always save my little press clippings from the high school newspaper or the local newspaper saying that I had played with my band. You know, I thought it might be the last time my name was ever in print! *(Laughs)*. And as we got more successful, I saved every article. I saved the tickets from the dances, I'd save the poster from the dance. I collected stuff, and I don't know why. I was the leader of each band, both of the Guess Who and of BTO, and I saved a lot of that stuff just for the bands' history, and after an accumulation of thirty years of it, I got asked by the Archive Museum in Canada's capital to donate it all to the museum for their archives.

So I went through all this stuff, boxes and boxes of it, some of which I hadn't seen for years. A lot of the stuff, I would come home from a tour and throw it in a box. It was all in some kind of chronological order, all just layered in each box. As it was, I think I donated tens of thousands of items to Ottawa; all my amps, guitars, foot pedals, my clothing, all the contracts, posters, over a hundred and twenty gold and platinum albums, and I had nowhere to put this stuff. I have had storage of several double garages full floor to ceiling with all this stuff stored in there, pretty much getting mildewed, because when you rent these little mini-storages, they're not heated and stuff, and so I was really thrilled to be able to send it to Ottawa and have somebody care about it and put it up in museum display cases.

Now they've created the Randy Bachman Room in the Archive Museum in Ottawa, and it's really cool. They have an Oscar Peterson and a Glenn Gould

Room, you know, classical and jazz Canadian guys, and now they're embarking on Canadian pop and country music. And they gave me a tax credit for it, which you apply against your income tax that you owe; they can't pay you for it, but they give you a tax credit, which if you're earning any money is just as good. You just don't pay as much tax at the end of the year. So they have all this stuff there; they're still going through it in Ottawa.

It took probably ten months to do it, to document everything. I had to put everything I was sending on computer, because I didn't want to just send all these boxes without looking at it. But I was able to shrink my collection. I still have it at home. I would send my two-inch masters to Ottawa, but I would take that and copy it onto a DAT. I'd send my video masters, but I copied them to High 8, so I was able to shrink everything I have at home to fit on a shelf instead of filling a whole room before, because with technology you can shrink everything to a smaller format. So all of my original stuff is there, and it was just kind of neat to do. Now I'm kind of an ambassador, and I encourage other artists to archive and save their stuff and send it to Ottawa.

SW: That's interesting. You can actually go to a museum and say, "This is my life."

RB: That's true, and I can go there any time with my family and my kids can see it. And over the years I've had many requests from people all over the world who are doing a Doctorate on Canadian music, or a newspaper article or a book, and they would call me. Or more specifically they're doing an article or their Doctorate or their Master's on the Guess Who or on BTO or on Canadian music, and I didn't have enough time to spend with these people and send them documents.

Now I just refer them to Ottawa. They can go to Ottawa, or they can call Ottawa and say, "Can we have this period of time?" And Ottawa then copies it all and charges them ten cents a sheet, because that's what libraries do; you can get information very economically and cheaply there. So people can now go there and do the proper research and documentation without me feeling that I'm cheating them out of a request because I don't have time to fulfill all their needs and demands. So it was a really good three or four fold purpose in doing that.

SW: That's really cool. When do you think your next record will be coming out?

RB: I'm not sure. Like I said, *Any Road* is just waiting. I'm either waiting for it to take off or to glide or to stop, and I'm still waiting. It's early January, and I'm not sure what's going to happen with it. I'll be finishing up my next album in the next two or three months, and I'll just sit waiting. I mean, Canada's been waiting for a year, and I'm waiting to see what *Any Road* does around the world. We're just talking now about releases in the Netherlands and Australia, and we'll see what happens.

I don't want to overlap albums and be trying to promote two albums at the same time in different countries. That would drive me nuts. I want to spend more time at home and be more in control of my traveling, and the way to do that is to not release this album until I know that *Any Road* has run its course. And I might know that in the next month, or that might take all of next year. I don't know.

SW: Well, I hope it all goes real well for you.

RB: Me, too, and thank you!

For more information about Randy Bachman, please visit www.randybachman.com

"I Don't Believe In Guitar Heroes"

Martin Barre *was chosen from a field of dozens of contenders (including soon-to-be* **Black Sabbath** *guitarist* **Tony Iommi***) to replace* **Mick Abrahams** *in* **Jethro Tull***, thereby ushering in the most successful era of* **Tull***'s career*

Though the band retained its bluesy edge on 'Stand Up', its second album, band leader **Ian Anderson** *soon began to change his focus from the standard blues progressions that were so much a part of British rock at the time to a more distinctive mix of rock, classical, and Scottish folk influences which eventually became* **Tull***'s signature sound.*

Barre*'s distinctive, diverse contributions to such timeless albums as 'Aqualung', 'Thick As A Brick' and 'War Child' helped elevate* **Jethro Tull** *to its status as one of the world's most successful headlining bands in the Seventies, selling out arenas in virtually every country of the world. His playing is familiar from any one of nearly a dozen AOR staples such as "Aqualung", "Locomotive Breath", "Bungle In The Jungle", "Teacher", and "Farm On The Freeway".*

In the Eighties **Jethro Tull** *settled into the second stage of its career, no longer dominating the charts, but continuing to release solid albums and tour successfully, playing to the massive, cult-like audience the band had cultivated.* **Barre***'s playing continued to shine on such albums as 'A', while his contributions to the overall sound of* **Jethro Tull** *continued to expand. In the mid-Eighties the band experienced a resurgence of sorts with the 'Crest Of A Knave' album, which featured some of* **Barre***'s best playing to date. The album earned* **Jethro Tull** *a Grammy for Best Hard Rock/Heavy Metal Performance, much to the chagrin of* **Metallica** *fans everywhere. The band released a boxed set and embarked on an enormously successful world tour to commemorate its twentieth year.*

Subsequent albums such as 'Rock Island' and 'Catfish Rising' have proved successful enough to sustain the band into its third decade. **Martin Barre** *continues to record and tour with* **Jethro Tull***, still a popular arena act. In 1994 he released his first solo album, 'A Trick Of Memory'.*

I spoke to **Martin Barre** *on January 29th and February 19th, 1995, from his home in London. He was extremely busy, recording a new* **Tull** *album during the week and working on a second solo album in his spare time. In fact, the guitarist's schedule was so packed that he asked me to fax him in the morning, Atlanta time, every Sunday at his London home to see if he could squeeze in a bit of conversation between sessions. This interview took place over a period of almost a month, with several weeks going by which yielded nothing more than apologetic faxes and the promise of next week.*

Barre *exudes none of the self-satisfaction that often comes with twenty-five years of success and fame; indeed, he virtually refuses to give himself any credit whatsoever. He approaches his music as a working man approaches his trade, resolving to do the best job he can. He's more interested in* *making good music than in being perceived as a rock idol. Before we began, **Barre** told me, "I don't believe in guitar heroes."*

SW: Do you remember the first guitar you ever owned?

MB: It was a fall-apart Spanish acoustic for a few months, and then my dad got on hire, whatever you call it in America, hire purchase, a Tuxedo, it was called. I've never seen one since! *(Laughs)*. It was actually a very pretty guitar, and very unusual even in those days. And it was fairly playable, but it was just a nice shape. I wish I had it now. I'd love it now. Probably sound terrible! *(Laughs)*. But it meant the world to me; it was just every dream come true, and I looked after it better than I looked after anything in my life. Fortunately my dad signed the bits of paper for me, as he did for many years after that for various instruments! *(Laughs)*.

I played with that…well, I was at school and in a band, and then the dates don't come to mind immediately, but it was probably around 1965, I bought a Gibson 330. Of course, that was the biggest step in my life, really, to get a proper guitar. In those days everybody played Fenders or Gibsons. There was no reason to go one way or the other, it was probably whoever your hero was that month; if he played a particular guitar, that's the one you bought. But I suppose that stamped my identity, because I bought a Gibson and stuck with them for quite a few years after that. I had a Gibson 330 and a Vox 8030. It actually sounded great! I should have never got rid of those, either. Then I was into serious noises and no excuses.

SW: Who were some of the early guitarists that influenced you?

MB: Very, very early on, there was only such a handful of guitarists anyway. The Shadows and Hank Marvin, Duane Eddy…anything. Anything and anybody who played guitar, I listened to and devoured it. But there was so little to get the inspiration from; you compare those days to now, there's just no comparison. I was desperate for anything to listen to, and it just wasn't there.

And then finally the blues started to come into England; you know, Sonny Brown, Terry McGhee, Buddy Guy, Muddy Waters. They had a thing called the Blues Train in England, with some vague connection with British Rail, so they traveled around on trains and played in railway stations. It was them playing their original stuff, so that was the introduction to the blues.

In Birmingham, where I came from, the blues was very strong. There were a couple of blues clubs, and I used to go down there and listen to people. In fact, the Spencer Davis Group was around in those days, and they were sort of local heroes—you know, with Stevie Winwood. This is when I was sixteen or seventeen, and they were actually a big band in those days. He's been around a hell of a long time. So the blues started creeping in.

Unfortunately, when I turned professional you couldn't make money playing blues; in actual fact, I had to play saxophone to make a living as a musician. The only professional job I could get was as a sax player. I doubled on guitar, but it was more R&B and soul. We used to be a backing band for people like Alvin Robertson, Lee Dorsey, and the Coasters, so I used to play my sax backing these guys. It was sort of sixty percent sax and forty percent guitar. It wasn't really for a couple of years, until late '67, that the blues came back with a huge explosion, with Fleetwood Mac and Traffic and Cream. So it was brilliant; I could sort of chuck the sax away and continue on guitar.

But a really good thing that came out of that was that I learned flute, because traditionally sax players in soul bands doubled on flute, for some strange reason. A lot of them played flute as a second instrument, so I learned flute. I enjoyed that a lot more than saxophone. I've always sort of kept on fiddling about with flute.

SW: You played some flute on your solo album.

MB: I just don't play enough to be a reasonable player, but it's still ingrained from all those years ago.

SW: Did you always know you'd play music professionally?

MB: No, it just fell that way. I've always thought that the equivalent to what happened to me would be like you being at college and having a bad year at college, and you just think, 'What the hell, I'm just gonna backpack and travel across the Himalayas for a year, just for the hell of it,' and for some reason you settled over there and became a doctor or something! *(Laughs)*. It was as silly as that.

There was nothing like that available in my day, so music was like a fantasy. It had nothing to do with talent, or thinking of what I wanted to do for the rest of my life. I just figured, what the hell, I'd had a bad year with my exams at University, so I just sped off for a bit to see what would happen, and then maybe I'd come back to my studies later. I went through three years of sleeping on floors and earning absolutely zero, and then at the point where it was all going to finish and I was seriously considering going back to my student days, the gig in Jethro Tull came up, and I auditioned for it, and after a couple of times I got it.

SW: How did you hear about it?

MB: In two ways; one way, my band supported Jethro Tull in England, and because I played flute, I think that they remembered me and my guitar playing. So on the one hand they were looking for me for the audition, and eventually found me through their spies. And the ad which was in the music paper, I'd actually answered it; well, I phoned up, but when I found out who it was, I didn't think anything more about it, because I was petrified.

And then when they found me, they said, "Come on over and have a go." And I did, but it was very daunting, a room full of guitar players waiting for their turn to play, and I didn't do very well, predictably. But then I called back and said, "How's it going? Have you found somebody?" And Ian hadn't. I think they'd been working with Tony Iommi, and things hadn't worked out, so I had a second go, and it went better. And that was it, really.

SW: Were you already familiar with their first album?

MB: Yes, because they were a very big band in England. And I have to say that as much as I've never really had heroes, if I did, they would have been one of them. But it wasn't that sort of relationship. But I did think that they were a really, really good band, exactly the sort of band that I'd dreamed of being in all my life, really.

In many ways it was fortunate that the music changed when I joined, because I was never a strict blues player, and I think Ian wanted to get away from the blues and found the perfect answer in me, who couldn't play the blues to save my life! *(Laughs)*. So we started off on the right foot.

SW: Once you got in the band, how were the working relationships in the band; how did the band work together and what was your contribution?

MB: It was virtually zero, because Ian was writing all of the songs, and they were very complete in the form he wrote them. And it was very early days for me, so I trod very warily. The first year was very tense for me; I was sort of feeling my way and getting to learn my trade, in many ways. But things opened up once John Evans had joined. The music had a bit more leeway, and it varies from song to song, album to album.

There have been people, me or someone else, who've had a lot of input into certain songs, and on another track on another album, very little. It's variable. I think when somebody's writing songs or writing music, some things allow people to experiment and develop their part, and other bits of music don't; it's important that people play the part that's already written, because it's a very important part of the music inherently.

SW: As the years have gone by, it seems like your guitar playing has grown more, not *dominating*, I guess, but more technically oriented. Do you feel like you're improving as you go along?

MB: Well, I have to, as everybody has to, because in guitar playing, the standard increases and improves with every year. So there's no way you can just sit back and do what you did years ago and expect to get away with it! *(Laughs)*. I work hard, as hard as I can, to improve my playing and to improve my music writing and everything else. All those things run in parallel—writing music, getting good guitar sounds, playing well in the studio, pitching, playing in time, technique—it's a whole bunch of things that keep you busy.

SW: Do you actually sit down and consciously practice scales and exercises and that sort of thing?

MB: No. I did for a while, and I do occasionally, just in case I can find something new and interesting in the relationship between scales and chords. I never, ever read books or do any of those little exercises in the back of guitar magazines, because I just think that it's much more fun to find things out for yourself, because there's a sense of discovery, and maybe you might learn things in a slightly different way that gives you a bit of style that you can call your own.

There's a lot of different modes and scales that don't particularly get used often in Jethro Tull music, but they might in something I do. If I've been fiddling about with something, and it might be a scale but it isn't a proper one, but it's pleasant to my ear, then I use it. I think that's the criteria I use for anything, is that if it sounds right, it is right.

SW: The last few Jethro Tull albums seem like they've come around to being a little more guitar-oriented than the albums of the early Eighties. Was that by conscious choice?

MB: No, I don't think so. I think there were a few very dominating keyboard players in the band at various times, and I don't mean that disparagingly; I think they're very good musicians, and they gave a lot of input into the overall musicality of Jethro Tull. But it was a new thing for the band, and I think keyboard players dominate; they fill lots of space, both musically and tonally as well. So people like Peter Vettesse and Eddie Jobson wrote a lot of music, and because it was written on keyboards, guitars and flutes and other things took a secondary role in the music.

Having said that, it was very good music, and very challenging to play. I enjoyed it just as much as I would an album where guitars were more up front. I mean, there's no less to play on an album that you might call less guitar-oriented; there's as much playing, and there's as much in terms of bits to do, but they're just not up front. It's just as satisfying to do.

SW: Do you enjoy playing more live or in the studio?

MB: I love playing live more than anything, and I love playing in the studio doing *my* music, because I love having a hundred percent control. I love having my neck on the line, where you've just got to come up with things constantly, to come up with the business of writing music. I really do enjoy it, because I obviously let myself into other areas of music that I want to be in.

If you go and do a session for somebody else, whether it's Jethro Tull or anybody else, then you're on alien territory in a way. You're playing their phrases and their ideas, and because of that it's harder to play. It's harder to feel music someone else has written. But when I write it, it's easy; I can feel it immediately, because I wrote it. And obviously that's the sort of thing that I like to play and can play well. But it's a lot more of a challenge to play Ian's music, and other people's, if and when I have done it. There's a lot more pressure on me.

SW: I had heard that you worked with Paul McCartney.

MB: I did a week of demos with him. But it was a very long week! *(Laughs).* And again, because you're really in at the deep end. It was rewarding as an experience. I even heard from somebody, although I don't know if it's true, that one of the tracks I played on was released in Japan. I haven't actually seen it, but that's what I hear. It was very interesting and a good thing to do.

SW: How did you come to be involved in that?

MB: He was looking for people for that album, and I think he went through everybody in England that had any reputation at all that plays. He did loads and loads of one-day demo sessions while he wasn't there, and out of all these tapes he picked groups of people to work with at his studio. So I think he must have done, as a guess, two dozen one-day sessions, while he wasn't present at any of them, and then he picked two or three dozen bands to work with out of those people.

SW: What other artists have you played with outside of Jethro Tull?

MB: I have, but I can't think of anybody really famous that would impress you or your book. Let me think…well, I played with John Wetton on his solo record, but unfortunately it didn't really see the light of day.

SW: That was *Caught In The Crossfire*, wasn't it?

MB: There you go. Obviously you're very knowledgeable. I was on that. Chick Churchill, I was on his solo album. I did an album by a Canadian band called Fahrenheit 451. The thing is, I don't do that sort of thing as a habit. I don't look for that sort of work, so usually I do it as a favor because it's a friend. And most people presume that somebody like me wouldn't have the time to do it, or the inclination, or the need to do it financially, so I think you rarely get asked. However, the case is I do them probably just for the fun; it's a bonus to be paid for it as well, but mostly I just enjoy working with other people.

SW: After you've been in the same band for so many years, do you find that playing outside of that format gives you a whole different perspective on music?

MB: I think so, because you're putting your neck on the line, and you find out a lot about yourself, because you're in a different musical environment and you're playing a different style. Very often you're asked to play something that you've probably never played in your life, or you've played very little of.

Ideally a guitar player should be a jack of all trades; you might have to play a country and western solo, or a bit of folk, or whatever. Anything and everything can be asked of him, and ideally he should be able to come up with something that sounds reasonably accomplished in any of those styles. I have done a country and western album as well, believe it or not. But I won't tell you about that one. *(Laughs)*.

SW: What prompted you to record your solo album last year after all these years in Tull?

MB: Well, I've written lots of bits and pieces here and there, but I think I just wasn't happy with my writing, and then I had a space of time that gave me enough time to write and get into the recording, and I just thought, 'Right, I'm ready to do it.' Don't ask me what it was; maybe it was just a hunch that I was ready. And I'm glad, because I was very pleased with what I did. Whether other people did, I don't know, but I enjoyed doing it, and I do actually believe that what I wrote was okay. It's nothing to do with being big-headed or having an ego;

I'm very critical of anything, particularly what I do, and I scrutinize everything that passes under my hands. But I enjoy what I did and would stand by it.

SW: The album turned out really well, and it was remarkably different from what some people might have thought it would be.

MB: Yeah, it was. They probably didn't know what to expect, having never heard anything I've done alone before. Really, I was taking a lot of liberty, because I just let loose and did anything I wanted to do. I've just started doing my second one, and I think that's a lot more focused, because there are things that I never want to do again, ever, like maybe sort of classical-sounding things. I've done one of those; I don't want to do any more. Because my band plays live, and the very early discovery that you make is that you need as much material that you can play live as possible. So the second album will certainly be more rock/blues, live playable stuff.

SW: When do you think that might be out?

MB: I hope to finish it in the summer. It should be out in September.

SW: And you've been working on a Jethro Tull album?

MB: We just started. In fact, we just started in the studio yesterday.

SW: When you work in the studio, do you like to fiddle around with lots of different amplifiers and guitars?

MB: Well, I do at home. It's difficult, because I made my album here, where I live, and I've got everything here. I've got guitars, amps, pedals; everything I own is at my house. Up at Ian's studio, I took a carload of stuff the first day, and I took a few amps up. And what'll happen is, each week I go up I'll take something else that catches my eye that I think might sound good, and hopefully I'll have enough stuff.

In many ways I get a sound and stick to it; I don't spend a lot of time using different amps. I get an amp that works for me, or a couple of amps that work for me, and stick to those for the whole album. I'm more interested in concentrating on the playing and the end result, once I've got a good sound. And I also believe that the player produces the sound, rather than the amplifier. As long as the amplifier does what you ask it to do, then beyond that it's how you play and what you play that produces the sound in the end.

SW: Since you've recorded the past five or so Jethro Tull albums at Ian's studio, is it easier to work there, as opposed to working in a bigger commercial studio where you have to go and book time and travel to the studio every day?

MB: Yes, it is. He's actually got a new studio which is a lot better; the one he had before didn't have a live room, so that was really difficult, because you had to play through power soaks on whisper volume and monitor on headphones. But now it's a proper studio.

In commercial studios you're just thinking about the money all the time. It's an outside pressure, and it's the last one you need, because you're constantly aware of the hundred pounds an hour or whatever that it's costing you, and you can't have an hour where you sit and have a coffee and think about music, because it's too expensive. I don't enjoy those sort of studios.

Also, having mixed my stuff at an expensive studio, I'm not convinced that you can't do a better job on a lot simpler equipment. Because the proof of the pudding is, you get your cassette; you stick it in the car, go for a drive and play it, and if it sounds good, then everybody else's car is gonna sound good! *(Laughs)*.

I don't really think that you should believe what you hear in million-dollar studios, because nobody else has that stuff. It might sound unbelievably good with that equipment, but you've still got to put it on a cheap, cheap cassette and then shove it in your local hi fi; cheap hi fi, medium-priced hi fi, good hi fi, you've got to try them all. And that's where you make your decisions as to what's going on.

SW: It seems like people are finding that out, because more and more people that have the finances to do so are recording at home now.

MB: Well, I've compared. I recorded all of my album at home, and I did one mix at home, and I swear I can't tell the difference. In fact, I prefer it. Everything else was done on computer, mixed by a mix engineer. But the whole album was done by me and my engineer, recording-wise, and then the mix was done by my engineer and another mixing engineer, so I was sort of a bit removed from it.

We were rehearsing in the daytime for a tour, so I'd come in the evening and my ears were shot from having been rehearsing all day, and it was very difficult to be objective. You might say, "That's not loud enough, and there's too much of that," but you're really making minor decisions, whereas to mix properly I think you've got to be there at the beginning of the day, put your drums up, get your drum sound, add the bass, whatever. It's a jigsaw, and you have to be there at the beginning. And I can only do that here, really.

I enjoy it so much more. Although it's all manual; there's no computer mix here. You sort of go for it. Instead of it being very predictable—you know, with a computer it moves in a very predictable pattern, but here you have to go for things, and you might miss a cue, or you might push an echo up twice as loud as you meant to. So you get things happening in extremes, and sometimes it can work for the better.

SW: When you're in a band situation like Tull that's ongoing for a long period of time, when you get together to rehearse for a tour, are there certain songs that you just say, "Oh Lord, do we really have to play that one again this tour?"

MB: I think we all feel that way. I enjoy playing anything, but I think it's much better to play "Aqualung" for twenty-five years than it is to play "Stormy Monday Blues" for twenty-five years, because that would really bore me. We play the blues in my local band, and it's great fun for a week, but I wouldn't want to do it for a living. I'm not good enough to enjoy it enough. Musically it's great, because it's not challenging mentally; the only challenge is playing the blues great, which is very hard to do. It's all about having great feel.

But with Tull music you're thinking all the time, and you're remembering. It's a lot more complex, and because of that you don't tire of things, because there's too much to think about. And sure, some things I could do without, and some things I couldn't, but it's such a minor point, it's not really an important factor. Because it's the songs you play the most that people love. You can't ignore five or ten thousand people going berserk when you play the riff of "Aqualung"; you can't stand there and say, "Oh, I hate it." *(Laughs)*. You can't, because it feeds you; they feed off you and you off them.

SW: With all of the member changes that the band has been through over the years, do you have to re-adjust musically every time someone departs?

MB: I don't think so. It's an enhancement in many ways, because you're mostly playing what's on the album, and there's only a few pieces of music that'll be strung together for a particular tour. Obviously that's exciting to do, especially working with someone new. Everybody that's joined has added a little stamp of personality on tour, and to the bits of music that we play, and usually it's an upward step. Nothing radically changes.

SW: When you go out and play in your solo act, is it always the same line-up?

MB: It has been. It's a big, nine-piece band, with two girl singers, two guitars, drums, bass, percussionist, and a saxophone player. It's great, but you don't make any money. *(Laughs)*. And of course, you lose money. I subsidize it, because I love doing it, but it would be nice if you could take a nine-piece band on the road and do the clubs and actually make a bit of money. Unfortunately, that's not the way. Probably in the next few years, if there is a band that goes on the road doing my solo album stuff, it'll be a lot smaller, I'm afraid.

SW: Would you like to come to America and do your solo act?

MB: I'd love to. Are you making me an offer? *(Laughs)*. Yes, please! I'd love to. If it's financially viable, i.e., you don't lose money, then I'll be there. So we'll see.

SW: Over the years you've played a variety of different guitars; you used to be primarily associated with Gibsons, then for a while it was Hamers and Schechters, and then Ibanez. What motivates you to change and experiment with various instruments?

MB: I just think it's the search for the perfect guitar sound, which doesn't ever exist, because no matter how good your sound gets, you hear somebody else whose sound you think is better than yours, so you carry on looking. You're trying to find the infinite guitar sound that doesn't exist. I just like experimenting with different things.

I used vintage Gibsons to the point where it was impractical to take them on the road, because they'd break or get stolen, and they're irreplaceable. I wanted to use something that if it got lost or stolen, I could phone up the next day and get another one exactly the same the next day, and because Paul Hamer was a friend of mine, I used Hamers for quite a while. And then when Paul wasn't involved with the company anymore, I left and went to Ibanez.

Actually, I used Schechters along with Hamers as sort of a Fender substitute; they're made for me in England by Chandler Guitars. But then I used Ibanez for a while, and finally got on to Tom Andersons. I've got lots of different instruments that I play, and I'm not really committed to using any one particular guitar. I just like to try and find different sounds, and if I find an instrument that I really like, then I'll start playing that.

SW: How many guitars do you generally take out on the road?

MB: You'd be amazed to know that I take *one*! *(Laughs)*.

SW: You're kidding!

MB: One.

SW: *(Laughing)*. That simplifies things!

MB: It simplifies tours quite a lot, because we've been doing a lot of Third World countries. We've played India, Turkey, Israel, Russia, all over South America…just all the weird countries that nobody else goes to, like South Africa. And it's very small margins of profit, if any at all, so we just fly our own instruments and we hire as much as we can. So literally every pound weight of luggage that's saved makes it more fruitful to coming out with a bit of money and making a small profit at the end of these tours.

SW: Do you find when you go over to those countries that things are not nearly as organized as you're used to?

MB: Well, that is the case, but we are, and that makes up for it. Usually we can overcome most problems, because the team that we take over are very, very good, and it's simple. I mean, I've got one guitar! *(Laughs)*. If I break a string, I change it. I don't have a roadie that changes it for me. I change it, I tune it, and I help set my gear up. I know how it works, and when it goes wrong, I know what's wrong with it. The whole thing is logical, and really puts it all in perspective how illogical and wasteful other bands are.

I've seen guitar players—whom I suppose I really shouldn't mention—but I saw somebody with a fairly big band, and he actually changed his guitar with every song! *(Laughs)*. He must have had fourteen guitars! I just thought, 'Well, but they don't sound any different.' On some songs he just played rhythm parts, and he changed guitars. And I just thought, 'Why?' I mean, he was making a lot of work for a lot of people. Maybe he was just being nice. *(Laughs)*. Call it job creativity.

We've had to do things that way, and as you say, because things aren't as well organized when you go to a place like India, the less that can go wrong on our side, the better, because then you can concentrate on the things that they get wrong. In general it's really good. You have to bear in mind that an audience in

India hasn't heard a Pink Floyd concert, and doesn't know the quality of sound that you can get at live gigs. But they're still not being cheated; we're still giving them the best that's available to them, and really they're just so pleased to see anything come out of the West as far as rock music, they're just delighted that you're there.

SW: Do you get a different response over there?

MB: Oh, yes. The people are just so nice, and genuinely pleased that you're there. It's a lot nicer than playing at the downtown theater somewhere in the USA, where you're one of about fifty acts that are going to appear there.

I mean, obviously the people are still pleased to see you, and they're very much your fans, but it's something about, people have too much of a choice, particularly in America. They say, "Oh, should we see Tull, or should we see Bon Jovi?" Or whatever. They're spoiled for choice, and it's a less meaningful thing. You know, "Aw, we saw Tull last year; let's see these guys this year."

And you can't blame them; they're lucky to have the choice. But when you do go somewhere people are just deliriously happy you're there...next time you go there, they probably couldn't give a damn. *(Laughs)*. But that very first time, it's something very special for them, so it's nice.

SW: Do you find that they're familiar with your music?

MB: Very much so. Obviously you research the country before you go over there. I think the only place where it really didn't go down good was at Mistonia, where it was a rock festival, and they were just completely out of their brains. *(Laughs)*. They were just totally into, like, Scandinavian heavy metal.

SW: Oh, no! *(Laughs)*. Tull meets Krokus!

MB: Well, not mentioning any names; I don't think they were there, but there were some fairly horrific bands there, and the audience just didn't want to know about us.

But anyway, going back to your question, I just use one guitar, and really, one guitar does the job. It would be nice to take two; it'd be nice to have a spare, or to have a couple of guitars for sounds. I take an acoustic as well; I take one electric, one acoustic. I do everything myself. I always have. I've always changed my strings every night, and tuned it myself. I wouldn't want or let anyone else do it.

SW: Which is pretty different from the way a lot of people feel.

MB: Well, I'm sure that some people have a crew that they trust. I would trust people, but I just think if it's your instrument, and you're playing it, it's part of your job as a musician to prepare your instrument for the gig. Because it's your neck on the line, pardon the pun, so if it's out of tune, you can't expect the audience to say, "Oh God, that guy's roadie..." *(Laughs)*. Only one person gets blames if it sounds bad, and that's the guy that's playing, so I like to take responsibility for as much as I can.

SW: Is there a particular Jethro Tull album that you feel represents your best playing?

MB: I'd have to say *Crest Of A Knave*, because it's probably got more guitar up front. On other albums, such as *Under Wraps*, there's a lot of guitar playing, but it's..."buried" would be an unkind word, but being blunt, it's a lot more back in the mix. And there's a lot of parts that were hard to play, and interesting, and creative, but because they're not up in your face, you don't hear them as well. In general, nine out of ten albums I enjoyed doing, and are very representative of what I do, but I think on *Crest Of A Knave*, because there's so much less instrumentation there, the guitar is probably clearer in the mix.

SW: Seeing you guys live, I'm always struck by how much heavier you are than on any record.

MB: I suppose so, but then, that's the way. I like playing loud, and I like giving it a bit of stick, as I think the rest of the band do. So it tends to be that way, and it always has been, except for the earlier albums. The albums contain production ideas and subtleties that you can't reproduce on stage, and the way to make up for that is to really give it stick when it is loud and heavy, and then really lay back when it's acoustic and light, so you've got two very strong contrasts.

SW: I read somewhere that Jimmy Page was sitting there watching when you recorded the solo to "Aqualung".

MB: Yes. They were recording in the downstairs studio, the Island Records Studio in London. I forget which album they were doing; they've all got numbers. *(Laughs)*. It was one of their famous ones.

We used to meet up in the coffee kitchen; there wasn't even a lounge, just a kitchen where you made coffee. And we'd see them in there on coffee breaks and say, "Oh, hey, how's it going?" Apart from that, we never saw them; you know, you're completely encapsulated in the studio.

However, he just happened to drop by the control room on this one occasion, and I was right in the middle of doing the solo, and he's sort of standing at the window waving. I thought, 'Now, should I wave back and do another solo, or shall I just sort of smile and go for it?' And I thought, 'Bugger, I'll just go for it." And that was the one that was kept.

SW: You toured with Zeppelin at one point, didn't you?

MB: The second tour we did of America was with Zeppelin.

SW: What was that like?

MB: It was very good for us. It probably was the tour that broke us in America, because obviously Zeppelin were huge. It's probably not that way anymore, but in those days when you opened for a band, you had half an hour—actually, it hasn't changed a lot—you have to go on while they're still coming into the auditorium, so you play to half a crowd who haven't come to see you. Most of them can't wait for you to finish so they can see the band they've come to see. You've got your gear set up in front of the main band's gear, so you've got no stage to play on. I mean, really, it's a shit gig! *(Laughs)*.

But you've just got to go for it, because you know you're either going to do this for the rest of your life, or you're gonna give everything you've got in half an hour and win some people over. Fortunately, we did. It was very good for us. The next tour we headlined our own gigs. It was a real good opening for us. We'd already done a long tour before that in America, but that was just an introductory thing.

SW: Out of all the bands you've played on the bill with over the years, is there one that stands out in your mind?

MB: It's hard to say, because only the first two tours did we support bands. We did the odd festival after that where we weren't top of the bill. We played with Hendrix a load of times.

SW: I never knew that.

MB: We played the Isle Of Wight when he was there, we did Randall Island when he was there, and we played with him in LA another time. There were a lot of big festivals, and they were great, because there were a lot of bands. I mean, we played with everybody, like Jeff Beck. It was fabulous.

The thing that was good about it was that you got to see everybody; all your heroes were up there on stage, and you got to see the gig for nothing, plus you're actually on the same stage on the same night with these people. Some people were brilliant and friendly, and it was nice to see them and meet them, and other people were total assholes and you thought, 'What was all the fuss about?' But I learned a lot, and it was good for me, because I was sort of wet behind the ears, and I got to play with every great guitar player of the day. It was sort of nerve-wracking, yet exciting. There was a lot of great gigs, but I don't think any one band stood out, because I just enjoyed seeing so many.

I would have to say that the most influential band we played with—in fact I think that they supported us—was Mountain. We became very good friends; they were one of the first bands that we got close to, personality-wise. And I mean, Leslie West, he's such a great guitar player. As much as anyone's influenced me as far as guitar playing goes, which is hardly anything at all, I would say Leslie West was the only one that came close to it. He was such a great player, and a nice person. That was a really memorable band, one of the all-time greats for me. They were just so good live.

SW: You've said that you enjoy playing live more than anything. Do you think Jethro Tull comes off better in the mid-sized theaters, or the larger outdoor venues?

MB: I think theaters, because it's such a visual thing. It's much better when Ian is closer to the audience. At outdoor events it's potluck; you get one that goes good, and the crowd is great, and the people are really there to see you and not the other bands, and you play when it's dark so the lights are good, and if you're lucky, the guy on the PA knows your music a little bit. It's real potluck, and the odd one will be really good, but then the next one will be terrible, because you might not be top of the bill, so you might have to go on when it's light, so you don't get any benefit of the lights at all. Plus you're in a mixed audience, where some or most of them are there to see another band.

In a smaller theater, the people that got the tickets got them quick. It's sold out, they all really want to be there, and you can see most of them. And the odds are that the sound is pretty good, and the band is consistent, so everything's going for you.

SW: What's the funniest thing that ever happened to you on stage?

MB: A lot of funny incidents. We used to dress up in suits, all the roadies and us used to dress up in rabbit suits. *(Laughs)*. That didn't last very long, but at the beginning of the show, the lights came up, and a rabbit came out on stage, and the audience laughed. Then a second one came out, and they laughed a bit more. Third, fourth, and then they giggled a bit and thought, 'What's going on?'

Finally there's about ten rabbits on stage, and the crew leave, and the idea was that all the musicians would then form a circle and then unzip the rabbit suits in front of them, so we could get out of the suits. But of course, the zippers stuck, and you couldn't see the zippers, so for about ten minutes we're trying to get out of these rabbit suits. The moment had passed at least half an hour ago where it was a good joke, and the audience was certainly getting restless, and we were just sort of stuck in these bloody rabbit suits! It was fabulously silly, it was so bad. *(Laughter)*.

Another one was when John Evans, again, I think he was in a rabbit suit as well, and he used to have a piss backstage in a beer can halfway through the gig, and he'd left it next to his rabbit's head. And we had to go back and change in the dark. Somehow he kicked over the beer can, and it got into the head. And when he walked to the front of the stage and put the rabbit suit head on, it was like, "Aaaaughhhh!" *(Laughs)*. He got covered in it! A few things like that. *(Laughs)*. We have a good one now and again—usually at our own expense.

SW: You mentioned to me that you don't really believe in guitar heroes…

MB: No, I don't.

SW: And yet you are a guitar hero to a lot of people.

MB: I'm…it's nice, and it's a great compliment, *if* I am. I mean, a compliment's a compliment, so the only way I can react is to try harder, so that if people do like my playing, then at least next year they'll think it's even better. I'd hate for people to see a deteriorating standard in any musician, much less myself.

I'm just too objective to think about things like that. I always hear the faults that need correcting; the things that are good you file away as "correct". That's okay, thank you, and it's gone. The moment's gone; I enjoyed it, but it's gone, and I'm waiting for the next moment to get right.

I'm always looking at the things that need to be improved. I never really savor what I do, or if you like to put it an easier way, I don't have an ego at all. There's nothing in my personality that has any room for that sort of attitude, and maybe that's a bad thing, because everybody needs confidence and a boost when things get tough. But maybe that's balanced by the fact that it doesn't become a problem where I think I'm better than I am. Or as somebody put it, "Hey, you sound better than you are." *(Laughs)*. That's one of those musician's jokes, isn't it?

All musicians are neurotic, and I'm probably more so than most, but I use it to my own advantage because it makes me try harder. It's a job that I love, and I'll play as long as people want to hear me play, and then when they don't want to hear me anymore, I'll just play for myself! *(Laughs)*. I just love music. I love listening to music as much as I love playing it. It's all the same thing to me.

SW: Did you ever think Jethro Tull would last so long?

MB: No, of course not. I mean, particularly in the early days, but it didn't seem to matter then, because you weren't married and didn't have children, and houses, and mortgages, and debts, and bank accounts. The only time I started worrying about how long it would last is when I had the same responsibilities everybody else had, and then of course you start to think about what's going to happen in the future.

When you're young you're like every other band; you're just having a good time, and you don't think about next year. It doesn't matter. You might be there, you might not, but what the hell. You're having a great time, and you just take it as it comes. But you can't plan ahead that far, and you still can't, really.

I suppose in reality we could plan ahead five years, and if people hated our next record and it got slagged and nobody bought it, we could still probably exist for five years before people got really fed up with us, but it would be embarrassing. You'd do concerts where they would be half full, and you'd think, 'Well, it's time to stop.' You've probably got a few years' grace, but I don't think we would do it; I think we would quit as soon as we realized that we weren't the flavor of the month anymore. But we'd give it a good shot even then. We wouldn't be put down easily.

SW: Jethro Tull is really the only one of the Seventies progressive rock bands that's managed to retain a steady audience all the way through its career. Why do you think Tull has managed to last and adapt, whereas so many of those bands just seemed to fall apart?

MB: We've got Ian Anderson, who's a prolific songwriter, and has written great songs for twenty-six years. Plus, we've changed a lot; we've offered different styles of music within the framework of what people would accept as Jethro Tull. Things have sort of meandered in style.

We've had albums that have been very different; we've had bad albums, which in some ways I think has helped us, because if you do something that's very constant and very predictable, I think that can work against you. With Tull, people don't know what to expect from year to year. They'll buy an album, and the idea that it would be the same or similar to the one before is sort of inconceivable, really, whereas you can buy an album of some artists and say, "I didn't need to hear it, it's the same thing as before." We work hard at what we do; we don't have a year off, or six months off. We always work, in one direction or another, at what we do.

SW: Not long ago you released the long-fabled *Chateau D'Isaster* tapes. What was the story behind that?

MB: There were punitive tax rates in England at the time, and we tried to save paying crazy taxes by recording out of the country. And this recording studio, which I think now is vastly improved, thank God, was available, and we went to live there and make this album, a double album called *Passion Play*.

But it was a disaster in many ways; everybody got food poisoning from the disgusting food they used to serve us. *Unbelievable* food! In the end we just ate omelets: breakfast, omelets; lunch, omelets; dinner, omelets. Nothing else, just omelets. We didn't trust anything else. They used to bring in things that looked like blackbirds or crows. And the meat, the best you got was horse meat, and God knows what else there was. It was horrific.

Then all the gear was going wrong in the studio and there was nobody there to fix it, and it was a dirty place. It was dreadful. And we had to quit in the end; we went back to England, and rather than try and retrieve what we did over there, we started again. No good trying to re-capture things that worked well over there and give them a second go; better to start fresh and have a better feeling about the music.

SW: So you just sort of skipped over that material for a while?

MB: Yes. "Skating Away" was the only track that we kept from those sessions; the rest didn't emerge until this new album. It was good music, but I think because we spent so much time recording it, it would have been too depressing to have to re-do the whole lot again. We just thought it would be a more positive thing to start from scratch.

SW: Particularly by the time you could have recorded it all over again and then gone on the road with it, you'd have been saying, "Oh, no, do we have to play this?"

MB: That's right. It was sort of past its 'sell by' date.

SW: Looking back, is there a particular Tull album you don't care for too much?

MB: It would be very unkind to say so. There are albums I don't think were quite as good as other ones, but I don't think it's fair to say which ones. It's my opinions, and not anyone else's opinions necessarily, and you're talking about tiny differences. If I don't like A as much as B or C, but I like D a bit better, I'm talking about minute differences, rather than I hate one, and I think the other one's the best thing ever.

I've enjoyed them all, and there's good and bad things on all of them. Some are better for me guitar-wise, and other things aren't, but that's the luck of the draw. It's according to those songs and the way the music's performed. One album might highlight a couple of people more than the other two, but you can't expect to have a free run the whole time.

SW: In 1985 or '86 Tull had a really big resurgence with *Crest Of A Knave*; the single I guess was supposed to be "Steel Monkey", but the song that really caught on was "Farm On The Freeway". Was that more or less by accident?

MB: It just evolved to be. I don't know why, but particularly in America people like that song a lot. It said "freeway", so it's an Americanism. People latch onto some things, and don't like other things, and that's the freedom of choice of the audience. You get feedback on the different things you do, and some things that I love, audiences don't like.

Some songs audiences have liked continuously; you have to include "Aqualung" and "Locomotive Breath" and a few of the other ones. Having said that, I sincerely hope we don't do all those songs next time out. I think it would be a real good time to have a good re-think of what we do live, because we've been playing a lot of the same material for a long time, and I think Ian would agree as well that it's time for a new look at things.

SW: Do you like to go back and pull off some songs from the earlier albums that people haven't heard in a long time?

MB: We do to a smaller degree. Every tour we try to put something in that's new from the back catalog. We try a lot of old tracks to see which ones work, and a lot of them don't. But then occasionally you pick one out and it's an old song and everybody likes it, it has something about it, some bit of magic, and it's great. It's fun to do some of the old things.

SW: The *Crest Of A Knave* album resulted in Tull being nominated for and ultimately winning a Grammy for Best Hard Rock/Heavy Metal Performance, which caused a flap with some people who thought that it should have gone to a heavier band like Metallica. What was your take on that situation?

MB: I didn't let it fuss me at all. We didn't expect to win. The record company didn't think we'd win. We were back in England; they didn't even fly us out for it. So we didn't say, "Hey, we're going for this." We weren't pushing for it at all. Maybe other people who were there at the ceremony thought that they should win, and they were there and ready for their award. But we weren't being presumptuous at all. We just thought, great, they've put us up for the nomination, and it's their choice ultimately which album they choose.

Sometimes, like with the Oscars, the Best Actor might be given to somebody not particularly because of the film, but because over the years they've done a lot for the film industry. And they just figure, this guy is the right guy for the Oscar, plus he's got a good film on release at the moment. It's his year; give him the Oscar. But there might be a better performance somewhere from another actor, and that's the way it goes. People have accepted that for years. It's the same deal; they just liked the album, they thought we deserved it, and that's great. There'll always be people who disagree.

We're a rock band; we're not a heavy metal band and never have been, but we're a rock band, and we play in rock arenas to rock audiences, and have done so for twenty-six years. It was a stupid category to mix heavy metal with rock music, but that wasn't our mistake. And I'll agree that you could certainly scratch out the "heavy metal" part of that section. *(Laughs)*. I'm looking at it right now. It's on my shelf. I quite like it. *(Laughs)*. I'm not gonna give it back.

SW: Tull has outlasted punk, disco, New Wave, and now grunge. What do you think of the current musical climate?

MB: It's both healthy and unhealthy. It's got a very quick turnover, which isn't healthy for people as artists because they've got a very short life span. And music trends are very much based on fashion, rather than musicality, which inevitably means that people do an album that sells crazy amounts, and then suddenly they're not the flavor of the month and people are looking for something else, a new set of heroes. Which is sad, because the bands that really are meaning a lot are the people that have been around a long time; Pink Floyd, Phil Collins...I can't even think of who, but the longer-serving bands are the important groups even now, and I'm not saying that it should be that way, but it must mean that their music is stronger, longer-lasting, and more people enjoy it. There's nothing really that's come up in the last five or ten years that can challenge that sort of importance in music history.

I'm not saying we're a part of it, but I don't think the grunge bands or the punk bands have left that sort of a mark in music history, and bands aren't doing it now. They're disposable. And it's because it's not that different; I've heard similar things before. It might have been ten years ago, twenty years ago, thirty years ago, but I've heard that sort of a thing somewhere before. It's not different enough. It doesn't have enough originality to really stand out and be everlasting.

SW: When you listen to music on your own time, what kind of stuff do you listen to?

MB: I like classical, which I listen to most of the time. But I also like Nick Kershaw, Celine Dionne, Jackson Browne, Tribal Tech...I even like Richard Marx. I just like good music, played well, sung well, with great production. There's a lot of it about; well, not a lot, but there's enough of it about. I can listen to Sting's latest album once a week at the moment and enjoy it, but I'm sure in six months I'll be a bit fed up with it and it'll go to the bottom of the pile, and it'll stay there another year until it becomes a novelty again.

I like those things in a small quantity, but with classical, because it's such a vast catalog, I can listen to most things. There's not a lot I don't like. Most things I enjoy enough to hear once, and sometimes enough to go out and buy it.

SW: If you had a chance to write your own place in rock history, what would you want it to say?

MB: I just like being part of a band that's meant a lot musically. All I ask is that people think I had a lot to do with the music of Jethro Tull. That's all I would ask, is that I was recognized as having done something—I'm not saying how much—but certainly as being a reasonable part of the success and the importance, however much that is, of what Jethro Tull is.

I've always been part of a band; I've never been a solo performer or, as you say, guitar hero. I don't think so many people particularly come to hear me, so much as the band that I'm a part of, and that's what I enjoy. When I go to see an orchestra, I enjoy the violin section as much as I enjoy the lead instrumentalist or somebody playing the double bass or the oboe. There's so much to hear, and each part is vital to that piece of music and can't be diminished. There might be the guy up front who's getting more money, in the case of an orchestra, or more recognition, but I look beyond him. There's so much more to music than what hits you in the face, and as long as what I'm doing is appreciated somewhere, then I'm happy.

For more information about Martin Barre, please visit www.martinbarre.com or www.Jtull.com

MIRACLES

Craig Chaquico's *success in the music world is something of a minor miracle. At age twelve the guitarist was involved in a serious accident which broke both of his arms and one leg, and had to undergo almost a year of grueling physical therapy. Encouraged to play guitar to help relieve the boredom of his lengthy hospital stay,* **Chaquico** *was only able to reach the high E string with his shattered hands. Nonetheless, his determination to play was so strong that he actually wrote a song while still in his hospital bed.*

Against all odds, **Chaquico** *emerged as a teenage prodigy, playing on solo albums by* **Jefferson Airplane** *singer* **Grace Slick** *by the time he was sixteen. He was invited to join the band two years later, at which point the name changed to* **Jefferson Starship***.*

In his twenty year career with **Jefferson Starship***,* **Chaquico** *earned thirteen gold and platinum albums, a Golden Globe award, and Grammy and Oscar nominations. His playing is featured on a number of radio classics including "Jane", "Miracles", "Find Your Way Back", "We Built This City", "Sarah" and "Nothing's Gonna Stop Us Now", and he has toured the world a number of times to great success.*

Not content to rest on his laurels after leaving **Starship***,* **Chaquico** *embarked on a solo career as a jazz/New Age instrumentalist which showcased a completely new, acoustic side to his multi-faceted musical talents. His debut solo album 'Acoustic Highway' was named Billboard Magazine's #1 Independent Adult Alternative/New Age Album of 1993, and also received a Bammie (Bay Area Music Award) for Best Independent Album of 1993. In 1994* **Chaquico** *released his much-anticipated follow-up, 'Acoustic Planet', which also came to rest at the top spot in Billboard's Adult Alternative/New Age charts, earning the musician a Grammy nomination and two additional Bammies.*

I spoke with **Craig Chaquico** *by phone from his home studio in California on January 6th, 1995, just days after he received the news that 'Acoustic Planet' had been nominated for a Grammy.* **Chaquico** *was clearly enjoying the rewards of having followed his heart and seeing it pay off, and it would be hard not to share in his pleasure. A thoroughly engaging conversationalist,* **Chaquico** *is also such an altogether affable, pleasant guy that it's easy to see why one of his publicists commented, "Craig is my favorite client. For someone who's been a rock star since he was in his teens, he's not into any kind of star trip. He's the nicest guy I've ever worked with."*

One interesting thing about **Chaquico** *is that he speaks quite rapidly; one simple question might easily yield several pages of answer. Transcribing this interview took much longer than usual because he had fit so much more material into the allotted time than any of my other subjects. During our conversation* **Chaquico** *was bright, funny and extremely humble, going so far as to thank me for deeming him worthy of inclusion in this book. It was my pleasure.*

SW: You were already in a major rock and roll band before you were out of your teens. How did that come about?

CC: I started playing guitar when I was ten years old, and when I was in high school I was in a local garage band. We played at my high school, and my English teacher happened to hear me play and asked me to join his band.

He was about fifteen years older than me, and all of the guys in his band were older and they all had day jobs, but they happened to have this band on the side. We were playing with a barber, so he got me a fake mustache to wear. *(Laughs).* So at the age of fourteen I was playing bars and clubs all around the state of California, and then going to school the next day.

Some of the people in the Airplane knew my English teacher, which I didn't know. They had gone to school with him. So they would come to our shows, and I would think, 'Why do those guys look familiar?' *(Laughs).* And then I realized that he knew Grace Slick. And she asked me to play on her first solo album, so on my sixteenth birthday I did my first recording session. And then every year after that I was asked to play on her records.

By the time I graduated high school and was in college, my band got a record deal on the Jefferson Airplane label, and we toured with what was called Jefferson Starship, even though we hadn't made a record of the band yet. Paul had used that name once on a solo record. All the people that had been playing on Grace's and Paul's solo records got together to do a tour. That included me, John Barbado—who had been playing with Crosby, Stills and Nash, and then he joined the Airplane for about the last six months of that band—and David Fireburgh, who had been with Quicksilver Messenger Service and played on all of Grace's solo records, and had also been in the Airplane toward the end. Pete Sears was the bass player; he had been playing with Rod Stewart, but he had also been doing these studio records.

All of us had been in different bands and had been doing these studio gigs for a couple of years, so eventually they decided to do a tour, get us all together and play live, and we called that Jefferson Starship. Of course that included Grace Slick, and Papa John Creach, and Paul Kantner from the Airplane. And my band opened! *(Laughter).* So I played in both bands. I played in the opening act and the headlining band.

And of course, being a teenager from Sacramento and playing with Grace Slick, making my first record at sixteen years old, I thought I was going to be famous and that was it. I've got my name on a record and wow, this is it! *(Laughs).* So I would go to San Francisco, and it was like this big fantasy to play with all these people that I'd seen before. And then I'd go back home and realize I still had to do my same homework, and ride my bicycle to school, and nothing really changed. So it was like this constant reality check-fantasy-reality check, starting at sixteen.

As I went through high school, each year I'd go and do a recording session, and just have a great time and learn. Even when I was fourteen and playing with my English teacher I had a lucky break, because I was playing with older musicians and I was constantly learning faster than a lot of people my age, and it really helped me evolve. I would sit in my room and listen to Clapton and Hendrix and Pink Floyd and Zeppelin and Santana and the Allmann Brothers, and just learn all those licks, as well as saxophone players, you know, and Wes Montgomery. All this different music, like Chet Atkins, that I would listen to over and over again, and learn from that, and then get a chance to play with older musicians on top of that, which would help me really focus what I was doing.

But as I said, it was always this thing of going down and playing on these records and seeing my name on an album, and then realizing that it was the real world and I still had to go to school and keep my grades up or my mom and dad would kick me out of the house! *(Laughs)*. So that went on and on, and as I graduated high school and went to college, I'd been on three albums already as a side guitar player. One of my biggest compliments was when Grace showed me a review in *Billboard* that said something like well, obviously Carlos Santana can't use his name on this album because of contractual commitments, or maybe it's Eric Clapton, but they've come up with this phony name of Craig Chaquico! *(Laughter)*. Just so he could play on the record. So that was really cool. It was a compliment, because even though they didn't believe that I existed, they thought I was an alias for somebody who was really good.

So by the time I was in college, I did the tour where I played with both bands. I'd taken six or seven weeks off from college to do that, and I figured after the tour I'd go back to school; you know, the same cycle of playing rock and roll and then back to the real world. As it turned out, on the way back from the airport from this tour, Grace said, "Well, Craig, you've got a choice. You can either go back to school, or move to San Francisco and join the Jefferson Starship and make an album with us." *(Laughs)*.

I was still a teenager, but by then I was nineteen, and we did the album *Dragonfly* in San Francisco. I lived in the Jefferson Airplane Mansion, as they called it, even though nobody lived there anymore. It was a four-story Victorian mansion that had been turned into their office space. The place was haunted, too! *(Laughs)*. So I lived there for the recording of the album, and then we did a tour, and of course I expected from there to go back to school, just like always. But the album did real well; it was a gold album, and they said, "We're gonna do another album, *Red Octopus*. Why don't you stay in San Francisco, and you can stay in the house?" So it was cool.

I wasn't an equal member of the band on the first two albums, but I was loving life, because I wasn't even twenty-one yet, and I was getting a chance to really live out a fantasy of touring around the world and playing rock and roll, living rent free. *(Laughs)*. It was cool.

And even when I first started recording, way back when I was sixteen in San Francisco, I can remember walking down the halls of Wally Hyder Studios…Grace and everybody would record at night, and I would get a ride up from Sacramento and record at night, but in the afternoons Santana recorded. And there was another young guitar player, Neal Schon, who was the same age as me. We were both sixteen years old. And he was playing with Carlos. They'd be finishing their sessions right when I was coming in to start mine, and every now and then me and Neal would pass in the hallway, and we'd look at each other like, "What the hell are you doing here, kid?" *(Laughter)*. He wasn't even old enough to drive. His mom would pick him up in front of the studio and take him home. It was just really bizarre.

It was this amazing journey from being just a teenage kid in Sacramento to playing in bars and wearing a fake mustache, and then recording, and then touring, and then being asked to join the band. Like I said, the first two years I wasn't really an equal member yet, but the second album sold millions of records, so the record label and everybody else said they'd better start signing everybody up, because this group seems to really be doing something right. On the third album I became an equal member, and I never did go back to school! *(Laughter)*.

SW: I guess not!

CC: I guess the band became my higher education, so to speak.

SW: The band was consistently successful during your time with them.

CC: Well, from 1974 to 1990 I was there on every album, and if you think about it, I'm really the only guy that's consistently there on every record...

SW: Oh, are you really? *(Laughs)*.

CC: Yeah, which is amazing, because I was the kid, and then I wound up being the longest member. I ended up writing more of the songs than any individual in the band, had my name on more songs than any other individual that was ever in the band as far as writing credits. I played on every song, was in every video, every tour...I always wrote material for each album.

You know, I love your title, *Unsung Heroes*, because usually someone who does most of the writing, or has been in the band the longest, or is the lead guitar player, gets a lot of notoriety, but I was always kind of in the back. When you've got people like Grace Slick and all these big stars in the band, it's easy to be overlooked. And also, when you start when you're just a fuckin' kid, everybody has a tendency not to take you as seriously. They just think, 'Oh, he's just that guy in the back that smokes pot and plays guitar.' *(Laughter)*. So it's funny to realize it myself. It didn't even dawn on me until I left the band, and then I said, "Geez, I'm really the only guy that's been here the whole time, and a lot of people don't even know who I am."

I can remember walking into Safeway here in Mill Valley right when I started working on my acoustic guitar project, and on the background music at Safeway was one of the songs that Jefferson Starship did called "Count On Me", which was the first time I ever did an acoustic guitar solo on a record. So I thought how ironic that I'm just starting this new solo project on acoustic guitar, and I walk into Safeway and I'm standing in line, and I hear the first time I ever played acoustic guitar on a Starship record. It's a twelve year old recording.

I'm listening to it and I'm thinking, 'God, this is really cool. I'm going to be in Safeway, and my solo's coming up in a second, so I'm gonna hear my acoustic guitar solo in Safeway right before I go back home to begin recording on my new acoustic record.' And I'm getting all proud, thinking, 'This is great. This is some history I can really be proud of. This is something that I accomplished.' And I'm starting to think all of this, and right when it comes to the guitar solo, I hear this click and, *(imitates the sound of a voice coming over the loudspeaker)* "Uh, price check in produce, please. Bob, could you go and check broccoli in produce?" *(Laughter)*. Through the whole guitar solo, all you heard was this guy talking about produce. So that's another reality check.

SW: That's pretty funny!

CC: There you go, that's how important that solo is today, in the Nineties. *(Laughs)*.

SW: Do you have a particular favorite album from the Jefferson Starship years?

CC: My favorite album was *Freedom At Point Zero*. It's between that or *Modern Times*. Not to say that I didn't like the albums before that. I thought that *Red Octopus* was really interesting. In fact, that album had two instrumentals on it, which kind of led to, you know, now I'm doing all instrumental music. That was a very memorable album. We had eight people in the band, from this old rock violin player in his fifties to this long-haired guitar player in his teens, and people from the Airplane and Crosby, Stills and Nash, and Quicksilver, all in the same band. Two lead singers, all these songwriters, and for me it was really exciting, because it really was my higher education at that point. I was playing with all of these fantastic talents, and I was at that age when I was absorbing everything. It was great. That was a lot of fun.

We had a huge record with that, and "Miracles" was a big single that I've come to appreciate more now that I've heard it over the years. But at the time, although I really liked it, I was still listening to Led Zeppelin and hard rock, and I was trying to add as much of that energy to the band as possible. And the band had so many influences that that was only one small part of the band, that harder rock vibe, and a lot of times the stuff that got the most notoriety was the slower ballads like "Miracles". Which I loved, and I was proud of it, but I was sometimes a little frustrated because I wanted to play more guitar.

Looking back at it, I really am proud of how I did "Miracles". It's almost closer to what I'm doing now than anything else we did. But at the time I was wanting to rock out more. I remember we were headlining these big shows in these big coliseums, and we were having people that were really rockin' like Foreigner open for us, who'd just done "Hot Blooded" and "Double Vision". We were supposed to be headlining, and here's the opening act and they were just kicking my butt, man, playing all the shit I wanted to play, you know, just rock and roll. Guys like Ted Nugent and Jeff Beck were opening for the Starship, and they'd just shred out there, and then we'd come out and do a lot of slower ballads, and I'd be like, 'Man, let's get this thing out of first gear!' (*Laughs*).

But that's just a young kid thinking, too, and like I said, I was just anxious to rock out more, and saw these other people doing it and just loved what they were doing. I would go to every Aerosmith concert I could on my day off and just absorb that stuff. So finally we had this big riot in Germany, and we lost a lot of equipment, and a lot of tragedy hit the band all at once. Grace quit the band, Marty quit the band, our drummer got in a car accident a couple of weeks later and busted his neck and his arm and his jaw, so it was pretty bad. We had no lead singers and no drummer, and we ended up getting Ansley Dunbar on drums and Mickey Thomas on lead vocals. And that was a point where we got a chance to do more of the hard rock stuff that I was pulling for, and I got a chance to write more, and *Freedom At Point Zero* was the album that had "Jane" on it.

At that point the band became more of a reflection of the type of music I was leaning toward, coming from the guy that used to listen to Zeppelin and Aerosmith and Foreigner and everything. So that's why that record means a lot to me, because it had "Jane" and a lot more guitar-oriented stuff on it. And then we moved on to *Modern Times*, which had "Find Your Way Back" on it, which is actually on my new album, too. That period was the most exciting for me.

The band went through so many changes, from the first incarnation that had Marty and did the albums *Dragonfly*, *Red Octopus*, *Spitfire* and *Earth*, and then it changed with *Freedom At Point Zero*, *Modern Times*, *Winds Of Change* and *Nuclear Furniture*. Those were our hard rock days, getting a little pop at that point towards the end. And then there was the phase of *Knee Deep In The Hoopla* and *No Protection*, with songs like "We Built This City" and "Sarah" and "Nothing's Gonna Stop Us Now". Through the whole time I felt like it was an evolving, exciting time. There were always people in the band that I enjoyed playing with. Even though some people left, other people came in.

But right towards the end, around "We Built This City" and the album after that, and then definitely the album after that, *Love Among The Cannibals*, which hardly anybody's ever heard of, I started getting disappointed with what was happening in the band, not just because we were getting more and more pop-oriented, but the guitar was becoming less and less a factor. It was becoming more where everything seemed to be focusing on one singer, especially when Grace left again. It got to the point where everyone I enjoyed playing with had gone, and musically I wasn't happy. It was just me and Mickey, and of course the manager was this dickhead manager that we had for the whole time (*laughs*), who actually I never really got along with.

In fact, there was a time when we were doing "Jane", which is one of my favorite guitar solos of all time…

SW: That's a great solo.

CC: In fact, I was at the Bammies, and Kirk Hammett…it made me feel a little old, but Kirk came up to me and said, "Man, when I was growing up, we used to wait by the radio for 'Jane', because that was the only good guitar solo that was on the radio back then!" *(Laughs)*. And I know what he means, because I remember really digging that solo.

But it was a long solo. It was twenty-seven seconds. Our manager came into the studio with a stopwatch and timed the solo and said, "That solo is twenty-seven seconds long. It's never gonna get played on the radio, because they don't play solos that long, and you guys are crazy to let Craig play that long on the song." And I was thinking, 'Fuck you, man; that's the way the song was written, and I helped write it.' And everybody in the band backed me up, and the manager got all pissed off and walked out and said, "Well, you guys are really fucking up, because that song is never gonna get any airplay with a long solo." *(Laughs)*. So now, every time I hear that solo, I go, 'Yes!' when I hear it on the radio, because it did get airplay, and I had to fight for every second of that solo.

So I always had a little bit of conflict between his philosophy of music and mine, and when everybody I enjoyed playing with left, it was just me and the singer and the manager, and he said, "Look, Mickey's going to do most of the writing, and he's gonna pick the songs, and it's going to be a lot more stuff you don't like to do. And we're gonna hire a bunch of guys to record the album in LA, and then you and Mickey will go down and overdub on it, and then we'll call it Starship. And then we're going to hire a bunch of other guys to tour, and you and Mickey will tour with them, and we're gonna call *that* Starship."

SW: Oh, *that's* interesting. *(Laughs)*. Gee, the fans will really eat that up!

CC: I said, "While you're hiring, hire another guitar player." *(Laughs)*. I didn't want to do any of that shit. That was a little too close to Milli Vanilli for me. So I quit, man. I quit in 1990, and I think I blew everybody's minds, because up until then I was always a team player, somebody that was happy to be part of the team and be, when there were eight people in the band, be one-eighth of the band, and when there six people, be one-sixth, and when there were four people, be one-fourth. But when it came down to two people, I wasn't one-half of the band anymore. I was back to being one-tenth of the band, and not even that, and it was just real frustrating, so I bailed. And they just never thought that I would do that. I guess Mickey and the manager just thought I needed to stay in a real comfortable situation.

I found that leaving the band was really scary. It was really frightening, because it was like leaving this really secure day job and going off into who knows what. And yet, I didn't know it at the time, but looking back at the success the albums have had since I've gone, you know, two back-to-back number one albums in *Billboard*, and now a Grammy nomination for my new album, and two Bammie nominations, it's great. I look back at it and I know that because I left and took a chance, it put me on the edge and made me more…it's like the guys that came back from Vietnam said that no one should ever have to do that, but while you're over there you never felt more alive. Everything is more intense because you're on the edge.

And I felt that way leaving this secure situation, and then all of a sudden finding out that my wife was pregnant, and everything's happening all at once. And I think all that emotion and intensity was reflected in the way the albums came out, because they had a lot more passion and feeling, whereas had I stayed in the band, everything would have been sort of pop and glossy, kind of dull or unexciting. This way, I think I had a lot more feeling. I didn't know it at the time, but looking back at it, I can look at the whole thing as a gift, even though it was super scary.

SW: Now there are two versions of Starship, aren't there?

CC: (*Laughs*). It's funny, because there are two Starships, and people say, "Would you ever play with Starship again?" And it's like, "Well, which one?" (*Laughs*). It's weird, because each one only has one guy that used to be in the band. Mickey got together most of the people from Elvin Bishop and did a version of Starship, and Paul got together most of the people from the Airplane and did a version of Starship. It's really confusing, because I was there longer than any of those guys, so when people hear that Starship is playing, a lot of them assume it's me! So I always try to make it clear that I'm *formerly* of Starship so they don't get it confused. Neither one of them has a recording deal, so it's...

SW: The Mickey Thomas version of Starship came here a while back, and I forget where they played, but I mean, *I* could play there! (*Laughs*). I could get a booking there.

CC: I know it's kind of weird, but I still talk to those guys. I joke around with them, though I don't think they see the humor in it as much as I do! (*Laughter*). For example, I know that a lot of the time it's billed as "Mickey Thomas' Starship". I told him, "You should just shorten it to your initials and call it the M.T. (*Empty*) Starship!" (*Laughter*). I don't think he liked that. And I told Paul, "You quit the band, and everybody had to pay you all this money so you wouldn't use the name, and then you just decided after eight years to use the name anyway. And you got all these people from the Airplane to do the band, but you're still calling it Jefferson Starship. Six of the original guys aren't in the band, but you're still calling it Jefferson Starship. Why don't you just call it Led Zeppelin? That way only *four* of the original guys aren't in the band!" (*Laughter*). He didn't see the humor in that.

I joke around with those guys all the time, and I honestly think they're both really good bands, but it's a little misleading because they're using that name. That kind of bugs me, because I had a little bit invested in that name, too. It's just a little bit awkward and sad that it ends up being, I think, misrepresented. It was something that was really great. We were really proud of it, and now to have it diluted, watered down, it bugs me a little bit. But hey, I guess it's not the first time. I know there's been three or four versions of The Platters, and three or four versions of Fleetwood Mac, and three or four versions of The Temptations. That stuff seems to happen a lot. I mean, at the same time! Two bands with the same name at the same time. It's weird.

But like I said, I loved everything I did with the band. Toward the end it got a little frustrating, and it was time to leave, and I'm glad I did, because that was truly a gift for me. It put me out there to do what I'm doing now.

SW: You commented on how the ensuing albums after changing the name to Starship were more and more pop-oriented. Was that the result of a conscious decision to focus more on pop music, or did bringing in the outside writers have that impact?

CC: That was part of it. I got to see a couple of different sides of the music business that most people don't get to see. Starting in the Jefferson Starship, that band had a little bit of history as an extension of Jefferson Airplane, so the band had a certain amount of creative license at the label. Usually when a band gets signed to a label, an A&R guy hears you, signs you, believes in you, and they kind of mold you and focus you and point you in the right direction. It starts from that point, and you listen a lot to the label.

When I first started with the band, we got to do whatever we wanted, and I don't think anybody at the label had a clue what was going on, because we were a bunch of hippies from San Francisco, and at that time everybody else at RCA was pretty straight. So they just let us do what we did, because we were selling millions of records, and they never said shit to us. It was like, "Yeah, okay, you wanna put a picture of a heart on the front of the album with tentacles coming out of it and call it *Red Octopus*, that's okay. We don't care. And you wanna have these weird songs, that's okay with us." *(Laughs)*. Because we were selling a lot of records.

And when the band started changing and members started changing and leaving, we got the chance to evolve. And it was great, because the second version, the rock version, also sold a lot of records, and it wasn't like we had to audition. It wasn't like we had to get discovered by an A&R guy. We already had the gig. We just gave them a totally different style, from "Miracles" to "Jane", and they didn't say shit about it and they let us do it. And the albums did really well.

Then there was a period when some of the people in the band were leaving, and Grace had done a solo record, and she worked with a great producer, a guy by the name of Peter Wolf. Not the guy from the J. Geils Band, but another great producer. He was bringing in some outside material that she used. We thought that he wrote some really good songs, so we invited him to write a song for us, an outside song called "No Way Out", and it did really well. It was the single off of one of our records. So all of a sudden the record label started getting involved, saying, "Wait a minute, now they're getting really good songs from outside writers, so let's try to encourage that."

So they started bringing in more and more outside songs, and started getting a little more forceful about what they wanted us to do. And some of the people in the band got a little frustrated with that, and some of the guys started leaving. Before you knew it, hardly any of the songs were being written by the band anymore, and the label was bringing in a lot of material and sort of pushing us in that direction. So then I got to see that side of it, of being more led around by the nose by the label, a little less artistic control.

And in any band, a lead singer has sort of an advantage to captain the ship, and in that case Mickey was getting more of a chance to plot the course of the Starship. So a lot of things were focusing more on his musical tastes, and mostly his vocals, and less and less on anybody else's musical tastes and what they contributed. And I remembered the band being more of a team effort, but it was becoming more of an individual's perspective with Mickey, and Paul started doing that a little bit, too.

Like I said, I've always been a team player. I like going along with the flow. And I did, and it was great, but I could see it changing and going into this...you know, when Paul was leading the band for a while, it started to get real out there, musically. Interesting, but out there. And then when Mickey started to do a little more and Paul left, it got to be a little more pop. And that was cool. It was good to be able to change and grow. But then toward the end, with everybody leaving that I liked to play with, and it just being all outside writers, it got a little awkward.

When we started writing in the band again on the last album, *Love Among The Cannibals*, Mickey was the one that was doing all the writing, and I didn't have much input or say, which kind of bummed me out, because I was there longer than he was, and had written more songs. So I thought, 'Well, I'll try this. I'll see if it works.' You know, with him writing most of the stuff and using outside writers. And it didn't work out too well. It didn't sell too many records, and boy, I don't think too many people liked the music.

And then when they said, "Well, we're gonna do what we just did, only even worse, on this next record," then I went, "Well, I'm outta here." And they worked like that for a while after I left, but I don't think it sounded as believable anymore, so nobody picked up on that approach, and the band got dropped from the label. And that's what led to what's going on today.

After I left, they tried it. They released a greatest hits record, which had a good amount of songs that I had written on it, and then it had some of the outside writer stuff like "We Built This City". It was a really good greatest hits package. But they tried a couple of new songs on there, songs with just Mickey and the studio musicians, and they didn't really seem to do much. So right after that the band got dropped, and then split up, and now there's Mickey's Starship and Paul's Starship and...

SW: That's a pretty convoluted story. It would make a great movie of the week.

CC: I think *you* should have a Starship. Sterling's Starship! *(Laughter).* I'll play in that one!

SW: *(Laughing).* You're crazy! But if the money's right, who knows? Have your manager call my lawyer, man. *(Laughs).*

CC: I was a little bummed out by the way it all sort of disintegrated, but

I also felt it was a gift to have the chance to do something different. When you think about it, when a band has been around as long as we were, it's pretty unusual. We really had a long run.

SW: It's probably one of the most unusual histories of a band that I can think of.

CC: Oh, man, me too! *(Laughter)*. But now I'm in a situation where I get to do this, and it's all kind of evolved from Starship. Even though some people look at me and say, "How can you be the same guy that played on 'Miracles' and 'Jane' and 'We Built This City', and now you're doing a totally instrumental acoustic guitar record?" And I tell them it's the same feeling that I get when I'm on Highway 101 in California. Up north it's Redwood Highway, and down south it's the Hollywood Freeway. And I think, 'How can this be the same road?' *(Laughs)*. But it really does have a connection there, and like the idea that I was able to do something different, instead of going and doing Craig's Starship or something like that.

A lot of people thought I was going to do more of a rock and roll thing, or join a band and play more hard rock guitar and have vocals, and do mainstream pop type music. And instead, I did the opposite in a lot of ways. I went acoustic, solo and instrumental.

A friend of mine named Clyde Fessler, who's now Vice President of Harley Davidson, told me, "What you did with your music is kind of like my philosophy of life. When everybody in a motorcycle pack turns right, I turn left. *(Laughs)*. That way I'm not locked in the pack. I get the whole road to myself, the view is better, and I'm not bumping into everybody." And he said, "That's what you did musically. Everybody thought that you would go with the pack and do what everyone else would do, but you turned left musically, and now you've got this whole road to yourself. You're not lost in the pack, and you've got more of an individual chance to be perceived." And actually, with the title *Unsung Heroes of Rock Guitar*, it's funny, because all the work I did with Starship has gotten me less notoriety than the stuff I'm doing now.

SW: That must feel good.

CC: Really, it's a blessing. It's really cool to be able to do what I'm doing now.

SW: It seems like part of the reason you didn't get as much name recognition as some of the other members of the band is because you didn't make headlines in any kind of scandals the way some of them did.

CC: Oh, of course. And even though I ended up being the guy that was there for the longest, I always felt like the new kid on the block the whole time. Not in a negative way; it didn't bother me, but I knew I was never going to be given the same amount of recognition or be perceived in the same way as someone like Grace Slick, who's always going to be a rock legend. She's one of my dearest friends today. I just adore her. For someone who was always a mega-superstar, she never, ever copped an attitude like, "Well, I'm the singer and you guys are just the band. I want my own limousine and..." She was always one of the guys, from the beginning to the end, and I've seen a lot of the other guys in the band just completely ego out. Grace never did that. She was always the biggest star, and the most down-to-earth.

I always felt like it was a natural thing that I never got that much recognition, because the whole band was geared around singers. And yet it's funny, because I've seen other bands spring up from out of nowhere, and there'll be a guitar player who gets immediate recognition and attention, and then disappears and you never hear from him again. But for that fifteen minutes of fame, he was more recognizable than I was. I was always just consistent, but not that flamboyant. I wasn't out getting busted or whatever. Although I did get busted once. I got arrested for riding a motorized skateboard on a bicycle path in Golden Gate Park. *(Laughter)*.

SW: Boy, I bet that just splashed across the headlines. 'Craig Chaquico— Rock And Roll's New Bad Boy'! *(Laughter)*.

CC: Yeah, I was really bad! But that was part of it. I never tried to hog the spotlight. I just tried to play what was right for the tune, and I think sometimes when you try to do the right thing, you're even less noticeable. So I was really happy with my work in the Starship, but I didn't get as much recognition as some other guitar players.

You know, it's funny, I'm thinking of your title, *Unsung Heroes of Rock Guitar*, and I know who my unsung heroes were. But first I have to tell you, when I was growing up, I had my heroes on my wall. I had posters of Jimmy Page and Jeff Beck and Jimi Hendrix and Eric Clapton and Duane Allmann and Carlos Santana and Johnny Winter and Rick Derringer. I had all these photos. All these rock guitar players on my walls were my heroes. Those guys were definitely *sung* heroes. They really influenced me, and I thought that they were the reason that I was going to be a great guitar player, if that was ever gonna happen. It was because of them and their influence.

But now that I've played on the same stages with a lot of those guys, and had records in the same charts with them, and now I've got my own record, and a Grammy nomination and all this stuff, you know, number one albums in *Billboard* and all this stuff on my own. Now that I've done that, and now that I'm also the father of a little boy, I realize that the real unsung heroes were my mom and dad, that bought me my first guitar, that had the day jobs that paid for the walls that had all these posters on them, and that encouraged me to play. At the time I didn't realize that, as a teenager, but those are the real unsung heroes, the people that back you up when you're learning. It's like, Van Gogh had a brother that would buy him his canvas and paint, because Van Gogh was so poor, he couldn't afford it. And nobody knows that much about it, but in a lot of ways it's those people that are the real unsung heroes that help the artists get their message out there.

So that's my version of the unsung heroes; my mom and dad. They were both musicians. My dad played sax and accordion in a jazz band, and my mom played keyboards and piano in church and on the radio for singers. And then they settled down and got more responsible day jobs that had a little more security, because they had a family to raise. I thought that was the most courageous thing to do. It made it possible for me to live my dream and play my music.

SW: That's great. You mentioned having to change people's perception of you, leaving a rock band and going into acoustic instrumental music as you did. Were you surprised when *Acoustic Highway* was such a big success?

CC: I was, because not only did I just leave a major rock band and do something totally different, but I did it at home in my own home studio. And this after working with the world's greatest producers in million dollar studios. I produced it and recorded it and did it in my own home studio on acoustic guitar, so it was a real big experiment.

I thought in my own mind that people will respond more to an emotion, a melody and a feeling, than how expensive the studio is. We respect studios and producers that come up with great material, but really, the first thing we hear is the song and the melody.

As a guitar player, a lot of times I'm drawn to someone who plays real flashy, but after a while it's like listening to someone type real fast. So what, what are you saying? Are you writing any poetry there? What are you writing? It's the same thing with a guitar player who plays real fast. I can be really interested for a little bit, but after a while I'll think, 'What else are you saying?' And if they're not saying anything else, then I'll get really bored, because it's like listening to someone type really fast.

I think that as musicians, a lot of times we forget that listeners are more drawn to a melody. Those are the things that really speak to them. Of course, flashy technique is exciting, and I use it as an exclamation point a lot of times at the end of a melodic statement that creates a mood, but it's not just flash for flash's sake. It's always about melody and feeling and textures. After recording in all those million dollar recording studios, there was never a knob anywhere in those studios that had 'FEELING' written on it that you could turn up. (*Laughter*). A knob that said 'EMOTION'. Those are the things that you have to add as a musician.

In my mind, I thought, maybe no one will get this, but I'd like to try to put feeling and emotion into music in my own home studio, where I can do it at 4 AM with a candle going, and really just take a chance and do it my way. And I got a chance to work with a really terrific keyboard player, Ozzy Ahlers, who has played with Jerry Garcia and Van Morrison and Clarence Clemmons. He really understood what I was trying to do, so together we wrote everything, and he helped me produce the album. We both just said, "Let's make this about melodies and feelings, and have it be a guitar record, but really concentrate on that. Not a thrash record; let's make it where it speaks to everybody."

And people thought we were nuts! My friends were going, "Craig, are you crazy? Doing this record with a keyboard player in your home studio, with no vocals? You should be in a band recording at the Record Plant, man. What are you thinking?" And we would say that to ourselves, too. But then we'd get into the studio and listen to the music and we'd get goose bumps, or we'd get tears in our eyes on some of the sadder stuff, or big smiles on our faces on some of the happier stuff. And we thought that if someone can listen to this and get the same effect, then we know we're doing something right.

The next thing we knew, a label heard it and wanted to put it out, and then the album came out and the radio stations wanted to play it. And when they played it, they instantly got phone response. People heard it on the radio and wanted to know who it was, and when they found out who it was, they wanted to buy it. The next thing we knew, we had a number one album. It was a great feeling of encouragement at the end of that, to know that during the process it was really scary, and it was a departure and it was experimental. But it goes back to, 'Build a stadium and they will come.' Follow your heart, do what you really feel, and I think it will translate to people.

It was just so encouraging to know as an artist that you can really follow a dream and have it turn out to be something that can really pay off. Because we all love music, but a lot of the time the music we like isn't in vogue right now, and a lot of musicians fall into that trap of following fads. You know, 'God, Nirvana's hot right now, I'm gonna start a Nirvana-type band', or 'I want to be the next Pearl Jam'. But you forget, there already is a Pearl Jam, and there already is a Nirvana! So you end up chasing the tail, and it never works out.

I think the guys that really have the better chance of making it are the ones who forget about what everyone else is doing and just do what they feel, because no one will believe your music if you don't believe it. That's why, when our record did as well as it did, it surprised us, but it also encouraged us to know that by doing the stuff we really believed in, it would be more effective than faking it. So that was just a great reward at the end of the tunnel.

It was difficult making an album at home. There's no budget. You're taking a big chance. But I talk to a lot of different types of people, and everyone says that a lot of times in life, the accomplishments that they are most proud of are the ones when they had to take the biggest risk, had to follow their instincts and do what they really believed in. So now, after a number one album and all these awards, the biggest reward I ever get is just when someone walks up to me and says, "I started laughing when I heard that song," or "I get goose bumps whenever I hear this particular song." Because that's where it all started. That was our test when we were in the studio by ourselves. Those were the things that we built on, so to finally have that translate is the biggest reward, to know that the emotion came out of it.

I'm also really lucky to have had the support that I've gotten on the business end. My manager, Laura Engel, and her assistant Shirley Greer have been with me since the very beginning of my solo stuff, and they've backed me up all along the way. They believed in my music when it was just a four song demo, and they've really worked hard to make all of this possible. It's important to work with people you can really rely on, and who really have faith in what you're doing.

SW: As a kind of bonus, I understand some of your music was launched into space recently.

CC: It's ironic to come from a band called Starship and to actually have music in space! *(Laughs)*. The Rochester Museum of Science approached NASA, which has a base in Rochester, about putting a time capsule aboard a satellite. The satellites go up all the time, anyway, and Rochester was only asking for a little bit of space, a little hermetically sealed CD-ROM that they could slip onto the satellite somehow, and NASA said okay.

So the Rochester Museum of Science put together a Compton's Encyclopedia, encoded it digitally on a ROM, and they took CNN's 100 Most Significant Minutes of 1993 and put that on there. They put paintings and poetry and music, recordings from all over the planet, from over 45 countries, on this CD-ROM. And in addition to that, they asked this journalist who lives in Rochester who he would recommend for some contemporary musicians they could put on there. They had Native Americans and Tanzanian witch doctors chanting, and they wanted to put something state-of-the-art, music-wise. He had just done an interview with me, and he said, "Well, Craig used to be in a Starship, so wouldn't it be cool of his music actually went to the stars? He's got this album called *Acoustic Planet*."

So they had me send them a DAT of one of my songs, and they put it on the satellite. It's really amazing that a song of mine from my solo album *Acoustic Planet*, after being in Jefferson Starship, is now in a geosynchronous orbit on a satellite that's supposed to be in orbit for millions of years now, along with songs by Peter Gabriel and Jimi Hendrix and others. The neatest thing about it is that I keep going back to my dad, thinking about when I was growing up playing loud rock and roll around the house. My dad would say, "Can you play 'Long, Long Ago' and 'Far, Far Away'?" *(Laughs)*. Kind of a musician's joke saying, "Can you just get out of here—can you play far, far away from here?" So now that I have a song in a satellite, I want to get the coordinates of the satellite, set up my telescope and have my dad over some time and say, "Hey, dad, see that star up there? Is that far enough away for you?" *(Laughter)*.

It's cool that I got a chance to do that. It's probably one of the things I'm proudest of. But someone reminded me, "Who's ever gonna hear it? It's kind of like taking your demo tape and dropping it in the middle of the ocean. Who's ever gonna hear it?" So I said, "Aliens might hear it some day, and they'll send messages back to Earth. They'll say, 'We really like it, but send more Chuck Berry next time.'" *(Laughter)*.

SW: You think so? Maybe so. Well, I wish you continued success with the new album. Congratulations on the Grammy nomination.

CC: Thanks for the encouragement. I appreciate it. You know, people ask me what it takes to make an album and get famous and all that, and I wish I knew! Nobody knows. So much of it is luck, and being in the right place at the right time, and I really believe a lot of it is doing what you believe in, too, but there's so many different things that you can't put your finger on.

Probably one of the biggest inspirations for me, though, was when I started getting into music, my parents encouraged me. My mom and dad were musicians, and they thought it would be a good thing for me to get into. But at the same time they realized that it could be a cruel mistress sometimes, and it doesn't always pay off the way you want it to. They always made me keep up my grades or they wouldn't let me do it. They knew from experience that it doesn't always pay the bills, and it's nice to have something to fall back on.

They encouraged me to play from an early age, and when I was ten years old, I started playing acoustic guitar a little bit. I never had one of my own, but I played some of my friends'. They could tell I was going toward music, but they didn't know guitar from shit, really, because my dad plays accordion and sax, and my mom plays keyboards. So they said, "Would you like to take music lessons?" And I said, "Yeah, that would be great." And they said, "Do you want to play an instrument like what your dad played?" And I thought, 'Yeah, if Dad did it, that would be cool.' So they said, "Your dad played accordion. Do you want to take lessons and play your dad's accordion?" And I said, "Yeah!" And then I thought, 'What is an accordion, anyway?' *(Laughter)*.

So they brought this thing out, and I ended up taking lessons on it for a couple of years, and I hated it, man. I mean, I just totally *hated* it. I kept listening to the radio, and there was no accordion music on the radio. And at one point we were going to my accordion lesson, and I was actually in tears in the back of the car, and my dad pulled over and said, "Hey, it's not supposed to be torture. It's supposed to be fun." And I said, "But Dad, I don't like this instrument. I want to play guitar." So my dad said, "We've paid for the accordion lessons. Just take this one last lesson, and you'll never have to take it again." And I was so happy, I had the best accordion lesson ever, because I knew after that it was all over.

Then my mom and dad bought me my first guitar, a ten dollar acoustic, which I still have. I'm looking at it right now. It's in my studio. And having been held back from it for so long and forced to take an instrument I didn't like made me love it even more, so I played it non-stop.

Unfortunately, when I was twelve years old, I was in a car crash with my dad. We were hit by a drunk driver, and it broke both my arms, my leg in three places, my thumb and my wrist. I woke up in the hospital after coming out of a coma, and the first thing I asked for was my little acoustic guitar. My dad was pretty banged up, but he was okay, and I was going to be okay, but at the time I was still in the hospital. And my mom and my doctor encouraged me to play this little acoustic guitar. Even thought my hands were in casts, my fingers stuck out, and I could just reach the high E string on the guitar. So that was the only string that I could play.

They knew I loved the guitar, so they told me to just keep playing. It was good therapy for my hands, and kept my muscles from atrophying while they were in a cast. So I wrote this song all on the E string that's on my new album. It's called "Center Of Courage", and it's subtitled "E-lizabeth's Song", because my doctor was named Elizabeth, and because it was all on the E string. And through my wheelchair therapy, and then crutches, and then corrective shoes, until finally I'm back to normal—physically, that is *(laughs)*—my doctor encouraged me to play the guitar.

So I put the song on the album, because there are places called Courage Centers in hospitals. That's what they call these places where people recover from physical trauma. I wanted to dedicate the song to people in a situation like that, because music can be very healing. I've learned a lot about that over the years, and I know what it's like to be a little boy and wake up in the hospital. It's very frightening, and it's also frightening for parents to see their kid there and wonder how they're going to get through it. So I wanted to write a song that showed that there's a light at the end of the tunnel. I got all banged up, and yet I was able to come through and play guitar, and all these things that were broken ended up working well enough for me to make my living at it, my hands and fingers. So that song is dedicated to Courage Centers, and specifically to some people I knew that have just gone through physical trauma, and used my music as a kind of healing aid.

My dad told me about Les Paul, you know, how Les Paul got his arm all fucked up, and he had them set it so he could play guitar, and now he's one of the greatest guitar players that ever lived, and he's got a guitar named after him. And he said, "You can do it, too. If he can do it, you can do it." So the encouragement was, if I could get through the therapy, which was sometimes very painful and discouraging, then my dad would get me a Les Paul guitar someday. So all these things, in a way, made me want to play guitar even more.

Looking back at it, those challenges, again, were gifts. Sometimes we don't see it, but the most challenging times can be the most vital and inspiring times. So when people ask me what it takes to get really good at guitar and be famous, I say, "Well, force them to take accordion lessons for two years, and then break both their arms and their legs!" *(Laughs)*. And then let them play acoustic guitar in the hospital.

So I guess some of the unsung heroes of rock guitar aren't even musicians. Sometimes they're people like your parents, or the doctor in the hospital that tells you to keep on playing. So check it out, on *Acoustic Planet* there's that song called "Center Of Courage".

SW: I've heard the song. I just didn't realize that was the story behind it.

CC: Yeah, and it's all on one string. Well, ninety-nine percent of it is on the E string, and it was written when I was twelve years old. And I just want to say thank you for thinking of me, and for even having the idea to do a book with a concept like this. I think it's really fascinating. I think a lot of people out there pride themselves on, besides knowing about Eric Clapton and all these really famous guitar players, everybody likes to know about someone that nobody else really knows about, and turn them on to something really good.

It's kind of cool to have a writer want to make a book about the people we've probably all heard on the radio, but they're not as well-known as some of the other people. God, there are so many great players out there, that a lot of the times don't get any recognition from anyone except maybe other guitar players.

SW: Hey, that's what I'm here for! Well, that and the money, of course.*(Laughs)*.

For more information on Craig Chaquico, please visit
www.craigchaquico.com

INDEPENDENCE DAY

Larry Crane rose to prominence as the guitarist behind the signature sound of **John Cougar Mellencamp**. On a string of albums stretching from 'A Biography' in 1978, featuring the AOR classic "I Need A Lover", to 1989's understated masterpiece 'Big Daddy', which contained the disdainful "Pop Singer" and "Jackie Brown", **Crane** provided the gutsy rock and roll backbone upon which much of **Mellencamp's** roots-oriented rock relied. In 1991, determined to give his own music a shot, **Crane** struck out on the solo trail, and in the years since then has earned much critical acclaim with his own brand of heartland rock and roll.

Crane grew up in the small town of Seymour, Indiana, playing in a variety of local rock acts before he was out of his teens, often with his childhood friend **Mellencamp**, who was actually asked to leave one such band because the other members thought he couldn't sing. After high school graduation the pair went their separate ways, with **Crane** seeking his fortune in the West, touring with a country band, while **Mellencamp** pursued his adolescent dream of rock stardom with little success. After **Mellencamp** secured his recording contract and recorded the forgettable 'Chestnut Street Incident' under the name **Johnny Cougar**, he looked **Crane** up and asked him to be the anchor for his touring band, an offer which **Crane**, eager to get back to playing rock and roll, readily accepted.

It was the beginning of a pairing which would last for more than a decade and produce some of the classic rock songs of that time, including "Jack And Diane", "Authority Song", "Pink Houses", and "Rain On The Scarecrow". **Crane's** gritty guitar playing proved the perfect complement to **Mellencamp's** heartland mythology, evoking both the rock and roll strut and swagger of the Rolling Stones and the wistful small town spirit of Middle America. Perhaps the crowning achievement of this partnership was 1985's 'Scarecrow', a song cycle inspired by the plight of the American farmers who were losing their farms in record numbers. From the proud "Small Town" to the angry "Rain On The Scarecrow", the album perfectly captured the nuances of life in rural America at a time when that way of life was threatening to slip away forever.

Crane also participated in the filming of **Mellencamp's** somewhat ill-fated movie project 'Falling From Grace', the title of which came from one of **Crane's** songs from the soundtrack. During this period, when **Mellencamp** was taking a two-year break from the music industry, **Crane** began to seriously explore his other options, feeling that the time had perhaps come to test his wings as a solo artist. He parted with **Mellencamp** during the sessions for the album which was to become 'Whenever We Wanted', concentrating on playing live with his band and working up material for an album of his own. In 1993 **Crane** tested the waters with the critically acclaimed 'Independence Day', an EP release which more than established his credentials as a solo performer. In 1994 **Crane** followed *up with his self-titled full-length release, touring extensively with John Prine to promote it, again to glowing critical reviews.*

*I spoke to **Larry Crane** on November 8th, 1994 by phone from his home in Indiana. In a startling contrast to his longtime friend and collaborator **John Mellencamp**, a rather brash and outspoken man, **Crane** is without a doubt the most reserved, soft-spoken rock musician I have ever interviewed. He has never lost the gentle country accent of his youth, and his conversation is filled with the colorful expressions so unique to the Midwest. Talking to him, it is almost hard to imagine such a quiet man being capable of playing with the passion evidenced by much of the music he made with **Mellencamp**.*

*   **Crane** is clearly pleased with his progress, and well he should be. If his solo efforts thus far are any indication, **Larry Crane** just may have what it takes to make people forget his past and concentrate only on his musical future.*

SW: When did you start playing guitar?

LC: I was thirteen when I started, really. I'd messed around with other people's guitars a little bit, but the first guitar that I had of my own was when I was thirteen.

SW: What kind of a guitar was it?

LC: It was a little tiny Gibson 3/4 model of an ES-125. Basically what it was was an expensive beginner's model that a friend of mine had, and of course it was the old thing where he had all good intentions to learn how to play the guitar, so his parents bought him a real nice guitar and amplifier and all that, and then he took lessons for about a month and gave up on it! *(Laughs)*. So I got to buy the guitar for cheap.

SW: How did you become interested in the guitar?

LC: My aunt had an old arch-top that used to sit around in the living room, and she was nice enough...when I was a real little kid, we'd come over and visit, and I was just drawn to the thing, so I'd always pick it up, and she was nice enough to let me play it. You know, normally if a little kid grabs your guitar, you snatch it back out of their hands. *(Laughs)*. But she was nice enough to let me sit and kinda peck around on it, and I would sit and peck out a little tune here and there. I can never remember not being able to actually pull some kind of a tune out of a guitar.

SW: So you just took to it right off.

LC: Yeah, just one string at a time to start off with. I'd just peck out little melodies, and that just piqued my interest. I always wanted to play.

SW: Once you had a guitar in hand, did you learn on your own, or did you take lessons?

LC: I learned on my own pretty much, just learned the chords. Got a chord book and learned those, and the little cheat sheets with the chords above them, and I kind of had an ear for that stuff, too. I'd hear something and I'd be able to play it. I could tell what chords it was going to. It was never really hard for me.

Somebody asked me one time, "Larry, when you first started out, how many hours a day did you practice?" And I said, "I never practiced, but I *played* eight hours a day." That's the thing. If you've gotta make yourself sit and practice, you're probably meant to play some other type of music. But just to bang around, I just always had the thing in my hands. Shoot, I used to fall asleep with it.

SW: Did you always know that you'd turn pro?

LC: I always wanted to. I really wanted to play guitar for a living, and I seemed to have an aptitude for it. By the time I was fifteen years old, in the little town that I grew up in, I was probably one of the best guitar players in town, including the adults. And if I thought someone was better than me, I would get with them and just sit and jam and play around with them until I could play everything they could, and then I'd move on. I was a real sponge. I'd learn off of other people.

I had a couple of buddies that kind of played around on guitar and bass and drums and stuff; we always had some sort of little rock band going, and we'd throw together a little equipment, and mostly rehearse. Once in a while we'd go out and play a little dance here and there.

I grew up in a town called Seymour, Indiana, and right down the road there was a little school in a town called Brownstown, and I think there was one month that we played there, in their little cafetorium, we played there six times in one month. *(Laughs)*. We played all their dances. It was more just a chance to get out and have fun, really, at that point. It was a fun thing to do.

Of course, all of us had aspirations of actually being able to make a living sometime doing that, and I really couldn't do that. I made a lot of money later on when I was in high school, at sixteen or seventeen.

SW: So by that time you were on your way.

LC: I remember the first time I realized that I was actually getting paid for doing something that I loved. I played with a lot of older guys, and by the time I was sixteen I was playing with guys that were in college, and I was always the youngest guy.

A lot of kids on the weekends would go to ball games and stuff like that, while I was over in Peoria, Illinois playing the Top Hat Lounge! *(Laughs)*. Back then they would allow you to come in and play. There was always a little table by the stage that you would have to sit at, and it was legally okay to do that. I think there was one place where I had to get a special liquor permit to be in there, but usually we'd just cruise in and I'd play, and as long as I stayed within the rules, we were okay. Everybody else was old enough to be in there.

That was quite a realization, that I could actually go out and get paid for something that I liked to do. That was pretty cool. I felt like, well, the rest of these guys, during the summer they'll go out and work farms and bail hay and stuff like that, while I...I did a little bit of that, but I didn't *have* to do it. So it was real nice. I enjoyed that part of it.

SW: How long did it take to go from those types of gigs to larger, more professional kinds of situations?

LC: Well, it was kind of a slow process. You know, me and John gigged around, because John was in a lot of those little bands that I was in. And when I got out of high school, I wanted to travel a little bit. You know, growing up in that little town, it's one of those things where you just wanted to go somewhere else. You were tied down to being there a lot of the time, and you didn't get far geographically.

So I hooked up with some people in Kansas City, an agency out there, and they hooked me up with a little country band, which wasn't anything that was gonna go anywhere, obviously. We were just playing tiny little clubs, and the guy that sang had been in the business for quite a long time. Great guy, wonderful voice, but it was just, you know, nobody really did any writing. It was just kind of, they went and played. They were playing just about every night except for a Sunday. And he paid me a salary, and all of my hotel expenses and everything like that, so that was real nice. I could just enjoy playing, and it was a new set list every night.

We took requests. This guy was like an encyclopedia of old country songs, and man, I learned a lot of them. He'd just tell me the name of a song, and the key, and away we'd go. I'd just hold on through the first verse and chorus, until I had it figured out, and then I'd go on from there.

So I did that for about a year, and then John Mellencamp got hold of me. I was out in Kansas somewhere. He said that he'd got a record deal, and he was wanting me to come back and help him put a band together. So at that point I hadn't played that much true rock for almost a year, and I really missed it, and that sounded like a good opportunity to come back and do that. So that was kinda the beginning of the John Cougar thing. That would have been '76.

SW: So you were with him even on those really early albums.

LC: The only record that I didn't do in those early days was the very first one, because when I was out west, he was busy making a demo tape, which ended up being the very first record called *Chestnut Street Incident*. I was out playing with that band then, but when it was time to put a live band together, that's when he called me.

We worked that record, and then the next record we went to New York to make, which at that time didn't come out. It was supposed to be on MCA Records; it was like a package deal. Now, every time John puts out a record, his old manager, who was a guy named Tony DeFries, who managed David Bowie…he was with Main Man, was the name of the agency. They handled Lou Reed, Mick Ronson, Dana Gillespie, a bunch of those people from that era from around the New York scene. So we went up there and made that record, and it never came out. That's when John switched managers.

SW: As you pointed out, he did have a manager who was noted for managing some glitter-rock acts, or whatever you want to call them. I understand DeFries had kind of a screwy marketing plan for him.

LC: Yeah, this guy was a little crazy in the way he looked at things, and John...at that point that was the only game in town, and I think this DeFries guy wanted to turn him into like a cartoon. But the one good thing it did do, it got his foot in the door and got him some fairly solid management with a guy named Billy Gaff over in London, who managed Rod Stewart at the time.

So we went over there and made one record. We lived there from 1977 to 1978 and made one record called *A Biography*, which had the song "I Need A Lover" on it. That's where that song originated. We lived there for a year and toured Europe a bunch, and all over Britain, and did that whole thing.

It actually did very well in Australia, that record did. It was not released here in the States, because we did not have a distribution deal here in North America, but it went everywhere else. And it was number one for like two months over in Australia. *(Laughs)*. And based on that, that was on Riva Records, and we brought Riva over to the United States and set up a deal with Polygram. So that's how all that got started.

SW: What record was the first one to come out in the States after that?

LC: It was just called *John Cougar*. That would have been right around '79.

SW: When you toured in support of that, was it still mainly opening for other people?

LC: Yeah, even at that point we were still opening for other people. Over in Europe we opened for Blue Oyster Cult, Nazareth, Thin Lizzy, John Miles. We opened for everybody. Even when we got back here, we released that record and started going around the United States mainly, and we were opening for some strange bands that you would never think of us opening up for. We opened for The Kinks quite a bit. We did three tours with those guys. And Kiss, we did a bunch of dates with them...

SW: *(Laughing)* I find that hard to picture!

LC: Well, it didn't last very long. But you know, just a lot of gigs like that. And then for the next record, *Nothing Matters And What If It Did*, again, we were still opening, and then the next record *American Fool*, when that album came out it did real well, and the tour we had planned was an opening act tour with Heart, who had a new record coming out at the same time.

Their record didn't do so well, and ours did really well, but we just remained on that tour, because it was a good tour for us to be on. We were filling houses. Heart was the headliner, and together we were filling up houses. And it worked real well.

SW: Was it a situation where you actually upstaged the headliner when it was all said and done?

LC: Sometimes. Like here in Indiana we did. At that point they were really suffering from the old "you're only as good as your last record" ordeal, and we came out, and we were really new and fresh to a lot of people, so we would have a lot of our audience show up.

We were in a no-lose situation. Even if we didn't bowl them over, it was okay because we were just the opener! *(Laughs)*. And then if we did, it was just the icing on the cake. We started really attracting a crowd then.

SW: What was it like on those early tours opening for other people? Did you generally get treated okay as an opening act?

LC: It's according to who you're opening for. You know, Heart especially, the Heart people were great. Plus we were in it for the long haul, and that means something. But it's according to who it is and how insecure they are. If it's some artist that's really worried and not very secure about his fan base, they can get a little funny about things. Of course we had problems, because we just did it for so long, but considering how long we did that, how many shows we did opening up, the percentage was pretty good.

It always seemed like it was some of the acts that really weren't that good that treated us the worst. The ones that were good, we normally got along with. And there have been some that we opened up for that a few years later ended up opening up for us.

SW: Like who?

LC: Ritchie Blackmore, for one. Ritchie's a nice guy; he's kind of a strange old duck, but he's real nice, and we always got along with him. But it was just funny to see the whole turnaround. We did a bunch of dates with him.

Actually, the one and only time that we had problems as far as the crowd pelting things at us was at Oakland Coliseum opening for Ritchie. I think Judas Priest was supposed to open, and the promoter told everybody except the people who bought tickets, and when we got there, they were expecting Judas Priest. We came out, and it was all these big-time vested biker guys. The minute they said John's name and we started playing, they just started picking up everything they could grab.

SW: Oh, no! *(Laughter)*.

LC: But that's the only time that happened. And then about two or three years later, Ritchie opened up for us at some sort of festival. Actually, we weren't even the headliner on that deal; it was one of these big festivals, and I can't remember where it was at, but it was one of those big summer jams, in a big stadium, and he went on before us. We got kind of a chuckle out of it.

SW: At what point did you start to headline?

LC: The first headlining tour was when *Uh-huh* came out, which would have been '83 or '84.

SW: How did that go?

LC: Real good. We wouldn't over-venue ourselves. We would go into places that we knew we could fill up. We'd rather play in a smaller place and sell out than play a big place and not sell out. So we were putting that show into theaters and that type of place. Around here in our home state we would play larger places, but that was just around here. And we had some hot spots around the country that we'd go play, and that worked out pretty good.

We knew where our audience was. If the tickets would sell out immediately, then we might move it to a larger place. But we always played sold-out shows, and that made everything look good, because if people come to a show, if it's sold out, then they think it's really going on.

SW: As opposed to the situation you were in with the country band before that, where the set list was different every night, on a major venue tour the set list is much more static. Do you find it harder to keep in shape as a guitar player when you're not constantly playing new material?

LC: No, not really, because I think that kind of thing is my strength. I'm not what you'd call a real big jammer, a soloist or anything like that. There's guys that do that really well, I just don't happen to be one of them. I play guitar *parts*. I like to play guitar parts and entertain.

I always consider it a good show when I felt like I split my attention exactly in half between working a crowd and actually doing a show, and the other half actually playing guitar. If it got too much one way or the other, I consider that a bad show. I like to walk that fine line between doing too much and not doing enough.

SW: So you're not interested in doing a long, drawn-out guitar solo spotlight?

LC: No. My whole thing is, there's great guitar players, great drummers, great bass players, great keyboardists, but there's damn few great bands. And it's much harder to do. A guy can sit in his room and practice his scales or do this or do that or whatever it is, but the heart and soul of rock and roll has always been with a band.

SW: The rhythm section particularly.

LC: Yeah. It's like when one guy makes a mistake, the rest of the band makes the same mistake at exactly the same time without even looking at each other. That's something very few people get to experience, and with me, Kenny Aronoff, Toby Myers and Mike Wanchic, we had that. We spent so many hours playing together that it was ridiculous. We could start stuff up without even looking at each other and be right there, like NRBQ is.

SW: How long did that same line-up stay together?

LC: Let's see, Kenny's first record was the *American Fool* album, so that would have been '82. Then after that record was done, that's when Toby came aboard, so about nine years with that exact line-up. Plus John Cascella on keyboards, so that was really the unit.

SW: In nine years you must have played literally thousands of shows.

LC: Yeah, and we clicked. You know, we were either in the studio or out playing. We just played so much, and practiced so much, that like I said, if one guy made a mistake, the rest of the guys made it right along with him without even looking up. Now that was a band.

Like the band I have now, I've had the same members now for quite a while, and I told them, "There's another level of playing that we will get to at some point, but it takes a long time." It's not that easy to do. It just takes hours and hours of playing together. And you know, none of us were really great musicians. Boy, when Kenny joined the band he was a horrible drummer.

SW: *(Laughing).* What was so horrible about him?

LC: He had, like, a thousand cymbals and a thousand tom-toms, and was playing jazz fusion stuff and Gino Vanelli and things like that and just overplayed, and couldn't play with a click. His kick drum was inconsistent, the snare drum would be loud one time and soft the next time.

And we just learned together, you know, these were the things that we needed to do, and we just worked on it until it was right. Kenny studied old Rolling Stones records and learned, what's Charlie Watts doing that's so cool, and how's he doing that? And really analyzed them and figured out what made those things work.

We were more into arrangements and songs and making records than we were our own instruments. I mean, we were interested in the fact of the instrument as long as it pertained to the band, but we weren't trying to achieve anything just for the sake of achieving something on an instrument. It's the old gunslinger thing: no matter how good you think you are, there's gonna be somebody better. And who's to say what's better? To me, I'd rather hear a really great guitar part than a really great guitar player.

SW: A great riff or whatever.

LC: Yeah, somebody that comes up with really cool parts. For instance, the new Pretenders record. There's a couple of songs on there that have really great guitar parts that are simple. Anyone can play them, but thinking of them is another thing, and to me that's where the writing comes in.

That's what I always did for John. I wrote the guitar parts, and to me that's where my creative input was. I felt like those songs were mine, too, because I put so much arrangement and guitar playing into them. But it was never anything fancy. It was all by the seat of my ass. I never did want to come up with anything too hard, because I couldn't play it on stage! *(Laughter).* You know, I might be able to get in on tape once, but playing it every night would be a different story, so I would never try to do anything that I couldn't play. But the thing is, if I can think of it, normally I can play it.

SW: You always see John pictured with a guitar in the videos. How much does he actually play in the band?

LC: He plays a little bit. He just sorta chords on the guitar, he doesn't really play parts or anything like that. He just sorta writes on the guitar. On one tour, I think it might have been the *Uh-huh* tour, he decided he was gonna play electric guitar on stage, which was like a nightmare for me! *(Laughter)*. So he set this little amp up, and he's got this black Telecaster, and we're playing this song, and all of a sudden this horrible sound starts coming out of his amp.

Well, he looks around and scowls at me, thinking it's me screwing up. And the longer we play, the madder he gets, because it's this awful sound. I mean, it's just distorted and nasty-sounding. *(Laughs)*. And he keeps turning around and making bad faces at me, so I said well, that's enough of that. So I walk up and while he's singing, I just walk up and switch the pickup switch back down on his guitar. While he was strumming the guitar, he'd batted the pickup switch onto the front pickup, and the amplifier was not set for this pickup at all, it's set for the back pickup. And he'd hit that and didn't even know it, and on top of that, didn't even know that it was his guitar making that awful noise!

And so at that point I said, "Hey, John, let me handle the guitar stuff," and we just gave him a fake chord, and I said, "If you want it for a prop, go ahead and take it up there and strum it, but please don't plug it in anymore." *(Laughter)*. So that was the end of his electric guitar on stage. It was kind of a short-lived career.

SW: So he's not really somebody who studies equipment and so forth…

LC: No, not really. *(Laughs)*. And plus, he's up there singing and doing his thing. He doesn't have time to worry about that. I'm sort of in the same situation myself, now. In the band that I have now, I pretty much play guitar and do what I do, but I don't try to get into anything very versatile as far as different sounds and anything. I keep it real simple, because I'm sort of up there where John normally was at center stage singing, so that keeps me fairly occupied there. I've got a really good guitar player in my band, so I let him handle all the difficult stuff.

But yeah, that was his one and only time playing electric guitar on stage as far as I know. Now, he may be doing it a little bit now. I don't know. But at least while I was still there, that was it.

SW: You had to put your foot down! *(Laughs)*.

LC: He plays acoustic okay. You can hand him an acoustic and he's fine with that. But I just thought it was crazy for him to do that when he had two guys standing there who had nothing to do but play guitar. Let him worry about all the other stuff.

SW: As the years rolled by, you guys kept having hits. Did that change the way you worked?

LC: Well, the band always changed. And again, my guitar playing changed as the band's sound changed. During *American Fool* and the *Uh-huh* album, I pretty much played Gibsons. I was using more of a double coil sound, a little thicker sound. And as we went on into the *Scarecrow* album and *The Lonesome Jubilee*, I got more infatuated with the Telecaster sound and started using more Fenders, which I had never done before. I'd always used Gibsons; Les Pauls, SGs and 335s. And so now I use both. But back then, when we played the old songs I would use the Gibsons, and then all the new stuff was played on Fenders. But really, that was about as radical a change as I went through.

I like to keep my guitar playing subject to what the song is. Whatever the song requires, that's what I'll do. I've never really used pedals or anything like that. I'm kind of a purist on that. I think if you start getting those pedals and stuff, really I think pedals mask people's style, and to have your own style is really what you want.

I was playing with Dave Grissom the other day, we were doing a session with Bob Johnston over in San Francisco, and I'd pretty much done most of the guitar on the record. I'd cut all the basic tracks, and we had Dave come in and just fly in some solos. And there was a guitar part that I was trying to relate to him what I wanted, and he said, "Why don't you just come out and do it? It's a lot easier than trying to tell me." So I just went out there and I grabbed his guitar, his settings, it was set just the way he had it, and did the part and came back in, and he said, "You know, it really doesn't matter what kind of guitar, whatever you grab is gonna sound like you. You could grab a four-string banjo and it would sound like you." So that was quite a compliment, especially coming from a guy that I consider one of the better guitar players around.

So I never used pedals or anything like that because I always felt that masked what style I had. I didn't ever want to mask that. And all my great guitar heroes that I thought were great guitar players really didn't use effects. Like Jimi Hendrix is not one of my guitar heroes. My guitar heroes are guys like Roy Buchanan, you know, people like that. They rarely used effects.

SW: Who are some of your other influences?

LC: It's according to what period of time. I've been influenced by so many guitar players. At one point when I was younger, I just wanted to be Rick Derringer. *(Laughs)*. I wanted to look like him, I wanted to play like him. When I was still in high school I looked exactly like him, because I'm short, and I've got the kinda reddish hair, and I had my hair cut exactly like him.

And from that phase, I wanted to be Johnny Thunder for a while, from the New York Dolls, and I still think he's one of the greatest punk guitar players around. And the other guy…man, his name is escaping me right now, the guy that played with Iggy Pop. Played with him for years; as a matter of fact, I saw them in the late Seventies, and he was still playing with him. But man, I can't think of his name for anything. And I like Martin Barre. I always thought Martin was a really great guitar player. And then I got really influenced by Mick Ronson and Jeff Beck. For a while there I wanted to be those guys, too. I wanted to play just like them.

Keith Richards has always been an influence. He sort of amalgamated all the different blues guys and old rock guys together and made this cool style that he does on his own, and I always thought that was kinda neat. Here's an English guy that would sound very American, very black at times, but not quite. He still put it in his own realm. And to me, "Tumbling Dice" is still the best intro in rock. There has not been a better introduction to a song. When that song comes in it's so cool, I can't imagine anything being any cooler than that. Even "Start Me Up", what a great come-in. An intro is half a song. It catches you when it starts.

SW: It's that hook that makes you want to pay attention.

LC: Yeah. But as far as pure players, you know, Roy Buchanan, I listened to him for years and years. Just as far as guys that play solos, I just thought he was the best. He was just playing balls-out, just shooting from the hip. Nothing real technical. He had that old beat-up Telecaster and a little Fender amplifier and a chord, and that's all he needed! Guys like that, I just thought he was great. To me, his solos and the way he played had more heart and less technique.

I'm not into the technical guys. I'm more into the guys that just come out and you can tell. It's like a singer; you know, a guy can be a great singer, and can sing real high and real low and be able to do all kinds of acrobatic stuff, but if their heart's not in it, you can just tell immediately. And that's the way guitar players are, too.

SW: You stopped working with Mellencamp just prior to *Whenever We Wanted*. What prompted you to do that?

LC: Well, it wasn't like I woke up one day and decided to do that. We were working on that record at the time that I left. John was wanting some commitments that I didn't want to make, and it was causing some friction between us. See, he'd taken a hiatus from the music business for two years.

SW: Was that when he was working on his movie?

LC: Yeah. See, I was working on the movie with him, too. I did a lot of the music in the movie, and actually had a role in the movie, so we were still working together.

SW: What role did you play in the movie?

LC: I played Raymie, the half-brother of the main character. Anyway, in between that time I'd gotten this small band together, and we were starting to do some stuff. I was doing a lot of writing, and to me, what has come up in the forefront as far as what I want to do on a day-to-day basis, and what seems important to me now, is writing.

You know, playing the guitar has always been great for me; I love being a sideman. I think I was a really good sideman, but I'd been a sideman for so long that it was time for me to move on. I just couldn't see myself being a sideman for another three or four years, because at that point I was thirty-three or thirty-four years old. To commit to another three records and three tours, hell, by then I'd have been almost forty years old, and I didn't want to start working my songs and doing my thing when I'm forty and might not have the energy for it.

So I've been doing this for the past three years, basically on my own, and I've got a new record out that's distributed by DNA up in Boston, and things are looking pretty good. It's got a lot of critical acclaim, and I've just been doing a lot of writing.

SW: Are you going to be touring nationally for this?

LC: Eventually. Right now we're doing a seven-state area release, so as far as playing out, I'll concentrate on those seven states. After the first of the year they want to do more of a broad national and international release, so hopefully our momentum will be going to the point where we can do something like that. I'd like to do some opening act stuff again. I think that would be good for us to do right now.

SW: You talked briefly about the movie *Falling From Grace*. Did you enjoy doing the movie?

LC: Yeah, I really enjoyed it. I'd done a little bit of acting earlier on, when I was in high school, so it wasn't completely new to me. What was new to me was doing it in front of a camera, which is a lot different from the stage. And there was guy named Ron Burris, who's an acting coach, that came in and worked with me for a month.

The part that I had was fairly big, and I'd never really acted on camera before, and I really wanted to do a good job because I enjoyed it. So I sat with him for a month, and we just went through the script, and he coached me and just worked on technique and different things. I really enjoyed the whole process. I've had a couple of other offers. I was supposed to be in a movie called *Bad Girls*...

SW: With Drew Barrymore?

LC: Yeah, but they started running out of money, and when they started running out of money they started pulling characters, and one of the characters they pulled was mine. But the main story had six stars, so it was a little tough for the supporting cast to get in there. I was gonna play the guy that, the bank robber that helped them out, I was gonna play his little brother. Another little brother thing. *(Laughs)*.

SW: Do you think you'll pursue acting more?

LC: A bit, yeah. The guy that directed that wants me to do his next movie whenever he does that. His name is Jonathon Kaplan. He was real hot on me being in this movie; he wanted me to come and do this thing, and when Twentieth Century started cutting the script, he said, "There'll be the next movie." So I said okay. It's real nice. I've known Jonathon for a long time, and I can basically go in cold. I don't have to go in and test or read. He can just call me in, and he knows I can do the part. So that's just kind of a little sideline, more of a hobby. It's something that I enjoy doing.

SW: In addition to your record release, what plans do you have for the future? Do you want to see this solo project through and do more records?

LC: I'd like to see it do fairly well. With the glut in the market the way it is now, it's a little unrealistic to expect to sell zillions of records. I think you'd have to be something fairly trendy. But I think as long as you're writing good songs, melody and lyric, there's always a place in the market for you. And that's what I concentrate on, is actual songs. So that's what I want to do. I want to learn how to write really good songs and pursue that as long as I can. Until I decide to do something else! *(Laughs).*

For more information on Larry Crane, please visit
www.larrycrane.net

FIGHT THE GOOD FIGHT

Rik Emmett is perhaps best known for the years he spent in the Canadian hard rock trio *Triumph*, a band which took its initial cue from the blues-based heavy rock of bands such as Led Zeppelin. Though the band had already signed a recording contract when *Emmett* joined, it was his trademark guitar playing, singing and songs which became publicly identified as *Triumph's* signature sound.

Emmett's unusually versatile electric and acoustic guitar stylings, drawing on influences ranging from rock and blues to folk, jazz and classical guitar, lent *Triumph* a degree of musicality sorely lacking in most of the band's AOR brethren. Coupled with his tendency toward literary allusions and intellectually informed lyricism, this resulted in *Triumph* being labeled "thinking man's arena rock."

Heavily influenced by such progressive rock stalwarts as Yes, King Crimson and Gentle Giant, *Emmett* often found himself at odds with the more straightforward tastes of his *Triumph* bandmates, drummer **Gil Moore** and bassist **Mike Levine**. As the band grew in popularity through such albums as 'Just A Game' and 'Allied Forces', he was increasingly frustrated at how his contributions to *Triumph's* music were finally represented.

In the early Eighties the band faced a court battle with RCA to extricate itself from its recording contract, and its fortunes improved thereafter upon signing with MCA. *Triumph's* seventh album, 'Thunder Seven', became the trio's best-selling album, and the subsequent tour proved to be the most successful yet. Over the course of the next few albums, *Emmett* found himself and his ideas being pushed ever further to the background, a situation which reached its nadir during the recording of 'Surveillance', his final album with *Triumph*. Dissatisfied with the limitations of *Triumph's* music and the politics of the band, *Emmett* announced his departure in 1988.

He then faced more than six years of legal wrangling in order to collect the share of royalties that was due him, during which time he recorded two successful solo albums. 'Absolutely' provided the radio hit "Saved By Love", establishing *Emmett* as a viable solo act, which was further borne out by the success of 'Ipso Facto'. *Triumph's* attempt at a comeback without *Emmett*, entitled 'Edge of Excess', sank without a trace.

I spoke with **Rik Emmett** by phone from his home in Canada during a break from recording his third solo album, 'The Spiral Notebook'. It was a critical time for *Emmett*; he admitted to a bit of nervousness at finding himself on "the other side of forty" in a business aimed primarily at people less than half that age. He seemed somewhat apprehensive about the reception his new album would receive, but what struck me about him was his obvious intellect and the careful way in which he expressed himself.

Though there is clearly no love lost between *Emmett* and his former *Triumph* bandmates, whom he rarely refers to by name, but rather terms "the guys in *Triumph*" or "my former partners",

Emmett avoids expressing any overt bitterness about the past. He refuses to be drawn into a war of words with his onetime bandmates, preferring to let the music do the talking.

SW: How old were you when you started playing guitar?

RE: I was probably eleven or twelve. The whole thing was happening with the Beatles and all that British Invasion stuff, and my grandfather had given me an acoustic when I was really young. I was left-handed, so I was sort of playing backward and upside down and dreaming about being Paul McCartney.

And then I won some lessons. I was in grade seven, and I won some lessons from a local music school. I had a teacher there named Jack Arsenault, and I actually started on sort of a lap guitar where you played slide. Originally that was the sort of lessons I won. And then you graduated to sitting it up in your lap properly. Jack Arsenault was a left-handed guy that played righty and suggested I should do the same.

So I took lessons for about the first six months or a year and then dropped out, because I was more interested in playing in a garage band, basement band kind of thing than I was in taking lessons and going through the Mel Bay book. *(Laughs).* So I guess by the time I was twelve or thirteen, I was launched.

SW: Were those the only formal lessons you took?

RE: No. If we follow this thing chronologically, as I went through high school, I ended up being more the singer and front man for the bands that I was in than the guitar player. There was always someone who was shyer than I was, so he got to be the lead player. I was more of a hambone and didn't necessarily mind fronting the band and singing, so I'd end up being more the rhythm player.

Once I got out of that phase, by this time of course the whole Hendrix/ Clapton thing had happened, and then the invasion of British progressive bands that really influenced the way my friends and I looked at the guitar, the whole Yardbirds alumni kind of thing. And then came that wave of Yes and King Crimson and Gentle Giant and all of that stuff. That really affected the way we approached things.

So when I graduated from high school, to finally answer your question about lessons *(laughs),* I went to a music college for a short period of time. It was primarily a jazz program, and I studied with a guy named Peter Harris there. Again, I didn't last long there, probably less than a year; I think a semester and maybe a week. And then I decided that instead of paying money to study music, I could go out and play it and earn money by doing it. So I left music school and went into the school of hard knocks.

SW: Have you ever held a job outside of music?

RE: I taught school for a short period of time. I was a teaching assistant with the Toronto Board of Education, primarily with special education. And I've had other part-time jobs as a teenager, but never any other full-time work, other than that teaching job, other than music.

By that time I was just primarily playing in bands, going out on the road, and I guess my career had started back in high school when I was still playing in basement bands and stuff. I started gigging in wedding and bar mitzvah things, and I got a job playing in a country and western band while I was still in high school. *(Laughs).* Three nights a week I was playing in a bar playing country and western, you know, saving up my money and buying a Tele and a Fender amp. So I guess that never stopped, and even though I taught school for about six months, I was still gigging at night and doing things on the weekend, and then sort of decided to try the rock and roll thing.

Fortunately, the first band I was in was a recording act, and then the second band I was in got a lot of local notoriety in the Toronto area, even though we didn't make a lot of money. That brought me to the attention of the guys from Triumph when they were starting up, and when I joined them they already had a recording deal, so I was pretty much always just playing music for a living.

SW: You mentioned a lot of British progressive rock influences. Did you play that type of music before you joined Triumph?

RE: I did. The bar band that I was in directly before Triumph was called Act Three, and it was just a trio. We used to play cover material from all of those bands, and the American bands like Return To Forever and that kind of stuff, too, and then just weird stuff. We'd do medleys of "Tubular Bells" going into "Perpetual Change" by Yes, going into, what's the one by Gentle Giant, "Freehand" or something *(hums the song)*, whatever that one was. We used to do all that weird stuff, and of course, people would sit nursing a beer in a bar and looking at us going, "What the hell is going on?" *(Laughter).*

It was a trio, so our drummer had a keyboard setup over his floor toms on his right, and every now and then he'd be playing with his feet and one hand while he was playing keyboards with the other. It was wild. Of course, in those days everybody had bass pedals on the floor that were hooked up to things, and I always had a slide guitar on a stand over to the side. We played a lot of that stuff, and I can't necessarily say we were good at it, but we certainly loved it. *(Laughs).*

That sort of stuff was closer to my heart than, perhaps, the Led Zeppelin and Deep Purple kind of stuff that I ended up playing in Triumph when it first started off as a bar band, which was a harder rock kind of a thing. I mean, I like that, too. Ritchie Blackmore was a huge influence on me when I was in high school. I loved his guitar playing and certainly emulated it a great deal. But I think my heart was probably more into the eclectic, progressive side of guitar playing than it was that standard, blues-based rock playing, that pentatonic approach.

SW: The song "Blinding Light Show" from *Rock And Roll Machine* is a bit more progressive than the typical Triumph song.

RE: That song came from the Act Three period. The other writers on that, Denton Young and Chris Brockway, were the guys that were in Act Three with me, and in fact, that was an Act Three song that I brought into Triumph. It was actually modified to be more Triumph-esque. The main theme, that *(hums the guitar line)* was originally a thing that was in seven, that went *(hums the same part in more complex time signature)*. It had this sort of weird, bouncing-around-between-time-signatures kind of thing, and of course I played it for the guys in Triumph and they said, "Can't we just straighten that out into 4/4?" *(Laughs)*. So we did. But yeah, those were the weird days.

SW: Obviously you have a very broad palette of influences. What were some of your other early influences?

RE: When I was really young, my brother had bought me a Segovia record called *The Guitar And I*, which had a lot of basic classical guitar studies on one side, and then him talking about his early life as a classical guitarist on the other side. I was into that, and one of the first relatively decent guitars that I bought was a classical guitar. I had Julian Bream recordings and Segovia recordings that I listened to a fair bit. As much as I listened to my Beatles and Byrds, I was listening to classical guitar stuff as well. So I always had fairly eclectic taste.

Then later on, of course, was the influence of going to college and being in the jazz program; there was a tremendous exposure to Kenny Burrell, Wes Montgomery, Charlie Byrd and Joe Pass. People would be walking around talking about Charlie Christian and Django Reinhardt and Eddie Lang and all that kind of stuff, so we were all trying to get into that as much as possible and get exposed to that as much as we could. That happened later on in my teenage years, but certainly that was a part of what I listened to as well.

SW: When you joined Triumph, was it difficult for you to narrow back down to a simpler approach?

RE: I don't know if "difficult" would necessarily be the right word to use. I think it was more of a question of, that's what the gig called for, so that's what you did. I always thought of myself as being sneaky in the sense that, if and when I could convince somebody, there would be little moments of slightly jazz-esque kinds of things, or little moments of classical guitar, that would sprinkle through the predominately blues-based arena-style rock that Triumph was. But the reason we had a record deal, and the reason that the band had popularity on a mass basis, I think, was more because of the straightforward aspect of its music, not necessarily the eclectic nature of its music.

Certainly in the ensuing time period since the band's big success, the late Seventies and early Eighties, I think that the nature of the music business and music critiquing, and the industry as it has evolved, has really drastically limited the ability of artists to make pop music that is eclectic. You really do have to have that narrow focus in what you do. That's the nature of the beast. That makes it easy to market, and easy to target a demographic and go at them. So I think a lot of the stuff that I personally thought was so neat in the late Sixties and early Seventies that made the music business interesting, and made a lot of pop music and pop guitar playing interesting for me, really did end up getting bled right out of the business.

I don't think it was necessarily because of what the artists wanted to do. It was more a question of, that's the way the business evolved, the industry and its environment, and the people that made money off of it by writing record reviews and working as A&R men. They're not actually musicians, but it's their job to try and figure out what it is that the public wants, and then sign and develop and promote the acts that they think will sell. And in the end, to sort of answer your question—again in a roundabout way—I think it's more of a question of, you just do what the job seems to call for.

I shouldn't make broad, sweeping generalizations. Certainly I think if you talked to the guys today in say, Soundgarden or Pearl Jam or some of those Seattle bands, or REM or whoever, they would probably say, "Oh, no, we do just exactly as we want to do, and nobody tells us what to do." But I think behind the scenes there's probably a lot more that goes on than they'd necessarily be willing to discuss in public about what they're going to do to put out a record in order to try and maintain or increase the amount of records that they sell.

And they'll find, as their careers go on, that there will be pressure from record companies and managers and all the rest of the industry for them to do exactly that—sell more records, or at least keep selling exactly the same, or fulfill the mandate that stylistically they've already established. And so then you start to think, 'Geez, I'm kind of limited in what I get to do in this particular job.' But I think that's just the nature of the beast.

SW: So you just have to try as hard as you can to do good work within those confines.

RE: I think so. And hopefully then you have enough commercial success and recognition that maybe somebody comes along and says, "Hey, would you like to try and do this? It may be kind of a stretch for you, but you might think it's fun." And then if you do that and it works out well for you...look at Mark Knopfler. He's a perfect example of somebody that was off the beaten track a little bit, but then he had this mainstream success. And then all of a sudden he was given the opportunity to do film scores, and play on other people's records, and then he collaborated with Chet Atkins. A lot of good things happened for him, primarily because "Sultans Of Swing" was a pop success. I think opportunity comes based on one thing, and notoriety comes based on that one thing, and if you're smart, you try and turn that into opportunities in other areas.

SW: You've done some playing in other areas. I'm thinking of the *Guitar Player* Soundpage you did. How did that come about?

RE: That was basically just me talking to the guys at *Guitar Player* magazine about trying to get my ya-ya's out in a different kind of way. They had this Soundpage thing that they'd been doing on a fairly regular basis, and I said, "Hey, I've got this idea. What do you think?" And Tom Wheeler, who was the editor at the time, and I think was a good, strong supporter of me over the years—which is something I really appreciate—he said, "Sure, that sounds good to us."

It sounded like the kind of thing that was right up the magazine's alley at the time. I don't necessarily think *Guitar Player* is of the same persuasion now, but certainly in those days they kind of enjoyed that whole aspect of cross-fertilization or cross-pollination or whatever you'd call it. *(Laughs)*. Inbreeding? I don't know. But that struck them as something that would be interesting to do, so they said, "Okay, here's your budget, and away you go."

SW: It sounds like it was very enjoyable.

RE: In many ways it was a dream come true. I mean, for me to be able to work with players that were the caliber of Ed Bickert and Alex Lifeson and Liona Boyd on a strictly guitar level was a terrific thing. We weren't concerned about whether or not it was going to sell records or whether or not it was going to satisfy any record company's marketing plan or anything. It was just a question of, I wrote this thing, and it was sort of weird and wild and wacky and wonderful. It gave everybody the chance to do their thing, but then sort of accompany other guys doing their thing.

So it was fun for me, and in a sense, maybe that spoke more to what was at the heart of me as a guitar player than some of the things I've done on really popular, successful songs that made the hit parade. It was terrific. Too bad it was just one song! *(Laughs)*. I'd love to be able to do a full album like that sometime.

SW: Have you considered a full instrumental album?

RE: I have, and there's been a lot of anticipation, especially over the years when I do interviews with people to promote different records. I still think that somehow I have something that I have to prove in more of a commercial pop sense before I would indulge myself completely on that level. I mean, at the end of the day, when people ask me what it is that compels me to keep functioning as a performing musician and recording artist, what originally made me want to pick up the guitar and play was that I wanted to play a song and sing a song.

I was always a singer and a guitar player. I always sang in choir when I was a kid, and the first creative act I ever did on a guitar, once I learned a C chord and an A minor chord, was to write a song, not necessarily write a guitar piece. I still feel that what's central to me as a musician is to be this three-sided thing; you're a singer, you're a guitarist, and you're a songwriter. And that's really what I still want to keep doing, so that's what I feel like I have to establish primarily.

If I went and did an instrumental guitar record, I think you run a few risks. One of them would certainly be that all of the people that were sitting around waiting for you to fail as a commercial pop artist would finally say, "Well, see, he's finally smartened up. He's forgotten about trying to write songs and sing. Now he's just making an instrumental record, and that's where he belongs. He should have been doing that a long time ago."

The further risk is that the general public doesn't really rush to the record store to buy instrumental records by guitar players. I mean, even somebody as phenomenal as Michael Hedges or as technically brilliant as Allan Holdsworth, they don't end up selling humongous amounts of records to the public. Steve Morse is a friend of mine, and he's a phenomenal guitar player, and he just doesn't sell that many records. I mean, he sells enough that he earns a nice living, and certainly the guitar community knows about him, but the general public, I talk to people and mention Steve Morse, and they say, "Steve Morse? Who's that?" So I think that's the danger you run. If you start making just instrumental records, then what if you're somehow perceived in the music business and the industry as, "Oh, an instrumental guy; he can't sell that many records."

And the danger for me is that if I did the first one and it didn't sell that well, then I think you wouldn't get any more chances! The record companies that were looking for you to be a commercial kind of pop songwriter now would say, "Well, you shot yourself in the foot, didn't you? We're not interested in you now. Look what you've done."

That's why I've always been a little bit shy. I've always felt I had to have more of a commercial base before I tried something off the beaten path, so that even if it failed, you'd still be able to indulge like that whenever you wanted to. I think when Knopfler steps out of Dire Straits and goes and does the Notting Hillbillies, or goes and does the film score for *Local Hero* or something, I think everyone involved on both sides of those projects always thinks, "Of course, he's gonna do another Dire Straits record in another year or two, and that's fine. That's good for him, and this is the natural course of business as usual." So I've kinda felt like it was too risky for me at this point. But I will someday, I guess. Maybe sooner than later! *(Laughs)*.

SW: You talk of pressure from record companies and radio programmers and so on. When you were in Triumph, did you experience that kind of pressure yourself?

RE: The nature of the band was such that the other guys, their strengths were more management and marketing and promotion, the other two guys that were in Triumph, and they didn't really make much of a secret about that. That was what they enjoyed and what they liked. So that made it sort of a unique and unusual band, even though the music that ended up getting made might not necessarily, from a critical point of view, have been thought of in that way. We functioned rather independently, isolated and insulated in our own little world. We had our own recording studio, and pretty much ran our own affairs, and managed ourselves. So in that sense we just did whatever we liked.

But it wasn't a nice, smooth, easy kind of situation. When we were on RCA, I think RCA got to a point where they said, "Well, these guys are only ever going to sell 500,000 records, so we're only ever going to make a certain amount of effort in order to fuel what they do." And there were also some rumblings at one point with RCA where the record company had gone to the other guys and said,

"Look, your strengths are management and promotion and marketing, so why don't you two guys sort of step to the back and let Rik front the thing more and be more the focus, and we'll hire some really good players to be part and parcel of what we're going to call Triumph, and then we'll really go for that."

Of course, the other guys hated that idea, and thought that RCA was being terrible and horrible, so they focused on a contractual dispute and took them to court and sued them and tried to get out of the record deal and lost, and that ended up in a big schmozzle. And then MCA came along and bought us away for 1.2 million of our own advance against royalties; they used that money to buy us away from RCA, so now MCA had a large investiture in trying to make sure that they brought this thing home.

So then, again, they sort of left us to our own devices, but it was kind of like, "Come on, guys, we gotta have a single. We need to have something that we can cross over to CHR radio." We gotta do this, we gotta do that, you know. "Gee, maybe we should import a producer."

So we jumped through a few hoops over the course of the next two or three records, which would have been after the *Thunder Seven* record; the *Sport Of Kings* record and then the *Surveillance* album, and in the end it was just too much for me. I mean, I'm not going to blame the record company or radio or anyone for any of that. That's just the way it was; it's the only reality I've ever known, and so I kind of think that's the way it works. I don't hold any grudges against any of that situation.

I think that it comes back to the fact that it was a commercial enterprise, and so those kinds of things tended to push into the background the kinds of things that…let me put it this way. If I had written a song that was, I thought, an excellent song, but it was based around using a classical guitar as its primary instrument, and so it needed to be a very soft kind of rhythm track, maybe no drums at all, or maybe the drums just came in in the third verse or something, that wouldn't have been considered for a Triumph album except as a C or D cut. Like, "Yes, we can do that, but that will be cut number eight on the record, and that won't be a focus track. We would never want that to be the lead single."

We live in a time where people focus in on the first single, and if it stiffs, you're pretty much in trouble. They'll go one more cut, but if that doesn't catch, your record is over. I was talking to somebody the other day about Don Henley's *The End Of The Innocence* record, which had four or five tremendous hits on it; you know, "Heart Of The Matter", "End Of The Innocence", "New York Minute". Now, can you name me the sixth cut on that record? How often do you program your CD player to play "Little Tin God" or "I Will Not Go Quietly"? And of course, the answer is that ninety-five percent of the people that bought the CD *never* listen to those songs. They would have a hard time saying it's a Don Henley song. That's the age and the time we live in. That's the way the business works.

So there were aspects of what I did as a guitar player in Triumph, and the music that I wrote, that just never really rose to the surface. The record company and the band itself had its priorities, and for me, personally, that's kind of a drag, because I was always the kind of guy that liked to listen to the whole record and then find these things that were sort of off the beaten track, and then tend to think that's where the heart and soul of what this person as an artist is all about. This is the stuff that completes the picture for me. But as I say, it's no big deal. It's just the way it is, I think.

SW: You did, though, get in a lot of instrumental licks over the years, such as "Midsummer's Daydream". Was that something you had to fight for, or was it something where they didn't mind you doing it?

RE: I didn't have to fight for it. I think they kind of came to expect it from me. Certainly at least the Triumph fans considered that a part of a Triumph record. There was a piece called "Embrujo", I think it was during the *Sport Of Kings* record, and Mike, the bass player, said, "Have you got a guitar piece? We've got to have a guitar piece on the record."

I think at that point in the band's career this was a standard thing. It had to be on there. It was almost as standard as you had to have a power ballad somewhere on the record. I think people almost expected that. Triumph fans expected that if they came to see a concert, at some point I was going to come traipsing out with a classical guitar and beat the hell out of it for a couple of minutes. *(Laughs)*.

SW: How long did it take for Triumph to catch on after you recorded the first album?

RE: It was a slow start. We formed in September of 1975 and put the first record out in '76 at some point in Canada. It didn't do tremendous, but it did well enough that the Canadian company said, "Okay, let's do another one." So we did a second album in Canada. It took a longer time to record. We fiddled around and wrote things and did some sessions where we recorded a cover of "Rocky Mountain Way", and then when we put that out, "Rocky Mountain Way" became a sort of hit single in Canada. It did pretty good at radio here, and I think that album actually ended up going platinum in Canada, and brought us to the attention of the American labels.

So RCA came up and saw us playing a big concert in Toronto and said, "We gotta sign these guys." That got us the American deal. It was probably '78 before the American thing started to happen, and then we did *Just A Game*, and it did terrific. It did great at radio in both countries, and we toured like crazy, and the record companies went to the wall to promote it. It did great.

Then we did *Progressions Of Power*, and that didn't do anywhere near as well. That was sort of a stiff. It didn't do very well at all. So then we kind of regrouped, and spent a lot of time thinking about the next record. We built our studio during the period after that, and when we came back with *Allied Forces*, I guess that would have been maybe '83...

SW: I think it was '81.

RE: Really?!

SW: Yeah, because I think '83 was *Thunder Seven*.

RE: No! God, is that true?

SW: *(Laughing)* I think so.

RE: I don't know, you may know more than me. I don't have anything in front of me. I kind of thought there was a longer period between them. Maybe *Progressions Of Power* was late 1980 or early '81, so that it seemed like a little longer period to me before *Allied Forces* came out. I seem to recall touring on *Allied Forces* for like, forever, and I thought that *Thunder Seven* wasn't until about '85 or '86. We're also forgetting *Never Surrender*. It came in there at some point between the two.

Triumph kind of went up and down. Each step up was higher than the previous step up, but we'd go two steps up, one step back; three steps up, one step back; three steps up, two steps back. Every second record were the good ones, to my way of thinking anyway. *Just A Game*, *Allied Forces* and *Thunder Seven* were really the three albums that I think of as the heart of what we were, what I thought the band was about. The other records I thought were weaker records. *(Pause)*. Did I answer the question? *(Laughter)*.

SW: Pretty much. *(More laughter)*. I think it's in there somewhere. Triumph was very much known as a concert act. Regardless of how your records did, you seemed to always be a big concert draw. Was that because of the fact that you toured a lot, or was it just a matter of the reputation you'd built?

RE: Probably a combination of both of those things. You know, the more you tour, the more you get the word of mouth about the band as that kind of band. "Oh, you've gotta see them live, it's great." Certainly from Triumph's point of view, our drummer, Gil, was really, really big on the whole aspect of the big show. He thought Kiss was a phenomenal thing, and he just loved the whole aspect of a giant production. He loved to go and see the Rolling Stones, to see what they were doing with their light system and what they were doing with their special effects. And he was big on coordinating with the light companies and the PA companies and that whole thing, aspects of the production that was going to tour, so the show would be geared toward bigger and better, lasers and flashpots, and there was always something more for people to see and more value for their concert dollar.

We were never from that less-is-more, minimalistic music school. No way, it's Barnum and Bailey time, here we go! *(Laughs)*. I mean, I think even now, for example, the Rolling Stones sell more concert tickets than they do albums. Over the years that's kind of been what they were, and I think Triumph was that sort of thing, too. It was more of an arena rock, touring extravaganza kind of thing. That was the reputation that it got, and of course critically we were hated. So we were never able to shift over into that *Rolling Stone* magazine, "We-love-these-guys,-they're-cultural,-social-kinds-of-icons." *(Laughs).* We were just traveling, hard-working musicians who were more sort of entertainer/performers than, I don't know what you'd call it…social scribes. *(Laughs).* Thought of as re-writing the culture of the youth of North America. We were more just kinda *(imitates bored voice)* "Yeah, yeah, they're coming through town." *(Laughs).* Lots of sizzle, no steak.

SW: And yet it seems, particularly through your efforts, I would imagine, that there was almost a literary undercurrent in some of what Triumph did, in the sense that, I know you had some literary quotes on one record's liner notes, and there were literary allusions in a number of your songs over the years. It also seemed that certain albums seemed to tie together; not necessarily concept albums, but they tied together thematically…

RE: I did what I could within the confines of what we were, and I think that some of the things I tried to do were either dismissed or completely overlooked. I guess one of the problems was, and maybe this was a legitimate…I shouldn't say maybe, I think probably it was a legitimate criticism of the band, was that musically and artistically, it didn't function at the same level as some of those ambitious concepts that I tried to put in there. It didn't get pulled off on all levels. We weren't able to pull them off.

I always liked Neil Peart's lyric writing in Rush, for example, and I always had a strong thing for concept records. The records that I liked were…call me crazy, but I thought that *Tales From Topographic Oceans* was a very neat, interesting, strange idea, and I would have much preferred to hear that than, say, an album of ten pop songs that Tom Petty writes. That's the kind of guy I was. So when I would write a record like *Thunder Seven,* and try to tie in aspects of James Joyce's *Finnegan's Wake* and Marshall McLuhan's ideas and bring those into the record, I think generally people thought I was being, I don't know, "pretentious"? *(Laughs).* That's probably the word.

SW: Maybe a little too high-brow to play it in the hockey arena?

RE: Exactly! And you know, maybe they were right. But the sensibilities that I had as a musician, the aspects that we discussed earlier, you know, a little jazz-influenced guitar playing and classical-influenced guitar playing, by the time the band had worked its way through a song that I had brought in, the song would end up getting beaten down into something that was Triumph-ized. *(Laughs).* If I had been bringing that into a room where I had, say, Bill Bruford sitting behind the drum kit, and Jon Anderson over there in the corner who was going to sing and maybe even re-write some lyrics, I'm sure the end product would have been entirely different from what it ended up being.

There was a gap between whatever original seeds and concepts that I was envisioning, or at least throwing onto the table, and the final product. They weren't necessarily going into the direction where they were as fully realized as they could have been. Maybe they did end up getting changed into something else. But that's the way it works. It's collaboration. A band is pretty much art by democracy.

SW: It's all compromise.

RE: It ends up being that. So maybe it was the wrong band for me to be trying to do some of those kinds of things in, even though I still look back on certain things, let's say "Stranger In a Strange Land" on *Thunder Seven*, and I still think it's a pretty neat little song. I think for me it has stood the test of time better than some of the other things. Even though it didn't get too much public acceptance or recognition, and certainly was totally overlooked in any sort of assessment of what Triumph was.

That's just one example. I could probably name six or seven others from other aspects of the records that pretty much got lost in the shuffle. On the Triumph *Classics* greatest hits package that came out after I'd left, I wasn't consulted about its contents. I've often wondered just how much it represents the majority of true Triumph fans' ideas of what *made* something a Triumph classic.

SW: You mentioned *Rolling Stone* and the fact that they never did like you guys. I may be mistaken, but I could swear I remember some letter to the editor that you wrote…

RE: Yeah.

SW: That was you?

RE: Yeah.

SW: What was that all about?

RE: They had done a fairly feature kind of story on what they termed faceless, nameless bands, and they had really pissed all over Rush and Styx and Journey and a few others. Triumph had not been mentioned, but certainly we kind of fell into the category of the music that they were trying to say "oh please"…*Rolling Stone* was saying where are the Pete Townsends and the Mick Jaggers and the Keith Richards of tomorrow?

Rolling Stone had its demographic and had staked out its territory, and so this was a pretty good way for them to take a shot at a bunch of people and cause a little controversy and satisfy a great deal of their demographic. A lot of their readers would look at a thing like that and go, "Yeah." But I felt very strongly that this was a very unfair thing to do to someone like Neil Peart, who was a terrific writer. He was a very good lyricist and a tremendous drummer, and to throw out those babies with that kind of bathwater just seemed really shallow and stupid and superficial. I mean, Neal Schon's a tremendous guitar player, and Steve Perry's voice, or Lou Gramm's…and they were saying these people are faceless.

I said that the people that are out there buying concert tickets and buying records, they don't think that Lou Gramm's voice is some sort of faceless, nameless thing. They don't think that Steve Perry's voice is. They don't think that Neil Peart's drumming is. You guys are off on the wrong tangent. And I went on to say in the letter that the reason you're off on the wrong tangent is because all of the people you're trying to sell Johnny Walker Red whiskey to and Kawasaki motorcycles to are not the people that listen to these bands.

Rolling Stone has its mandate and wants to sell to a certain Boomer demographic. So the bands that came after the Boomer generation and sold to that audience get urinated all over, which only serves to make that Boomer generation of bands, which is your Pete Townsends and your Rolling Stones, it only serves to make them seem even more larger than life, more amazingly incredible and more classic.

Naturally, *Rolling Stone* edited the letter and left out all that stuff about attacking them for their demographic marketing skills, and they just printed a letter that said, like, *(imitates moronic voice)* "Why do you attack these bands and these artists, and if you think they're so faceless and nameless, why don't you just put them on the cover and that would solve the problem? Sincerely, Rik Emmett from Triumph." So they make you appear like you're an idiot by sucking the meat out of the argument. You live and learn. That was the last letter I sent to an editor anywhere.

I've done a few in my crazy youth. I sent one to an English magazine, too, at one point, and just really fucking went crazy. *(Laughs)*. And they printed my whole letter, all two pages of it, with a big picture of me with my mouth open behind it, sort of saying, "The Thunderer Speaks". This was when the *Thunder Seven* record had come out, so it was like, yeah, Mr. Mouthpiece. *(Laughs)*. And I think I talked about the, if I can remember some of the things, the slime trails where lowlife, scuzzball writers…*(Laughs)*. Anyway, it was fairly vitriolic.

SW: *(Laughing)*. It wasn't a very favorable letter!

RE: So that was kind of like, thanks, that's the end of my career now, thank you very much. I don't think I'll ever do that again!

SW: One thing I was going to ask, and I guess you've already answered it in a sense *(laughs)*, is do you pay attention to the reviews you get?

RE: This is going to sound like a cliché, but in fact it's the truth: I used to, but I don't much anymore. I think maybe it's a sign of age, or maybe it's a sign of some sense of self-preservation. *(Laughs)*. As you get older and read a review, if somebody is taking just incredibly cheap shots at you, you realize that it's not about the music at all. It's not about you and what you're doing. There's some other dynamic at work. And if there's some other dynamic at work, then it's not worth it. I've got better things to do than to waste my time and energy on this sort of thing.

There have been some reviews I've read over the years that have been good reviews; they've been negative, but they've been good in the sense that they've been helpful because it's a legitimate criticism of the work. As I do new work, I take some of those things into account. But having said that, it's very few and far between that you find that kind of stuff.

Essentially someone who writes critiques of records, it's a sound byte medium, and they do it to be sensational and cause a little controversy, or else they're doing it to promote whatever it is that they've got on their agenda. There has been a widespread thing in the last fifteen or twenty years in North American pop music reviewing and critiquing where there are some things that are just sacred.

For instance, nobody will ever write a bad review of Richard Thompson. He will always get an excellent review from every reviewer. Now, it may be that Richard Thompson is above and beyond reproach, or above and beyond any aspect of criticism. *(Laughs)*. Maybe he's just about as perfect as perfect gets. But that's hard for me to believe, that somebody could be so universally great, whereas somebody like the guys from Journey, how could they be so bad?

I think it's kind of a shame that we now have a business where it's really easy…I shouldn't say really easy, but it's a lot easier for a grunge band that's got some heroin addicted person or drug abusive person. I think of them as damaged goods. Somebody who is damaged goods, and has a message about being damaged goods, stands a much better chance in the critical community and the industry it fosters than somebody who's just trying to make good music and be a good musician and try and make the best records they can. Now it may be that, for example, Michael Bolton is truly the devil, but I kinda doubt it. *(Laughter)*.

My feeling is that the kind of people who are living in suburbia, and drive to work every day, and listen to radio stations that are playing Bonnie Raitt and Sting and Michael Bolton songs, they're not so evil. They're not so terrible. These are just people that want music to be something in their lives that can function as a transportation and a communication for various aspects of their souls. Recreation, that's what they're looking for, and I don't think that's so bad. I don't think you have to constantly be challenged by people that have damaged personalities.

I give full marks to the Neil Youngs and the Kurt Cobains of the world. That's great. But for me, I can't take too much Neil Young guitar playing, because it's just not that good. I can't take too much Neil Young singing, because it's just not that good. I love to hear Neil Young sing that song about Philadelphia, but I couldn't take an entire album's worth of that, because for me it's just not nice enough to listen to. And I think it's kind of a shame that some people's tastes—like mine for example—become something that is just subject to ridicule and an object of ridicule constantly and critically, while other people's tastes are things that are championed and become, like, wow, mainstream now, no question.

SW: You know who else your analogy applies to is Tom Waits. The guy never gets a bad review, and he really can't sing at all.

RE: Now, I can understand somebody saying that singing is not what that's all about. But if you're going to love a record for that reason, then when somebody puts out a record where singing is indeed what it's all about, then you have to judge it on that level. You can't say that Michael Bolton's singing drives you crazy, so his record sucks. Geez, you can't love Tom Waits for one thing and hate the other guy for the exact same thing. It's hypocritical.

I'm trying to think of what Kurt Vonnegut said the other day. Vonnegut is, of course, a very satirical guy, and he was promoting something that he'd written that he'd sold to television. And he was cutting down mainstream American television and films, and they said, "Yeah, but you're here doing this." And he said, "So what you're saying is that I'm hypocritical? Well, I'm a U.S. citizen! That's just part and parcel of what I am and what I do. It's our way of life to be hypocritical." And that's right. I think in the end we're all hypocrites in one way, shape or form.

SW: You left Triumph after *Surveillance*. A lot of people were relatively surprised, but you obviously felt it had been building for a long time. What actually prompted you to leave?

RE: The combination of a lot of things, but essentially I just didn't want to make records with those guys anymore! *(Laughs)*. That's what it boiled down to. And now I've done enough interviews and I've seen this kind of thing discussed in print enough that I realize that sometimes it can look like you're being...your tone of voice doesn't translate well. I don't mean it in any kind of horrible, terrible, egotistical way. The bottom line is, I just didn't want to make more records with those guys. I've made a lot of records with them.

There was the combination of a lot of factors. I would write songs and I would end up giving two-thirds of the songwriting credit away, and that meant I was giving away two-thirds of the publishing. And when I decided I wanted to leave, in fact those guys said, "Well, you don't get *any* of the publishing. You're fucked!" *(Laughs)*. And we had to fight a big, long lawsuit battle about it. So to me that's a perfect indication of how there was a real problem that existed in that partnership and how other people viewed it, and that there were real imbalances and injustices that existed in it. "Midsummer's Daydream" is a perfect example of a song that was a guitar piece...

SW: So obviously the drummer didn't write it.

RE: Well, the drummer collects one-third of the songwriter's royalties, and the bass player collects one-third. They now collect two-thirds. Ever since I was in the band, they had been collecting two-thirds of the publishing, and as soon as I left, they kept *all* of the publishing! *(Laughs)*. So that means that essentially I'm earning thirteen cents on every dollar that song earns. It's a guitar piece that I wrote and recorded. Something's wrong about that. So in the end I just felt that was an unfair situation, never mind the frustrations that existed on other levels of trying to get records made to sound half decent, and the process of going through submitting material and having certain kinds of things rejected.

The band was devolving into...on the last album you'll see that there's songs from outside writers. I mean, I never had any problems writing material.

That's what I think of myself as, is a writer. But now I was in a band where I was being denied the opportunity to put material onto records, because the other guys in the band, particularly the drummer, wanted to have opportunities at hit singles that he was the singer of. And a band is a democracy, and everyone's entitled, you know. I just felt that Triumph was becoming less and less of a thing that I could feel was a good representation of me and what I wanted to try and do as a member of a band, and it was becoming more and more of a representation of what the other guys wanted. And I thought, 'Well, they can have it, then.' *(Laughs).*

SW: I remember hearing the *Surveillance* album, particularly a song called "Rock You Down", and thinking, 'Wow, surely they could have done better than this.' A lot of it was surprisingly bad.

RE: Well, when I originally wrote "Rock You Down", the lyric was about social change. It was a song about how every generation comes along and they feel they have to be rebellious and revolutionary. When I wrote it, I envisioned it as being very Pete Townsend/Who-ish. That "Won't Get Fooled Again" ballpark is what I was looking for.

And on the last day, the very last day of recording for the record, we'd gone so overtime on the mixing and overdubbing phase of that record that we had gotten down to the very last day that they could FedEx out the master tapes and still get the artwork and layout together in time to meet the projected release date. And the drummer, Gil, went into the studio and recorded a whole new set of lyrics that he had written for the song that he hadn't shown me. There'd been no previous discussion about it or anything. So when I heard the final mix of the song and heard those lyrics, I went, "What the...what is this?! What happened?"

And because they had done that, they had to change some of the mix of the song, and take out some of the guitar parts and change it around, and they turned it into this kind of...whatever it was. *(Laughs).* I won't say anything negative, but, you know, it was something entirely different than what I'd intended. And in fact, in the liner notes there had been quotes that I'd yanked from *Bartlett's Famous Quotations* that were supposed to be associated to the lyrics that got printed on the inner sleeve...

SW: And that one said something like, "I hold it to be true that now and again a little rebellion can be a good thing," or something like that.

RE: Geez, there you go. You're obviously fairly well researched on all of this. That's what the lyric was about, was that every now and then, a little rebellion's a good thing. "Rock You Down" was kinda like, that's what I'm gonna do; my music is the thing that I use as my expression of outrage and rebellion. And here was this lyric about, you're good-looking and I want to fuck you! *(Laughter).*

SW: *(Laughing).* I've had the thought before that, man, this quotation really doesn't have anything to do with this song!

RE: Oh, I was beside myself. I couldn't believe that that would actually happen in a professional situation. So that was one of the straws that broke the camel's back, that one.

SW: I guess so. I read an interview once—I don't want to get into any kind of negativity here...

RE: *(Laughs)*. Trash talkin'!

SW: Yeah. *(Laughs)*. But I did read an interview once with those guys after you were gone in which they claimed that they never knew you were going to quit until after you'd played your final show with them. They said they read in the paper the next morning, "Rik Emmett Plays Final Show With Triumph". What was the story behind that?

RE: That's complete, absolute bullshit. The bottom line there is that, after I left, it was very important to them to try and continue on. They wanted to keep the thing going. They were going to own the name, and they were going to own all the assets.

These are very complicated kinds of things; when a band has been established over a long period of time, if a guy leaves, there's the question of who owns what. All these flashpot systems that we had custom made, and hydraulic drum kits, and in our case we had management offices that were filled with office furniture, and we had a studio that was worth hundreds of thousands of dollars that was full of microphones and playback equipment and God knows what. Never mind the fact that there's publishing catalogues that have a hundred titles in them that are sitting there. So there's going to be a discussion about who owns what and who gets it and how much.

So it was very important to them to make it seem like I quit, because in the partnership contract it states that if you leave, you're only entitled to this kind of a thing. Now, behind the scenes for a good year prior, we'd been talking about what are we gonna do, how are we gonna go about this, how are we going to make this separation and ending of the partnership work? There were other problems that existed. One of them, a very fundamental one, was that the other two guys had sucked way more money out of the partnership in the last year than I had. So there were inequitable partnership draws. One guy had taken ninety thousand dollars more out of the band than I had.

SW: You're kidding!

RE: So that was a very fundamental problem that existed, and if they could make it look like I quit—you know, "Boy, he just quit one day and walked out"—then someday in a court of law they would be able to stand up in front of a judge and say, "He quit. He walked out. Why should I have to pay him the money back? If only he'd stayed in the band, we'd have been able to play gigs and make enough money to pay the thing back. But he didn't, you see. He quit on us, so we had no way of earning the money to pay him back."

The truth of the matter was that we'd started talking about it, and through that last year, when I was still in the band but wanting to get out, they had said that we had this debt. We'd taken a large advance from a T-shirt company from merchandising, and they wanted their money back. We'd gone out on a tour and hadn't earned their advance back. So we had to come up with something like a quarter of a million U.S. We had to pay these guys back. So the guys were saying that we needed to play some gigs to earn this money back.

And I said, "Well, if I walk from this partnership, if I leave, and you don't pay me back one-third of what the assets are worth, but you do make me play a bunch of gigs so that I pay off all the debt, so I walk away and leave you debt-free but you won't give me my share of the assets, what is the reasoning behind that for me? What is the rationale?" So I said no, I won't do that. I'll tell you what I will do. I'll stay in the band, and I'll play as many gigs as you need to pay off the debt, as long as I always get one-third of the revenue from those gigs. Because that's fair. I'll play the gig, you give me one-third of it, you keep two-thirds. You can use it to pay off the debt. You don't have to; you can use it to do whatever the heck you like, as long as I get my one-third.

So they said okay, fine, that's a good deal. We shook hands on it. So we went out and played a bunch of dates through the summer of '88. We went down and played one in Texas, played one in Florida, played one in San Francisco, and then by Labor Day of that year we played one in Toronto. Well, after the first two or three of those gigs, they hadn't given me the one-third of the money. *(Laughs)*. You didn't have to be a Rhodes scholar to figure that one out. They had booked just enough gigs to be able to earn enough money to pay off the debt, and then they were gonna tell me to go fuck myself. *(Laughs)*.

So I thought, 'Well, you don't have to be an idiot.' I played the gig in Toronto, and then I said, "That's it. I'm not going to play any more." They knew that was gonna be it as well as I knew that was gonna be it, but that's not the story they decided they were going to float to the general public, because that's not the story they were going to try and tell when they finally went to court. Which, in the end, they never did, by the way. This June they settled out of court. *(Laughs ruefully)*. It wasn't great, but I finally got some money.

SW: Well, that's good, at least.

RE: Well, it's typical of the rock and roll business.

SW: Does that leave them owning your past, free and clear?

RE: Yup. And in fact, the only reason they wanted to settle with me, I'm absolutely sure, was that they had a deal where they were gong to sell the publishing catalogue to someone else and get just a gigantic pot full of money, probably in the neighborhood of a quarter of a million or something. So they settled with me and got me to sign papers that say I have no claim against that catalogue.

So all the money that they owed me for gear and all that stuff that was ancillary…the publishing catalogue became the central issue, because of course that was the thing that was worth something. Everything else was pretty much worthless, and of course, after they put out that last record, the Triumph name was pretty much worthless.

SW: That record didn't do anything.

RE: Nope.

SW: Are you familiar with the music on that record?

RE: I heard it once.

SW: What did you think of it?

RE: It didn't surprise me. *(Laughs)*. I've probably already said way, way too much that you're taping, you know what I mean? *(Laughs)*. And a lot of this stuff can come back to haunt you and bite your ass. I just don't want to say anything . . it's not in my best interest to appear to be somebody who is bitter and vindictive. Really, I don't care, it's been so long now.

I tend to think of it in a very philosophical way. It's like when a marriage goes bad, you only make yourself look stupid if, years after the fact, you're still going around bad-mouthing your ex-wife or ex-husband. At some point you just have to say whatever is, is, and whatever happens, happens. Whatever they do now hasn't got anything to do with me, so it's really not up to me to talk about it.

Certainly the music that I heard made me feel very strongly that I'd done the right thing to leave. And as I say, that record didn't surprise me when I heard it. But I don't mean that in any kind of a negative way at all. I just mean it in a purely kind of neutral way. *(Laughs)*.

SW: I don't want to persist with this line of questioning, but does that mean that in playing your own songs from the past, you're paying them?

RE: What happens is, yeah, essentially yes. If "Magic Power" gets played on the radio, those guys earn two-thirds of the writer's share of that song, and I earn one-third. And I think if they've made the deal to sell the publishing to someone else, then someone else will be earning the publishing money.

And if there's any kind of a third party licensing deal—like for instance there was a thing that happened recently where NFL Films for ESPN used an old Triumph song, which is a third party licensing deal—if that happens, then in fact I'll be making more than I was making, because what was happening there was that my old partners were just keeping all the money and screwing me, whereas now if there's a third party publisher, they will pay the writer's royalty out. So at least that will happen.

But essentially, if you're asking me when "Fight The Good Fight" and "Magic Power" and "Never Surrender" and all those songs get played on the radio, who's making most of the money, then the answer is that my former partners are making two-thirds of it.

SW: How about when you play them live? Do you have to pay some sort of...

RE: Usually with live performances, nobody's paying anybody anything, and what happens is that clubs and concert promoters make blanket fees to the performing rights societies. And then based on some sort of formula that the performing rights societies come up with, they divvy up the money and send it out. So of course, Elton John gets gigantic paychecks from that kind of money, while guys like Rik Emmett get very minuscule amounts.

Of course, the thing that bothers me a little bit is that I end up promoting songs—this is like the John Fogerty/Credence Clearwater problem—you end up feeling like you're out there promoting a song that makes somebody else more money than it does yourself. And then people say, "Well, don't carry that grudge. Those songs are you, so you're promoting yourself, and that's good." But I say, "Yeah, but I've got new songs. Let me promote those." But they go, "No, we don't like that. We want the nostalgia." So it's tough. You're kind of caught in a bind. There are some songs that...it wasn't until after the *Just A Game* album that Triumph decided to start splitting the royalty credit three ways.

SW: How did they even arrive at that?

RE: That was actually my suggestion. Gil was the general manager of the band, and Mike Levine was promotion and marketing and all that stuff, so those guys were honestly, legitimately spending an awful lot of time on the phone, doing business and working hard. And then when it came time for everybody to get a paycheck, everybody's paycheck was the same, except for when royalties came from airplay from the performing rights societies.

If you're the principal writer and you had written the single, then of course you were going to make way more money than anybody else. This is the old, "Mick-Jagger-and-Keith-Richards-made-way-more-money-than-Charlie-Watts-ever-did" theory. The scenario I envisioned was, "Oh my God, these guys are handling the money and the business, and it wouldn't be too hard for them to start screwing me if they wanted to."

So I went to them and I said, "Look, I don't want to be in a position where my songs are starting to do so well that you guys are starting to feel like you're getting ripped off. I appreciate the fact that you're doing all of the business representation and so forth, so in that spirit, let's just split the songs three ways." And they were obviously...

SW: More than willing to do that! *(Laughter)*.

RE: Of course! Now in retrospect, I think what a fool I was. But you can never be that young again, and you live and learn. *(Laughs)*. But the reason I did it initially was that I felt it was the best way to be fair to everybody.

In any case, there are some songs that had never originally been registered as being written by all three guys. So those songs from *Just A Game* like "Hold On", "Lay It On The Line", "Suitcase Blues", "Fantasy Serenade", that stuff I'm the only writer. So I still like to play that stuff live and promote those songs, and hope that people will gravitate a little bit more toward some of those songs than they might toward some of the other AOR staples that Triumph had like "Magic Power" or "Fight The Good Fight". Because if they play "Hold On" on the radio, I end up getting all of the writing money! *(Laughs).*

SW: In leaving Triumph to pursue a solo career, were you nervous about going out on your own in terms of the name recognition and how well it might do for you?

RE: I knew there were certain crosses I would have to bear, and things that I would have to overcome. I mean, I'm always nervous. I did a seminar this summer for a group of eight year olds, and I was nervous before going on to do that. *(Laughs).* I'm nervous about everything, always. I think that it's good. I think you need to have a certain amount of butterfly nerves in order to do well. I think it's part of the whole performing urge, which is a very complex, strange thing. Why are we so egotistical as to want to do this in the first place? Why are we so self-punishing? *(Laughs).* Why put ourselves through this?

So I was nervous before I decided to set out on my own, but I was inspired by the challenge of it and looked forward to that, and felt it was just another step along the way in evolving toward whatever it is that I'm evolving toward.

SW: What cuts from your solo albums thus far do you consider to be real standouts?

RE: On the *Ipso Facto* album, I thought I had done something good with "Out Of The Blue". I thought I'd captured something good in that. And I think there was some stuff on the last record that really pointed the way to the future for me, songs like "Heaven In Your Heart"; I thought I'd captured something in there that seemed to be more for the future.

I was kind of disappointed in the harder-rocking kind of stuff, and as I get older, I'm less inclined to feel that that's at the central core of what I'm trying to do. So songs like "Bang On" and "Rainbow Man" and "Straight Up", I kinda feel like I'm leaving that behind. But songs like "Meet You There" and "Can't Lie To Myself" and "Out Of The Blue", I felt those were more an indicator of the future. And the lyric that I had written in "Calling St. Cecilia", I felt I captured something there that I felt strongly about, whereas I didn't necessarily feel as strongly about some of the other things.

On the first album, *Absolutely*, there were certain things that were obviously a lot of holdover from the Triumph stuff, and I had a little bit of pressure from management and record companies not to wander too far away from the old, accepted Triumph sound. So a song like "Saved By Love", for instance, which did very well at radio and got licensed for a film, and did real well for me, it just struck me as kind of a Triumph song. But lyrically I felt there were a couple of tunes, like "Big Lie" and "World Of Wonder", that had been fairly strong lyrics for me.

"World Of Wonder" I know is a song that never would have been able to get onto a Triumph record, so I was happy to be able to do a song like that, just for the aspect of the Latin rhythms and what the bed tracks were doing in a tune like that. It was whole new territory for me, and I really enjoyed it. The record that I'm working on right now has got some songs that seem to me to be evolutionary offshoots of that kind of thing.

SW: What are your future plans after this record?

RE: If the record does well, then I'll be able to tour on it extensively, which would be great. So that's not a plan as much as it is a hope. There will certainly be at least one video, probably two, made for this record, and if I can't tour extensively then I will tour intermittently, and just start thinking about how I'm going to put together a deal to make the next record. And if I don't get a big enough budget from somewhere to do that, then I guess I'll just sort of scrape along, maybe do some production here and there, maybe play on some other people's records here and there, and just start earning a living again in the way that I did twenty years ago, and try to see my way to how I start doing it all over again, which is probably not easy when you're on the other side of forty now. *(Laughs)*.

When I shopped the first time after leaving Triumph, there was a record executive that said to my manager, "We're not interested in a guy like Rik, because the record business is pretty much about teenagers making records for teenagers to buy." And when you hear something like that, you realize there's a fairly cynical, cold, hard business out there. But there's a real truth to that. Soundgarden and Pearl Jam and those types of bands are making records that speak to their generation, and those people buy those records. You're not going to find too many forty year olds that are buying those records. I'm not saying there aren't any, but we're just talking in generalities of what fuels the economy of this industry.

As long as fourteen and fifteen year old girls will buy Madonna records, she will be the Queen of Pop. As soon as they get older and they won't buy Madonna anymore—and that will surely happen—then unless she has found a way to regenerate herself to the new fourteen and fifteen year olds coming along, she will start to slide down, and she will face the inevitable prospect, someday, of what will you do to preserve your dignity...*(Laughs)*. Well, maybe she's a bad example! *(Laughter)*.

SW: *(Laughing)*. I think "dignity" is the wrong word to use in conjunction with her, actually.

RE: Yeah. *(Laughs)*. Oops! But at some point, nobody will be willing to say, "Here's a bunch of money to go and make a record, because we think we're going to be able to make money by giving you this money." That won't happen anymore. And then what do you do? In her case, you start becoming a guest on *Hollywood Squares* or something, I guess.

But for somebody who's in a rock band, or a guitar player, I guess you gravitate towards production. Or what we talked about earlier, instrumental records and sort of offshoot projects. I have some friends in the business that have wound up writing for films and TV scores and that kind of stuff, so I'm hoping that maybe I'll be able to slide over into that. I could always earn a living doing session work here in Toronto, so that's no problem. I guess it will all work itself out.

For more information about Rik Emmett, please visit www.Rikemmett.com

CHANGING ALL THE TIME

The name **Peter Frampton** was virtually synonymous with rock superstardom in the mid-Seventies. His 1976 double live album 'Frampton Comes Alive' rocketed him from a comfortable, modest-selling career as a highly respected guitarist and songwriter to the single largest concert performer in the world, and to this day ranks as the largest-selling live album of all time.

In the two decades since then, **Frampton** has had to struggle to rebuild his musical credibility and his self-confidence, both of which were shattered by the media backlash which ensued as a result of his enormous fame and the overexposure it created. Post-'Frampton Comes Alive' reviews focused more and more on the boyish good looks which made **Frampton** a prime candidate for constant exposure in the teen magazines; one reviewer even dubbed him "the Farrah Fawcett of rock", and other critics followed suit, branding **Frampton** a one-hit wonder whose hairstyle and clothes were more important than his music.

It's a charge which has haunted **Frampton** since the earliest days of his career when, as a teenager in the British group **The Herd**, he was named "The Face of 1968" by a British music writer. Partly as a reaction to that, **Frampton** moved on to form **Humble Pie** with former **Small Faces** guitarist **Steve Marriott**, but left that group after only a few years, feeling that the band's direction did not leave enough room for his songwriting ideas.

Frampton's early solo albums such as 'Wind of Change' and 'Frampton's Camel' garnered favorable reviews, but after the enormous success of 'Frampton Comes Alive', the media seemed determined to focus on **Frampton** as a celebrity rather than a musician, and his management, in their determination to milk his career for whatever it was worth, only added to the feeding frenzy by deliberately marketing **Frampton** as a teen idol.

Plagued by personal problems, including well-publicized bouts with drinking and drugs, a car accident which left him wondering if he would ever play the guitar again, a palimony suit filed by onetime girlfriend Penny MacColl, and a split with his manager and mentor Dee Anthony, **Frampton** followed up with several disappointing albums like 'I'm In You' and 'Where I Should Be'. Coupled with his starring role in the disastrous movie flop 'Sergeant Pepper's Lonely Hearts Club Band', it was enough to seriously affect his career, not to mention his already shaky self-confidence.

After the relative failure of two subsequent albums, 'The Art of Control' and 'Breaking All The Rules', **Frampton** retired from recording and touring in the early Eighties. He returned in 1986 with 'Premonition', then again in 1989 with the excellent 'When All The Pieces Fit'. A projected **Humble Pie** reunion with **Steve Marriott** in 1991 fell through when **Marriott** was killed in a fire that engulfed his home. The following year **Frampton** embarked on his first tour in several years and was well-received, proving that he still retained an audience and bolstering his confidence once again.

I spoke to **Peter Frampton** by phone from his home in Arizona on November 1st, 1994, *just weeks after he had completed a three month tour for his latest release, 1994's self-titled 'Peter Frampton'. The tour had gone well, and* **Frampton** *was clearly in a good frame of mind. He lived up to his reputation as one of the nicest guys in the business; throughout our conversation he was polite, funny, and seemed to have come to terms with where he was, where he had been and where he was going, making sure to emphasize, "I'm not through doing what I'm going to do."*

SW: You've been playing guitar for what, about thirty years now?

PF: Oh, God! *(Laughter)*. I guess so. I started playing guitar seriously in the end of 1957. '58 is when I got my first guitar, so I was playing ukulele, or banjolele as it was called.

SW: Banjolele? What's that?

PF: A banjolele is a ukulele, but it was shaped like a banjo, so it's a smaller banjo. The English vaudeville star George Formby used to play a banjolele. It was just a four gut-string instrument, and it was tuned to the tune of *(sings)* "My-cat's-got-fleas!" *(Laughter)*. That's how you knew how to tune it.

SW: *(Laughing)*. I guess they didn't have electronic tuners at the time…

PF: No, so you had to remember *(sings)* "My-cat's-got-fleas", or "my-dog's-got-fleas", depending on the day. Which was obviously completely different than a guitar tuning. Then for Christmas when I was eight, in 1958, I pleaded with, I sent many letters to Santa Claus, and my dad relented and got me a guitar, and that was it.

SW: So he interceded on your behalf.

PF: Yes, he did. He had played guitar in college dance bands pre-war, I think; pre-Second World War. And he knew a few chords, so when I got a guitar I basically…well, he showed me the chords on the banjolele to start with, and when I graduated to the fifth and sixth strings *(laughs)*…there was a terrible noise when I started playing guitar because I didn't know what to do with these other two strings, so he showed me how to stop them up and put extra fingers on them. He showed me, like…are you a player?

SW: I sure am.

PF: All right. So he showed me your basic C, G, F, F minor, D, your basic "down there" chords in the first three frets.

SW: Those are the same chords my dad taught me.

PF: There you go. And I took it from there, really.

SW: Did you ever take formal lessons?

PF: A little bit later on, when I was eleven or twelve, I took three or four years of Spanish classical guitar. Bored me to tears, you know. I hated it, but looking back on it, it was good because it showed me fingerings. You know, where the right finger's supposed to be, and how you *are* supposed to use the little finger on your left hand.

SW: Did that improve your technique later on?

PF: I think so, because it helped later on when I got into my jazz thesis, you know, my jazz period of listening to everybody I could. The more sophisticated jazz licks, you have to use your little finger. It's not just the first finger and the third finger as in more like blues playing. So I guess it made that a lot easier.

But at the time I wasn't very interested. You know, I appreciated the beauty of Julian Bream and Segovia, and these wonderful pieces that were written for guitar, but I was much more interested at the time in Hank Marvin and the Shadows, and Buddy Holly, and Eddie Cochran and people like that.

SW: Early on, did songwriting go hand-in-hand with guitar playing for you? Did you always view yourself as a guy who wanted to write songs, or did you just consider yourself a guitar player?

PF: I was more of a tune writer than a song writer to start with, because at the time I started, my biggest influence was this guy called Hank Marvin, who was a legend in his own time. He was the lead guitarist of the Shadows, which was Cliff Richard's backing band. He was the man with the first bright red Stratocaster with a maple neck in Europe.

I believe that Cliff Richard had gone to America to try and find fame and fortune there, which didn't quite come off the first time. But he brought back Hank a red Strat, which everyone would salivate over in England, including myself. Of course, this was roundabout '57 or '58 when I was starting, and the Shadows really were the instrumental Beatles in Europe before the Beatles.

I started writing in about '61 or '62. I formed a band, was part of a band called the Truebeats, and started writing instrumentals, a la Shadows/Ventures-type instrumentals. That's how I started, and I was about ten or eleven then.

SW: So you've actually never worked another job in your life, have you?

PF: I've never had a regular job, no. *(Laughs)*. I've never worked a day in my life.

SW: That's a nice statement to be able to make.

PF: Yeah, right. Well, that's what people say.

SW: Too bad it's not really true, obviously.

PF: *(Ruefully)*. No, I don't think so. *(Laughs)*. It's like that Dire Straits song, you know, "Money For Nothing". That's the opinion of the guy who's selling refrigerators.

SW: I bet if he had to drag himself all over the world by bus to make a living, he wouldn't have that opinion anymore.

PF: No.

SW: After that, you were in the Herd at a very young age.

PF: I left school at sixteen and then joined the Herd during the summer vacation, and I would have either gone back to school and done two more years and then gone on to college, music college probably...but the opportunity was there, and I took it, and it was only a year and a bit before we became very successful. It was '67 or '68.

SW: Did it take you by surprise? Did you think it would be so successful, or was it something that you got into that just exploded under you?

PF: We went after it. We were very popular locally and we built up a following very quickly, and then we got a residency at the Marquee Club in London, which was sort of what every group wanted to do, because that was a great showcase club where many bands, including the Who, the Stones, you name it, they'd got their start. You know, a record producer or manager would come down.

And that's exactly what happened to us. I believe the record producer Steve Roland came down, who was producing a band called Dave Dee, Dozy, Beaky, Mick and Tich (*laughter*)...

SW: (*Laughing*). Could you spell that, please?

PF: D-A-V-E-D-E-E-...(*Laughter*). He was actually the singer in the Hollywood Argyles, that had that song, I don't know, it must have been the late Fifties or early Sixties, called "Alley Oop". I'm sure you're thrilled with that. (*Laughs*).

But he became a record producer and moved to England, and spotted us, and then he told the managers of this band that I won't repeat—you've heard it once—and they were very big in England, and all of a sudden we started doing their demos for them. I guess we were being tried out to see if we were good enough in the studio for these two managers, Howard and Blakely, to write songs and start us off, which is what happened.

We had one single out called "I Can Fly", which was 1967, because I remember we were trying to do backward voices frontward, sort of like *Sgt. Pepper*. Then we released another single which they wrote called "From The Underworld", and it was a big top ten hit in Europe, and that was it. Off we went.

SW: You were in that band for how long, about two years or so?

PF: I think so, until '67 or '68, and then at the end of '68 I formed Humble Pie with Steve Marriott.

SW: Was that a reaction to having been in the Herd? I know you were named The Face of 1968 or some such...

PF: Yeah, and Steve had been named The Face of 1966 or something, so we were basically reacting to the fact that we realized that people weren't as interested in the music as we thought they would be, and we wanted to be in a band that was playing music that we liked, rather than being pinups. So that's what we got together for. We were just jamming on R&B and blues and you name it.

The Small Faces at that time had sort of come through the teenybopper stuff with a record called *Ogden's Nut Gone Flake*, which was a very serious record, one of my favorites still. But the Herd hadn't, and so I just left, and really hadn't a clue as to what I was going to do. Steve was helping me form a band which he wasn't going to be a part of, and then one day he just called me up and said, "I'm going to leave. Can I join your band?" So I said, "Okay, sounds good." So that was it. We were formed within the week, because he had already introduced me to Jerry Shirley, and Greg Ridley of Spooky Tooth. So that was it, we were a four piece.

SW: So you formed Humble Pie as a way of getting into more guitar-oriented music?

PF: Yes, exactly, and Humble Pie was like my guitar apprenticeship. That's the way I look at it, concentrating much more on guitar playing and much less on singing.

SW: A lot of your playing on those early Humble Pie records is considered absolutely classic today...

PF: Well, thank you.

SW: It's true. Yet you left that group after just a couple of more years, just when they were becoming very successful. What prompted you to do that?

PF: I guess I was coming of age, and really, Steve and I were two very strong individual characters, which is what made Humble Pie so good. We couldn't have been any more different if we tried, and it was difficult for me, because the material that we were doing was no longer as broad-based as it started off being.

We started off being very acoustic as well as being very heavy rock. I wouldn't have classed it heavy metal. We ran the gamut of material to start with, but as we went on, our direction seemed to get narrower and narrower, and it got into an area where there was less and less room for the acoustic side, which I still needed to do. And I think Steve did, too, but we all realized that the audience wanted us to do the heavier stuff. Which I enjoy immensely, and all of us did, but the sort of songs I was writing at the time didn't really fit into Humble Pie's format anymore. And Steve and I weren't getting on as well as we should have at the time, and drifted apart, basically.

I think that when we formed the band, Steve was someone that I really looked up to, very much so, as a teacher of I guess singing and songwriting, and playing in a certain sense, like in his blues sense. He had a lot of soul. Now it was time for me to go out and do stuff on my own. It was just a natural progression for me, even though we were to get back together before he died, in the end, which was wonderful.

SW: In the period between leaving Humble Pie and recording your first solo album, there was a time in there when you did some session work.

PF: Yes, quite a lot.

SW: Did you like playing sessions?

PF: I did, because they were all people that I admired. I wouldn't want to have been just a session guy to do whatever came along, but I've only ever done sessions for people that I really liked their music, and it was a mutual respect, and I got asked to do it.

When you get me, you get me and my style. I don't come in and play like somebody else. I come in and play like me, so it's always been very nice to see how my style fitted in with other people's work that I would not normally have thought of playing with, but admired their work. John Entwistle, Harry Nilsson, Nicky Hopkins, George Harrison, people like that it was very enjoyable to work with.

SW: You played with Harrison, and your first album featured appearances by Ringo Starr and Billy Preston. For a guy who'd grown up in the era of Beatlemania, what was that like?

PF: The day that I got, for my first record I got Billy Preston and Klaus Voorman and Ringo all to come on the same day, the record company couldn't believe it. They *didn't* believe it. So most of the record company came down that day to see. I think they thought I was bullshitting.

So it was a very exciting and nerve-wracking day for me. You know, sitting down on the piano stool next to Billy Preston, who's played with Ray Charles and all these fabulous people, and I've got a Beatle over in the corner, and then Klaus Voorman, who's virtually another Beatle, over there, and I'm conducting them. It was very nerve-wracking to say the least, but it turned out fabulously.

Ringo had already played on a couple of tracks on the album, so I'd gotten used to him being there, but not everybody else. And of course all of their entourages came with them as well, so it was like doing a gig! But very exciting. I mean, what can you say? Through doing the *All Things Must Pass* sessions with George Harrison, I'd gone around and asked all these people, "Look, when I do a solo record, would you come and play?" And they'd gone, "Yeah, sure kid." *(Laughs).* So in the end they were very surprised to get a call from me, and they'd said yes, so they couldn't say no now. So in they came, and it was very exciting.

SW: So you've worked with at least two of the Beatles.

PF: Yes.

SW: Later on, you appeared in the *Sgt. Pepper* movie. Was it that much weirder for you, the whole experience of that movie, because you already knew them?

PF: It wasn't a pleasurable thing at all, really, because I was told that Paul McCartney had already signed to do the movie, to be, actually the part that Billy Preston ended up playing. He was going to be the savior of the heartland, as it were.

But of course, I was, uh, *fibbed* to by the producer himself, Robert Stigwood, so I don't think I would have...you see, growing up, to re-do something by the Beatles or the Rolling Stones, unless you could do a version your way, to make it your own version, like I did "Jumping Jack Flash", which you really have to listen to carefully to work out that it is "Jumping Jack Flash", or the way Joe Cocker did "With A Little Help From My Friends", which is completely different, that's fine. But to re-do the Beatles stuff or the Stones stuff note-for-note, like a cover version of it, had never been my idea of...well, it was almost sacrilegious.

But all of a sudden I roped myself into doing it, and I wasn't thrilled with it. It backfired, obviously. It wasn't a terrifically good thing for me to do. I didn't really want to do it in the first place, but you know, they gave me a lot of money! *(Laughter)*. You know, I've never been motivated by money. Even the Herd, we never earned any money in that band. Humble Pie, we had a little bit of money, but not that much. So there were a lot of people around the time of *Frampton Comes Alive* who, if I worked, they made a lot of money, too.

SW: Oh, absolutely.

PF: So we're talking about some very greedy businessmen. And all of a sudden, I wasn't being motivated by money, but they were. And I was getting pushed in various ways. Obviously I said yes, so I have to count myself to blame, but people were managing me for themselves, as opposed to for the bettering of my career, shall we say, or the longevity of my career.

SW: So looking back, not only the film itself, but you don't really remember the soundtrack with any fondness?

PF: No, not really. I enjoyed playing guitar on it. I did a lot of guitar playing on it when George Martin was there. And when he wasn't around, I didn't have to, but I did a lot of work on it to try and make it, if that's what they wanted, I tried to make it as authentic as possible.

But I don't think George Martin enjoyed doing it, the way it was. They should have had somebody else do the soundtrack. As wonderful as it was to work with George Martin, he only knew how to do it one way, but he didn't have the Beatles to re-do it. So therefore, you get slick studio musicians in there, and it wasn't done with studio musicians. It was done with the Beatles, and there are only four of them. To get somebody, anybody...if you get the Stones to come in and try to re-do a Beatles number, it's not going to sound like the Beatles, is it? It's gonna sound like the Stones! So whoever came in and re-did it, it wasn't going to sound that way. It was just a mistake.

SW: You mentioned wanting to move on from Humble Pie because the diversity was gone. Your first few solo albums are extremely diverse. There seems to be everything from blues-based hard rock to kind of a folky touch here and there, and maybe even a few jazz guitar influences. Are your listening tastes extremely wide?

PF: Yes, I think so. Always have been, really. Ever since I started listening to guitar, singling it out, I'll find it anywhere, whether it be jazz, whether it be folk or blues. I guess jazz and blues are probably my favorite styles to listen to.

Now, Stevie Ray Vaughan reigns, even though he's no longer with us. I'm a huge, huge fan of his, as well as obviously Eric, and I'm sure Eric was a huge fan of Stevie Ray Vaughan's. As well as picking up the latest, which unfortunately will be the last Joe Pass record, because I believe he passed away recently.

Django Reinhardt was introduced to me, his music was introduced to me by my parents. During the war they would dance to the "Hot Club De France", by Django Reinhardt and Stephan Grappelli, and when I first heard it, I thought it was rubbish. *(Laughs)*. This wasn't the Ventures or the Shadows, you know what I mean? I didn't quite understand what they were doing.

Then as the years would go by, I'd hear my father playing it, and then I started playing the records, and it's always been there for me. It's soulful jazz, a gypsy playing jazz, and I've always had a soft spot for Django, apart from the fact that it was nigh on impossible for him to play what he was playing with only two working fingers on his left hand.

SW: Yeah, that's amazing.

PF: And in the end I got, from Jerry Moss from A&M Records one Christmas...the record company that he would distribute A&M through in France was Barclay Records, and Barclay was the record label that put out Django's stuff. And Eddie was a very close friend of Django's and had a four-string Henry Selmer guitar, a Mackaferri guitar like the ones you see him playing with the very long bridge, and the D-shaped hole. And lo and behold, I got one of those guitars for Christmas. So I own one of Django's guitars, which is such an honor.

SW: I read somewhere that you recorded with that guitar.

PF: That was on "Rocky's Hot Club" on *I'm In You*, which is sort of a "Hot Club De France" type of chord sequence. It sounds very authentic.

SW: Do you collect guitars and hold on to them for their sentimental value?

PF: Yeah, I mean the ones that I've got left. I lost a lot of guitars. My black Les Paul, unfortunately, went down in a cargo plane crash in South America. After I lost that, I virtually...I don't get too close to any guitar. I say that, but I obviously have. If that's taken away from you...that was like my crutch, that guitar.

SW: That guitar was so widely identified with you and your sound.

PF: Exactly. It was very special, and it was a very light Les Paul. It was a 1954 body, and then it had been made into a Custom, it had been made into a three-pickup. It started off as a Black Beauty with P-90s.

The guy that gave it to me, his name was Mark Marianna, from San Francisco. He had found it and routed it for three humbuckers, and sent it back to Gibson and had them re-finish it. So it was like a mutt, actually, but it was just a very, very special guitar.

I'd had an SG that I was playing with Humble Pie, a red SG, a 1960 or something, and for some reason I wanted to get a cherry 335. A great guitar, beautiful guitar. I swapped the SG for the 335. I didn't realize how badly they fed back. So I'm playing with Humble Pie, Marshalls on eleven, and of course, every time I turn up to do a solo, it's like *(imitates the sound of feedback)*. My solos were feedback! *(Laughs)*.

We were playing the Fillmore West, and after the show Mark Marianna comes up to me and says, "I noticed you were having a little trouble tonight."

And I said, "Gee, you're not wrong," so he said, "I've got this guitar I think you might like to play tomorrow night. I'd lend it to you." So I said, "Oh yeah? What's that?" And he said, "It's a Les Paul."

I'd never really had any luck with Les Pauls. They were always a bit muddy for me, but I thought, 'What have I got to lose here?' So I said, "Thanks very much." So he said, "Look, I'll meet you for breakfast tomorrow at the coffee shop, and I'll bring it 'round."

So he brought 'round this guitar case, opened it up, and there it was! It was completely refinished by Gibson, so it looked brand-new, except it was a 1954, and three pickups. And I looked at it and gulped because it looked so gorgeous. I picked it up, and it was so light for a Les Paul, and I thought, 'Oh my God, this is me.'

I played it that night, and I don't think my feet touched the ground the whole night! And then of course, I came off stage and said to the guy, "Oh, Mark, how much?" *(Laughter)*. "Can I buy it?" And he said, "No, sorry, you can't buy it." So I said, "Oh, okay, I understand." And he said, "No, I want to give it to you." So I said, "I beg your pardon?" *(Laughter)*. "Could you say that one more time?" And he said, "I'd like to give it to you, because I see how much enjoyment it gives you." He said, "You deserve it." I said, "I can't believe this," so obviously I've stayed in touch with the guy ever since.

SW: That's a wonderful story. What kind of guitars do you use primarily these days?

PF: John Suhr is a terrific luthier who used to work at Rudy's Music Stop up on 48th Street in New York, and his guitars were called Pensa-Suhrs, but now he just makes Suhr Guitars, I think they're called. He was sort of modifying Schechters for a while there, and then he sort of gradually got into making his own guitars.

So after I lost my Les Paul, I bought myself a 1960, very expensive cherry sunburst, which I got rid of. It was really, really expensive. I forget how much they are now. I mean, you could buy a house now for what they cost! *(Laughter)*. I think I bought for like, six and a half thousand in 1980, something ridiculous, and then sold it for ten grand a year later. It was too-thin sounding for me. It was very trebly; it didn't have the warmth. I wish I'd held onto it, but I figured I'd sell it and move on.

And then I started playing John's guitars, and started to really love them. He would say, "Well, I'll make you one; what do you want?" And I would say, "I want this and I want that, I want this wood and that wood." And so he'd make me that, and after about the third guitar he made me, I was in the music shop up on 48th Street and I said, "What's that?" And he said, "It's mine," so I picked up this one-piece maple Stratocaster shape with one humbucker by the bridge and two single coils, by the bridge and in the middle, and it was like picking up my

Les Paul that Mark Marianna gave me. And I said, "Oh my God, this is great. Why don't you just make me one like you make for yourself?"

So he did. He made me the clone of that, and that's been my favorite ever since, basically. But there again, since I lost the Les Paul, yes, I play the John Suhr guitar more than any other; that's my main stage guitar. But then I do have, Roger Griffin from Gibson made me a replica of my Les Paul. I have one of those, I have Telecasters from Fender, I have Telecasters from G&L, which are great. All different guitars. So I've been playing about five or six different guitars on a regular basis.

SW: You mentioned doing your own version of "Jumping Jack Flash" on your first album. I read that the Stones considered you as their guitar player before they hired Mick Taylor. Did they actually approach you about being in the band?

PF: No, it was before they hired Ron Wood. I was on the short list with Ron Wood. It was basically because the first band that I'd been in the studio with before the Herd was a group called the Preachers, and Bill Wyman was the producer and manager of the band.

The original drummer of the Stones was a guy called Tony Chapman; Tony introduced Bill to the Stones, and then of course Tony got thrown out of the band, and they got Charlie Watts. So I guess Bill had always felt that he owed Tony a favor, so he produced a couple of singles and an album that I don't think ever came out. I stayed friends with Bill for…well, I still am.

I didn't know that Bill and Charlie had put my name forward on the short list, and I was driving home from Manhattan—I was living in the county north of Manhattan—and heard the news on the radio, and just heard my name mentioned as a possible member of the Rolling Stones. So I had to pull over, actually, at that point. *(Laughs)*. It was a very nice feeling, obviously. That was in 1975, and it was the following year that *Frampton Comes Alive* came out, and I asked Mick Jagger when I met him, "Was I really on the short list?" And he said, "Yes, you were," so I got it verified from the horse's mouth.

SW: He appeared on *I'm In You*, didn't he?

PF: Yes, one of the tracks on the *I'm In You* record. *(Note: The song was "Rocky's Hot Club")*.

SW: You got great reviews for the most part during the early years of your career when you were struggling, but after the live album hit, you experienced a tremendous critical backlash. Why do you think that is?

PF: Well, no one likes success, you see, for other people to have success.

SW: Do you pay a lot of attention to the reviews you get?

PF: It's very hard not to pay attention to reviews. When you're struggling, people always want to be the ones to discover you and say, "Well, I always knew. But now, of course, he's sold out." They're always very quick to turn.

It's the build-you-up-to-knock-you-down syndrome. When you're in the public eye, when you've climbed up the ladder, it's time to knock you down. It's just the nature of the media, I think. What's left to do, once you've made someone into a star, but to start pulling them to pieces? It just seems the nature of the business.

SW: Does it really bother you to receive a bad review?

PF: Well, it's not thrilling! *(Laughter)*. You know, I try not to read reviews, because I do take them personally, and you can't expect everyone to love what you do. There are going to be people that think you're the best thing since sliced bread, as well as there are going to be people that think that you stink. It's just personal opinion, but it does play havoc with your own feeling of self-worth as a musician. It shouldn't, but it does! If I told you enough that I thought you were a terrible writer, you'd start to believe it after a while.

SW: Especially if *everybody* started saying it! *(Laughter)*.

PF: Yeah, if everybody did, right! Exactly. So it's just getting it in the right perspective, which is very difficult to do when you're in the middle of it.

SW: Do you think it would have been easier for you, as per the reviews that you got during and after the *Frampton Comes Alive* era, if they hadn't focused so much on the way you looked and the whole image?

PF: Yes, but I think it was…*(long pause)*…it was very difficult for them not to. The thing is that the way I looked was almost a drawback. I've often said I wished I looked like the back end of a bus, which is an English phrase or saying; that I hadn't had the visual appeal that I had, because it does confuse the issue.

If someone is heralded for the way they look, it's sometimes very hard to take what they do very seriously. You know, "He looks good. He can't possibly be a great player." And it's unfortunate that that's the way it goes, because magazines like to sell magazines, papers like to sell papers, TV shows like to sell TV shows and so on, and people are first attracted by the way someone looks. And obviously, I became a pinup very quickly, very easily.

It's very hard. You can control the media, but you can't stop it doing what it does. I just don't think that a great job was done to control. I think that it was *fed*, because the management at the time believed the old saying, "Any publicity is good publicity". But not when *every* magazine has got you on the front cover. It's overkill.

SW: Your lyrics seem to come straight out of personal experience. Do you view them as a kind of diary?

PF: Yes. Very much so. You've hit the nail right on the head! *(Laughs)*.

SW: Is it somewhat uncomfortable to write all those personal thoughts and then put them on sale?

PF: Not really, no. That's how I write. It's like the last album I did, the one just called *Peter Frampton*, is probably what I feel is one of the best records I've ever done, and lyrically as well, and that's totally from what was going on in my life at the time. I mean, one has to write from personal experience. I'm not the sort of person that can make up stories, so that's the way I write.

SW: By the time you were in your mid-twenties, you were one of the most famous, recognizable people in the world. How did that impact the way you lived your actual day-to-day life?

PF: Being very recognizable obviously has its difficulties, but it never really bothered me that much. It comes with the territory. It's something I had wished for, but never quite thought that it would happen, and it surpassed any dream I had ever had of success.

It's something that you just have to deal with. Obviously your privacy is the first thing that seems to disappear. When you go out, it's very difficult to go anywhere without being recognized, but as I say, that sort of goes with the territory.

SW: Once the phenomenal notoriety of that period began to cool down a little, did it take you a long time to re-adjust?

PF: No. I mean, obviously I still get recognized, but it's calmed down a bit. It's been a lot of years since *Frampton Comes Alive*, that period. It's enjoyable in some ways. Obviously you don't want people to stop asking for your autograph, but you'd prefer, if you're in the middle of a nice meal, that they don't yank the fork out of your mouth to ask for an autograph then.

My hair is short now, so people don't recognize me anywhere near as much. It's a nice feeling to be able to go places and not be bothered. But I'd still like for them to ask for my autograph occasionally. Is that all right? *(Laughs)*.

SW: Sure. *(Laughs)*. These days it's a standard practice to take the tapes from a live performance and overdub them extensively before releasing the recording as a live album. In the case of *Frampton Comes Alive*, was that overdubbed, completely live, or a mixture of the two?

PF: It was, I would say, ninety-nine percent live. The only things we replaced on the live record were things where the signal didn't make it to the truck. The piano on "I Wanna Go To The Sun" just didn't; the mic wasn't working. Bob replaced that, and my rhythm guitar on "Show Me The Way" did not come through because they forgot to move the mic from one cabinet to the next. *(Laughs)*. Because I used a different amplifier on that. I used a Twin Reverb on that for the clean rhythm sound.

SW: That can cause a problem. *(Laughs)*.

PF: Yes. Nothing was coming out of the Marshall that they were micing at the time. So those two things, and I believe the acoustic guitar on "Baby, I Love Your Way". The quality was not very good on that. Again, the rhythm guitar on that, I replaced. But that's it.

SW: So it's actually a very fair document of a live concert.

PF: It really is. I mean, there's no way to re-do guitar solos or vocals and have the audience that loud, because you'd be able to tell.

SW: A lot of the time you *can* tell, because you hear a lot of live albums where it sounds like they played the studio recording and just stuck some people in the background.

PF: *(Laughing).* Right, exactly.

SW: In the years following *I'm In You*, there was a downturn in the sales of your records. Was that difficult for you to deal with?

PF: Not the easiest of things, but the main thing for me has always been, as long as I can go out there and play…I have an audience, I can make records if I want to. I've got something that very few people have. Well, *nobody* else has the biggest-selling live album of all time, so I'm happy with that.

I haven't finished doing what I'm going to do, but it's just that every career has its ups and downs. As you get older, you realize that. It was harder at the time, but I wouldn't change a thing as far as my career is concerned. I'm going on. I shall do another record and, you know, keep going.

SW: What kind of plans do you have for another record? Are you planning right now?

PF: Yes. I'm going to do another live record! *(Laughs).*

SW: Oh, really? That's great.

PF: Yeah, I'm going to, hopefully at the beginning of next year. It was planned to be done at Christmas, but I couldn't get it together in time. But next year, I'm pretty positive now that it's going to happen. This year we toured for three months, and next year I'm pretty sure we'll do at least another month's worth of dates so that we can do a live record.

SW: That sounds great. You must be looking forward to it.

PF: Yes, I am, because that's when I feel the most confident, is live. Obviously there will be numbers on there that no one's ever heard before, new songs. Probably two or three new songs on there, and some stuff that will be new to a lot of people because they haven't been aware of the records that have been out recently. So there won't be any repeats. It will all be new stuff as far as the public is concerned.

SW: Interestingly, you got together with Jeff Porcaro and Steve Lukather on *Breaking All The Rules*. How did that come about?

PF: *Breaking All The Rules* was a record that we wanted to…I got together with producer David Kirchenbaum, who was head of A&R for A&M at the time, and we wanted to do it as live as possible. At that time I didn't have a drummer, and I wanted to use Jeff, and David Kirchenbaum recommended, "Why don't you use Steve Lukather as well, on guitar, so that you can play solos live while we track?" So that was the whole idea of that, and obviously they both became good friends from that, and it was a great experience playing with them.

SW: Was that radically different from the way you had worked in the past?

PF: Yes. I usually overdubbed the solos, but on *Breaking All the Rules*, most of them were live. On "Friday On My Mind" and "Breaking All The Rules" especially, those two were totally live.

SW: As your recording career has gone along, to my ears anyway, it seems like you've become progressively looser and more confident in the studio, especially on the last two albums. You say you feel more comfortable playing live, and the last two records certainly seem to have a more relaxed feel to them. Is there anything you did differently on those records that made them that way?

PF: I just think that I feel more confident in the studio now. Both of those records were virtually done homemade, so they were done at my leisure. They were done when I really felt there was no pressure to record them. I think the last one is more of a live feel than *When All The Pieces Fit*.

When All The Pieces Fit was a little bit too computerized for me. I did most of it myself, whereas with the last record, Kevin Savigar and I basically did the whole thing, and it was more of a human record than machines. In fact, we didn't turn on the machines until after we'd finish writing the songs, and then we only used the machines to help us put down a demo, and real musicians were used after that.

SW: The last few records also have, not necessarily more, but a different kind of guitar playing, more the high-energy kind of thing that people really used to associate with you. Is that a deliberate return to your roots, or did it just fit the mood you're in?

PF: I guess it just fit the mood I'm in. I think that I'm just more natural in a recording situation now, as far as playing. I've never been able to do more than three or four takes, because it just gets worse. With me, you've just got to find the right moment, and usually it's when I don't really think I'm doing it for real. It's when you get it by accident, when I think I'm just doing a demo solo, you know. That's when I get something I like.

SW: A lot of the songs on *When All The Pieces Fit* lyrically deal with a common theme of starting over. Was that just another reflection of the state of mind you were in?

PF: That was sort of the beginning of when, even though I was using computers, I decided to write more the way I used to write, which was with an acoustic guitar or a piano. And this last record was even more that way. I had my Taylor twelve-string, and I'd just put down loads of ideas on a cassette, and then pick through them and work on those ideas that I really liked, which was very much the way I'd written *Wind Of Change* and *Frampton's Camel* and those early records.

There were no drum machines in those days. There was no MIDI. A song has got to stand up on its own with a voice and an acoustic guitar or a voice and a piano. It's got to stand up on its own without a thousand gadgets going boom-ch-ch-ca-ca. *(Laughter)*. *When All The Pieces Fit* was written a little bit with computers, and some of the songs on there don't quite stand up on their own as much as the last record. I feel that any one of the songs on the last record, I could play with a piano and a voice or a guitar and a voice and they would still sound good.

SW: I saw you sing "Waiting For Your Love" on Regis and Kathie Lee.

PF: Oh, right, yeah! *(Laughs)*.

SW: That was great version of that. I actually liked it better than the recording.

PF: Thank you!

SW: One last thing. Your project that you had begun to get back with Steve Marriott was tragically cut short by his death. How did that affect you at the time?

PF: Well, we were just about to sign a recording deal, a publishing deal… everything was right there. We'd written four or five things already, and we were ready to go, so yes, it was a bit of a shock. And it took quite a while to realize what I wanted to do after that, because I'd put all of my eggs in one basket, as usual. *(Laughs)*. It was going so well, and it was so exciting to be back working with Steve, that when it came to a grinding, shocking end like that, I didn't quite know what to do.

In the end, it took me about a good six months before I realized that I just wanted to go out and have fun and play live. So that's when, in February of '92, I went out and did what was going to be a six or eight week tour which, through the demand and the ticket sales, went to seven months. And that's when I realized that there was a huge following out there still for me, and that's what got me a new record deal and started everything.

So out of something terrible, at least it reactivated me, and I got back into it. It was just something that no one would have thought was gonna happen. It was a shock, and these things you get over.

For more information about Peter Frampton, please visit www.Frampton.com

THE POWER AND THE GLORY

Gary Green was the guitarist in the British rock band **Gentle Giant**, one of the most creative and innovative of the early Seventies wave of progressive rock which included ELP and Genesis. **Gentle Giant** attracted a large underground following through its conceptual lyricism and long, convoluted musical arrangements, releasing a string of highly respected albums throughout the Seventies before breaking up in 1981.

Since then, there has remained a cult-like interest in the band from the underground progressive rock community, particularly in Europe. With the release of most of the group's albums on CD, there has been a **Gentle Giant** revival of sorts as more and more fans and musicians alike have acknowledged the band as one of the most influential of all of the progressive art rock ensembles of its time.

Growing up during the cultural and musical upheaval of Sixties England, **Gary Green** took up the guitar just prior to the rock and roll explosion of the British Invasion era. Initially attracted to the instrumental groups of the day such as the Ventures and the Shadows, **Green** then became immersed in the blues, playing in several blues-oriented bands and honing his chops in the club and pub scene.

Responding to an ad in **Melody Maker** to audition for a new group that was being formed out of the ashes of the erstwhile pop group **Simon Dupree and the Big Sound**, which had enjoyed several chart hits in England, **Green** wound up joining **Gentle Giant** at its inception, working with the band for six months before recording its first album. **Gentle Giant** emerged as one of the vanguard acts of the fledgling progressive rock genre, fusing elements of rock, folk, and classical music to create a new style of music which defied immediate categorization.

Over the course of the next decade, **Gentle Giant** recorded a string of influential albums including 'Free Hand', 'The Power And The Glory', and 'Three Friends', which contained the group's closest call to a hit single, "Working All Day". Unlike such progressive contemporaries as Yes, ELP or Jethro Tull, **Gentle Giant** was unable to bridge the gap between longer, more progressive pieces and the shorter, more melodic songs that were crucial to radio programming. Consequently, the band received little radio support, touring extensively to keep itself alive and developing an extremely devoted following in the process.

By the beginning of the Eighties progressive rock had fallen out of favor, its leading lights either crushed under the growing weight of their own pretensions, or faded into the twilight world of lackluster album sales, and it became more difficult than ever for **Gentle Giant** to maintain its career. Growing career pressures, along with newfound family concerns, spelled the death of the band in 1981, and **Green** went on to play on **Eddie Jobson's** 'Green' album, a minor classic of the *progressive rock genre. He settled in America with his wife and spent the next fifteen years pursuing his love of music in various bands in and around the Chicago area.*

*I spoke with **Gary Green** on December 7th and December 8th, 1994, from his home in Illinois. Though **Green** has never made the kind of fortune from music that many of his contemporaries did, he speaks with no bitterness about his career. **Green** is very articulate and insightful about the creative process and the role of the musician, and dismisses the very notion of mainstream success.*

*We spoke at an exciting time for **Green**; his band **Big Hello** was finishing up the sessions for its debut CD, and **Green** was looking forward to the possibility of being able to tour. He also professed to be very pleased at the renewed interest **Gentle Giant** has been receiving, which resulted in his being asked to fly to Italy to perform with a well-known progressive band over there. And while **Gary Green** might not be the most familiar name in the music world, in the estimation of his fans he is most certainly a musical giant.*

SW: How old were you when you started playing guitar?

GG: I was fourteen or fifteen, as I remember. I'd always had an interest in music, and my older brother Jeff played clarinet at school, and he had brought home a guitar and started to learn to play. It was laying around the house and I picked it up, and he showed me a few things, and I took it from there. That really would have been just prior to the Beatles. Just about that time.

SW: Do you remember the first guitar you got?

GG: I remember buying a real cheap electric guitar off a friend of mine for the, it seemed to me, exorbitant sum of five pounds back then. *(Laughs)*. And I remember propping it in the corner of my bedroom and looking at it from my bed at night, proudly thinking, 'Yeah, that's my guitar.'

The first guitar I had was one of those semi-hollow deals. It was called an Elite. I wish I still had that. It sounded pretty good, as I remember. Not that my musical sound antenna was terribly sophisticated back then. *(Laughs)*. But you know, it sounded great to me.

Then my mom and dad bought me for Christmas a Hofner Lucky Seven, and that was a terribly thrilling Christmas. I think it must have been the Christmas of '63 or '64. It had an action about an inch high, and sort of high-tension hawsers for the strings, but I struggled through and learned the Beatles' "Hard Day's Night" on it, and it was great. It had a cutaway, so that was really cool. You know, it looked like a real guitar. This Elite thing didn't, but the Lucky Seven did.

I ended up painting it black and carving "Down With Prohibition" in the top of it. I don't know why; I hadn't even touched alcohol by that time, but it seemed like a very cool thing to do. *(Laughter)*. I used to collect bottles for some reason, and I would soak the labels off all these various different alcoholic things, and I plastered a whole bunch of alcohol labels over the front of it, too. And then it had "Down With Prohibition" on it, so it was a juxtaposition guitar! *(Laughter)*.

SW: That's fairly interesting. Quite frankly, it makes you sound like a bit of a madman! *(Laughter)*.

GG: I think I'd seen Donovan on *Ready, Steady, Go* in England, and he had carved on his guitar "This Machine Kills", which I think was a paraphrase of Woody Guthrie's "This Machine Kills Men". I think that's a Woody Guthrie phrase. But anyway, that's what Donovan had carved on his guitar, and I thought, well, that looks cool...

SW: Good enough for him, good enough for you! *(Laughs)*.

GG: Well, so much of that early stuff is done by imitation; that's how you learn to play. And you don't—or I didn't, anyway; I'm sure there are some players that do—have any sense of discipline about what it is that you must do to learn an instrument. That's not what makes you pick up an instrument to learn it in the first place. It's just that it's cool, and you like music, and you want to play. So you learn by imitation. Then you start to find out that well, if I did *this* like *this*, I could actually perhaps play *this* a little better. But it starts off as pure imitation. We're all clones in the beginning, I think.

SW: Who were your early influences, other than the Beatles and various alcohol bottlers?

GG: The Shadows were the big one in England, I'd have to say. That was Cliff Richards.

SW: Everybody I ever talk to from England always names them. I wonder if there would have been any music out of England in the Seventies if not for their influence.

GG: Oh, yeah, they were the Ventures of England. They were a musical twangy-guitar quartet, all playing Fenders...well, no, they didn't play Fenders, they played these Burns guitars, with scroll tops on them and stuff like that, but they had that Ventures sound, and they had a number of instrumental hits. "Apache" was the big one that I remember. *(Laughs)*.

To this day, if I'm tuning a guitar and I can't hear an interval, I go back and remember this tune "Apache" that the Shadows did. *(Hums the tune)*. That's a fourth, so it's like most of the tunings of open strings on a guitar, so it always reminds me of "Apache"! *(Laughs)*. So they were really influential, on me, anyway. I learned all those instrumental tunes they did. "Dance On" was another one, and "Foot Tapper". Great stuff, really good. And then as they subsided I guess the Beatles started to come along, and all the rest of it.

During that period of time, my dad was pretty influential on all of us kids. My dad always used to play a load of jazz in the house all of the time. He was a big Duke Ellington fan, and Count Basie and Benny Goodman. Sunday morning we'd get up late, and always wafting up the stairs there would be Frank Sinatra or Benny Goodman blasting out the radiogram as we tried to struggle awake.

My dad didn't play anything real well; he had been a drummer, a little bit, in an RAF band during the war, but he only played in the band, I think, to get out of all the rest of the duties. *(Laughs)*. He now fancies himself as a trombone player, and has a trombone and slides around a little bit. But anyway, it was his musical influence that got us all interested in it. And my mom loved music, too. Not that she was a professional or a singer or anything, but she just loved music, and it rubbed off on us all.

That seems to be where it comes from. It always seems to start from some sort of a parental thing. I don't know if *always*, but a lot of players I speak to, there's been a lot of that in their lives, and it rubs off.

SW: Did you take lessons at that point?

GG: No, I never took lessons. My brother Jeff is a wonderful guitar player; he's played with Stephan Grappelli and a bunch of people over in England. Jeff showed me a few chords and stuff, and then there was the Burt Weedon *Play In A Day* book.

Burt Weedon was this guitar player in England who had this instruction book, kind of like Mel Bay, if you like. *(Laughs)*. Burt Weedon was famous for saying, "Now I'm going to play this tune, and I'm going to play over a thousand notes in under a minute." Not any different notes, just millions of duplications. It was like *(hums the tune very fast)*. It was terribly hokey. *(Laughs)*. But anyway, he had this instructional book, and it had, you know, "Michael Row Your Boat Ashore" and that kind of thing. *(Laughs)*. Most British guitar players sort of plodded through this book, I'm sure. So I looked at that, but no, I didn't have any formal lessons or anything.

I wish now that I had. Of course you go through all these periods where you think, 'I don't want to be a trained musician, it would destroy the intuitive side of me', and all of that. I think that's crap, actually. I used to think that, but I don't think that's the case. I think it can only help. Today I wish I knew more about the theoretical, practical application side of music. It would be just great to gather four or five people in a room and throw up sheet music and wham, there it is, you're playing a piece right away. That's pretty much magic, that is.

SW: When people hear Gentle Giant's music, with the convoluted time signatures and complex arrangements, the natural assumption is that all of the players are immersed in theory and classical training.

GG: That's not really the case as far as Giant goes. Kerry, obviously, is a very schooled musician. He's a graduate of the Royal Academy and all that. Raymond, too, played with the National Youth Orchestra. Derek read or understood music a little bit; not to a great extent, and the same with Phil. John and I, not a bit! *(Laughs)*. We were just kinda from-the-belt players. I grew up really playing stuff like early Beatles, and then getting into blues and playing that a lot, and then there was jazz, and that's my whole background. But no, I'm not a schooled musician at all.

A lot of the music from Giant, I think people will be disappointed to hear, from my point of view, would be that some the stuff was just parts. Kerry would write parts and not exactly just hand them to me; we'd go over them and amend them here and there and make suggestions. But pretty much there was already kind of a skeletal outline as to what the part and what the music was going to be. It wasn't, "Here's an idea; let's all throw in ideas." You know, it's a pretty strict format. It has to be if you're talking about that kind of music. It's not jamming music.

SW: It's not like Led Zeppelin, where you can say, "Let's just stay on this riff for an extra ten minutes…Gary, you take the solo and just go crazy."

GG: No, it's not like that.

SW: What kinds of early bands were you in before Gentle Giant?

GG: The first band I was in was called the Insects, and later changed its name to the Outcry. *(Laughs)*. That was a high school band, and we played the R&B stuff of the day, like "Long Tall Sally" and a lot of Chuck Berry stuff, and some Beatles stuff. And then I found this friend of mine at school who was a harmonica player, a pretty good one, and he introduced me to the blues. I used to take my guitar to school and we would play during breaks in the classroom, just jam the blues in the corner, and that was pretty much when I started to find that I was starting to get really serious about guitar playing.

I really found that here was a music that wasn't just that you were bashing and smiling inanely; you were actually thinking about what you were playing, and you felt things as you were playing. You were able to elicit oohs and ahhs from people by things that you could do; they would like what you were doing, and their attention was right there with you at the same time. I'm talking about the interplay between the two guys, really. You play off each other on that. So that was really the time I started to get serious about guitar playing, I think, was when I was fifteen.

SW: Were you in several other types of bands?

GG: No. I was just playing that pretty much, and playing at home with my brother, and then after I left school I went to work. I still had a love for the blues and was playing the blues all the time, and then my oldest brother Mike was a drummer, and we wanted to get a band together, and he had a friend who had apparently grown up with John Mayall, and so we got a blues band together called Kokomo Phoenix.

We did a residency at this pub in north London for a few months, and it was interesting. Several times there was an opening act called Duster Bennett; he was a one-man band kind of thing. He had a bass drum on the floor in front of him, and an old Gold Top Les Paul he would play, and a harmonica, and he was really good. And his manager was Peter Green, who came to a couple of gigs at the pub.

He would sort of sit off in the corner and watch Duster Bennett and watch us. I never got to talk to him, but his presence affected me a great deal because I really loved Peter Green. You've probably heard that a lot from people, too, as far as his being perhaps a little more influential than Clapton with some people. I saw him with the Bluesbreakers several times, and very early Fleetwood Mac, and was just astounded by that wonderful feel he's always had.

So that was Kokomo Phoenix, and then a band called Fish Hook came along and decided they wanted to snag me, so I joined them, and that was really semi-pro. We actually went traveling to go play places, so that was really a step, uh, sideways, I suppose. (Laughter). Not a step up, but another step sideways. We played for quite a while, probably about a year. I forget why that eventually broke up. I think the drummer had lost his job at a factory or something and couldn't pay the payments on his drums anymore.

SW: Well, that will do it. (Laughs).

GG: Yeah, those kinds of things really affect a band in those early years! (Laughs). Nothing to do with splitting up because of musical taste differences; we split up because the drummer lost his job and couldn't afford the payments on his drums! So that was Fish Hook.

Then I went into a year's period of depression or so. I think I was probably about seventeen or eighteen at that time. My parents, meanwhile, had moved from London out into Essex, which is actually very close, adjoining London, but nevertheless, it seemed the other end of the earth as far as I was concerned at the time. They moved out into Essex and I moved with them, and I got a job in town, in London, and commuted every day back and forth and got terribly bored, awfully despondent and depressed, and then one day answered an ad in *Melody Maker*, and it turned out to be an audition for this band Gentle Giant.

I hadn't been in any professional bands before Giant, only semi-pro stuff, and really the only band that was semi-professional was Fish Hook, because we had a van and went traveling around. Kokomo Phoenix would have been playing in somebody's living room if it hadn't been playing in this pub. (Laughs). It wasn't a paying thing at all. So my musical experience in that kind of thing was pretty limited.

SW: And those bands were obviously radically different types of music than Gentle Giant.

GG: Yes, it was.

SW: Were Giant already together when you joined them?

GG: Mostly, as I understand the story. They had been a pop band called Simon Dupree and the Big Sound, which had enjoyed a couple of hits in England. They were a pop band with flowery shirts and big heels, and they wanted to change that. I think they got sick of doing that and wanted to do something more meaningful musically. And prior to my doing the audition I think they'd gotten hold of Kerry. I'm not sure how that came about. And they needed a guitar player, and advertised.

I think my joining was very, very shortly after Kerry joining, because when I went in to audition, I remember the bass drum still had 'Simon Dupree and the Big Sound' on it, which sent shivers up my spine, because I knew who Simon Dupree and the Big Sound was, and I didn't want to do that! (*Laughter*). I said, "Oh, no!"

SW: "Have I come to the wrong place?" (*Laughs*).

GG: The audition was really good, actually. I think there were probably about forty or fifty guitar players, and they all had a point in time at which to show up. It was at a pub in London called the Pied Bull, which has been the seat of a lot of musical stuff going on there. So they kind of liked me at the audition. You know, I went through a few hoops and stuff. Ray threw a couple of tricky little phrases at me and said, "Can you play this?" And I'd say, "Yes, I think I can play that." That kind of stuff.

SW: Did they hire you on the spot?

GG: No, then they said, "Well, we'll have to think about it." And then I got a call a couple or three days later asking me to come down to Portsmouth, which is down on the south coast of England where they lived, for further rehearsals, a bit more intensive tryouts. It was going to be a whole day thing.

And that's what I did. I went down and played with them, learned more parts of the tunes that they had. They must have had a fair bit of the first album written, and it was still kind of formative, as I remember, because I learned some of the parts for the first album at that second interview, and tossed ideas back and forth, and spent basically the whole day there. Probably about six hours, with them all playing tunes and learning parts, basically to see how we all interacted.

I don't think it was probably a question of musicianship by then; it was a question of how it was going to work personally. And it seemed to be pretty good, at the end of which Phil Schulman said, "We like you a lot. We think it's going to work out. We think it's going to do amazing things, this band, so you're hired." And it was at the amazing sum of twenty pounds a week, which I couldn't fathom. It was a fortune to me from having had nothing. But then, any kind of regular income would have been, I'm sure! (*Laughs*).

And the amazing part was we weren't playing any gigs at this point. The management who had managed Simon Dupree and the Big Sound, which was Gerry Bron and Bron's Associates, sponsored the band through six months of rehearsals just to be able to get this new band together. They'd been fairly good friends, and I guess Simon Dupree and the Big Sound had done all right by the Bron Agency, so Gerry put up the money to pay everybody's wages for about six months so we could rehearse, which was real nice of him.

SW: That's a great situation.

GG: It was ideal, and almost necessary for a band like Giant, where it was very complicated music, really, for its time. There was no guarantee that there was going to be a market for this at all. When I joined it was March 1970…

SW: So none of the breakthrough progressive rock bands had really hit any big sales yet at that point.

GG: All the others were developing, too, like Yes and Genesis...

SW: And even ELP or King Crimson were new at the time.

GG: I remember hearing that first King Crimson album in the car. It was a very early gig; it must have been within 1970, because we used to have this terrible old car that we used to travel to gigs. We got into the car after some gig and turned on the radio, and here was this thing; it was the middle of "21st Century Schizoid Man"*(hums the rapid passage from the song)*, and we all just stopped dead. We all just piled into the car like, "What the hell is that?" It was really good. I think it was our first exposure to the fact that there was another band around that was going to try and play actual music. 'Uh oh', we thought, 'Let's get working!' *(Laughter)*.

SW: Did you rehearse for six months and then go out and start playing live, or did you go and start recording an album?

GG: I think during this period we'd done a couple of demos. We went to Pye Recording Studios at Marble Arch and recorded two tracks which were later not to be used, because they were nothing like the rest of the music that was coming out. They were more tunes, with chords. They were quite nice little tunes, but they were kind of a hang over from the days of Simon Dupree, transitional sort of tunes. They were mainly to see how we were going to work in the studio, and would the management be wasting their money? And meanwhile I think Gerry Bron was talking to Phonogram. Vertigo was the progressive label of Phonogram at the time.

I can't remember when we went into the studio to make that first album. We went into Trident Studios in London. That was quite an experience, just being in a studio, for me. I'd never really been in a real recording studio at that point. Kerry hadn't, either. I think we were the two most naive players in regard to what you get exposed to. All the others had been in the studio, so it wasn't new to them, but it was to us, and it was quite an experience. A bit strange, actually.

Trident seemed odd to me in that the control room was upstairs, and you looked down into the room from a long way. Not that you could really see from the board or anything. And the tape machines weren't even in the same room as the control room. They were down the corridor, and you had to talk to the tape operator via the intercom if you wanted to roll back to a spot and then run it from there. It was pretty confusing. This was before there was auto-locate and you could just go back to a spot. You'd tell them to go back to there, and they'd make a mark on the tape, and they'd just go back to the squiggle.

SW: That's fairly primitive compared to how things are now.

GG: Oh, yeah. That was recording.

SW: Were you pleased with the album when you were done with it?

GG: I was thrilled with it, just because it was a record I was on, for a start. *(Laughs)*. But beyond that, I think I got a sense of what this band could be. I was pretty naive at the time. I think I was nineteen. So to be on a record was quite thrilling; it was probably, at the time, the coolest thing a kid could do, because it was already cool to be in a band, so to be on a record as well...I don't know, I'd like to feel that I wasn't affected too egotistically by all of this. I don't think I was. But I was quite thrilled. I thought it sounded good, I really liked the tunes, I liked everybody. I thought it was going to be a really good project to be involved with. I felt committed to it from minute one.

SW: When the album came out, how did it do?

GG: It didn't do any great guns as far as charts go. I wasn't terribly concerned with all of that. I was not mature in the music business at all; I didn't know anything about it. I was fairly happy to be rolling along with the fact that there was an album out with me on it. It got good reviews.

Of course, when you're involved in any project like that, you get tunnel vision. I did, at least. You get tunnel vision about it in that your whole world is focused on this one thing. You've got this album, so everything you see and read is pertaining to this. You listen to the album a bunch, you look in the music papers all the time, and there's a picture of you and a review of it, so you think that you're plastered all over the place.

In a more objective light, it probably didn't do hardly anything. But it did get good reviews in terms of, there's a new musical force here that's emerging, and it should be watched. Basically it seemed to me that was the thrust of a lot of those early reviews.

SW: Were the relationships between the band members themselves friendly?

GG: Pretty much. The three brothers in the band at the time, Ray, Phil and Derek, they were Jewish; not that that means anything at all, but Jewish people, in my experience—because I've got cousins that are Jewish—they tend to be very loud, very vocal in their feelings. They're able to say what they mean, have what seems to me like an incredibly intense argument, and then forget it in a nanosecond. Which blew me away, because I've always been one of those people that if there's friction in a room, it sort of soaks into me and affects me and it lasts with me a long time.

So stuff like that would upset me emotionally, and I couldn't get used to the fact that they could shout back and forward and it mean nothing, pretty much. It's just an outpouring of their feelings at the time. It's just brotherly love, I came to realize later on, but it was very upsetting to me, and I think it caused Martin, the drummer at the time, to leave later on.

I think he and Phil had words. Phil is a very smart man, quite an intellectual in his own way, but sometimes he could be kind of cruel to Martin or to people. Sometimes he couldn't think too much; he didn't know that what he was saying was really affecting somebody so badly. He didn't realize that, I think. He was able to belittle people, and I don't know that a lot of it was intentional. A lot of it was a by-product of his tough upbringing.

But it was very friendly; I don't want to give you the wrong impression. The brothers would argue back and forth and call each other all sorts of names, but it would be over in pretty much nothing. Derek and Phil rubbed each other a little bit wrong most of the time, but there was great friendship between the band. The relationship of the band was always real strong, particularly I have to say probably Ray, Kerry, me and whoever the drummer was at the time.

It was Martin on the first album, and I got on fairly well with Martin. I lived with him for a little bit at the beginning of the band. I lived with him about four or five months, I think, and then ended up living in Portsmouth. And then the next drummer, Malcolm, I got on fairly well with, too. He was okay. And then when John joined the band, we were kind of soul mates. We were always real tight, John and me and Kerry and Ray. And Derek; I lived with Derek quite a while, as well. We got on very well.

We did a lot of personal things together, the whole band; we'd go out fishing and all this kind of stuff. It wasn't just a purely musical business venture, it was a bunch of friends. It really was. We'd seek out each other's company in the evening and go out and have a drink. We were always together, pretty much, when we all lived in Portsmouth. And our wives were friends, too, so it was a nice little community.

I think it was probably because we felt like outsiders from the main body of the musical community. We weren't in the mainstream of things by any means. We didn't live in London, we weren't with the hip crowd, we didn't hang out in the clubs or anything like that. We drew our strength from each other and our own sort of family. That's really what the strength of Gentle Giant was, a lot of it. It wasn't typical of bands hanging out and doing what normal rock and roll players do. It was nothing like that. It was very normal, I must say. *(Laughter)*. At least that's the impression I get now, in retrospect.

SW: The band was together for a long time, during a period in which progressive rock came along, hit its peak and then faded away. Did you play on the bill with a lot of the other progressive rock bands of the day?

GG: We played with Yes a few times. Probably ten times or so we played with Yes. We played with Jethro Tull an enormous amount of times. The last part of our first American tour we toured with Jethro Tull, and we subsequently did a bunch of tours in Europe with them. We went to Italy and Germany and all over the place with them, and got on very well with all of them.

That really helped to establish Gentle Giant, I think, because their music was similar. Not musically, necessarily, but in its attitude and its theatricality on stage, and it was a very complementary bill to have those two bands on the same stage. It worked well for Tull, as well, having us open up, and for us to be exposed to such a huge audience helped us enormously, and really was the thing that helped us gain whatever prominence we had.

We played with Coliseum, as well; they were a bit more R&B/jazzy. They were more musically progressive, I guess. I don't know, what is progressive music? It gets lumped in with Yes, Genesis, Jethro Tull, Gentle Giant...that's progressive music, I guess. Now, see, Charlie Parker was progressive! *(Laughs)*.

We played with loads of people, lots of diversity. Our first tour of the States was with Black Sabbath, which was a very strange bill. *(Laughs)*. We played with Focus, and they were very good live.

We played with Greenslade, which was an offshoot of Coliseum. Dave Greenslade was the organist with Coliseum, and Coliseum was a band that John Hiseman, the drummer who had formerly been with Graham Bond, formed. It was him and Dick Heckstall-Smith, who was a saxophone player who had played with Graham Bond alongside Jack Bruce and Ginger Baker in the famous Graham Bond band. I speak to a lot of people, and nobody knows who Graham Bond is over here. Do you know who Graham Bond was?

SW: Only by vague reputation.

GG: He was a musical giant in England. John Mayall gets a lot of credit for being the father figure of bands like Cream, that had Eric Clapton in it, but the other side of that was, okay, Eric Clapton came from John Mayall, but Ginger Baker and Jack Bruce came from the Graham Bond Organization. Graham Bond was the organ player and alto sax player, and there was Dick Heckstall-Smith, who played tenor and alto, and Bruce and Baker.

That was a tremendous band. Baker would do his famous fifteen minute drum solos, and from that band they got together and made Cream. I'm surprised no one really talks about Graham Bond as being more influential on the scene. He died tragically. He fell under an underground train in London.

But Graham Bond had a band called Magic, and John Weathers played with that band. And Giant had played some show in the north of England, there were several bands on the bill, one of which was Graham Bond, and I remember this drummer floored me. I loved him, and when we were looking for a drummer to replace Malcolm Mortimer, who had broken his leg and his arm on the eve of a British tour, who the hell could we get? First of all we tried for Mike Giles, who was with the original King Crimson on their first album...

SW: *Giles, Giles and Fripp?*

GG: Yes, and we tried to get in touch with him. We were looking for a permanent drummer, and his response was, "Well, just send me the music and I'll learn it." And that's not really what we were looking for. We wanted someone to be with us a little more, who was part of it, and we got to thinking and remembered John and tried him out, and it was wonderful.

We never did play with Genesis. I saw them once, actually, without Peter Gabriel, much to my chagrin. God, I can't think of who else...

SW: You mentioned playing with Jethro Tull a lot. Was that when you were on Chrysalis?

GG: There was a lot of that association, because Ian Anderson had a lot to do with the running of Chrysalis, I think. Because Terry Ellis, one-half of Chrysalis, Chris-Ellis, was Jethro Tull's manager, and he became our manager.

SW: How did that work out?

GG: Pretty good. We had to get ourselves out of a previous management deal which had not been to our benefit at all. We'd suffered the usual trials and tribulations of naive musicians getting ripped off, and deals being made behind our back that we didn't know about and hadn't authorized. We got very fed up with the maneuvering behind the scenes and went seeking other management, and had a meeting with Terry Ellis.

I think we'd already toured with Tull, and probably word from Ian Anderson had gotten to him that we were a good band and he liked us, and therefore Terry Ellis would give us the time of day at least to listen to us. And we then bought ourselves out of our former management contract and went with Terry Ellis, and also with Chrysalis at that point. So it would have been just after we played with Tull that we got together with them.

That was a pretty good period for the band. I think we felt a lot less manipulated and maneuvered, and freer to pursue what we wanted to do. This was a really good period for the band.

SW: You switched labels a few times in the course of your career. Was it just in search of a label that would represent you better?

GG: I think we always felt that the distribution or marketing of the album was never as we would have liked it to have been. Derek always fancied himself a manager. Now he actually is! (Laughs). You know, he's high up in record companies and stuff. He was always interested in that, and was always keenly following the progress of the band, and what they were doing to market it, and how sales were going and all of that stuff. He was very on top of that all the time.

And there was a feeling of dissatisfaction generally early on with how things were being handled in that way. I don't think we, at the time, really realized that it was probably an insanely hard thing to sell, progressive music, what we were doing, so it wasn't going to garner the kind of sales we had thought about. It wasn't to be, simply like jazz is never going to be the best-selling music. You know, it's just not in the cards. But I think we thought that it should be. (Laughs). We felt damn good about what we were doing, by golly, and it ought to be out there and people ought to be able to buy it. And since it wasn't happening, it was frustrating, so I think we were searching for some pot of gold that wasn't there.

Although I have to say that we always had creative control over our product, totally, one hundred percent. It was never an issue. So it wasn't that; it was pretty much the marketing end of things. I think it was born out of the frustration that it wasn't selling like we thought it should sell, or we weren't getting the prominence that we thought we should get. Which, of course, is ludicrous! (Laughs). But nevertheless you're dissatisfied, and you keep trying for something better. Like anything, it's born out of a need.

SW: There used to be some strange stories about Chrysalis, particularly Terry Ellis. Did you ever experience any problems working with him?

GG: Not personally, no. They seemed to give us quite a bit of freedom. We always had creative control over every aspect of what we did, music and cover and stuff like that. They seemed to be fairly good people to work with, I always felt. But having said that, I realize that it was more my formative years. I was sort of a naive lad there for a while, and did not take too much interest in a lot of that, so I probably missed a lot of stuff that other people would say was different than I saw it.

I don't know, I find that a very hard line to run. It seems to me that either musicians are musicians, creative people, and they get on with their job, which is making music, or they are management/business types, and then they go toward that aspect of the business. And it seems to me that the two don't mix particularly well.

It seems to me, perhaps naively again, that the best musicians are the ones that don't really concern themselves with that. And while that may be to the detriment of seeing what they do gets out to the public and how it's handled, it certainly still makes for a better piece of music or a better piece of art. You can be one or the other, it seems to me, but perhaps not both. In a few instances there are people who do well in both. Frank Zappa comes to mind right away.

SW: How about Derek Schulman?

GG: Right. Derek was always led toward management and the business side. He was always into counting numbers. Derek was also artistic as well, but I think he was, percentage-wise, leaning more toward the business aspect of stuff more so than the creative thing.

SW: Do you keep in touch with the other members of Gentle Giant?

GG: I haven't done, no, although I did see Kerry, I guess that would be five years ago now, and it was as if we had never parted ways at all. After the band broke up I moved to the States fairly directly, and as a consequence did lose touch with everybody because of the physical difference. I haven't really spoken to anybody. I haven't spoken to John, for instance, who was perhaps the one I was closest to in the band, and Kerry next, and then Ray.

I did speak to Derek a few times after I initially moved here. He at that time was working for Polygram, and he knew Eddie Jobson and knew he was doing a project and suggested me. So through Derek's connection I got that little gig there.

SW: The *Green* album.

GG: Yeah.

SW: It's interesting that Derek will most likely go down in history as the man who signed Bon Jovi, rather than for himself...

GG: Than for Gentle Giant! I know. Which is kind of a sad sort of epitaph, a little bit. Well, I don't know, I suppose I say "sad" because I'm not a Bon Jovi fan, I guess! *(Laughter).* I don't know, I guess they serve a need or something. Do they?

SW: I guess somehow they must.

GG: I'm not sure how that works. Does the fact that something sells justify its existence? I don't know. That sounds terribly pompous. I don't mean to sound quite like that, but just because something sells a lot doesn't mean it's good, obviously. There's so much commercialism in this country, you can sell shit to a horse stable if you convince them they need it. *(Laughs).* All it takes is a good salesman to do that. It's sort of irrelevant as far as the worth of the product that's being sold.

You know, it's a shame. People I guess are generally gullible. I mean, look at the occasions down through history where someone is sold down the river, or something's been palmed off on them just because somebody can make money off of it. It's not a terribly altruistic world.

SW: And that makes it perhaps even more frustrating for something that's genuinely good music, like Gentle Giant, to not achieve the recognition it deserves.

GG: I don't know, perhaps that's kind of a pompous attitude, too. I think we all felt we were making music that was, I hesitate to say "groundbreaking", but it was innovative for its time, definitely. Having said that, that's never going to be a huge commercial success, anything that's sort of on the edge. Obviously it garners interest among people who are so inclined in those areas of music, but it's not generally something that will go to an instant success like Bon Jovi, which kind of sounds familiar before you hear it.

SW: It's just rehash by its very nature.

GG: It's largely derivative. Gentle Giant was none of those things, so it always needed fresh ears and an open mind to listen to that and accept it for what it was. Thankfully, those people are still around. I don't want to give the impression that I'm despondent over the future of music in any way, not by any means. There's always room for good music, there's always plenty of people out there to support it, but it's never the mainstream of market sales. It's never going to be. But that I can live with, I think. Because it still means that people like Richard Thompson can make a good living.

And in some instances, too, huge success often spoils a band's artistic direction, it seems to me. I thought it was going to happen to U2, but they seem like they turned around and pulled themselves back together. But for a long time there it seemed like they had sort of lost the appeal they'd had a little bit. And a band like Midnight Oil; I really love them, but it seems to me like they've catered more to mainstream stuff of late, in the last two or three albums. But perhaps that's inevitable. I mean, Gentle Giant did that, too.

I don't know what that is about a band. It's like the first two albums are groundbreaking, really good, and then they discover a formula that seems to work for them and continue on in that vein, trying to please other people rather than please themselves. I don't know if it's really a conscious decision that bands do that, or whether it's the fact that since they're now on the market and you're now familiar with them, then everything you hear from them subsequently sounds familiar because you already know what they do, or whether in fact it is a sort of selling out. I'm not decided about that issue, but it always intrigues me.

SW: Some of the later Gentle Giant albums were radically different from the original intent of the band.

GG: They did change, and I think that was really due to the search for a hit album. It seemed to me that Derek perhaps mostly, and then Ray to a lesser degree, really wanted to push for hit records. You know, they really wanted to have a hit top ten album, whilst with the first few albums I think Derek was content to be changing ground musically, radically, from what they had done before when they were a pop band. They were very keen to shed that skin and not be known as that, because there was a stigma attached to it. But it had made money, whereas in Giant the tours always finished up losing money, and the albums never made back the money that was spent on them.

So it actually becomes, for a band making albums like *Acquiring The Taste*, for instance, a real day-to-day survival thing. If you don't have enough money to pay your own bills, then either you change, or the band doesn't exist. So you pick the lesser of two evils and try to maintain your musical integrity, and that's a shitty tight rope to have to walk. So you try to do that. It's difficult, though. Yes, the albums changed, but we weren't ever the best band to try and write hit material! *(Laughs)*.

It seemed to me a foregone conclusion that it wasn't going to happen. We should have stuck with the kind of thing we did best, which to me was around the time of the *Octopus* album, or *In A Glass House*, and been content to produce that kind of music, which we all loved, and make a reasonable living. Not a good living, but a reasonable living. And perhaps that would have made the band last longer. I don't know. How long does a creative project like a band last?

SW: It's hard enough to keep it together in the best of financial circumstances.

GG: You know, a band like Cream, for instance, was together for what, two and a half years! *(Laughs)*. And still legendary today. And John Mayall's Bluesbreakers with Eric Clapton was only about nine months. It's hard.

There seems to be a peak at which a band is really good, creative-wise, and then something gets lost. Not to say that the individual members lose any of that creativity or spark; it's just something about the mix of the band. Something doesn't work anymore. I don't know what it is, but there's a peak that most bands hit relatively early in their career, and then it goes down a little bit, and some are able to keep that going, and some are not.

SW: Look at how long some bands have stayed together. I guess it's no wonder they sometimes lose their way. Look at Yes. Not that I'm on the Yes-bashing bandwagon or that I dislike Yes' recent efforts; in fact, I spoke to Trevor Rabin for this book. But over all these years and all the member changes, they've certainly had their ups and downs musically. And because the current lineup focuses more on shorter, more pop-oriented material it makes it a little strange when they play the old songs live, because it doesn't seem like the same band.

GG: I don't think there's anything wrong with playing the old material. It doesn't sound like you do, either. But you've got to play them with the right spirit. You can't just toss them off because that's what's expected of you. It is expected of you to some extent, but you can still do it well.

That's the hard thing about being on tour, especially with an elaborate road show like so many bands have anymore. The kinds of huge shows that bands have on the road now, it's such a production, with everybody having to know cues all around, that you pretty much have to run the same show every night for a year, let's say, so you get burned out playing them that way. You really do, rather than being able to call a tune and play it.

That's tricky. But having said that, that's your job! *(Laughs)*. You know, your commitment is to be able to produce the goods on the night. That's the focus of it.

SW: When you were on tour with Gentle Giant, did you play better toward the beginning or toward the end of a tour?

GG: Probably toward the end, although having said that, there might be perhaps more spark about it at the beginning of a tour, because you're not sure what's happening, so you're on your toes.

That kind of nervousness helps you play well. You think that perhaps you're not, because you're nervous about playing, you're not sure what the arrangements are, you can't remember the way the show's supposed to run. But that gives you a certain edge and keeps you alive, and then once you get rolling and the machine gets smoother, you tend to start taking it for granted. So the band plays the tunes better, more professionally, toward the end of a tour, but there's a bit more spark in it all at the beginning.

SW: In rehearsing for Gentle Giant tours, would you just play straight through the show time after time?

GG: Sometimes we would do that. We used to do that toward the end of rehearsals. We'd rehearse all the tunes that we were going to play, and then sort out an order for them, and what kind of effects we would want. And then we'd run through it just because of our own physical instrumental changes that we would have to make, just to see how viable they were. And then we'd have to bring in the lighting guy and see what he would want to do, usually with our suggestions.

And then we'd have full-blown rehearsals at Pinewood Film Studios in London. That's kind of a popular tour or stage rehearsal place. You hire a soundstage and set up the whole PA and everything, and you run through the whole show probably four times. I think that's the maximum we ever did it, actually. Not too elaborate. But then, bigger shows probably need much more run-throughs than that. I don't know.

SW: You mentioned U2 earlier. When they came to Atlanta last time, they hired eighty extra crew guys in town, in addition to the full crew they brought with them.

GG: Was that the *Zooropa* thing?

SW: Yeah, the Zoo TV tour.

GG: That was hugely elaborate, wasn't it?

SW: What a headache it all must have been.

GG: Must have cost millions to put on. But quite spectacular. I didn't see it. I saw a little bit on television and it looked great, I have to say. I would have liked to have seen it live.

SW: It was pretty awesome. At that point, though, it's almost like the recent Rolling Stones tours, where it's like, "Oh, and they're playing songs, too!" *(Laughs).*

GG: Right. I must say I'm not a fan, particularly, of huge stadium shows. I never was. You feel a bit like a circus event passing through town. You don't really feel like people are there to hear the music. That seems to be the case.

I don't know what it's like in Atlanta, but around here when a tour comes, and it goes through the smaller cities, the events are attended just because they're events, not because of who they are. It's kind of like a carnival atmosphere going on. There's pretty much barkers in the foyer selling hot dogs and popcorn and all that stuff, and it seems the band is incidental to the whole process.

What I really liked to play were the smaller theatres, you know, three-to-seven thousand seat theatres. The sound is much better, you have a real stage, people have got good seats, and you can hear properly. That's much more to do with listening to music than a sort of sports event, which is what arena events tend to be.

SW: It seems that way. Here in Atlanta there's so much entertainment nonstop, but even so, it doesn't matter what you attend, it has that same theory at work. I avoid those big shows because there's always a problem. It's a hassle before you even see the band.

GG: That's right. You've gotta park miles away...

SW: Exactly. We have the Dome here, and it'll pack 80,000 people, and you get your Rolling Stones or your Elton John and Billy Joel out there, and it's just too crazy. Two incredibly loud pianos and 80,000 drunken idiots...now that's entertainment!

GG: And it always sounds terrible! It seems to me that you can only play a particular kind of music in a stadium like that and have it come over well. U2 are a good example of that. They play sort of mid-tempo tunes with notes that aren't too close together, so there's enough space between the notes that it gets around the natural reverb of a place like that. So you can kind of hear what they're doing, because they're playing slowly. If you've got something a bit more intricate, like Frank Zappa for instance, you couldn't make out a thing of what anybody was playing!

SW: It would be just a dull roar.

GG: A cacophony, really. We played with Zappa a couple of times. One was in a huge place, I think it was in Oakland. It was an enormous place. Of course, we had the privilege of being backstage to watch from there, which is my favorite place to see anybody from because you can hear everything. But I would always go out front and have a listen to see what it was like where people were sitting, and you'd get out there and it was insane. It was Frank Zappa, and you couldn't tell who it was!

And the same when we played with Yes, too, because some of their stuff is pretty intricate. You get way back in the hall, like the Cobo Hall in Detroit, and you don't know what they're doing. It kind of sounds like "Close To The Edge", so it must be! *(Laughs)*.

SW: I've had several bad experiences seeing Yes, and it's not even their fault. They played fine, it's just that the places are so huge, you're using opera glasses and saying, "I think that little one must be either Steve Howe or Jon Anderson!" *(Laughs)*.

I saw that *Union* tour, which was at a huge outdoor amphitheatre, and the guy in front of me had been drinking and was yelling at the top of his lungs. I had been waiting ten years to hear Yes play "Awaken" live, and this was going to be my shot, and just as they started into it, the guy in front of him got tired of him yelling and turned around and shoved him, sending him sprawling right into my lap, not only knocking me right off my feet, but spilling his beer all over me as well. That's a really special memory for me. *(Laughs)*.

But anyway, I digress. I wanted to ask you, do you have a particular favorite Gentle Giant album?

GG: No, in a word. I'm trying to think. I've been asked that question a bunch of times, obviously, but no. I suppose the one that comes closest to it is *Octopus*, but I have tracks off of every album that I like. It seems to me that there's always one or two that you're not real happy with for whatever reason. That's always a hard choice. Right around that period it seems to me that the band was strong, confident, doing good things.

SW: How about a least favorite?

GG: I used to cite *Interview*, actually, as a least favorite, but since they've come out on CD and I've got them, I listened to it, and I thought, 'Wow, there's some pretty good stuff on there!' *(Laughs)*. So I have to really listen to the whole catalogue again, and then I'll be able to give you a better evaluation of both of those questions. Obviously being closer to the situation back then, *Interview* was driving us nuts back then.

SW: How so?

GG: We used Advision Studios a lot for previous albums, and when we went in to make *Interview*, it really seemed like we were going in and clocking in and putting in our eight hour shift. It felt too workmanlike. We were already into a routine of like, well, okay, we know we've got to make a record in three months' time, so here we go, we start the writing process in rehearsals…It was just too down pat.

And it may have been more the circumstances that surrounded the making of it, rather than what we actually made in the end, because as I say, since I've now heard it with all these years in between, there's really some very good stuff on it. There's Kerry's composition called "Design" on it, which is just voices and percussion, which is really kind of a landmark piece now. It's bizarre, but there's really some fine bits in there. *(Laughs)*. Really good writing. So my attitude toward it has changed a bit. It's a better album than I gave it credit for at the time.

SW: Simply because of the way it was made.

GG: I think we just felt we were in a rut. That stirred us; after making it, we figured we didn't want to make another studio album and go all that route again. We didn't even think we'd go to other studios, which was pretty dumb. We probably could have gone anywhere in the world to make it and had fun doing it, but instead we figured we were going to go back to Advision, and we didn't want to do that.

So we said, "Okay, let's make a live album", which is how the live album came to be. Which was real fun making, because it wasn't draining in the sense of going to the studio and clocking in. It was just a by-product of doing what you love doing, playing live. It's being recorded, and at the end you've got an album, too. *(Laughs)*.

SW: Did you record the live album over a bunch of dates, or just choose specific ones?

GG: We just recorded, I think four gigs was all, in Europe. So it just had to come out of four gigs. Brussels, Paris, Munich, and I don't remember what the other one was. So then we obviously had to listen to all of the concerts and decide which bits we were going to use. We didn't just take one concert and use it; we used the best take of whatever it was and put it on the album.

SW: Did you wind up going into the studio to re-dub certain parts, or was it completely live?

GG: We did re-dub some things. Kerry had to re-do a keyboard on one, because at the Brussels, Belgium gig, just before we were to start one of the tunes, there was this horrible smell, and it was the keyboard kind of up in smoke behind us. *(Laughter)*. So he had to play the whole tune on what we felt was the wrong keyboard. It didn't give it the right sound, so he overdubbed the right keyboard in the studio. So it sounds a bit strange, but it's there, nonetheless.

Derek did re-do some vocals of his. I'm clean, John's clean, Ray's clean, I think. So it's pretty much in the vocals. Otherwise it's just as it happened, which is nice.

SW: Which demonstrates remarkably tight playing from a band performing such complicated music.

GG: We did achieve a real good level of playing live. It was very fun to be in, a great live band. We had some thrilling times, literally, on stage, like wow, did we really pull that off like that? *(Laughs)*. It was really good. That's the most satisfying feeling in the world, when you do that, and that's why you do it. And it doesn't happen all that often. You know, even Giant, as well as it did play live, we still had some real clunker gigs.

But mostly we were very consistent, and occasionally brilliant, it seems to me. You could probably count those on two hands, those kind of gigs, but I think we actually captured one of them on the record. I think maybe Paris was one of those gigs. I think that's where the "Free Hand" track comes from, because that's quite a blistering track on there.

SW: When you played live, did you have a lot of guitar changes to go through?

GG: Quite a few, because the music changed an awful lot from what the instrumental lineup of a tune would be. And obviously you're concerned with the transition of a show from one tune to another, so it did mean quite a few instrument changes.

For me, I didn't have too many guitars. I had an acoustic guitar, and two electric guitars that I switched between. I also played drums and recorder, and sang a little bit.

Kerry had the most changing around to do, from vibraphone to cello, recorder and all these various keyboards, which is ludicrous looking back on the amount of keyboards he had. When we played with Yes, Rick Wakeman had waves and banks of keyboards. It was insane. Of course, today…

SW: They have one! *(Laughs)*.

GG: Yeah, they have it all MIDI'd up. It's a damn sight easier.

SW: When I saw them, Tony Kaye had one little keyboard, and he played it all night.

GG: That's right. It would have been a much easier time to carry that.

SW: On the other hand, ELP still carries around that huge rotating keyboard setup.

GG: Well, I guess that's part of the visual thing of what ELP is.

SW: Yeah, because Emerson still gets out there and stabs that organ to death and drags it around and all that…

GG: Was it the...I guess it was the original guys, Emerson, Lake and Palmer?

SW: Yes. They did do one reunion tour that was actually Emerson, Lake and Powell, I believe, but that was 1986.

GG: Oh, Cozy Powell?

SW: Yes. I think they chose him because his name had to end in 'P'! *(Laughs).* Replacing a member of a band that has the names in the title is a little strange.

GG: To have to get a drummer with a surname of 'P'...it's odd.

SW: What types of guitars did you play in Gentle Giant?

GG: I had a Gibson Les Paul Standard, a vintage one, which I just sold, actually. A Telecaster...I had a Hangstrom twelve string that got stolen early on, which was a shame, because it was a nice guitar. And an acoustic guitar, a Yamaha F-150. But that was it.

I've never been much of a guitar buff as far as collecting them, although I really like guitars. They still seem to me like they're tools. If it's a good tool, you can do your job with it. If it's not, it's no good; throw the thing away. It doesn't matter if it's an ancient, vintage piece of equipment, it's really how the thing plays.

That's kind of all of our attitudes about it. None of us were particularly sentimental about instruments. They're literally that, they're tools. They're a medium through which you express something, and if they work, they're great. If they don't, they're just a pain in the ass.

SW: There's a real diversity of guitar sounds in Gentle Giant's music. In certain sections there's real subtle, clean-sounding chording, and in other places there's enormous power riffs...

GG: Right. Those were all achieved with the same arsenal of guitars I just described. I really didn't pull anything different into the studio. It was just done with different amps, different settings and that sort of thing. That's all it really was.

SW: When you played live, were you set up to send all the clean sounds through one amp and all the distortion through another?

GG: I only had one amplifier, and I really didn't have any kind of elaborate effects, either. All I really had was a chorus and a wah-wah and a volume pedal. There's pretty much one sound I used live.

It seems to me anyway that in guitar playing, you achieve different effects by the way you play. Obviously you can do it with effects pedals and rack mount stuff, but that really wasn't available to us then. But it still seems to me that, especially in acoustic playing, you can achieve a multitude of tones and little nuances by technique. That's really how it's done. It's in the wrist, it's in the fingers, how you produce the sound. That's how I would approach all that, really.

In the studio it's different. You've got a bunch of toys and time, and you can sort of piddle around and get different kinds of things. But live, I was never very technically minded, either, and I was always kind of impatient with things like that. I liked the idea of just plugging straight into a stack and just, let's go. *(Laughs)*.

SW: You just wanted to keep it as simple as possible.

GG: Yeah, and there's real advantages to that. You know, someone like Trevor Rabin can have a ten foot pedal that produces great noises, too, but I don't know. It's something that I'm getting more aware of these days, to be able to use things like that, but unless they're radically different, it's not so much the sound that conveys the difference of the part, it's the way it's played. And that is really what I relied on to achieve those, rather than a specific sort of tone change.

SW: I know just what you mean, because I've always played with just one amp. Although in my case, that was probably more necessitated by poverty, as opposed to conscious choice! *(Laughs)*.

Tell me about the band you're in now. What is the music like?

GG: I've got a band called Big Hello, and it's very stripped down music, a three-piece. It's kind of like power pop, mostly chordal stuff. It's not a lot of parts and stuff right now. I'm enjoying it because it's a three-piece. It's a challenge to be the only guitar player in a band, because you're carrying a lot of weight.

I'm singing lead vocals now, which is something I haven't done, but it's one of those things that if you practice, you get better at it. I've been doing it more and more. I'm more confident; I'm finding my own voice. I feel pretty good about my singing these days, whereas I was nowhere near of a singer in Giant, at all. But the situation demands that I am, these days. *(Laughs)*. So I'm doing it, and I'm enjoying it.

The fact of singing and playing is a whole different aspect, rather than just playing. You have to split your brain a little bit and let one side concentrate…I don't know, you can't ever let just one side concentrate on the singing and one on the guitar, it's that you try to listen overall. And for that, Giant was wonderful. When I would remember to, I would try to consciously listen to the whole piece of music as it was fit together. The tendency I think for most players is that you're really just concerned with your own sound and how you're playing, and you trust to instinct that you're with the other guys. I try these days, and I did then, to listen to the whole thing and see how everything fit together.

In a small way, it's kind of a meditation state. You're kind of drifting. It's a funny state to try and describe. You try to listen to everything and your own role in it and what you're playing, while at the same time concentrating on yourself. And singing and playing together is kind of like that, especially if you're playing things that are contrapuntal to each other. It's very enjoyable, because it's kind of mind-expanding, and it gives you a better overall feel of what you're supposed to be doing.

Any instrument is supposed to be subservient to the music, it seems to me. I'm not a big one for flash, Yngwie Malmsteem sort of stuff. The tune is the important thing. The piece of music you're playing is the main event, and what you do is kind of secondary to it, and your job is to support to your best effort that piece of music. I feel that's the role of the player in any ensemble playing.

SW: Do you have ambitions to get back into a situation where you can go out and tour and record and all of that again?

GG: I really would like to do some real serious recording again, and I would like to be in a band that's touring again. Because really, you can make your music and you can do it all in your basement, and all that's fine. That's admirable, and I want to do that as well, but there's a certain ego gratification that you want people to hear what you do. That entails going out in front of people, and I like that. That's an immediate comeback right then and there from people as to what you're doing.

It's fun to be playing in front of people. I like the volume, I've got to say. I think a lot of guitar players would tell you they like the physical rush of playing in a band, because it's loud and exciting. It's a pretty primal kind of deal, but it's exciting. *(Laughs)*. Why try and deny that when I mean, we are animals, you know. We have those kinds of feelings. I like it. Okay, I'm guilty!

And it's just plain fun. It's really good playing in front of people and with other people live. That's wonderful. There's nothing like it, in fact. It's great to be playing and building songs track by track on your own, but you miss a certain magic that you get when playing with other people.

Obviously a lot of people have come back to that realization. A lot of interviews with people that I've read, startlingly to my mind…I read something about Alex Lifeson saying Rush decided to do the last album they did mostly live, and he was kind of astounded that he was enjoying being in the studio playing with Neal Peart at the same time, and I thought, 'Wait a minute, that's how it's supposed to be! Where did you go so far off track?' I hear an album like Richard Thompson's newest effort, and you know its all been played together. *(Laughs)*. Maybe that's wrong, but it sounds like it. At least they've come up with the right result in the end.

SW: When Gentle Giant decided to split up, what prompted that?

GG: Derek and Kerry didn't want to tour anymore. By 1980 I think all of us were married except perhaps Ray, who had been married early on in the band, got divorced and then was single I think until 1981. I think he got married after Giant split up, but in any case he had a girlfriend and they were to be married, so for all intents and purposes everyone in the band was married.

And Kerry had just had his first daughter, and Derek had had his first daughter, and they were both feeling the pinch of being away and not seeing them grow up. And that's not a good thing. That's very hard. They both didn't want to tour from that point of view.

They both enjoyed playing, there's no doubt about that. But the family aspect of it, plus the fact that we had not gotten the kind of success that I think

Derek had really hoped that we would get, and felt that he was able to have, so he then felt that he should start getting on with his life and go into the record business. Which he did, and has done very well, as you know.

And really, that was the end of the band. We felt that perhaps the three of us, John, Ray and I could have continued on, but it wouldn't have been Gentle Giant. There was no way of replacing Kerry or Derek, and it was not that kind of band. I don't think that if any one of us had left, it would have continued on. I think we all felt committed enough to each other that this was the band, and if there was going to be personnel changes, then this wouldn't be the band anymore. So that was it.

And it had been ten years, and like I said, we felt that perhaps we're not going to be able to do this huge success thing. But I don't know, I wish we could have continued making studio albums. I don't know what the viability of that would have been, if record companies would even allow you to do that. Having said that, that's stupid; you can record whatever you like and put it out, and I'm sure there would be a market for it. XTC managed to do it pretty well. I think a lot of bands can do that.

That's something I would like to be able to do, is record and put albums out. And I'd like to tour, but it would be nice if you could sell enough records that you wouldn't need to. So the answer is yes, sure I would like to. That's what this band, Big Hello, is looking to do.

I'm hoping that we can change the music a little bit to become more musically interesting; it's really simple right now, and I'd like that to change. It has to be more musical for me. I'm playing a lot of three chord stuff, and I like it, and it's great fun doing it live. While you're doing it, it's a lot of fun, but when you come off stage and you get home and you're thinking about it, you wonder what it is that you're doing. It's wonderful when you're doing it, but it gives you doubts when you're away from it, and I'd rather not have those doubts. I'd rather be thinking more positive things about it.

SW: Well, good luck with it.

GG: Thank you. I think it will be good. We're putting out a CD on a label down in Champaign, Illinois called Parasol, which I think goes all over the world. This is power pop, I think, and the guy liked it enough that he's going to stick it out. It's not a real big deal, but we'll have a CD of it. And there's a lot of things...because technology is so available, it's getting cheaper and cheaper all the time, a lot of people have fairly serviceable studios anymore. So there's great possibilities for lots of good music to come out of all this technological wave. Of course, it's happened.

SW: I think already a lot of the indy labels are beating the major labels in the quality of the music they put out. The majors are still playing a big numbers game, and because of that they just wind up signing bands that sound like music that's already out there and doing well.

GG: But there's always room for good music. I'm just entirely optimistic about music and my role in it, and what I can do in the future, because there's always room at the top! *(Laughs)*.

KISS HIM GOODBYE

Bruce Kulick is the longest-serving guitarist in the history of the superstar rock group KISS. In his eleven-year stint with the group, the guitarist performed on such hit records as 'Animalize', 'Hot In The Shade' and 'Crazy Nights'. He was featured in a solo on one of the band's biggest hit singles, the power ballad "Forever".

Prior to his time with KISS, Kulick had served his rock and roll apprenticeship on the road with Meat Loaf on the 'Bat Out Of Hell' tour, as well as playing with Billy Squier. He had also recorded two albums with his own band Blackjack, a hard rock group which featured a little-known singer named Michael Bolton.

I spoke with Bruce Kulick during a time of change for KISS. The band had recently released 'Revenge', easily the best KISS album of his tenure, and had undertaken a series of conventions, which led to the idea for an MTV Unplugged episode. At the time of this interview the MTV Unplugged episode had been taped but not yet aired; already KISS fans the world over were buzzing over the fact that original guitarist Ace Frehley and drummer Peter Criss had participated in the taping. The rumors were flying that the original band would reunite and again don makeup for a full-blown world tour, but Kulick was not concerned; he had heard those rumors ever since joining, and dismissed these as just more of the same.

As it turned out, shortly after this interview took place, the original KISS did indeed reunite, and Kulick was released from his contract. Not long after the announcement was made, I received an unexpected call from the guitarist late one night, well past midnight. He was calling to inquire about the status of this book, which was mired in delay. "I'm really looking forward to this coming out," he said somewhat morosely. "Now I feel more unsung than ever."

I was surprised that Kulick had remained largely unrecognized, despite his years of effort in a top-selling band. But, when I made my initial inquiry about an interview for this book, I directed my call to the Director of Publicity for Mercury Records, explaining that I was checking on the availability of Bruce Kulick. I was stunned at her reaction.

"Who is that?" she snapped. "I don't even know who you're talking about." Although somewhat aggrieved by her rude tone, I patiently asked her if she knew who KISS was. Again, she reacted with borderline hostility. "Of course I know who KISS is," she said loftily. "They're one of the best-selling bands on this label."

"That they are," I replied. "And Bruce Kulick has been their lead guitarist for almost a dozen years. Perhaps you ought to write that down somewhere." In typical record company fashion, she dealt only with the principals of the band, Gene Simmons and Paul Stanley. Suddenly I knew why I was having to include Bruce Kulick in a book entitled 'Unsung Heroes of Rock Guitar'.

SW: You just finished doing a Kiss convention tour. How did that come about?

BK: It was really through the fans, in the sense that there have been Kiss conventions going on for about ten years, maybe even longer. Gene knows the first date; I don't. The fans would show up in hotel ballrooms and they would trade, and they would share whatever they had, show slide shows or whatever, because so much stuff of the band has been bootlegged through the years.

They can't get enough of us, and that's very flattering. They want every performance, anytime. *Anything.* When we were researching for our own videotape after the tribute album was put out, on some of the video stuff I think some of the fans had a better generation than we did, believe it or not. *(Laughs).* It was kind of funny. So we have this fan base that has a thirst that probably can never be satisfied. *(Laughter).* They're into collecting and cataloguing it all like no other—there's even a Kiss book on prices for memorabilia.

So I think the band realized, especially Gene—he's always been so proud of the band, and he always kept everything from day one. He still has the Village Voice ad from when he and Paul were looking for the other members. Tucked away in his mom's basement is everything from the history of the band. One of those things—not at his mom's house, obviously, but at a warehouse *(laughs)*—is the costumes. I remember him mentioning ten years ago that this was something we could show, and I didn't really get it at the time. Back then it wouldn't have meant that much, but now it does. You add another decade, and all of a sudden things start to look a bit more interesting, even more fascinating than ever. So who better to put on a convention than the band?

We wanted to celebrate the whole past and present of the band. We actually had costumes on display. We even had one set of costumes from the 1985 *Asylum* tour, which were really silly-looking. *(Laughter).* But that's cool, because it was part of that glam era. We all looked a bit glittered out. We wanted to show the fans everything, like a Kiss museum of sorts.

Actually being there and answering their questions was the unique part, because anybody could do a traveling museum. It's been done a lot, especially after people die. They took the Liberace museum on the road, for instance, and people go to Memphis to see Elvis Presley's Graceland, which is fascinating. But to actually have the chance to go one-on-one with the band and ask whatever you want, besides all the stuff you get to see, and maybe buy and swap—and on top of that, we did an acoustic performance.

Obviously, to do a regular concert would be impossible. You can't do that in a hotel ballroom. So we did a loosely structured show; although we got really good with knowing a lot of songs in an unplugged version, it was still very loose in the sense that we took requests, and sometimes we'd only try a chorus and a verse because nobody really remembered it. *(Laughs).*

SW: What was the most unusual song request you got?

BK: Sometimes they would ask for stuff from the solo records. And *The Elder*—which actually sold the least records in the history of the band—has some very strong die-hards, real core Kiss maniacs.

SW: Personally, I really like quite a bit of *The Elder.* It really showed a different side to the band. I think some of the hard rock fans just didn't want to hear Kiss attempt a more progressive rock style.

BK: *The Elder* wasn't a bad record. Kiss just maybe wasn't the right band to do that kind of a record, and maybe not at that time. I wasn't there to speak personally, but just from what I can tell, at that point the band was going through a lot of changes. Some of the fans would love to hear a whole concert of *The Elder* material.

As for weird song requests, I don't know every Kiss song. I can't, because there's just too many. Occasionally people even requested songs that were pre-Kiss, which didn't make any sense, obviously, so we didn't do it.

SW: Are you referring to Wicked Lester, the band Gene and Paul had before Kiss?

BK: Right. We were like, "No thank you". *(Laughter)*. But even if we couldn't do everything that they asked for, we saw a lot of similar requests, so we were able to handle all of them as best we could. We weren't going to do a whole set of unprepared material. That's not exactly worth the admission. We wanted to have some substance, so the band would know what we're playing and singing. So we threw the rest in for fun; no request too wacky. We just tried to do whatever we could.

What was really wild was the question and answer session. We got really crazy stuff like, "Can I have one of the hairs from your chest, Paul?" *(Laughter)*. Really weird stuff. Some people had testimonials, and some had really good questions. Some of it was just total adoration, which is cool, but it doesn't get anything answered. But it was really successful, and the kids really enjoyed it.

I shouldn't say *kids*. We really have different generations; we have professionals, and we have teenagers, and little toddlers come along with their parents. We seem to be getting whole families. We didn't think people would want to bring their children, so we didn't think about it, but we certainly don't want to charge admission for a little kid. Sometimes we said, "If you have a kid that you left at home, go get them."

I realized how powerful the band and music can be, especially to a youngster. Maybe a twenty-year-old, sweaty, screaming fan is our hardcore fan, but what really gets you in the heart is when you see some seven-year-old saying, "Can I have a guitar pick?" And they have the big eyes. *(Laughs)*. We had some even younger. It's just amazing. The kids know the songs.

In fact, we had a seven-year-old kid in Detroit get up and play drums with us. We didn't let other people up—we did let them sing, though. We passed around some wireless mics and let them sing along with us, and we backed them up, which was a lot of fun. But this kid could really play drums, and he got up and did "Do You Love Me". And his sister, who is ten, came up and sang "Let's Put The X In Sex", and did all the moves that Paul did in the video and everything. It was hilarious.

That happened to be the night that MTV came out to see whether this was something they wanted to be involved in. They weren't sure if they wanted to do an *Unplugged* with Kiss. They were really blown away by what they saw, and it didn't hurt, because we're still kind of a black sheep. We get all this respect from the fans, but on the other hand, it's a very controversial group to be a part of. That puts me in an awkward position at times. The band in general always has to ignore the critics; if they want to talk about us, fine. If they don't, fine. This is about the fans with us.

It's really similar to the Grateful Dead, but with hard rock, even though this band has done so many other styles. And the Grateful Dead, of course, has always had that hippie following. Their cultural niche is very defined, whereas with Kiss it's more just rock and roll, and standing up for what you believe in, "Don't-take-shit-from-anybody" kind of thing, without a lot of posturing, although maybe we've been guilty of some of that, too, through the years. *(Laughs)*.

I'm always humbled by our fans. Their dedication is extreme. And there's all these issues of the old band versus the new band, or Kiss in makeup versus Kiss in '95…

SW: Speaking of which, Ace and Peter took some part in these conventions in a couple of locations, didn't they?

BK: The offer was always for either one of them to come in and sit in if they wanted to. Peter took the opportunity when we were in LA; he lives here in LA. He actually came in and sang two songs, which was very cool. Ace didn't, whether he wanted to or not, or whether it was just because of his schedule. But when it came down to MTV asking about an *Unplugged* and Gene once again extended the opportunity, they both decided it would be a great thing for everybody to be involved.

SW: How did it come off in terms of personalities? Is there any remaining conflict between the original four members, or between Ace and Peter and Eric and yourself?

BK: I think that, like in a divorce, it's a little awkward for both Peter and Ace. Peter seems a little uncomfortable, because we know there have been times when he was very unhappy with or angry at Gene and Paul. Obviously, Ace and Peter don't have any personal gripes with me or Eric except that we're in the band and they're not. But it is awkward for them.

I have a lot of respect for Ace, and I know Ace respects my playing, but it was still a little strange, because there we were trading riffs. But we made the best of it. We made it fun. I think it was harder for Ace to come in, because he hadn't really been in touch with Gene and Paul, while Peter had already come to the conventions. But there we were; after the first day of rehearsals we all climbed into a car together and drove back to the hotel. *(Laughs)*. All six of us in this big car! It was pretty funny. Paul was driving, and I thought that was worth a picture. I hope some fan got one, because there were some fans outside while we were all piling into the car.

There is some tension, and it's understandable. It's interesting for me to observe it. It's just like life; any partnership that dissolves, or any marriage that ends in divorce, is a little awkward. But ultimately the goal was to have that special moment, play together and be professional, and everyone was extremely so, so it came off well.

Obviously, it just stirs up the old thing of, "There's going to be a Kiss reunion! When? Where? Why?" Sometimes people have really intelligent viewpoints, and sometimes they're completely warped. But they're entitled to say whatever they like, and the band's only going to do whatever the band feels like it wants to do. And I know that unfortunately—even though it was a great thing, with those guys coming out and all six of us playing—the downside is that everyone's going to talk. Maybe they're misconstruing things, and maybe they're going to talk about things that aren't true.

SW: It seems like for the past few years, hardly a couple of months goes by without one of the rock magazines printing that Kiss is currently rehearsing for a full-blown reunion tour with the original members in makeup. *(Laughs)*

BK: Oh, yeah. *(Laughs)*. I'm already hearing things about us doing *Unplugged* with only the original guys in makeup. *(Laughs)*. A year ago, just before we went to South America, one of the English papers, *Kerrang*—I like that magazine, actually—reported that I left the band to spend more time with my wife, and that Steve Stevens from Billy Idol's band was replacing me. They did say that they thought it was just a rumor, but still, it was in print, so that always makes it more than just a rumor. We got a good page out of it, though, because then Gene called up and did some press about what was going on.

So we're always hearing these things, and you can't control that. I realize that. I'm planning on getting a computer soon, so of course I'd like America Online or one of those services. I'll go in and read the stuff, and Gene's been doing it some. But you have to realize you can't believe everything you see.

SW: The Internet is a double-edged sword for bands in some ways. You're able to interact more closely with the fans, but a lot of it is just high-tech gossip. *(Laughter)*.

BK: It's so much gossip, it's unbelievable. And everybody loves a little dish or a little gossip once in a while, but when you read it and you know the truth, it's a little weird. It's sometimes tough for present members like myself and Eric—and maybe more so for me, because I've been there so long already.

SW: A lot of the fans don't take the time to stop and realize that you're actually the longest-lasting guitarist in Kiss history.

BK: Right. It'll be eleven years in September. But at least the fans are still talking about this band. They might argue about what direction we should go in, and they're always going to have their opinions. Our last studio album, *Revenge* in '92, really made a lot of Kiss fans proud, because very rarely does a band that's twenty years into its career make a valid album that they can be proud of. I wish I could say that about certain bands that I'm into.

But the last couple of things we've put out weren't new material, so it just fuels the argument, "Oh, they're just biding time for the reunion," and stuff like that. There's so much speculation, and quite honestly, the only reason that we haven't put out another studio record is because we weren't ready. A lot of other things were coming our way. We put out a live record, and that was a long time coming. And then there was the tribute album. I can't imagine the band doing that ten years ago—of course not! But at this point, Kiss was a band that was primed for that.

Eddie Kramer was starting to put together the Hendrix tribute record while we were doing *Alive III*, and I was fascinated by who was doing what. I heard McCartney was going to do a track, and Clapton, all these different people, and as usual a lot of people didn't in the end. And we got hit with that really bad, too, but at least the time was right to do it.

And then we got offers to headline this stadium tour called the Monsters of Rock in South America and Chile, and then we went to Australia right after that, and Japan. So we've been very busy, but because we haven't had a record out, it just fuels rumors.

We're real confident with our new songs, and anxious to get going. We would have been in the studio earlier, but the guy that we want to record with needed a little more time. So we'll start in October and that will quiet everybody down, and when the record comes out next year, hopefully they'll all be into it just like *Revenge*.

SW: How long does it generally take you to do a record?

BK: It's got to take two months, and that might include the mix. *Revenge* took a long time because we did it in segments, and we were writing a lot in the studio, which we don't want to do this time. That's another reason we've been waiting—most of the stuff that I wrote with Paul was all produced and arranged in demos in my home studio, and it sounds great. I'm going to have demo-itis, I just know it. *(Laughs)*. I have a real nice sixteen track.

There are more and more people getting into their home studios, but I'm the only one in the band that has any patience for buttons. *(Laughs)*. Gene and Paul have never been technologically friendly, I guess, so they never got into it. I know the difference between what sounds good and what doesn't, and I just go for it. We spent a lot of time working on that stuff, and then Gene's material is a little more loosely structured—which is going to give us some flexibility—but I still know basically what we were doing. It's going to be great to finally get in the studio. I'm very anxious to do that. It will shut people up who think we're just biding time for something different.

SW: Do you rehearse before going in so that you're already tight on the songs when you get to the studio?

BK: Yes. We won't have to rehearse as much as other times, because Eric played on all the tracks already, and I played guitar on all the tracks. So we won't need a lot of rehearsal. We really spent a lot of time on the arrangements before we recorded the demos. That's one of the great things about having a studio in the house. It's improved so much, and the price has dropped so much…

SW: A growing number of artists aren't even going to commercial studios anymore.

BK: Because of our reputation, we've got to do a huge 48-track production, but if this were a new band, I could probably do it at home and tweak it and put it out. I'm happy enough with the sound. A lot of bands are doing that now on ADAT or whatever. I like analog better, because I'm an old-fashioned guitar player. I like the warmth and the more distorted sounds, not the digital, clean sounds.

What we were doing on *Revenge* was really a return to our roots, and I was pulling out all of my pedals from the Seventies. And now that sound is so big... I'm not saying I spearheaded it, but I certainly realized that a lot of the material was nasty-sounding, and rack effects weren't going to make it sound right. I didn't have a rack, but I was used to being in the studio and saying, "Okay, put a little Harmonizer on it." And that worked on some records, but it was totally the wrong approach for *Revenge*.

I had a Distortion Plus on the floor, and my vintage wah-wah, and a lot of other pedals that were very, very strange. I've never had so much noise coming out of my guitar! *(Laughs).* But we made it work. One of the things I always tell people when I do clinics is that when you plug into a big Marshall amp, if you don't have mastery of your instrument, it's really going to show. Every little finger noise is going to be a lot louder and more obvious through a hundred watt stack. When you make all that work for you, it becomes part of your sound—like Hendrix did, who was one of my big heroes. Then it becomes part of your expression.

Of course, Hendrix did it with a lot of pedals that were, in some ways, kind of cheap and funky. Making all of it work is kind of like painting with colors—choosing the right kind of chorus and flange and distortion. Even the order that they're put in will affect the sound. It's almost like alchemy, turning all of that into something special. And obviously, he's one guy that I've learned a lot from. I'm convinced that if you put the same rig in someone else's hands, it would have been very obnoxious. *(Laughter).*

SW: Do you enjoy doing guitar clinics?

BK: Yes. At the conventions, both the drummer and I did clinics, which is something I've done before on behalf of Marshall or ESP Guitars. It's a good way for me to get one-on-one and for people to get to know me, as opposed to just thinking of me as the quiet guitar player in the band. *(Laughs).* Obviously if you do that at a music store or a guitar show, you've got a lot of guitar freaks there already, but this was in the middle of all that Kiss mania. It was interesting and a lot of fun. They'd ask me to play solos, and sometimes I wouldn't even remember any part of the solo! *(Laughter).* They'd help me out: "It's in the key of G." And it would pop into my head and maybe I'd be able to play part of it. It's funny, because they know every one, but I can't remember everything unless I review it.

I enjoy that a lot. It's like a mini-concert. I've done a couple at the Musician's Institute here in LA, and I actually brought in a bass player and drummer and jammed on a couple of songs. Anytime I do that kind of stuff, it's fun. It's not the same as the band—I always feel even taller and bigger when I'm onstage with

Kiss—but it's a chance to say, "This is me, this is what I can do." I take a lot of pride in that.

SW: What have you learned about playing guitar from being in Kiss?

BK: Playing guitar is an ongoing learning experience; it's kind of like being a cat and landing on your feet at all times, no matter what happens. The power goes out, you break a string, you fall—whatever it is, you've got to learn how to be flexible enough to get back on your feet like a professional. Obviously I had quite a bit of training before I joined the band, but now it's like I'm in college, going for my Master's. *(Laughs)*. I'm always learning something.

I always tell kids not to stay in their bedroom and play. There's a lot of guys who play in their bedroom and never leave the house, and sometimes they sound great, but they can't even jam with anybody because they've never done it.

SW: You can't learn how to play in time from a metronome, because in a live playing situation, the tempo isn't perfectly consistent. You've got to learn how to stay in the pocket even if the beat accelerates or slows down, and that's a lesson you can only learn from experience.

BK: You learn so much from playing with other people, even if they're way better than you, or even if they're worse than you. Obviously, it's better if they're more advanced than you are. I've played with some guys that are Julliard graduates, and I always felt very intimidated. But they loved my playing because I had that real rock feel, even though they were consummate jazz players. That really helped me, and made me strive for playing better.

But this isn't just about music. Being a guitarist is more than that. Sometimes it's the show and the attitude, and I've always struggled with that in the sense that I was always into music just for the music, and here I am in a band that's famous for the whole performance.

SW: Kiss is a concept unto itself in that way.

BK: Exactly. And we've done enough gigs lately to show people how well we play together where we didn't have the pyro and the lasers and the bombs. When we have it, it's *really* great. *(Laughs)*. I know people were blown away when we did the club tour. We played great, and it was so much fun. I was just as nervous there as I would be in front of a hundred thousand people, maybe even more so.

SW: Are you prone to stage fright and nerves?

BK: I get a little anxious before certain shows. Sometimes I don't care as much because I'm already in the groove of it all. But that first gig when you've been off for a little while, there's always a little anxiety. You spend your whole day preparing for that couple of hours of playing.

I've learned so much about performing by being in this band, even though I don't think anyone expects me to light my hair on fire! *(Laughter)*. You know, Gene spits fire, and Paul dances and plays guitar, and I find that if I get too wild, I don't play well and the music suffers. I think I give them the freedom to be able to do what they do by being entertaining, but at the same time making sure that I'm playing.

SW: Even though Paul is an accomplished rhythm player, I've noticed many times that he'll take his hands off the guitar to make some sort of gesture, and you'll be left to carry the weight of the guitar playing in the song.

BK: Right. And as long as I'm embracing the crowd, I always get a great reaction from them. I think that they know that I'm really into playing guitar onstage. I always think the pictures are funny when I see them. At the conventions there were some guys selling photos—guys who run fanzines and stuff like that—and in one of the most popular ones, I look like someone is sticking something up my butt. (*Laughter*). That's the way it looks to me! And I wondered why anyone would be attracted to that, but really, it looks like I'm just so into what I'm playing, and my face is just distorted and contorted from this moment that's been captured. And to me it looks like it hurts!

I sing everything that I play in my head; it's kind of a weird process. You can see my lower jaw moving when I'm playing a lead, but I'm not conscious of it when it's happening. So it's interesting that they like these wild-looking poses, but I guess they're into showing your emotions.

SW: What do you think of the Kiss tribute bands that are out there?

BK: It makes us feel good because it shows there's a lot of respect for the band. We've seen some that are really good, and some that are really bad. Part of the appeal of the band in the makeup is that they're wearing a mask. You turn into something else. You could be physically wrong or even facially wrong, but as soon as you're painted and in costume, everybody looks the part. It's kind of like Halloween. Some of these bands out of costume don't seem like they look right, but then they get in the makeup and it's surprising how believable it is.

It's very hard to do Paul. There are a couple of good Genes—there's one guy that's really good at Gene that traveled with us on the convention tour. The guy that does Ace well also works with us sometimes. So there's a couple of bands that are really good at it. It's very flattering, and obviously Gene and Paul, especially, get a big kick out of it. Some of these bands have the money where the costumes are really cool, and some of them you can tell they threw it together with aluminum foil, but it's all in the spirit of the thing.

SW: Let's talk about your musical background. How did you first become interested in the guitar?

BK: It seemed like there was always music in the family; my cousins played piano, and my uncle played violin. Everybody played a little bit of something, but no one made a career out of it. For some reason, I don't know what artist he liked, but my older brother, Bob, suddenly had a guitar in the house. It was just a cheap acoustic. Nylon strings back then, actually.

I was born in '53, so by the time I was ten in 1963 the Beatles hit in America, and I was definitely bitten right there. And at the same time, since my brother was older, he would get into some bands that I probably wouldn't have been exposed to, like the Yardbirds. He even knew Hendrix in the Village back before Hendrix was famous. So I was constantly exposed to some stuff as I was growing up that was really hip. I was into the Stones when maybe my friends were into the Monkees or whatever. So I really had a great opportunity, and it's the same things with Kiss fans. A lot of them, their older brother or someone turned them on to it, and they're still into it now.

First I learned a couple of chords from my brother, and then I took lessons down at the local record shop. They actually had a guy teaching guitar there, and he was impressed that I already knew some stuff. And I just took it from there. It was always very natural for me, and I just kept playing.

When we moved to Queens, I remember starting to play with people in junior high, and when there would be show and tell or entertainment, I would perform. I don't remember what I played or who I played with, but I remember it was great because you'd get out of a couple of classes! (Laughs).

I don't feel like it was just about meeting girls, even though it didn't hurt. I was able to play "Yesterday" and swoon some girls that I liked, which definitely went down. But it also made me a bit of an outcast. All these kids would be in cliques that I didn't feel like I fit into, and they would pick on me because I was kind of a loner. I was just into my guitar, and whatever girl I was dating or trying to meet. I didn't care about sports or the macho clique thing or hanging out.

I always felt a little bit isolated, but I was never lonely, because of the music. I was so into Hendrix, and then when Zeppelin came along, I knew I was hearing something incredible. In fact, Paul Stanley and I experienced many of the same concerts back then. We were at the same concerts—we didn't know each other, but he grew up about ten minutes away from me. Gene also, although I don't think Gene was a big concertgoer. He just knew he wanted to be a musician. But Paul and I both saw Zeppelin at the World's Fair Pavilion in 1969, and it was amazing.

I saw Hendrix at the Garden. I even bootlegged him. I still have the tape, too. I transferred it to DAT not too long ago with Eddie Kramer. I was really into the whole music scene. Living in New York, it was very easy. The access was there. By then I was old enough to have a friend that drove, and I'd go to a late show and come in at four in the morning. I was totally consumed with guitars.

SW: What was the first band you played in?

BK: I didn't actually play lead guitar in a band first. I was in a high school band where I played bass. I really loved Jack Bruce, and I thought, 'My brother's a guitar player, so I'll be a bass player.' I have some old tapes of us jamming that are pretty funny. It always sounded really good through a tape recorder. We would plug straight into a reel-to-reel and it would get kinda distorted, so we thought it sounded great. (Laughs). And my hands got stronger that way. At first I didn't play lead guitar very well because I didn't have the strength, so by playing bass I built up some power. That improved my ability; I would practice lead guitar at home, and then people would say, "You're a better guitar player than the guy in the band." So that's when I switched to guitar.

I moved on from there and started to get involved with different bands that could play and make some money, and at the same time I started to go to Queens College, and they had a good music program there. They didn't accept guitar playing as anything there—not that I was really trained; I was very knowledgeable, but I wasn't technically trained. And unless you play classical guitar, they don't know what it means.

That made me learn piano, which I picked up pretty quickly. I learned how to read and play simple Bach pieces, and I got turned on to Chopin and Stravinsky, and all of a sudden this whole world opened up to me. But I got fed up with college after two years. I wanted to be able to gig. I wasn't doing anything big in any bands, but I realized if I was in college I wouldn't be able to gig and do what I wanted to do. I also felt stifled by the whole classical angle of the school. I enjoyed having my mind opened to it, but I knew I wanted to follow the current music scene, as opposed to just studying the classics.

So I left school and as part of a compromise with my parents, because they didn't want me to just be an idiot, I started taking jazz lessons, which was very intense. That opened my mind in a whole different way. By then Jeff Beck was doing stuff like *Blow By Blow*, and I didn't understand some of the chords he was using. I realized how cool jazz can be. Not that I wanted to be a jazz musician, but I was really embracing all different kinds of music. I could really dig playing a Chopin piece on piano, but then I'd want to learn how Joe Pass did this solo version of a jazz song. I realized that if I wanted to be able to play, I needed to get some chops going.

SW: At what point did you start earning your living from music?

BK: The first bands that I started making money from were top forty dance bands, but the stuff I really liked playing was Steely Dan. This was when disco started to take off, and there I was, a rock guitarist stuck in a disco/top forty type of thing. But that was a challenge; I played either a Strat or an SG through a little Fender Reverb, and I realized then that I had a good enough ear to figure out most guitar players' leads, so that kept me very versatile for the band. I felt like I had a good ear to choose songs; if we were going to do a Hall and Oates song, I'd have an idea which one would be good for us to play.

From there I hooked up with a guy named George McCray, and this is funny because it's so non-rock and roll. He had a big disco hit called "Rock You Baby", which was a number one hit in Germany and America, and I got an offer to go on tour with him, so I did. *(Laughs)*. It was funny, but it was really good experience. I went to Europe, and he actually got their equivalent of a Grammy award, so we went on Radio Luxembourg and played live with a whole orchestra and choir, playing his big disco hit. *(Laughter)*. I still have a copy of that.

That was 1975, and I didn't really know Kiss then, although my brother had met Gene and Paul. He happened to have auditioned when they were looking for a guitar player in '73, when they got Ace. They started to take off in '75 or '76, so I knew of them, but only vaguely. At that point my brother started running into them a little bit more, because he was a session guitarist in New York. He started helping out, doing a little bit of ghost guitar work for them on *Alive II* and then on Paul's solo record. So he had that Kiss connection, which would later obviously make it easier for me to get the opportunity with them.

But back in 1975 and '76, all I cared about was getting some chops. I was just trying to learn to play and have the experience traveling and all of that. When I came back off the road from those disco things, I really wanted to do a rock gig, and that's when Bob auditioned for and got the Meat Loaf gig. They wanted dual guitarists, so I went in, and at first I don't think they were that impressed with me.

I ultimately got the gig, and the two of us did the dual guitar work, but there was something about the Meat Loaf gig that always bothered me. It was a lot of work for very little money, let's put it that way. And there was a lot of aggravation, because Meat Loaf back then was like Baby Huey on drugs. He was very difficult, and that's part of why he had such a bad time after that record. And part of why he's done so well recently is because he's really straightened himself out. He doesn't act like a maniac anymore.

That gig was very exciting, though. I remember being really touched by playing Queens College. I had gone there for a couple of years, so doing the gig there was very exciting. And that *Bat Out Of Hell* album was really huge, especially on the East Coast. I remember going out to California, and that was the one state where we wouldn't sell out the arenas. Everywhere on the East Coast, we were playing gigantic places. It was good experience. That's the first time I really understood big arena touring, and it whetted my appetite for what came after.

SW: Was that around the time you worked with Michael Bolton?

BK: I was pretty blown out after the Meat Loaf gig, but this guy—Michael *Bolotin* at that point, who later became Michael Bolton—he was a really talented singer from New Haven, and occasionally my brother and I would go out and back him on a couple of gigs. We'd do some covers and some of his original songs. He was working on putting together a solo deal, actually; he'd met this lawyer, Steve Weiss, who dealt with the business management of Led Zeppelin, which obviously meant some clout.

Michael was shopping a tape at the time that only had a couple of songs on it, but they were really good. They were kind of in the Bad Company vein, and at the time, Bad Company was huge. Michael was looking for people to work with, and I really wanted to do it, so the next thing I knew, we were rehearsing and auditioning for the record company. Coming right out of the Meat Loaf gig, it was good timing for me to be involved with that.

That turned into Blackjack, and we got a record deal. Again, it was a difficult time in the business sense. The music was always fun, but the business end was aggravating, with the record company always telling us who to record with. But I got to work with Tom Dowd, who was a legend to me from all the work he did with Clapton. We went down to Miami to record the album, and it was a very exciting time.

The first album had quite a big buzz about it, but it didn't go gold like the record company expected, in a month. *(Laughs).* Things were getting really crazy, and certain people's egos were really on the line in their corporate structure, and it had nothing to do with the music. It was a situation where I was writing all of the songs with Michael, and I really felt good about being part of a band, and to have people tell you what to do and try to control that…it was a real learning experience.

I always try to explain to people that there's music, and then there's the music business. That side of it is very weird, and there's a lot to learn about it. I really respect bands that just do it their way and don't care what anyone else says or does. And really, that's what Kiss does now. We don't ask the label who should record us, or what we should record. We don't have to. But that's what Blackjack had to go through.

We were able to do two records. I think the second record was purely contractual, otherwise they would have already dropped us. *(Laughs)*. The guy that signed us was fired within a year, so that was history. But we did some exciting gigs. We did a whole leg of a tour with Peter Frampton, which was a lot of fun. That was after his big live record, around '79.

So there were good things that came out of that, and once it ended, I had to decide what I wanted to do. I didn't know if I wanted to start my own band, or hook up with someone else, or what I wanted to do. There was a band called the Good Rats that was really popular in the tri-state area around New York and Jersey, and they were changing some members, so they asked me to join. I didn't want to deal with the music business anymore; I just wanted to be in a band where I could go and play a couple of sets a night, get paid and go home. *(Laughs)*.

I can't say I regret it, but I now realize I was taking kind of a beaten-up position at the time; instead of trying to forge ahead and pushing on, I retreated. I felt so burned from Blackjack—not from Michael, but from what we both experienced, which was incredible hype and then they drop you like a pancake. *(Laughs)*. I didn't want to deal with it anymore, so I did that gig for two years, and in that time I was really continuing to hone my chops and my sound and my ability.

Michael at that time was writing songs and trying to score a solo deal. That's when he changed his name to Michael Bolton. He called me up and said, "I'm going to tour with Bob Seger and do a record. Do you want to do that?" And I went, "Yeah." *(Laughs)*. "I'm ready."

It was a little awkward, because before we were more like equals in Blackjack, and now I was just going to be his lead guitarist, but I still knew that it was the right thing to do. So we toured with Bob Seger and we did some other gigs. We did the King Biscuit Flower Hour. I have that on tape. In fact, we did a couple of Blackjack songs, which was fun.

And then MTV started playing Michael's song "Fool's Game", which was from that first record, and I played on that record. He didn't really take off until later, after he became more of a pop/R&B singer, less of a rock singer. But I did a couple of records with him, which kept me busy.

Right at the end of Blackjack I did a Billy Squier album. He had just left Piper and gotten a solo deal with Capitol, and I did an album with him called *Tale Of The Tape*. I played guitar on that, and by his next record, he was huge.

He actually wanted me to play with him, but I still had some obligations to Blackjack, and that was my band, so I didn't want to say no to that. So I stuck with Blackjack and we got dropped, and I was kicking myself for a while there. But if I had been busy with Billy Squier, I might not have been able to walk into Kiss so easily.

SW: When did you first work with Kiss?

BK: In 1983 I was helping Michael out, and then in '84 I got the call from Paul Stanley. It was funny, too, because it was a holiday weekend, and at the time I was back at my mom's house, regrouping my life. I looked at the answering machine, and it looked like it said zero messages. As it turned out, it said twenty! *(Laughs)*. He tried calling twenty times.

So he woke me up the next morning and said, "Can you help out with a song in the studio? I'm at the studio right now. Come on down." This guy named Mitch Weissman, who worked with the band a little bit, was always a fan of mine. He knew I was a good guitarist, and they'd already used my brother enough to help out, so they figured that I would be a good guy to come in and help out with the song.

They had just gotten Mark St. John in the band, who was only in for a very brief time. He's a talented guy, but I think they got him for the wrong reasons. He was really into Allan Holdsworth and that kind of music, which I didn't think was going to fit into Kiss. But they wanted a real gunslinger that could really play, and he was a powerful lead guitarist, even though his approach was more fusion than what I think Kiss is based on, which is more blues and rock and roll.

I don't know if Paul wasn't happy with what he was playing on the song, or if that's when Mark started to get sick, but he asked me to help out. So I came in, and he liked what I played. I had a Floyd Rose vibrato bar, and back in 1984 you were on the cutting edge if you had that. So I remember Paul saying, "Don't cut your hair." My hair was long, but it wasn't really long yet. I didn't know why he said that, but as it turned out, about six weeks later he said, "This guy is sick, and we're doing a European tour. We're not going to stop and wait, so why don't you come on in and rehearse with us?"

So I started working with them, and in fact, I was rehearsing so hard and trying to get in shape for the tour that I pulled a nerve in my arm and missed two weeks of rehearsal! *(Laughs)*. I was thinking, 'How stupid can I be? How can I blow this?' But I followed what the doctor said and took care of myself. I had light strings on the guitar when I got back into it, but I was ready to go. *(Laughter)*.

Off we went to Europe, and it really started to click. We were all getting along and playing well together, and I realized they were going to ask me to join, even if they tried to give Mark a shot. I never felt evil about it, like I was trying to take anything away from him; I was just trying to show them I was a hard-working guy and I was into the gig. And I was rewarded with being asked to join the band. It was kind of an odd way to get in, but that's the way it happened. And here we are, eleven years later.

SW: You came into the band in an unstable period, and you were the third guitarist in rapid succession—first Vinnie Vincent replaced Ace, and then he was soon gone, and then Mark St. John came and went quickly because of his illness, and suddenly you were in. What kind of reaction did you get from the fans?

BK: At first there was a lot of confusion as to who I was. The true Kiss fans knew I wasn't Ace, and they knew I wasn't Vinnie, but they weren't sure if I was Mark or what was going on. It was a little confusing, because we never made a big statement about it initially, especially in America. The European press was told something like, "Former Blackjack guitarist Bruce Kulick will be filling in for an ailing Mark St. John." I remember the clippings from that. So the kids over there that read *Kerrang* knew all about it.

In America, the lead time on the magazines is about two months, so nothing could get into *Circus* or *Creem* or whatever to say, "Bruce is filling in; although he may not be an official member of the band, this is who you're going to see." And a lot of kids would just say, "There's a rock show in town; let's go!" As long as they were entertained, they were happy. They didn't care who I was.

The die-hard Kiss fans were really pleased, because as much as they knew Vinnie was talented and he wrote good songs, they never bought him in Kiss. They never felt it was right.

SW: He didn't sound good on the older material at all.

BK: I don't think he even attempted to, which was a real slap in the face to the Kiss fans.

SW: I remember seeing the band with Vinnie. I was still pretty young, not more than twelve or thirteen, and he started playing "Detroit Rock City", but he was playing the opening riff way up high instead of down in the lower strings like it is on the record, and it sounded horrible! *(Laughs)*. I wasn't even sure at first what song he was playing.

BK: I have some live tapes of him that they gave me when I first had to learn the show. I was mortified by what I was hearing. I really wish they'd just had me learn parts from *Alive* and *Alive II*, and then maybe learn songs from *Creatures* from the record. It was really awful. They were falling apart then, I think. Vinnie's talented, but he had his own agenda. He wanted to prove what a great guitarist he was.

SW: I remember some interviews he gave from that period where he was somewhat dismissive of what the band had done up to then. His attitude was, "I'm the best guitar player this band has ever had."

BK: Yeah, and that's not what Kiss is about at all. It's really a team effort kind of vibe. So it was pretty easy for him to self-destruct and blow himself out of the water with the band.

So by the time I came along, Mark St. John had been on the record, and it was a mystery who I was. I remember reading reviews that said, "New guitarist Mark St. John did an able job on guitar with his exciting fretwork." *(Laughter)*.

It was like, "Thanks a lot." There was a lot of confusion, but the feedback was positive, and it got back to Gene and Paul that people thought I was playing well, and I looked like I fit with them.

I wasn't running around a lot at first, but by the time I got to America on tour, I was more used to maybe running up the pod, running back down...I would go from stage left to stage right. (Laughs.) So the reaction was, "This is the guy." They were sick of the lack of any consistency in the guitar player, and certainly I knew that one thing I would bring to the band, besides my playing, would be stability. They realized that I would be there, I wasn't on my own agenda, and I'm a team player. And that's what Kiss needs.

SW: You're the only guitarist they've had since Ace left who sounds good playing the older material.

BK: Thanks. It's the same as when I played with Meat Loaf; Todd Rundgren played some great stuff on *Bat Out Of Hell*, so why screw around with it? That's how I felt about Ace's parts. At the recent conventions, a lot of times I got asked, "What solos from the vintage stuff do you find challenging?" And there are songs that stand out, like "100,000 Years" and "She". There's some great guitar stuff in there. Ace may not have been the fastest guitar player, but he certainly was extremely lyrical. And when you're learning the riffs, it has nothing to do with what boots he's wearing, or what his costume looks like, or his burning guitar. You're just listening to his playing.

The more we got into some of the older stuff, the more I realized that only on maybe ten percent of any of that material does the solo not really mean anything. Ninety percent of it is important to the song. And that ten percent isn't the real classic stuff; it's stuff like "I Was Made For Loving You". You don't think of the guitar solo when you think of that song. It's really a nothing guitar solo, so I just do a little different version. But when it comes to "She", and "Deuce", and "Firehouse" and songs like that, you really do have to get the essence of what he was doing. There's a lot of great riffs in there. So I think the fans appreciate that I do that.

SW: Coming into a band that was already so well established, and with two personalities that were the original founding members, was it intimidating?

BK: Definitely intimidating, because you can't argue with guys that have had that kind of success. Although in time I realized that what has made them successful is the way they are able to work with each other, not against each other. It's a very strong partnership in how they're able to complement each other. Even though at times it is a little bit of competition, I feel like it's healthy. There have been times when I felt like it wasn't healthy, but ultimately, once everybody gets down to work, it works out.

I'm never competing with them, and I don't want to, because I don't feel like I need to. I want to let my talent do the talking. I'm not the most verbal guy. Gene and Paul seem to be able to explain what they do, and what the band is about, so effortlessly and with such great analogies. I was always kind of shy, even when I had my own band in Blackjack. I was never dying to talk to the press. I can carry a good conversation—you hear me talking your ear off now! *(Laughter)*. But I don't do it as colorfully as they do.

SW: Gene and Paul are very interesting in that over the years, they seem to have created fictional celebrity identities for themselves that are separate from the private individuals. They rarely comment much about their personal lives; they talk mainly about Kiss and their professional interests, and when they do, they play those celebrity roles. You don't really do that.

BK: Right. And I don't think it would work if I did, either, because there would be so many guys trying to compete for attention. So I think my personality fits the band that way. They are always supportive of me; they want me to jump in and have my say and be interviewed. And I do, but I've always been very respectful of their ability to keep the press interested.

When it comes to music, if anything, at times they're intimidated by my ability. Not that that means anything, because ultimately the band is the most important thing, so they want me to use my talent. There have been times when Gene has said to me, "You're playing that too well." *(Laughs)*. And at first I was very offended by it, but it didn't take long for me to get what he meant. Maybe playing with a little more slop—not everywhere, but on certain parts—that looser feel makes it work better. I'm working with Paul, and Paul's more of a Keith Richards-type rhythm player, with that feel, and not a session player. I'm more like the guy that could do a session, but I can also work with Kiss. I can cross that line. So they always consider me the musician of the band, and the fact that I know how to twiddle the knobs a little bit doesn't hurt.

I think what's important is that I know what they're capable of, and they know what I'm capable of, and we all get to use and hopefully bring to the foreground our best abilities. I'm not a great singer. I could probably carry a song the way Ace does, but I'm not dying to sing a song. I also don't have a real big range. If I were a really great singer, and had always sung lead in my previous bands, I'd be a little frustrated, because there would be too much competition.

SW: It's interesting that the band has gone from initially having four vocalists, to now just having two.

BK: That's true, although Peter and Ace sang a lot less than it seemed like. It's just that the couple of songs they did sing would always be highlights. For instance, "Beth" was the biggest single hit the band ever had, which maybe made Peter a little bit delusional about the band...

SW: And possibly his own vocal abilities, as well. *(Laughs)*.

BK: Exactly. And part of the demise of the band was Peter feeling like, "Hey, I did this. I don't need you guys." And Ace had the only hit out of the solo records, "New York Groove", which is a great song. He actually didn't write it, but he sang it great, and you felt it. And in some ways I regret not pushing trying to have a song that's a good vehicle for me to sing. If you think about it, I could probably do as good a job as Peter or Ace, or even Eric Carr, who took over singing some of Peter's parts.

Eric never really got to show off how well he could sing in the band. His voice wasn't always suited to what he was singing. Sometimes he would sing "Black Diamond" and end up screaming it, just because he was competing to be heard over all the volume. And I think maybe he thought that would make him sound tougher. But I think he had a better voice than that, that we never really got to hear. You hear it real well on "God Gave Rock And Roll To You" in that a capella vocal part; the lower, kinda Beatle-esque part is Eric's voice.

Our current drummer Eric Singer has a good voice, and hopefully we'll see him sing something. It remains to be seen whether he'll write something and sing it, or whether we'll write something and give it to him to sing. That's definitely something the band is looking at. It would be great even if I just sang a line in a song, because I could do that. But it's not one of my strong desires.

And Paul has gotten so much better as a vocalist—not that he didn't sing well in the makeup years, but he's really improved his range and power. It's intimidating when the guy belts out a song that I'd be struggling on. But then again, the fans don't really care. They're not necessarily looking for a quality thing; they just want to get a little bit more intimate with you, so maybe if you sing something, they feel like they're sharing something with you. It's something that I think about, and I regret not being a better singer, but it doesn't mean that it's out of the question that I might sing a line or a verse, or even a whole song at some point. That would be nice. And Eric, we'll certainly get some sort of vehicle for him to sing, because he has kind of a high, punky voice which fits the band.

SW: When you joined the band, what was your level of contribution to the albums at first?

BK: On the *Animalize* record, I just did a couple of little pieces on it, maybe one song and the end of another. And I wasn't credited at all; it still said Mark St. John. Then we did a fairly successful six-month tour. *Animalize* had done very well; it had "Heaven's On Fire" on it, which was a big hit for the band. It was a good follow-up to *Lick It Up*, which was a period where the band was rebuilding itself. Before that, *Creatures Of The Night* was a great record, but they still couldn't convince everybody to buy it.

By the time they put out *Lick It Up*, MTV was in business, and it was a whole different audience then that got into the band even if it had no makeup. And maybe that's why; if they'd had makeup, maybe it wouldn't have been looked at the same way. It was like a rebirth for the band. The makeup thing had run its course, according to them. And you can see that as the years went along, the costumes got a little stranger, and then they cut their hair for *The Elder*, and they still had the makeup on, but it looked a little weird. *Creatures* was okay, but by then people had lost interest, I guess.

They were also frustrated with the fact that no one took them seriously because they wore makeup. There are so many great songs that they had written, and nobody could compare to that kind of stage show, but they still weren't taken seriously. And a lot of kids were into the band, too, and that makes the critics give you a hard time. So for *Lick It Up* the makeup came off, and then *Animalize* was a very successful album and tour to follow up, and then it came time to go into the studio to do the next one, *Asylum*.

By then, unfortunately I think the band was heading in a little more of a pop direction. Paul has that tendency sometimes; Gene's not that comfortable with the pop stuff. Although he can write Beatle-type songs, it's better when he's dark and ugly. So we went in to do *Asylum*, and I co-wrote three songs on that album, but I definitely was letting myself take direction, rather than forcing my own point of view upon them. I didn't think it was a situation where I should do that, even though Paul always told me to be as creative as I could and play with all the styles that I could that were current. That's when the whole flash thing was getting popular; Floyd Rose tricks and hammer-ons and all of that.

That got old after a few years, as any style does. But I was proud of my work on that album. I guess the highlight of *Asylum* was "Tears Are Falling", and we did a cool video for that. We toured and everything went well. We didn't have a real big hit single off that record, which was unfortunate, but we regrouped and then we did *Crazy Nights*, and I had four co-writing credits on that one, which was great. That's when we brought in Ron Nevison to produce, and here again, he's a great producer, but he's a little pop, so Gene was a little bit uncomfortable with that, while Paul was pretty happy.

SW: How did you feel about the album?

BK: Even though I felt like I got a real good guitar sound on that record, again, you can have a great lead tone, but if the material's a little poppier, what's the difference? It just doesn't grab you by the throat. Not that there's anything that I'm embarrassed by on any of those records, but it was just a poppier era for the band.

After that we started getting back on track with *Hot In The Shade*. Even though I don't think it's a particularly strong record, it did have a sense of us trying to strip down all of the slickness that was happening in the Eighties. And we had a big ballad hit called "Forever" which came about through my relationship with Michael Bolton and through Michael meeting Paul at a hotel here in LA. They wrote "Forever" together, which is a wedding song now! *(Laughs)*. People have it at their weddings. That will the Bruce Kulick tribute, to see some guy in a wedding band do my acoustic solo from "Forever". I was always proud of that solo.

After *Hot In The Shade* we went out and did a great tour that year. We toured the States for over six months, and that's when we started really expanding the set and including some of the old stuff like "Deuce". We went from doing fifteen songs to twenty-three, which the kids really appreciated. Plus, we were doing a big show, with the lasers and big lights and all.

From that we got a sense of what the fans really want. They want a mixture of everything, and they want us to play a lot of songs. That's when we started dropping the individual solos, because it was stupid. Rather than me going out and doing a five minute guitar solo, I'd rather do a five minute song and have a great solo in the middle. The solos were mostly posing, anyway. I guess Eric Carr was the most disappointed about that, because he always liked his drum solo. He always had an interesting drum solo spot. I think he still did it on the *Hot In The Shade* tour, but the rest of us didn't do any solos.

SW: How did you wind up doing a cover of "God Gave Rock And Roll To You"?

BK: We got the chance to cut a track for the second Bill and Ted movie, *Bogus Journey*. Actually, it was originally titled *Bill And Ted Go To Hell*, but they wouldn't buy that because Kmart wouldn't stock it. *(Laughs)*. So it wound up as *Bill And Ted's Bogus Journey*. That's when the band realized that maybe we could do an album better than *Hot In The Shade* if we got Bob Ezrin back in the fold.

The only way to know if Ezrin was in the mindset to work with the band was to try him and see if it worked out, and here was the perfect opportunity. So we had him come in and help us produce the song, which was a remake of an old Russ Ballard song that Argent had done. We changed some of the lyrics, because some of it was too psychedelic for what we were trying to get across. And it was great working with him. We realized that it would be good to work with him on a record, and we put that song on the next record. We just used a different mix than the film.

SW: Right around that time was when your drummer, Eric Carr, was diagnosed with cancer.

BK: In 1991 he started to get sick, and within six to eight months he was dead.

SW: At what point was the band informed of his illness?

BK: I was the closest in friendship with him; we used to do certain things like go to the Van Halen concert together. I remember in April of that year, he got sick, and when they did an X-ray to find out what was going on with his chest, they found some sort of growth on his heart. They didn't know what it was, and I remember him telling me that they were going to have to cut him open and look at it. That was right when we were cutting that track, so he didn't actually play drums on "God Gave Rock And Roll To You", but he did the video with us.

They did the open heart surgery and removed this growth, and they realized that it was cancer. And when you get cancer by the heart it's very dangerous, because the heart pumps all those cells to every part of the body. So he went through chemotherapy, and it was terrible, because at the same time the band was trying to rehearse and move ahead with writing. We knew we had to do a record. It was time to get ready to go into the studio.

When he got back after the heart operation, that's when we did the "God Gave Rock And Roll To You" video. He was so into it, because I think he realized that he might lose what he loved the most, besides living, which was being in Kiss. It was just a terrible thing to see happen. Eventually he had an aneurysm from the cancer, and the last few months he was in the hospital and the family didn't want anyone to see him. I'm kind of glad I didn't, because it wasn't Eric at that point. When you're that sick...

Then there was the funeral, and because he was Italian, it was an open casket.

SW: That's very difficult.

BK: Oh, yeah. It was unbelievable. I remember Paul and I saying, "That's not him. That's not Eric." We were in denial. We knew it was his body, but it wasn't Eric, because Eric just had a certain life force. There was no one like him. There was just no one like this guy. He was so funny and unique and sensitive and talented, and great to the fans. He was a tremendous individual. He had the biggest heart of anyone that I ever met. He was always the most generous and giving to everyone, including the fans. So it was a very sad thing to see happen.

And actually, we had already cut basic tracks in the studio, so right after we got back from the funeral, it was like, "Okay, Bruce, time for the solos." Because there was no way those guys were going to be able to sing. So I had to get right to work, which was actually good therapy for me. It kept me busy. That's when we decided to take an old track that he had a drum solo in and overdub on that, which we called "Eric Carr Jam". That was a nice tribute to him.

He left a legacy behind of his work, and there's actually some other songs which might end up on a box set. There's also an idea for an animated show called *The Rockheads* which Gene is still pitching. There are people interested, so it would be great if we could get that off the ground. It was a sad thing, but fortunately, Eric Singer was able to step in.

SW: Where did he come from?

BK: He had worked with Paul on the solo tour that he did between *Crazy Nights* and *Hot In The Shade*. Paul had to spread his wings for a little bit. Gene was mogulling with a lot of different things, so there was an opportunity for Paul to do that. And he realized that as fun as it was, there's no place like home. And that's the band.

We all knew Eric Singer was a talented drummer, but we weren't sure if this guy with blond hair was going to fit! *(Laughs)*. I remember jamming with him, and we still weren't sure. We knew he played great, so we decided that's what we needed—not an Eric Carr clone; we needed fresh blood that was really talented. And Eric has done a great job. He sings well, and he plays great, but no, he doesn't have dark, curly hair. So what?

We went on tour for *Revenge*; first we went to England, and then we came back to the States and put together the stage show with the Statue of Liberty, which would give the finger at the end. *(Laughs)*. It was a little difficult to travel with that set, believe me. Not all of the halls were big enough to handle it. We always had some technical problems. But it was still a fun show, and we got to film it and record it for *Alive III*. And then we did the tribute album, which I didn't have to do much on.

The most exciting thing about that was going down to Nashville to work on "Hard Luck Woman" with Garth Brooks.

SW: What was that like?

BK: He's a total gentleman. I guess I'd flip if I could see his bank account balance, but I couldn't imagine success happening to a nicer guy, and to someone who just doesn't seem to be affected by it. He's just a great guy. I've seen some videos of some of his live stuff, and I can definitely see how he was influenced by Kiss. He uses fire and pyro and all that stuff.

That was a lot of fun. It was great to see how these country guys work, as opposed to all the rock and roll records that I've been involved in. We were in Nashville for a few days, and then we wound up doing Leno with him, which was very exciting.

SW: I saw that. I never would have believed it otherwise. (*Laughs*). It was surprisingly good.

BK: We were kinda backing him, but hey, he is Garth Brooks. At least he was doing a Kiss song! (*Laughs*). That was very flattering for us, especially Paul. He was really thrilled with the whole thing.

SW: What does the band want to accomplish in the rest of the decade?

BK: The story continues on. Whereas a lot of the Eighties bands have gone by the wayside, I think we've proven to our fans and the rock world in general that we can continue, because the band wasn't really based in that Eighties fluff sound, even though we went through that period. The band has always had an interesting history, and a record like *Revenge* reflects that history more so than anything we did in the Eighties. Not that we're embarrassed by everything from the Eighties; certainly there were some great songs, and some of the tours were very exciting. Unfortunately, now that seems really dated, and labels have dropped a lot of the bands that were part of that style.

SW: A lot of the bands that were MTV and radio staples a few years ago are now out scratching a living on the club circuit.

BK: Right. And what sets us apart is not only our history, but also our commitment. Kiss has always been about more than just, "Let's have a party and get laid." It's a different approach. It's obviously a blessing that the band's been around as long as it has—I don't necessarily think the Eighties would have happened for it if not for the Seventies. The band made a lot of money in the Eighties, and it was like a rebirth, and now I feel like we're going through one again in the Nineties.

SW: On the *Alive III* album, did you go back and re-dub certain parts in the studio to round out the live tapes?

BK: I'm not going to lie and say nothing was touched. The night they wanted to use the performance of "Forever", I flipped out, because I'd missed the first note of the solo. There was no way I could leave that, so I just dropped in the note. Unfortunately, on some of the stuff we really wanted to put on there, the drums didn't sound the way we heard them live. That's just the way they were recorded. You never know what's going to happen when you're recording a live show. You're hearing it onstage, but it's being recorded by someone in a mobile truck parked off to the side of the arena. (*Laughs*).

I think the biggest problem with *Alive III* was that it wasn't a double record, and a lot of people wanted it to be. We definitely had enough good material to do a double record, but the record company said that twenty-five dollars for a double CD would be too much for our fans. I don't agree with that. But we wound up doing a single disc. And even so, there's still an hour's worth of music, which you couldn't squeeze onto a single record.

But there's something cool about vinyl records, the way you can hold them and look at them. *Alive III, Revenge* and the tribute album were all released on vinyl in limited editions. They look cool, they feel good, and a lot of kids bought them at the conventions. I'm into vinyl. I look for certain records. I hate when they're noisy and scratchy, but if you find something newer and in pretty good shape, it's a great thing to have. There's no doubt that CDs are more convenient, but what happened to the packaging? *(Laughs).*

SW: I couldn't agree more. I grew up listening to bands in the Seventies, and so many of the albums had cool packaging, like Kiss did with the tattoos and posters, or Jethro Tull did with *Stand Up*, where there were actual pop-up figures of the band when you opened the jacket. It's pretty hard to squeeze something like that into a CD cover.

BK: I'm pretty sure that we'll continue to put out a limited amount of vinyl so that people will have a choice. Maybe even colored vinyl.

SW: Despite the fact that you've been in Kiss for a long time, have played a lot of great music, and are obviously a guitar hero to the dedicated Kiss audience, you don't receive a lot of attention from the guitar magazines. Why do you think that is?

BK: It's not the kind of band where one person stands out. I've learned a lot going into the studio and seeing the way Gene and Paul work. It's always about what works for the song. Each song is more important than one person's ego regarding what's going to make him stand out. I've seen Paul be so patient with Gene, and vice versa, when they suggest things where I think, 'That's just not going to work.' They still try it, and I've got a lot of respect for that. It might take us a little longer, but everyone's suggestions and contributions are entertained.

I think the band has become stronger because Gene and Paul are very open to hearing ideas, even from Eric, who's only been in the band a few years. So the vehicle is on all four wheels and running. There's no doubt that Gene and Paul are the front wheel drive. *(Laughter).* They created this monster. But they really rely on the other two tires moving and carrying that weight. If you don't carry it well, then it gets bogged down.

That's what happened, at times, during the Eighties. Gene got involved in other things, like movies, so the band got more pop. The new stuff that Paul has written for this next record is still Paul, but it does have a lot of attitude. Paul doesn't always have to be real pop. I mean, Paul wrote "God Of Thunder". He didn't sing it, but he wrote it.

SW: Do you have musical ambitions outside of Kiss, such as producing or playing with other artists?

BK: We're pretty busy, so I don't feel a strong need, but since there's some stuff that I write that doesn't fit Kiss, I like to try and get some of that stuff done. One of my goals is to write a top ten hit for someone. I didn't say a number one, because that's pushing it. *(Laughs).* But a top ten single. I don't have to be the artist; I just want to write it. I don't care if it isn't Kiss; in fact, it's more likely not to be Kiss, because it's so hard to get a top ten single for a rock band these days. Even our last big single hit, "Forever", only went to eleven.

I'd also love to produce a band and have it be very successful. But right now, a lot of my aspirations are satisfied by being in Kiss. The fact that we're able to keep the band alive, and still vital and important in the Nineties is quite an impressive feat, I think, considering how hard it is to keep bands together and how many changes there have been in the music business.

Outside of that, I think I've improved as a songwriter. I'll have the most co-writes ever on this next album, more than any of the previous albums, which is a sign that if I really apply myself and let go…sometimes when I was preparing to write, I used to think, 'What would be good for the band?' instead of, 'What do I feel right now?' And it's hard for anyone who's in a creative field, because you have to think of who you're writing for. Even for someone like yourself, writing your book, you may want to go off on a certain tangent, but the publisher may think you're crazy. And you have to answer to them.

SW: That's been known to happen. (*Laughs*).

BK: We also have people to answer to—our fans. Even though we want to be true to ourselves, we also have to keep in mind what the fans will accept. Like on *Revenge*, Gene had an idea for a harmonica solo on one of the songs, and I thought it was nuts! But we entertained the thought; we actually had the guy come down, and he was a great player, but I hated it. What he played was great, but I didn't think it fit on a Kiss album. It's funny, because when I brought it up at some of the conventions, the kids all laughed and agreed.

SW: That would seem more appropriate for someone like Aerosmith.

BK: Right. And we don't want to be Aerosmith. So that's what I mean. That's the process we go through. With writing, obviously the more things you come up with, the more chances you have that some things are going to stick to the wall. So I try to keep being creative. Working on our new material, I pushed the issue so much, and came up with so many different riffs that Gene really liked, that he kept reminding Paul to get going. And Paul wasn't resisting; it's just that he wasn't yet focused as to what the direction of the material should be at that point. And then some of the stuff we started working on, Gene was really happy with, and Paul was excited, and more importantly, some people that we trust that we know have their ear to the ground said, "This stuff is great."

I was so flattered. That's why I'm so excited about the next record. I wouldn't be so much if I knew there was only going to be one of my songs on there, but since there's going to be a good number of co-writes, it makes me feel like I'm really contributing to the band. Even though I always give a hundred percent, if I can contribute creatively, too, then that's a big turn-on for me.

SW: You recently did this huge career retrospective book called *Kisstory*…

BK: Yeah, the *Kisstory* book is quite amazing.

SW: Now there's a rumor that the band has authorized an official biography. Is there any truth to that?

BK: No, not that I know of. Believe me, they wouldn't authorize anything unless they could be involved. Gene's at the point where, because of the *Kisstory* book, he's like in-house publishing. He bought enough computer equipment that we can publish our own stuff.

The next thing coming out is *Kiss Nation*. Marvel Comics put out *Kiss Classics*, which was the first two comics that Marvel did in the Seventies together in one issue. But *Kiss Nation*, which is also on America Online, our fan club thing, is going to be a comic book. One of the guys who draws the X Men is drawing the comic, and the other half of the magazine will be fan stuff—news from us, photos, and other things like that. Kind of like *Kisstory*, but small. Some of our personal items, and then we asked fans to send us whatever. Like if you have a Kiss tattoo, or you drew a picture, or anything like that. One of the great things about our fans is they give us all these cool gifts.

SW: What happens to what they send?

BK: We've got it all. We keep it. There's a guy who makes these great caricatures of us. I've had two done already by him, and then the third one was his idea of me in makeup. I was The Sorcerer. *(Laughs)*. It was really cool. The guy's very talented. There was a contest in *Livewire*, the rock magazine, where you could win a Bruce Kulick guitar by sending in some sort of Kiss thing—why you love Kiss, or something related to the band -and Gene picked that guy. I'm glad he did, because he's done some great work. So he got flown to the convention in New York, and we presented him with a guitar. We love doing that kind of thing.

SW: You guys must get asked all the time how long you expect Kiss to continue. Do you have any idea, or do you actually plan for the future?

BK: No. The truth is, when you see the Rolling Stones, Jagger's in his fifties now, and it's okay. I think Kiss will have run its course when nobody really cares about the band anymore, because then you're just not able to carry on and do what you do. I really think this band has the capability to carry on like the Stones. I can see us playing a gig in the year 2000, absolutely. There's no reason not to.

I can't see any reason why our record sales won't stay constant at gold. That's certainly nothing to be ashamed about. I'm even hoping that we'll have a few more platinum albums or even something more successful than that, but if not, to just be able to play, and have appreciative crowds, is great. Why stop? As long as the business is there, the fans want us, and we're doing quality work without compromising, we never want to give this up.

For more information on Bruce Kulick, please visit www.Kulick.net

PLAYING FROM THE HEART

*Howard Leese has been the lead guitarist in **Heart** for two decades, during which time he has been responsible for such classic solos as "Magic Man", "Barracuda" and "Crazy On You", to name just a few. Though the band is fronted by the **Wilson** sisters, **Ann** and **Nancy**, it is **Leese** who provides the group with much of its musical backbone.*

*Growing up in Los Angeles, **Leese** began playing guitar at age eleven, playing in several local bands while in his teens, one of which, **The Zoo**, gained enough local notoriety to convince **Leese** that his course was set on music. Tiring of the club scene, **Leese** moved to Vancouver and spent seven years as a first call studio musician, playing guitar and keyboards on a steady stream of recording sessions while carving out a nice living.*

*It was during one such session that he first encountered **Heart**, who had yet to secure a recording contract. **Leese** played electric guitar on the band's 1975 debut album 'Dreamboat Annie', then made the decision to join the band when the album became somewhat of a surprise hit. The band went on to have several successful albums throughout the remainder of the decade, establishing **Heart** as one of the most popular rock acts in America.*

*The early Eighties were a time of professional turmoil for the group. Faced with extensive personnel changes, **Heart** produced a pair of disappointing sellers, 'Private Audition' and 'Passionworks', after which the band left Epic Records and signed with Capitol. Working with veteran producer **Ron Nevison**, the band returned to form on 1985's self-titled 'Heart' album, which became its first chart-topper, producing the hit singles "What About Love", "Never", and "These Dreams". 1987's 'Bad Animals' provided a million-selling follow-up, spawning the number one hit ballad "Alone". **Heart's** subsequent albums all proved to be strong sellers, sustaining the group's popularity into the Nineties.*

*I spoke with **Howard Leese** on May 31, 1995 by phone from his home in Seattle. **Leese** had recently completed work on **Heart's** forthcoming acoustic project entitled 'The Road Home', a career retrospective which features the band in an intimate club setting. He was excited about the new arrangements and the opportunity to work with producer **John Paul Jones**, who also played some bass on the recordings. **Leese** had also been playing some shows with his side project, **The Howard Leese Group**, and was preparing to celebrate his twentieth anniversary in **Heart**.*

SW: What have you been up to?

HL: This past weekend I drove down to Oregon and played a big biker rally. They have bike runs, and these guys will go out and camp for three or four days. I have a little fun band that plays around here in the clubs and stuff, my heavy guitar band, and we went down and played some hard rock and roll for two thousand bikers. It was fun.

SW: What's the name of your band?

HL: The Howard Leese Group.

SW: Is it all original material you're playing?

HL: No, none of it's original. Well, I do a couple of solos that I wrote, but mainly it's just real heavy Seventies guitar music, Deep Purple and Robin Trower and stuff. There's a lot of lead guitar. It's fun.

SW: Speaking of Deep Purple, I just read today that Steve Morse joined them.

HL: That will be a fun job, because it's quite a body of work. Just to fit in and play all of Blackmore's parts would be hard enough, and then if you can throw something of your own in there, that would really be something.

That would be kind of a fun job; they just give you the song list and tell you to learn them, and you get to go and get inside Ritchie Blackmore's brain and learn all the parts. That's fun. Satriani did it for a while, too. Anybody who's that good is qualified to do something like that. It's just kind of a challenge. You wouldn't want to do it for years and years, but to go in there and do it for a tour or something would be fun, to step into a great player's shoes and try it out.

SW: I'm looking forward to hearing what they sound like with Steve Morse, because his style is completely different.

HL: He doesn't seem like the obvious choice, but then again, he's a master of so many styles, he can probably just play his style without too much of a problem. Morse is an unbelievable player.

SW: He's just amazing. Even on the albums he did with Kansas, which I didn't think were really their best work, his guitar playing was incredible.

HL: I like some of that stuff. I've always liked Kansas. So, who else is in this book you're doing?

SW: You know Craig Chaquico, don't you?

HL: Sure. I've known Craig since back in '78 or so. We used to open for the Starship all the time, and he and I would skateboard before the shows and dink around. Plus when we recorded the *Heart* album in 1985, that was done in Sausalito, and those guys were in recording at the same time, so I used to see him every day in the studio.

That was wild; when we were in the studio doing that record, we were in Studio A, Journey was in Studio B, Starship was in there, Aretha was in there—everybody was in there all at the same time. It was incredible. And then a few months later the FBI closed the studio down because of someone who owned it, or one of the investors. Something was fishy somewhere. It was really weird! *(Laughs).* But that was a great time, all those bands making records at once.

SW: There must be something in the water in Sausalito! *(Laughs).* Let's go back in time a little bit. Do you remember your first guitar?

HL: The first one I ever had was a little solid-body electric, a Stella. Just a horrible guitar. It made my fingers bleed. *(Laughs).* I had that for a few months, and then when I could play a little bit of a tune on that one, my next door neighbors were this great Mexican family, and they had a guitar, and they loaned that to me. It was a little steel string acoustic, and I played that for about a year.

Then one day this friend of mine and I were singing folk songs for our fifth grade class, and everybody loved it so much, they asked us to leave the guitars overnight and do it again the next day. So we left them overnight, but we left them back by the heater. When I came back in the morning, the pick guard looked like a grilled cheese sandwich. (*Laughter*). It was all melted, and the guitar was cracked and ruined, and it wasn't even my guitar. I felt so horrible for this family, because they weren't rich. I lived in a poor neighborhood. It was such a drag that I ruined their guitar. I couldn't live with that for quite a while.

SW: What did they say about that?

HL: They were good about it. I think we made it up to them at a later date. But then I got a little electric guitar and an amp. My first decent guitar was a Gibson 335 that I got when I was fifteen. I got it because I was going to play the Teen Fair in LA, and that was deemed a big enough deal where I should have a decent instrument. I still have that 335, too.

SW: Did you grow up in LA?

HL: I was born in Hollywood, and I grew up in central LA.

SW: How did you first become interested in music?

HL: It just sort of came naturally to me. One day when I was nine, I was visiting some friends with my mom, and they had a piano, so I sat down and started tinkering around on it and came up with the Davy Crockett theme! (*Laughs*). I took piano lessons from nine to eleven, and when I was eleven I decided I wanted to play the guitar instead, so I stopped playing piano and started playing guitar.

I played nothing but guitar for about seven years, and then I started playing keyboards again when I became a studio musician and started having to do keyboard sessions as well as guitar sessions. And that was good, because when I joined Heart I replaced a keyboard player, not a guitar player. When I joined there were already two guitar players, so I joined as a keyboard player, which was weird for me because that was kind of my second instrument. So I had to really brush up and get quite a bit better on the keyboards to handle the job. They were doing stuff by Yes and things that were fairly difficult, so I had to learn a lot of keyboards.

SW: Early Heart was doing stuff by Yes?

HL: Oh, yeah. We'd do two sets of Led Zeppelin, two forty-five minute medleys. That was our draw as a club band. We were like a little Led Zeppelin. We played all that Zeppelin stuff, and then we did another set of English progressive rock, Moody Blues and Yes and stuff like that. It was weird and different. Then we had our original set; we'd do a couple of sets of covers and then our original set to close the show, and then eventually when we went to playing concerts, all we had to do was forget the two cover sets.

SW: Who were some of your early guitar influences?

HL: Dick Dale was the first guitarist that I saw live. I saw him at the Teen Fair, and he came out with a left-handed metal flake Stratocaster with lots of reverb on it. And I said, "Wow, that's wild." (*Laughs*).

I think B.B. King was the first electric blues guy that I got into. The early

Clapton stuff with the Bluesbreakers affected everybody of my generation. And the first Hendrix album, of course. *Truth*, the Jeff Beck album; the first Queen album and, you know, the Beatles and the Stones and all the more popular bands. But as far as guitar-wise, I'd say those other records were more important.

I knew every lick that Keith Richards ever played; for their first ten albums I was a big Stones fan. I saw the Stones in '64 and '65.

SW: What kind of music were you playing in your first few bands?

HL: I had a band called The Zoo while I was still in high school, and we did some pretty big concerts. We opened for Canned Heat and Spirit and some of those touring bands. We would do big concerts on the weekends, and it was a lot of fun. We did TV shows and stuff.

And then I wasn't really in a band after that for quite a while; I went up to Vancouver, Canada, and I was a studio musician. I got tired of playing in clubs and stuff; I thought that was kind of a dead-end thing, so I became a studio musician. I moved to Vancouver, and I worked there for about seven years. I was the top studio guitar player in town until the Heart project came in. It was one of the records that I played on, and I ended up joining the band.

SW: They had gone up there to do their first record?

HL: Right. The first couple of records were done in Vancouver. They were up there playing the club circuit and living up there, and I was up there working. In fact, I produced the very first Heart demo about a year before they got signed. They came in to do a demo, and everybody was too busy, so it fell to me to produce it.

SW: What was the demo like?

HL: It was just some stuff from their live show. It was a medley of Bo Diddley beat songs like "Willie and the Hand Jive" and stuff like that, and "Sixty Years On" by Elton John, which was kind of strange.

SW: Not the kind of stuff people think of when they think of Heart.

HL: Well, we still love Elton John. He's great. And our style isn't that far apart from his.

SW: After all the sessions you had done by then, why did that one in particular appeal to you enough to join the band?

HL: They asked me to join at first and I said no, because they were still playing six nights a week in clubs, and I was just doing three or four sessions a month, and I was doing better than they were. And I didn't have to travel; I lived in Vancouver, and I really loved it up there, and I knew if I joined I'd be gone immediately, so at first I didn't want to do it.

But then the record came out and started doing pretty well, and the songs that I played on like "Magic Man" and "Crazy On You" were the popular songs. And then again they said, "You really should be playing these parts, since you played them on the record. You ought to join." And by then they were doing well enough where they said they probably weren't going to play clubs much longer, so I joined, and we indeed only did seven more weeks of clubs before we started doing concerts.

SW: Good timing! *(Laughs)*.

HL: Yeah! *(Laughs)*. That was great. And I'll be celebrating my twentieth anniversary this September 27th.

SW: That's a very long time. You guys have outlasted a lot of changes in that time...

HL: Seen 'em come and seen 'em go! *(Laughs)*.

SW: To what do you attribute that longevity?

HL: We didn't go disco when it was time to go disco, and we didn't go punk when it was time to go punk. We just ignored the trends and stuck with what we thought was cool, and what we thought our fans would think was cool.

It's hard when you're making a record. You're working in a vacuum; it's not like playing live and going, "Oh, they like this song better than that song." When you're in the studio you're just sort of going, "Well, maybe this will be cool, or maybe it won't be cool." *(Laughs)*. You don't really know.

So you just go by your instincts and do the best you can, and then some of the time people love it and go crazy and think it's the best thing in the world—and you know, *nothing's* the best thing in the world—and other times they don't like it as much, and it's just as good. It's just a hard thing. You just go in there and do what you think is good.

SW: When you're working on new material, how do you divide up the guitar parts between you and Nancy Wilson? How do you decide who is going to play what part?

HL: Generally it's pretty straightforward; she does the acoustic stuff and I do the electric stuff. That's generally how it is, although I occasionally do something on the acoustic and she occasionally does something on the electric. But generally I do the lion's share of the electric stuff.

SW: A lot of times you see her in the videos playing the electric.

HL: Yeah, right. That leads to a lot of misunderstanding. But those are *videos*! *(Laughter)*.

SW: Look, everybody, I'm not plugged in! *(Laughs)*. Back when Heart started out, there were very few rock bands with women in them, and even fewer where the women played dominant roles. Did that create any additional pressures for the group?

HL: When we first started out it was kind of strange, because back then women were looked at in music as more of a novelty, like, "Oh, how cute! They have a girl in the band! Does she play the tambourine, or does she really sing?" *(Laughs)*. There were only a few bands, like Jefferson Airplane and Janis Joplin, that were real hard rock bands with women in them.

So it was still pretty new when we started doing it, and in a way it was kind of weird, because they didn't take the girls as seriously as artists as they should have. But then in another way, because it was different, it may have worked to our advantage. I don't think it was really a disadvantage. And nowadays there are women players everywhere doing every style of music, so I don't think it's strange at all.

We never looked at it as male or female; we just thought it was cool that Ann could sing hard rock. You know, she sounded like Robert Plant, and we thought, 'Cool. Hard rock with a girl singing.' And in a way it works out better, because a woman's voice is a little higher in range than the electric guitar. You know, usually a male singer and the guitar player are right in the same range, and they have to tap dance around each other, whereas Ann's a little higher up. It actually works out good for the guitar players.

SW: Speaking of Robert Plant, do you guys still do "Rock And Roll" in your live set?

HL: No. We only did it for seventeen years, so...*(Laughs)*. I think it was a tour or two ago that I finally said, "That's enough." Plant had come to see us do it in England, and then the tour following that Page had come to see us do it in England, and I said, "The two guys who wrote it who are around have seen us do it, so we don't need to play it anymore."

Van Halen do it sometimes now. But we did carry that torch for quite a long time. That was the one vestige of our old club Zeppelin set. And recently we've been doing "The Battle Of Evermore", which we used to do years and years ago.

SW: You did that as the Lovemongers?

HL: Well, they did it too, but we did it in Heart in '75 or '76 back then.

SW: When Page and Plant came to see you separately, did either one comment on your performance of their song?

HL: We didn't talk to Page. I think he left after it was done; he didn't come by to visit. But Plant stayed and visited with us. He said, "Is that the same key? I can't believe it was that high!" *(Laughter)*. I said, "Absolutely, that's the same key." He was real nice about it.

SW: Do you take part in the Lovemongers as well?

HL: No, that's their little side thing that they do, mainly for benefits for charity to raise money for good causes around here in the Northwest. I've played with them on occasion. We had this one thing here where everybody from the Northwest came down and did an acoustic show. It was us, Queensryche, the guys from Alice In Chains, and various permutations. Everybody played with everybody else. So I have on occasion been on stage with them, but in general I don't. That's their little fun deal, and we keep it separate. When we work together, it's Heart.

SW: Heart was a very successful band from Seattle long before grunge came along. Did you ever think that Seattle would become such an influential rock and roll town?

HL: I don't know if I ever predicted it, but I've always ran around everywhere telling everyone how many great bands there were here in Seattle. I remember in the late Seventies and early Eighties I'd come back and do interviews around here, and they would ask me about other bands, and I would say, "There's a band in Seattle that's big in Europe and big in Japan, and no one's even heard of them in America. They don't play in Seattle because there's nowhere for them to play. They're an all-original band called Queensryche, and they're really good. You'll hear about these guys." And it took them a long time to break in America. They were big in Europe and Japan years before they broke in America.

SW: I remember about ten years ago they came around opening for Kiss, and even Kiss at the time were saying how they were going to be huge one day.

HL: So we've been supporting bands around here for a long time. One of the guys that used to be our publicist—who actually lived in the guest house right here behind my house and has known us for years and years, and came up through our organization in the business—is the guy that now manages Alice In Chains and Pearl Jam and Soundgarden and all those bands. So there's a lineage here from different influences that we set up.

Bands here all use our accountant, and they all use our studio. It's really cool. It's great that there's such a fertile music scene here. All the bands play with one another, too. When Spinal Tap was in town, me and Cantrell got up and played with them, and then Nancy and McCready got up and played with them. *(Laughs)*. All four of us, in two platoons, jammed with the Tap, man. *(Laughs)*. I did "Break Like The Wind". I was Beck and Satriani and whoever else. Me and Cantrell had to cover all those crazy guitar parts on the end of that.

So we've done that quite a bit. And you know, Ann was on *Sap*, and Layne sang a song on our last record. Originally Cornell sang it, and then the guys in his band got a little ticked at him for doing it, so he had us take him off and we got Laine to do it. But it's cool. It's not like LA, where there's kind of like different gangs. You know, the bands there are very separate and competitive. Here it's more of a family deal.

SW: So you've seen a lot of those bands come up through the clubs there locally.

HL: Definitely.

SW: Do you still like to go out to the clubs and see what's going on?

HL: I still play them. I opened for the Tubes about a month ago, and I did five Robin Trower shows about three or four months ago up here. I like to play the clubs. It keeps your chops up.

SW: When you're on tour and you play a similar set list every night, do you find that it's easy to play the songs on automatic pilot after playing them so many times?

HL: I don't think so. When you're on stage in front of a gigantic crowd of people, it's so damn exciting, I don't think you could go into automatic pilot even though you've played the song a thousand times. And some of the songs and some of the parts are still challenging; we wrote them that way in the first place so they wouldn't be boring.

There are certain songs that my hands can play all by themselves, so I can look around and enjoy the moment and not really have to concentrate on what I'm playing because I've played it so many times. But that's just muscle memory, and everybody has that.

SW: Do you rearrange some of the older songs so they don't become stale?

HL: Absolutely. In fact, we just rearranged our whole career, pretty much.

We just did a really great project up here that will be coming out in a couple of months. We did a live album in a local club up here. We did five nights of an acoustic show in a local club.

We had John Paul Jones from Zeppelin come in and produce it, and he wrote these beautiful string charts, and we had some guys from the Seattle Symphony come down. We booked five nights, sold them out in eight minutes, and recorded it for a live album. Originally John Paul Jones was just going to produce it and conduct the orchestra, but the more he got into it and the more he saw the level we were playing at, I think he was more comfortable with playing more and more. So pretty soon he started playing a little piano and a little mandolin, and pretty soon he was playing bass, and we played "What Is And What Should Never Be" with him on bass! (Laughs).

We just had a heck of a time. It was a really galvanizing show. And now that the record's done, the record company called us up last month and said, "We should have filmed this thing. We didn't know it was going to come out this good. We want a video of it." So we did it again. Two Friday nights ago we did it at a place called the Moore Theater here in Seattle. We did two shows in one night, and we had a bigger section from the symphony, and we filmed it.

We took all of our songs and completely re-did them in acoustic versions, with no electric instruments at all. So you have songs like "Alone", which is done with just Ann and I. I play the nylon string classical guitar, and we do almost a baroque version of it. And our other songs, we do songs like "Mistral Wind", songs that are normally big, heavy electric ones. I do "Barracuda" on a twelve-string, to give you an idea of what it's like! (Laughs).

So we had to reinvent a lot of our songs, and it was really satisfying to take just the structure of the song and forget the style of the song that you did it in at the time, and just take the actual structure of a song and interpret it in a completely different way with different instrumentation. I learned songs that I played on the guitar on the mandolin, and on the piano. That's really nice and challenging. It keeps it from getting stale. It keeps your body of work alive, and not just, "It's recorded. It's over." The work continues to live and breathe as long as you keep working with it.

SW: Are you going to try to recreate these arrangements on the road?

HL: We'd love to; I don't think we're going to tour with this, though, because it's a live album, and you usually don't tour behind a live album because there's only one new song. Plus, Nancy wants to stay home this year. She's trying to have a family.

That's one of the reasons we did the video, because we weren't going to do it live. We have the live video of it, and we'll probably do Letterman and the Tonight Show and a few TV things, but that will probably be it.

SW: What kind of a time frame are you looking at to do another studio record?

HL: As far as starting on the next studio record, I don't know; maybe

Christmas, maybe next spring. I don't know. I'm just starting to write a little bit, and I think the girls are writing.

We did a new song for this filming. We titled the live album *The Road Home*, so we thought we should write a song called "The Road Home". That's the only new one we've done recently, but I think everybody's going to start writing for the next studio effort pretty soon.

SW: After having a lot of success in the Seventies, the early Eighties was a rough period for the band in terms of experiencing some member changes and a label change, and after you moved to Capitol, the album *Heart* was a big comeback for the band. Were you surprised by how successful that album was?

HL: Pleasantly surprised, I must say. *(Laughs).* When the Seventies were over and Michael Derosier and Steve Fossen left the group, we had to re-define our sound. When you change members, especially the rhythm section, it's going to change the way you sound. The girls gave me the responsibility of finding the new rhythm section, and I really enjoyed that. I got to pick Mark Andes and Danny Carmassi, and we put together what I thought was a real good band.

We did one record together, and we were still finding our sound. That was the *Passionworks* record with Keith Olsen. It was a good step in the right direction. We were sort of getting our feet under us with the new band, and then we went on tour with that record, and I think that's when we really locked it down.

So when we came back in to record our second record with that band, we changed labels, we changed management, we changed producers—we changed everything but our lawyer. So we had a lot of fresh blood and a lot of people who wanted to work hard for us. I think we just had the opportunity to do something good, and had we not done a good record, then none of that would have happened. But we made a good record.

We weren't really self-conscious about it. We sort of realized that if we didn't have a hit record here pretty soon, we might not have a record deal. *(Laughs).* So we'd better make a good record.

So we took our time; we cut the tracks in LA, and then we went up to Sausalito and did all the overdubs. It was the first record that we did that had significant writing by other writers, specifically Bernie Taupin and "These Dreams". So that was another big change, and I think all of those changes put together worked out good.

SW: What was it like working with Ron Nevison on that record?

HL: Nevison is a very demanding producer, and sometimes difficult to work with, but when it's all done and mixed and in the can, you say, "Boy, he really is good!" *(Laughs).* And the other beautiful thing about that record is that the engineer was Mike Clink, who went on to become Guns N' Roses' producer and is now one of the hottest producers in the world. I think that was the last record where he was just an engineer. He went on to become a producer immediately after that.

So the next record we did with Nevison, Nevison engineered it himself, the

Bad Animals record. I think that's a really good piece of work, because boy, being the producer *and* the engineer, that's a lot of responsibility and a lot of work.

He knows his stuff. He's a great producer, and I'd work with him anytime. But he was hard on us. He was hard on me, and he was hard on Ann. Very demanding. I thought by the second record we had a much better working relationship, and *Bad Animals* was a lot more comfortable.

SW: Nevison really brought out a glossier side to the band.

HL: I think so. He had been doing Ozzy, but he had done some pop records, too, and I think he had a specific idea of how he thought we were going to sound and what he was going to do. I think the biggest question was just finding the right songs. Those records aren't particularly hard. They're pretty polished. Our main complaint was that those records are a little bit slick.

SW: The last few albums since then have all been very successful. Now that the band is in its twentieth year, does it worry you to go out and try to repeat that success with all of the changes that have come about in the last few years in radio and video?

HL: No more than usual, I don't think. You always wonder of this is going to be your last record or your last tour, and that's what keeps you moving. As long as we're making fresh music and making records that are hits, and not doing a nostalgia show like, "Do you remember this one from 1972…" *(Laughs).*

I don't think we're ever going to do that. As long as our current music is popular and we feel like we're doing work as good as we always have, then I don't see any reason to stop. When you start losing it, then it's better to bow out gracefully, but our last record was one of the best we've ever done, and this acoustic show we just did was really satisfying. It's the kind of musical thing that most people never get to experience. It was really beautiful the way we played with the orchestra, really satisfying and a lot of fun.

So I don't know. Ann says we're going to just keep going until the last one dies! *(Laughs).*

SW: What kinds of guitars are you using these days?

HL: I love guitars. I've got lots of guitars. Right now in my fun band I play nothing but Les Pauls. I've got some nice old Les Pauls. In fact, I just got a really beautiful 1960 sunburst a couple of weeks ago from a friend of mine down in Texas. We traded. I'm always using different guitars, and I'm always trying new things.

I have the first two Paul Reed Smiths, maple flame top guitars. The first one has been my main guitar forever and ever and ever. But I have over a hundred. Old Strats, Firebirds, and all manner of classic vintage American stuff. I'm really into that. I go to all the guitar shows, and I go to shows around here and display parts of my collection and wheel and deal.

SW: Do you bring in a lot of guitars when you're in the studio?

HL: *(Laughs).* We sure do! It's ridiculous. There's sixty or seventy guitars everywhere. Nancy brings twenty acoustics, because they all sound different, and I bring thirty or forty guitars of my own just because they all sound different.

Every amp and every guitar are all different, and when you get all of those combinations, there are thousands of permutations that you can get.

And if you're doing a record and there's going to be six or seven different guitar parts, and every one of them has to have a little different unique sound of its own, you need quite an array of sounds to choose from. It's just like a painter; how many colors do you want in your painting? If you want to go just black and white, that's cool, too, but I like to have all the different colors.

SW: When it's time to go out on the road, how do you choose which guitars to take?

HL: Generally I take guitars that are a little bit sturdy, and I still like to take vintage guitars, but certain ones are just too valuable to take on the road. But generally I take the same stuff. I like taking the good stuff on the road. I take a '58 Les Paul and an old Strat and a couple of PRS's and a few acoustics and a couple of mandolins. I just get the song list and figure out what sounds I'm going to need to make, and what guitars I can do it with.

SW: Do you worry about them getting stolen?

HL: I don't worry about it, but they do get stolen. One got stolen from me just the other night at the theater show. It was a shame, too; it was a beautiful Carvin maple electric/acoustic that they just made for me. All they wanted was a picture of me playing it, and I was going to get some pictures that night, and the day of the dress rehearsal somebody walked out the door with it. Never even got a picture of it. Never even played it!

SW: That's terrible. I would be beside myself.

HL: I've lost a few. I don't worry about it too much, but that's why you don't take your very, very favorites. Like Carlos [Santana] has had his two PRS's stolen.

SW: That's right; he wanted them back so desperately that he placed ads all over the place, and all the guitar magazines have run stories asking for their return.

HL: When those guitars were built, I already had the first two ever made, and Paul Smith called me up and said, "Carlos loves the guitar, and he's ordered two of them. Can he borrow your spare one while I'm making him his guitar?" And I said, "Sure; it's Carlos." *(Laughs)*. So I sent it to him, and he recorded *Zebop* using my number two, and then he sent it back. I use the number one, and the number two is still in its case.

So then Paul called me up again and said, "Do you still have number two?" And I said yes, and he said, "Carlos doesn't know it yet, but his two guitars are gone, and he's on Letterman tonight." And I said, "Oh my God."

SW: That's terrible!

HL: So he said, "Can I borrow that guitar again while I make him another one?" *(Laughs)*. So he just borrowed it again while they made him a backup. See, that would kill me if I lost number one, so I do have to be careful.

But you don't want to not play your best guitars, because they sound the best, and that's what you want to do; you want to go up there and sound the best that you can. Plus, I feel like the kids want to see where their money goes, and if they pay you enough to buy a good, expensive guitar, I like to spend their money back on them. That's where it goes.

We always have the big lights and big stage and giant stack of Marshalls. I want them to see where their money goes, and that we're not just buying cars and houses with it. We're out buying gear so we can put on a better show for them. That's the way it should be, I think.

SW: Is there one album or any certain song that you would point to as your best playing?

HL: I like the solo in "Alone", the solo in "What About Love", and the solo in the end of "Bad Animals". Nevison tricked me on that one. He told me he was just getting the level. That was the take before take one, before I was supposed to play my first try, and he said, "Just do it one time for me to check the levels." So I did it, and I said, "Okay, I'm ready to start," and he said, "No, you're done." *(Laughs)*. And I said, "Aw, come on, let me play. I just got here." And he said, "No, that's good. That's it."

I don't sit around and listen to my own stuff that much. But I do have my moments. The end of "Stranded", the solo there.

SW: Do you enjoy playing more in the studio, or live?

HL: That's a tough one. It's really apples and oranges. I think the studio is more satisfying on one level, because everything that you're doing is brand-new, and you're creating, and you're making up stuff that hopefully will be around for a while. Whereas when you're on stage, you're playing stuff that you've already done.

But then there's a certain creativity to being on stage, too; like you said before about being stale, if you're good and you're clever, you can go even farther on stage. There's the freedom of the stage; because it's not being recorded, you can be a little bit more reckless. Plus there's the audience and the lights and the moment and the volume and that whole thing, and that's intoxicating. So being on stage might be more fun, but being in the studio might be a little bit more satisfying in the long run.

SW: When you hear old songs of yours on the radio, do you go back over your performance after the fact and say, "Oh, I should have done this, I should have done that..."?

HL: *(Laughs)*. You always second-guess yourself, and if you're ever completely happy with what you've done, then you probably didn't work hard enough on it. You always think, 'What were we thinking when we did that?' But most of our stuff wears pretty well. Some of it does, some of it doesn't. Sometimes I hear stuff and say, "Hmm, that wasn't very good."

But then I was driving in LA late one night about two months ago, and they put on the whole *Dog And Butterfly* album. They were playing that on the radio. I heard stuff like "The Lighter Touch" and "Mistral Wind", the original version of that, and I thought, 'Man, that was cool.' It's still cool now. That was a long time ago, and it was kind of ahead of its time.

You hit and miss, and not everything you do is great, but if there's anything you do that you're happy with then that's pretty good for an artist, because most artists are tortured, they're never happy, and they die penniless. *(Laughs)*. And then five hundred years later people realize, "Hey, Van Gogh was pretty good, wasn't he?" *(Laughter)*. So being in a successful rock band, as far as being an artist, is pretty good. You have it pretty good, because you're appreciated in your own time, at least.

But you always say, "I wish I'd had this sound then", or "Listen to how primitive that is, because that was sixteen tracks and now we're on forty-eight tracks digital." *(Laughs)*. But you know, we've been making records for twenty years, so the technology has changed quite a bit.

SW: They're doing amazing things these days. I interviewed Trevor Rabin for this book...

HL: Oh yeah, their whole last record was done at his house direct to hard disc. Alan White is a good friend of mine; he married a girl from Kent, Washington, right here where I live. They used to live around here, and I'd see him all the time. I used to see him in the airport, and I ran into him and Tony Kaye while they were doing that record, and he said, "We're doing it all at Trevor's house, and it's all sampled onto hard disc."

It's like, "Should we repeat the chorus? Okay!" *(Laughs)*. No need to play it again; you've already played it once. That's pretty scary. We still do it the old-fashioned way. We all play together. We all have to look at each other and have to be able to see the drummer's foot to see where the beat is going to be. It's still pretty analog. We record on digital machines, but everybody's still playing at once, and Ann actually sings while we cut the tracks. We usually keep part of that vocal, too.

SW: That's very unusual these days. Most people go in and want to use a whole day to record one vocal.

HL: She's really good, and you get her excited and that's when she performs the best. She's not one of those people that can sing at half level, either. She sings all out every time she sings. So we record her whenever she's singing! *(Laughs)*.

SW: You have this side project going as well, the Howard Leese Group; if Heart never made another album, what would you do in your career?

HL: I'm starting to produce a few things around here in Seattle. I produced a rock band, and I'm producing a funk record. It's all on a computer, and I'm just going in and getting the sounds for them, and I'm going to play guitar on it.

I'm also making some guitars right now. I'm doing a real small run of these really beautiful guitars. I made the first one for myself, and people liked it so much that I'm having to make a few more. I'm probably going to make about ten of those. So that's kind of fun.

I'd probably just do what I'm doing now, just stay involved in music and have fun. I enjoy the free time that I have now, because we have a lot more free time. For the first fifteen years we never stopped for a minute. *(Laughs)*. "I know I have a house somewhere, and I guess it's pretty nice, but I haven't seen it!" *(Laughs)*. So it's actually nice to be around for a while and have some time in the Northwest here.

But I think we're going to travel a little bit this summer. Me and Ann are going to do a few shows. She's doing this R&B rock/blues thing; we'll take a little band out with horns and do a few shows just for the hell of it. That will be fun. Heavy and funky.

SW: If you could write your own place in rock history, what would you want it to say?

HL: Boy, I don't know if a person should write their own epitaph! *(Laughs)*

THE MAN BEHIND THE METHOD

Doug Marks has probably taught more people to play the guitar than any other person in the world. Since 1982, he has sold over half a million copies of his **Metal Method** *instructional tapes in more than one hundred countries worldwide. In the process, he has virtually re-defined the market for instructional videos, as well as discovering and nurturing several newcomers who went on to successful musical careers.*

A largely self-taught guitarist and self-described "street musician", **Marks** *honed his chops in a succession of hard-working club bands in the Southeast for years before moving to Los Angeles in the early Eighties to take his shot at rock stardom. Quickly disillusioned with the local music scene and desperate to make a living,* **Marks** *started the original* **Metal Method** *course out of his living room in 1982.*

Over the next few years, **Metal Method** *proved so successful that it allowed* **Marks** *the financial and artistic freedom to put together his own band,* **Hawk,** *and release an independent album in 1986. Though the group disbanded, various members went on to play in bands such as* **Judas Priest, Bullet Boys** *and* **Guns N' Roses.** *Having focused so much time and energy on* **Hawk,** **Marks** *spent the next several years rebuilding* **Metal Method.**

I spoke to **Doug Marks** *on June 6th, 1995 from his home in California. He was in the middle of shooting a new video, the first in a new series on songwriting, and was very upbeat.* **Marks** *speaks with a great deal of humor and insight about music, the music business, and his unique role in it. He admitted some frustration at the lack of recognition he has received from the industry at large, and seemed very pleased at the opportunity to set the record straight.*

SW: Tell me about the Metal Method.

DM: I created the first version on audio cassette in 1982, and then introduced it on video in 1986. It's a six-tape course that teaches all the basics and includes a few advanced techniques and theory.

The basic course is normally revised every two years in response to students' questions and to include new techniques. I think I've finally got it right, because it hasn't been revised in three years, and for the first time I don't really feel a revision is necessary.

SW: You've been in business for thirteen years. Did you have any idea at the beginning that your course would be around for this long?

DM: I've never known from day one how long the guitar lesson business was going to exist. I certainly didn't think it was going to last as long as it has. I mean, no way! I thought maximum, maybe five years, but even that seemed unimaginable in the beginning.

Initially I thought of the course as a vehicle for me to make a living and put together my dream band. I tried putting together the dream band without success, and for the past five years diversified a bit. I opened a recording studio and ran it for a year, and tried my hand at various other ventures.

Well, after beating my head against the wall in a few different directions, I finally decided that what I'm put here to do, and what I do best, and what people are willing to pay me to do, is give guitar lessons on video! Whether I like it or not. *(Laughs)*. So I decided I'd better get motivated again and focus on guitar videos. Last fall I really got into gear and got the business going better than it ever has. I sold more stuff last December than I've ever sold in any previous month.

SW: That's remarkable.

DM: I'm proud of it, especially considering that people are saying hard rock is dead. The fact is, regardless of how it appears out there, I'm selling more than ever.

I realized that if I want to stay on top, I've got to start turning out some new products. So my goal right now is to crank out a new video each month. Some of the stuff in the future will feature other players. But I've got many ideas for my own new lessons, too. I'm currently working on a new video.

SW: What's it about?

DM: The basics of songwriting. It teaches a simple technique for consistently writing professional-sounding songs.

SW: Are you going to offer an entire course on songwriting?

DM: Yes. This video is actually the first in a series of four songwriting lessons. The second in the series explains the equipment used for songwriting, and then the third teaches lead composition. The fourth video takes the song that was composed during the first three videos into the studio. It teaches tricks for making a professional-sounding recording on a limited budget. And believe me, that's a valuable lesson.

SW: That's for sure. Stumbling through the studio the first couple of times can be hazardous to your bank book! *(Laughs)*.

DM: Exactly. When I opened up the studio and ran it last year, I learned a lot from the experience. I picked up some valuable tips on how bands can get the most bang for their buck in the studio. This new video series contains many of the same things that I would recommend to every band that came in, but most bands wouldn't take my advice.

The mistake that I've seen bands make over and over again is not coming in prepared. Most bands come in with a tiny budget, and they think they can spend two hundred dollars and get out of there with a professional-sounding recording. So they try to lay down the basic tracks in about an hour and move on from there, and what happens is they go through everything too fast.

And then they go back and try to doctor this lousy recording, when they didn't get the foundation put down right in the first place. So they wind up spending a thousand dollars or more, and when they're finished, they're very dissatisfied. Plus it's not much fun to work with them.

SW: *(Laughs)*. I can just imagine. You get to take the blame!

DM: Exactly. And it's just a matter of their inexperience. So there's a great deal of valuable information I'm trying to get across in this video, and hopefully my students will be more willing to take my advice. When you're actually selling studio time, the bands don't trust you.

SW: They think you're just trying to get them to spend a thousand dollars.

DM: Right.

SW: Do you ever see yourself expanding to maybe teach a little bit about the business side of music? Or is there even a demand for that with your students?

DM: There's not a big demand. I cover certain aspects of the business, but my lessons are primarily aimed at beginner and intermediate guitarists.

The music business is like a pyramid; the pros are at the top, the amateurs at the bottom. I gear my course for the bottom because that market is huge. When I design a product for advanced players, sales are abysmal because the market's too small. Plus, experienced musicians are much less interested in music education.

SW: That's true, they're not as apt to accept advice and criticism. They want to feel like they know it all.

You know, it seems strange to say this, but I was thinking about all of my favorite guitarists, the ones I grew up listening to, wondering which one I would name if someone asked me who my main influence is as a guitar player. Out of all the great guitarists of the world, which one influenced me the most? And it's actually you! *(Laughter)*. In the sense that, no matter how much I might like some famous guy's playing, he didn't teach me barre chords!

DM: *(Laughing)*. I appreciate that! Not to sound immodest, but I hear that often. And it's true! I mean, I've replaced, for a lot of people, that first small town guitar instructor, or at least supplemented that small town guitar instructor, and that's where most people learn their chops.

SW: Let's talk about your musical history a little bit. Do you remember the first guitar you ever owned?

DM: Yes, of course. *(Laughs)*. That's like asking me if I remember the first time I had sex! My first guitar was a Marco Polo acoustic.

SW: *(Laughing)*. I don't think I'm too familiar with that company.

DM: I've never seen one before or since. It cost about twenty-five dollars new, so it wasn't exactly a fine musical instrument. *(Laughs)*. A lot of kids write to me and say, "All I have is an acoustic guitar. Can I still learn from your lessons?" And of course, the answer is yes. Sure, it's a lot easier to learn on an electric, by far, but of course you can learn on an acoustic.

And as long as you don't get discouraged, the more difficult the instrument is to play, probably the better off you're going to end up for it. Because when you give up that first lousy acoustic with the big, thick neck and strings on it, it's a breeze from there on out. It separates the men from the boys and the girls from the women. *(Laughs)*.

SW: What kind of early musical influences did you have?

DM: I have an older sister, so my influences go way back to post-Elvis, pre-Beatles stuff. The first type of music that I listened to, through no fault of my own, was Bobby Vinton, Bobby Vee, Bobby Rydell...*(Laughs)*. All the Bobbies! Neil Sedaka. I still remember the lyrics to much of that stuff. My sister had poor taste in music, what can I say? *(Laughs)*. It certainly warped me.

Then of course the Beatles were an early influence; I mean, they influenced a million people to pick up the guitar.

SW: More like ten million.

DM: Definitely. I can't really say that the Beatles were the thing that changed my life, because I can remember even before then I had decided to become a musician. I'm not sure why, but I guess it's because I was fascinated by Superman and Batman, and rock stars seemed like the closest thing to a real live super hero. *(Laughs)*.

I can remember playing outside when I was small; I was singing, and one of my little friends said to my mom, "Doug's quite a musician, isn't he?" But I thought he said *magician*. And I considered that quite a compliment. A magician sounded like much more fun than a musician! But as time has passed, I've found that magicians and musicians have much in common.

SW: More than the audience ever suspects, I'm sure. It's a professional musician's job to make it seem like magic, like it just comes naturally.

DM: In live performance, as well as in the construction of songs, it's all done with mirrors.

SW: If most people were to meet their big guitar heroes and see how human they are, they'd probably say, "Is that it?" *(Laughs)*. I know I've said that a few times.

DM: Sure. I told a guy that was a big fan of MTV that it was all lip synching, and he was so disappointed it was like telling a kid there's no Santa Claus! *(Laughs)*. The trick has been exposed.

Even in my first band, the groupies thought we were so cool until they watched us rehearse and heard the arguing. Our illusion was, we acted as if we liked each other. *(Laughs)*.

I heard an interview with David Lee Roth recently, and someone asked if he misses all the fun he had in Van Halen. And he said, "If the truth were to be known, it was *never* fun." The trick is to make it look like fun.

SW: Oh, there's more truth to that than people imagine. When I first started interviewing people a few years ago, it really opened my eyes to how little some of them care about the bands that made them famous. *(Laughs)*.

I remember meeting Neal Schon a couple of years ago, and he really wasn't into Journey at all. He was like, "Screw Journey. All that band did was hold me back musically. The music I'm playing now in Hardline is way better." Which is kind of ironic, since he's now involved in recording a new Journey album! *(Laughs)*.

DM: That's funny.

SW: Yeah, it's crazy. So, when you were coming up and learning music, did you take lessons?

DM: Yes. The first guy I took lessons from was in one of those little music stores. He didn't even know how to play barre chords. I learned from the Mel Bay books.

SW: *(Sings)*. Michael row your boat ashore...

DM: You were there? *(Laughs)*. It was frustrating, because I definitely wasn't learning what I wanted to know, and I was unable to find a rock guitar teacher. I started playing guitar when I was thirteen, and I didn't find a good teacher for about five years. Didn't even get in my first band until I was nineteen, and still wasn't much of a player then.

I used to bother all the hot local guitar players in my hometown, one guy in particular. He sounded professional, played by ear, knew a bunch of songs and leads, but couldn't read music. I tried to convince him to be my teacher, but he refused. He didn't think he had anything to teach because of his lack of formal music education.

I didn't care about formal knowledge; the stuff he knew is what I wanted to learn. My course is all about teaching the things he thought had little value. My slogan is, "I'll teach you what you want to learn."

SW: Yeah, that's probably what hooked me! *(Laughs)*.

DM: When I started teaching guitar, I tried to become the teacher that I never had. It's difficult to explain, but I often feel as if I'm teaching "Young Doug". So I have a lot of empathy for my students. I've been there.

SW: You mentioned some early bands you were in. What material were you playing then?

DM: The first band played cover tunes: Alice Cooper, Deep Purple, Black Oak Arkansas, the Johnny Winter version of "Rock And Roll Hootchie Koo", and some Stones songs from *Sticky Fingers*.

SW: When did you turn to heavier rock—were you always into real heavy rock-oriented playing, or did you get into it later when it became more popular?

DM: I've always been into heavy rock; Zeppelin, Black Sabbath and that type of stuff. I think what changed my life and approach to the guitar, like a billion other guitarists, was the first time I heard Jimi Hendrix. I can still remember the first time I heard "All Along The Watchtower". Love at first listen. He was my biggest influence. Even today, I still look to him for inspiration.

SW: You just can't go wrong with Hendrix.

DM: Naw, he's just amazing. To me, he is the guy that will be remembered as the musician of this century.

SW: And a lot of these guitar heroes that are so recognizable in their time will be completely forgotten.

DM: In every generation there's always an artist that stands above the rest. To me, he's the man. I thought that twenty years ago and still think the same today.

SW: The more music that comes along that's really less and less original, the more you look back and realize how truly original and inspired Hendrix really was.

DM: He certainly was. One thing I mention in my lessons is how important it is to copy songs from recordings. Many musicians think that if they copy songs, they won't sound original. Jimi Hendrix was one of the most creative, original guitarists ever, yet he copied songs constantly. He performed *Sgt. Pepper's Lonely Hearts Club Band* live two weeks after it was released.

SW: And I understand he used to like to jam with just about anybody. That's how you pick up the little things that make your style.

DM: He had an incredible passion for playing.

SW: He was into King Crimson and ELP, which I always thought was kind of strange. At one point they invited him to join ELP. They were going to change the name to HELP! *(Laughs).* It just goes to show you how diverse his tastes in music were.

DM: Of course, he was also a very big Bob Dylan fan, which is surprising.

SW: It is, because there's really no great guitar in that stuff, but I guess he could perceive the innate quality of the songs. And his versions of Dylan's songs were always much better than the originals. *(Laughs).* Of course, *anybody's* versions of Dylan's songs are always superior to Dylan, but that's another story!

DM: A guitarist that influenced me nearly as much was Robin Trower. He's not considered an innovative player because he was working within Hendrix' framework, but he had his own little niche within that type of music. I've got all of his early CDs, and still listen to and copy his stuff. I love the chord inversions and just so much about his music. He is a very melodic, spiritual player.

SW: Before you started the guitar lesson business, did you always make a living solely from being in bands, out on the road and that kind of thing?

DM: Yeah. I was at the bottom of the pyramid. *(Laughs).*

SW: *(Laughing).* As we have all been at one time or another...

DM: I spent a long time at the bottom, and while I was doing it, it was like, "What in the world is going to come of this?" I mean, no permanent address, no life outside the band. It was tough.

But looking back, I consider those days the best time of my life. So far, anyway. And what came of it is my Metal Method course. I teach from experience.

SW: Were you familiar with theory at that point in your playing career?

DM: No. I didn't really understand theory until I started giving private guitar lessons. My students would ask me questions about theory, and I would either look up the answer or figure it out on my own.

I'm completely musically uneducated. *(Laughs).* There's a lot I don't know about playing guitar. How this happened to me, and continues to happen, is somewhat of a mystery.

SW: That's pretty funny. How did you manage to put together so much knowledge of theory? Just by picking it up in bits and pieces?

DM: Yes. I had identified many pieces of the puzzle from figuring things out on my own. So I could see the holes left by the missing pieces, and had a pretty good idea of how the whole thing should fit together. While attempting to explain theory to my students, I learned it myself.

Still, I'm basically a street musician. I try not to pay too much attention to theory and the technical aspect of playing guitar. By staying a little naive, I stay in touch with the audience I want to please. I don't really play for professional musicians; they're not who I'm trying to reach. I play for the people, man. *(Laughs)*. Music is simple; you don't need to know the theory behind it to write a melody.

SW: I've known plenty of really good musicians over the years who didn't even know the names of notes up and down the neck. In fact, Billy Sheehan doesn't, supposedly, and it hasn't hurt him any. Rick Richards from the Georgia Satellites played with Izzy Stradlin on his solo album and tour, and he claims Izzy doesn't even know the names of chords or the proper fingerings! But the guy has written some classic riffs.

DM: Irving Berlin, who wrote some of the most popular and memorable songs of the past century, couldn't read or write music. He played by ear. The Beatles couldn't read music, but they sure could write songs. That's where I come from. You don't have to know how an engine works to drive an automobile. *(Laughs)*.

The more analytical you become about music, the further you get from art. You move from right brain to left brain. When I write, I seldom think about key, scales or the proper chords. I just try to play what's in my mind.

SW: How did you wind up in Los Angeles, and what prompted you to start the Metal Method once you were there?

DM: Desperation. It was either that or fry burgers at McDonalds. *(Laughs)*. I came to Los Angeles to become a rock and roll star. Most of my cover band work was in the Southeast, based out of Atlanta.

SW: That's where I am.

DM: That's right; Marietta, Georgia. There's a music store I used to shop at there. That was a long time ago, almost seventeen years ago. I left there in '78. From there I moved to Denver, which is where I first started giving private instructions. And from there I moved to Los Angeles.

When I got to LA, it was totally different than I expected. I knew there would be a lot of competition; that didn't worry me. I thought I was a pretty accomplished player when I moved here. The problem I didn't foresee was, there are a lot of musicians out here, and most of them aren't very good. So there are an awful lot of people to sort through, and it's very difficult to put together a situation where you're playing with good players.

After showing up for my 200th audition, and the musicians sucked as bad as they did at the last 199 auditions, I became discouraged. I couldn't find anybody to play with! One problem is that many of the musicians in Los Angeles have never played in cover bands like musicians do back East.

I was accustomed to playing five hours a night, six days a week. In Los Angeles, bands typically play one set of material, one night a month and don't get paid for their performance. So they never have a chance to develop the same level of professional skills as the musicians I was accustomed to working with.

SW: The kind of guys that are in the movie *Airheads! (Laughs).*

DM: Right. I was being kind. *(Laughs).* So I had developed a whole different set of professional skills than the people I was meeting here. And it's hard to convey your experience to other people. It was frustrating playing with guys that didn't know how to perform on stage. I was frustrated and desperate to get something started. The something I got started turned out to be the guitar lesson business.

SW: How did that come about?

DM: Before moving to Los Angeles, I had been giving guitar lessons in Denver for two years. I had about seventy-five songs written in tablature, and I decided since I wasn't going to be teaching these students again, why not sell them everything? One student had access to a Xerox machine, so I told him, "Look, make fifty booklets of this stuff, and you can keep a booklet for free."

So I took my fifty booklets, sold them for fifteen dollars a pop, and left Denver with seven hundred and fifty dollars that I wouldn't have had otherwise. Before this, I always thought that if you want to make a buck, you must give a buck's worth of effort. This was the first time I realized it's possible to make money with little effort; just create a situation where everybody wins. Deal making at its finest! Just think up something clever, kinda like Tom Sawyer convincing people to paint the fence for him! *(Laughs).* I'll give you this, I'll give you that, I'll collect the money, and we're all going to be happy...

SW: And I've got a painted fence! *(Laughs).*

DM: And I've got seven hundred and fifty dollars in my pocket that I wouldn't have had otherwise. That made a very big impression on me. I got to Los Angeles and found it difficult putting a band together. So within a couple of months of moving, I started putting together a booklet on theory to sell to my students in Denver. I wasn't ready to let go of them yet! *(Laughs).* There was still money to be made.

That's how I first became involved in mail-order. I didn't intend to start a mail-order business; it was done out of necessity. I also started giving private instructions in Los Angeles. My gimmick was the first lesson for free. Pretty soon I had forty students coming to my single apartment for lessons.

I was married at the time, and since a single only has one room and a bath, my ex-wife, Londa, would wait in the bathroom while I was teaching. What a life. Plus, she worked full-time as a graphic artist and financially helped support me while I was putting together the first version of the course. And she illustrated all the manuals. Without her help, there would be no Metal Method.

SW: How did that small seed of an idea expand into the Metal Method?

DM: The idea of selling a booklet to my students back in Denver was successful, so I decided, why not take a shot at putting an ad together and running it in a magazine? My ex-wife and I put together a tiny one-sixth page ad that advertised "First Lesson Free", and used the line "I'll teach you what you want to learn." Both lines had helped me establish my private instruction business. All I needed now was money to get started.

At the time I had a couple of guitars; a '65 Stratocaster and a '62 Stratocaster. I had made up my mind that I was never going to give them up. They were my most prized possessions. I was sure that one day they would be buried with me. But then I remembered something about my hero, Jimi Hendrix, something that he did at the Monterey Pop festival; he sacrificed his guitar, lit it on fire and threw it into the audience. Legend has it that he believed that if you sacrifice something you really love, it will take you to the next level. It certainly worked for him, so I decided that I would, in essence, sacrifice my Stratocasters to start my business.

I sold the guitars and used the money to invest in a few ads, placing them in a couple of magazines. And I put together a little pamphlet with a free lesson for those responding to the ad, but I hadn't even begun writing the course when that first ad came out! *(Laughs)*. Before I knew it, I was getting orders for the non-existent course advertised in the free lesson brochure.

I recorded the first version of the Metal Method in that one room apartment. This is how sophisticated I was—I actually plugged my distortion box directly into one channel of the recorder and a microphone in the other! *(Laughs)*. And I became a master at writing excuse letters: "The course isn't done yet. I don't know how long it will take me to complete it. If you want your money back, I don't blame you, but if you hang in there, it's going to be great." I'd already collected a lot of money, and there was no turning back because I'd already spent the money! *(Laughs)*.

I worked on the course, continued to advertise and write excuse letters, and after five months of stalling, it was completed. When I finished, I didn't think the course was worth the advertised price. So along with their order, everybody received a refund check of five dollars for each lesson purchased.

When creating lessons I normally hate them when I'm finished, because I'm such a perfectionist. It's my students that give me the confidence to go on. Many of them wrote to me saying that I was crazy for refunding their money, that the course was worth far more than advertised! *(Laughs)*.

SW: By the time I started taking the lessons, around 1986, you were very well established. I can remember flipping though the magazines and seeing your picture so often that it seemed almost like you were some sort of rock star yourself. I think the fact that you were so visible is what prompted me to give the lessons a chance

DM: Well, the sixth-page ad worked so well, I figure why not try a third-page ad? I made twice as much money with the larger ad and no additional work. So it didn't take a genius to decide to try a full-page ad. I tripled my income, once again with no additional work. From that point on, the course has been successful. That was about twelve years ago.

SW: That's quite a story. Of course, as time went by you must have gone back and re-recorded the entire course.

DM: Oh, of course! I revise it every couple of years. The stuff I was doing in the beginning was very primitive; I duplicated my own cassettes and didn't know how to hook the recorders up properly. I chained them together, input to output, input to output…the last deck in the chain got the heavy distortion version of the course at no additional charge! *(Laughs)*.

I would scrounge around looking for bargains. Found a guy with a warehouse full of used, filthy old cassettes of various lengths and bought them for a nickel apiece. Londa and I cleaned and sorted them, and I actually started recording my lessons on them! Everything was done out of desperation. It had to be done to survive. Today I'm able to afford the quality that I wanted back then.

As primitive as my cassettes were in the beginning, the lessons were really good and my students loved them. I have never thought of myself as selling tapes. I sell the lessons that are on the tape.

Many people see what I have done with mail order and say, "Oh, this is fantastic, I've gotta start my own mail order business." But the thing to consider is, I never wanted to start a mail order business. It was the only means that I had to distribute my product. When I started, a friend gave me a book that she had ordered. She responded to a "get rich quick" scheme, and the "get rich quick" scheme was actually a book about mail order. It was trash to her, but a gold mine to me. So that's how the whole thing got started.

I still create lessons the same way I did thirteen years ago; I have never created a product, then advertised it. I always advertise it, then create it. I put an ad together that appeals to me: "Hey, wouldn't it be great if this product actually existed?" I sell myself on the idea, then my students, and then I'm forced to create the product because it's too late to turn back. They've already sent the money.

My students are my boss. I can't force myself to create a lesson without that kind of pressure on me, because there is no necessity. I make a decent living without creating new products. And recording new lessons can be a grueling process because I'm such a perfectionist. I agonize over every second of the lesson, from writing the script to the final edit.

SW: You could have called the lessons anything; you could have called them the Guitar Method or the Music Method or whatever. In choosing to call your course the Metal Method, were you predicting that metal was just going to blow up in the next year or so as it did?

DM: I'm a hard rock/metal guitarist, so I didn't really have a choice. Plus, when you try to please everybody, normally you please nobody. So I limited my market, knowing that I would seem more legitimate to my students if I said, "Hey, I'm a metalhead. If you want to learn this kind of music, this is where it's at."

I was the only one who was willing to be pictured in his ads, so my potential students could see that I'm a metal kinda dude. Even today, few of my competitors include a photo in their ad. I don't know about you, but I like to know what the person looks like that I'm taking lessons from! *(Laughs)*. I wasn't trying to go after the metal market. I was part of it.

SW: Whether you could have predicted it or not, especially in Los Angeles and then right after that, all over the place, metal just went crazy in popularity.

DM: Right. When I arrived in town, bands like Motley Crue were starting to make waves at the local clubs. So the writing was on the wall. The cartoon character in our first ad was actually a caricature of Nikki Sixx. That was before the Crue made it on a national level.

That was an exciting time in Hollywood. The first time I saw Motley Crue at the Whiskey, there was no problem standing against the stage front and center and hanging out all night. The next time, maybe a month later, they cleared the club out after their first set and brought in a new crowd at eleven o'clock that had been lined up around the building.

Shortly after that they played the Santa Monica Civic Center, and my ex-wife thought it would be cool to stand in the crowd front and center; she was almost crushed, nearly suffocated. A friend that went with us stayed in the crowd and wasn't sure whether it was his sweat on his jacket or someone else's! *(Laughs)*.

It was amazing. I wasn't predicting anything. I was part of the scene. I would have preferred to have been performing at the time, but that just wasn't in the cards.

SW: You've been in business now for thirteen years. In that time, obviously you've sold tons of lessons. How many countries is the Metal Method in now?

DM: I stopped keeping track of that about five years ago, but at the time I had sold lessons in more than eighty countries, so I'm sure it's well over a hundred by now.

SW: During the years you've been at it, metal exploded and became, for several years, just about the most popular form of music out there, and seems to have been displaced now by grunge. Is that reflected in your sales?

DM: No, not at all. I don't really see a big musical change. I mean, Soundgarden is the type of music that I've taught all along. I have never been someone who taught much of that Yngwie sweep arpeggio stuff. I worked that style into my videos, but I don't really emphasize it.

And I don't really see what all the fuss is about. Sure, the music's changed a bit, but not greatly.

SW: What's really changed—and this is what hooks the kids—is the image that drives it.

DM: Yeah, but I've seen this image come and go two or three times. This reminds me of the Allmann Brothers image of the early Seventies. It was the same non-image; you know, blue jeans and flannel shirts. No difference. It goes in cycles.

SW: It will eventually get back around to where people are wearing space suits or whatever. *(Laughs)*.

DM: Sure, the Kiss image will rear its ugly head again. *(Laughs)*. Big hair and makeup seems to be present in every decade at one point or another. Image is part of the merchandising, but the music itself hasn't changed that much.

SW: That's true. Who are some of your favorite younger bands out there now?

DM: My favorite guitarists? I like the guy in King's X, Ty Tabor—although they're not really a younger band. I like Soundgarden, Alice In Chains...and I'm not mentioning guitarists because I don't know their names! *(Laughs)*.

I haven't bought the Corrosion of Conformity CD yet, but I really like the sound of it. What's not to like? I was always a huge Thin Lizzy fan, and they've borrowed heavily from that sound. Once again, everything moves in cycles. What goes around comes around.

SW: Do you still go out in Los Angeles and try to keep up with what's going on in the club scene?

DM: Not much, but when I do it's still fun. I live about forty minutes from Hollywood. If I lived closer, I would be there every weekend.

SW: In the mid-Eighties you recorded an album with a band called Hawk. Was that the culmination of your efforts to put a group together?

DM: It was. As I mentioned, part of the reason I started the guitar lesson business was to be able to invest in a band and not be at the mercy of the record companies and such. So I put together a band and called it Hawk.

We got a lot of attention in Hollywood. We sold out the Roxy, and all in a very short period of time. We were outrageous. Glam was happening at the time, and we were completely over the top. My ex-wife, Londa, was very good at makeup and costume design. She's a unique artist, and she created a unique image. I was never comfortable with the glam image, but that was part of her contribution. Without her involvement...well, half the money was hers, so it was her project, too.

Londa also helped me find the musicians, and we definitely found some hot players. Our drummer, Scott Travis, went on to play in Racer X and Judas Priest, and I believe he's currently in Fight with Rob Halford. The bass guitarist, Lonnie Vincent, played with the Bullet Boys.

I still believe there were nights when we were the hottest band in the world. But we never got beyond Hollywood. I have no doubt that we would have been signed to a major contract if I had kept the band together. We came real close to getting signed, but I just didn't want to get involved with that particular group of people, because it was killing me.

SW: It seems as if the band was pretty much your brainchild. If I remember correctly, all the songs on the album were credited to you, as well as the production. What was the extent of the other musicians' contributions?

DM: We didn't have management, so I was the advertising executive, manager, and financier, on top of which I still ran the Metal Method business. All I really wanted to do was play guitar, but there wasn't much time left over for that.

I wasn't getting much help from the other band members. They were all on salary and were only expected to play music. What a life! *(Laughs)*. A couple of the guys were young and immature and caused endless headaches, so I just decided I didn't need the hassles and made plans to record an album without the group. I used the name Hawk, but it was a solo project.

SW: So the people on the album were none of the same people you had been playing with?

DM: No, it was an entirely different group. I really wanted to continue working with the drummer, Scott Travis. The problem was, he really wanted to continue to play out live, and he was playing with the musicians from the original group under the name New Hawk. That really got under my skin, and I told him, "As long as you're playing with them and using that name..."

It was a question of loyalty. I just didn't feel that what he was doing was very loyal, especially considering that I'd really given him his start in the business. I paid for him to come out here from Virginia, set him up and got him going, and I felt like I deserved a little bit more than that. We talked quite a bit about it, but he just felt that between doing my album or staying in the group, he'd rather be in the group. So I ended up doing the album totally on my own.

SW: How did you find the people that actually played on the record?

DM: After disbanding the original group, I sent out a newsletter to 40,000 of my students offering a thousand dollar reward to anyone that located a vocalist for me. That's how I met Jim Gillette, the instructor on our Vocal Power video. He responded to the newsletter.

We eventually chose David Fefolt as the vocalist. I recorded the album at Pasha, and the engineer there recommended Matt Sorum, who is now the drummer in Guns N' Roses. I found a bass player, but had a falling out with him a couple of days before going into the studio, so I wound up playing the bass by default.

I did all the rough tracks in my home studio and recorded the vocals there. The vocalist never even set foot in Pasha. The vocals were all recorded at my home studio. Matt Sorum helped me with drum programming, and he was actually listening to the drum machine in headphones while he was playing. I'm very budget conscious; hey, it's my money! *(Laughs)*. So I used every trick in the book to record the album as inexpensively as possible.

SW: After recording the album, did you ever play live at all with the new line-up?

DM: Really, the only people in the group were David Fefolt and myself. I held auditions, put together a group, and rehearsed. After a month of rehearsals I didn't feel that the combination of musicians really worked well together. The players were all good, accomplished musicians, but for one reason or another—and I've never quite put my finger on it—I never felt that it gelled as a group. Basically, I put together a group that I didn't want to be a part of.

Maybe my expectations were wrong. Given time, we might have been pretty hot. I was impatient; plus, once again I was footing the bill, so I decided to cut my losses. In pursuing the group, with the overhead of salaries and advertising costs and so on and so forth, I wound up spending about eighty thousand dollars, most of the profit I had earned from the Metal Method. That was my nest egg, and I blew it all, and I didn't feel like I had a lot to show for it.

One reason why I let the original group fold, and gave up so quickly on the second, is I'm not a tightrope walker who works without a net. I work *with* a net, and that net is the Metal Method business. When the going gets tough, I'm always able to fall back on my business. Once the personality conflicts start, Metal Method starts looking pretty cozy. There's no one to argue with but myself. The guys that make it in the music business normally have nothing to fall back on. It's either succeed, or get a day job.

SW: After the album came out, it actually got very positive notices and reviews.

DM: I generally got good press and a surprising amount of airplay. I can think of only one place where I got slammed, and that's *Kerrang*. They expected, because of the times and because I give guitar lessons, they thought I was going to be some sort of Yngwie Malmsteem guitar god, which I'm not and don't want to be.

I was going in a more musical direction, not just, "Hey, look at me play fast." The thing that's most important to me, by far, is the song, not my individual guitar playing. Because if you don't have a good song, you don't have much of anything.

And at the time that this guy in *Kerrang* gave me a negative review, Hawk was the top selling independent release in England. I wound up selling about thirty thousand units, and you don't see that too often from a strictly independent release.

SW: Now that it's over and the dust has settled, is it something you think you'll ever pursue in the future, in terms of putting another band together?

DM: I think about it constantly, but I hate the auditioning process. I would be in a band right now if I didn't have to go through the drudgery of putting it together. Plus, my top priority at this point is Metal Method. When I spent all my time pursuing band efforts, the guitar lesson business suffered, and it's taken me years to get it back into shape. I don't want that to happen again.

SW: And in a lot of ways, as I said before, you have more of an impact on other players by far doing the lesson business than you would by cranking out albums.

DM: I think so, too. But at the same time, I feel best about myself when I'm in a performing situation. But like I said, I'm in a position where if I pursue that, I will probably lose ground in the guitar lesson field. I'm not the risk taker I was in the mid-Eighties.

SW: What kinds of guitars and amps do you favor?

DM: I use either Marshall or Carvin amplifiers, depending on the sound I want. Carvin amps are great for leads, clean rhythm guitar and some distorted rhythm guitar. I use Marshalls primarily for rhythm guitar.

My favorite guitars are made by Carvin. The neck-through-body design gives them incredible sustain, and the action can be set very low so they're easy to play. I occasionally play Charvel Jackson guitars, and I have an Ovation Legend acoustic.

SW: Do you feel that you get the recognition you deserve in the music community, in terms of people acknowledging the contribution you have made through the Metal Method?

DM: When I'm in nightclubs or music stores, I constantly meet students that tell me how much my course has meant to them. When I was operating my recording studio last year, many of the guitarists I met said they learned how to play from my tapes. So I get a lot of recognition from individual musicians I meet.

And it's rewarding when I find out that a lot of top players know who I am, too. I don't come in contact with many of them, but they know who I am, because my picture's been in the guitar magazines more than theirs has! *(Laughs)*. Of course, I paid for it.

I'm sure many of the young guitarists in top groups learned to play using my tapes. Considering that I've sold over half a million lessons over the past thirteen years, there must be several of my students in top bands. Yet I haven't been acknowledged as an influence by any major player.

SW: I do find that surprising, because you know they grew up reading the same magazines I did, and you could hardly escape the ads for your stuff.

DM: It doesn't surprise me. Major guitarists seldom acknowledge their teacher. Guitarists often mention their roots, meaning groups or artists that influenced them, but they're reluctant to mention the guy that taught them barre chords and scales.

And face it, it's not cool to say you learned from a mail order course. It's a lot cooler to say you sat down in your room and copied Hendrix records, and that's how you became so good. That's okay. I didn't do this for the recognition. I did it for the money! *(Laughs)*.

SW: What is your goal for the Metal Method in the next few years? Are you planning ahead for it, or will you stumble into it when you get there?

DM: Well, I'm sure there will be some stumbling involved. *(Laughs)*. My immediate goal is to introduce a new product each month. I do have long-range plans, but there's no sense in telling my competitors what the game plan is. For years I wouldn't even talk about the things I've discussed with you. I was afraid of creating more competition.

Today the market is saturated; it's extremely difficult for a newcomer to find a way to make a profit. I sure wouldn't have been successful if I had started in 1995 instead of 1982. I'm able to stay on top because of my reputation.

SW: Do you plan to continue with the Metal Method indefinitely?

DM: As long as people want to learn what I have to teach, I'll be here. I have no place to go! And it's still very rewarding to do this after all these years. It's an interesting type of acknowledgment that I get for the Metal Method. I like to think of it as slow applause.

You know, when you're on stage it's nice to have that instant gratification, whereas with the Metal Method, I might create something and not hear the applause for four or five years. But it's there, and it's nice. I enjoy the recognition that comes from having influenced people through the lessons.

For more information on Doug Marks, please visit www.metalmethod.com

BIG HIT GENERATOR

Trevor Rabin is best known as the songwriter responsible for "Owner Of A Lonely Heart", "The Rhythm Of Love", "Big Generator", and "Lift Me Up", all of which helped re-define Seventies progressive superstars Yes into a mainstream pop success in the Eighties and Nineties.

Rabin was born into a prominent musical family in South Africa in the midst of apartheid. Surrounded by music from his early childhood on, Rabin took to it easily and was already a successful session musician by his mid-teens. He then formed a band called Rabbit which went on to become the most successful rock act ever to emerge from South Africa. He and the other members of the group actually had to hide from the screaming mobs of fans who pursued them everywhere they went.

Leaving the group, and the country, Rabin went to London and spent several years as a successful producer, during which time he also recorded three solo albums. The material he had written for his upcoming fourth album caught the attention of former Yes bassist Chris Squire, who asked Rabin to join him in a new band he was forming with drummer Alan White.

That band became Cinema, which recorded an album based mainly around Rabin's material. Joined by singer Jon Anderson, the band changed its name to Yes, and the resulting album, '90125', was released as a Yes reunion. Spurred by the single "Owner Of A Lonely Heart", which shot to the top of the charts in America, '90125' sold over four million copies, by far the group's most successful album to date. The follow-up 'Big Generator', which Rabin produced, also sold several million copies.

In 1989 singer Jon Anderson departed Yes to re-unite with other ex-Yes members in a group called Anderson, Bruford, Wakeman and Howe, facing an unsuccessful lawsuit from Chris Squire to prevent them from playing any old Yes material. After that project was completed, eight past and present Yes members united for an ill-fated album entitled 'Union', featuring two drummers, two guitarists, and two keyboard players. After a tour marked by dissension among the various factions, Yes returned to its prior lineup for 'Talk' in 1994, once again featuring Rabin at the production helm.

I spoke to Trevor Rabin on February 1st, 1995 from his home in Los Angeles. At the time, Rabin was very excited about the possibility of Rick Wakeman re-joining the band for its upcoming album. As with all things Yes, it didn't work out as planned; instead, Rabin resigned from Yes in May, a few months after this interview took place.

SW: Do you remember the first guitar you ever owned?

TR: I don't remember the model, but it was a Harmony semi-solid body, which I absolutely loved, and then broke.

SW: How did you break it?

TR: It fell. I dropped it in the middle of a gig, actually. The strap broke and it fell, unfortunately. I was quite upset about it.

Someone had a Strat that I borrowed, and I had never played one before.

I mean, I was only fourteen, I think. And I thought, 'Oh, this is pretty cool!' *(Laughs)*. My inspiration at the time was Hank Marvin, so I was definitely aware of the Strat.

SW: A lot of players have named him as an influence to me.

TR: That's odd. I wouldn't have thought so. I would have thought, particularly in America, that's someone that's lesser known.

SW: A lot of the guys I've spoken with are British, so that must be it. Who were some of your other early influences?

TR: I think primarily Hank was the first guy, and then there were a lot of diverse influences. John McLaughlin had an impact on me, and obviously Hendrix, who had an impact on everyone. The kind of flamboyance, the kind of abandon with which he played the guitar. John McLaughlin had an initial influence on me getting my technique together, and sound-wise I think Hendrix was the initial influence. I liked his sound as much as anything else. He was quite an influence on me on that level. But also I just love Wes Montgomery, Herb Ellis, Barney Kessel, all those old guys.

SW: So you have pretty wide tastes in music.

TR: Yeah. I was doing a ton of session work, and one of the interesting things I did, which I've never been able to find the record since I did it, but I was doing a ton of sessions at one point when I had just turned sixteen, and I was approached to do an album called *A Tribute To Herb Ellis*. And I said, "Well, I haven't played that stuff much." You know, the bebop thing. And the guy said to me, "Oh, it's not that difficult. You can do it." *(Laughs)*.

So I said okay, and he gave me some records and some of the manuscript, and I looked at it and I thought, 'Fucking hell, this is not easy!' *(Laughs)*. And I did the album. It didn't turn out too good; I mean, I was a sixteen-year-old kid. But it certainly got me involved in understanding some of the parameters of bebop and how difficult it can be, and how enjoyable as well.

SW: How did you get into session playing so young?

TR: I was in a band in South Africa called Conglomeration, and the same guys, we just changed the name—sort of like Spinal Tap—and ended up calling it Rabbit. We used to do a lot of band competitions and things like that, and we were playing one night, and this producer was there, and he came to me after the show and he said, "Would you like to play on some records?" And I said, "Shit, yeah, I'd love to play on records." At this time I was fourteen, and I went and did a couple of sessions that I thoroughly enjoyed, and it kind of led on from there. I just kept on doing that kind of thing.

SW: Were you already able to read music at that time?

TR: I started with piano, so my reading was pretty good, actually.

SW: You grew up in a musical household, didn't you?

TR: My father was the leader of the Johannesburg Symphony Orchestra for fourteen years, so I was really the black sheep of the family playing rock and roll. But I studied classical piano for many years, and did a lot of competition work, and really never had a lesson on the guitar. I taught myself guitar from the piano.

SW: What was the musical climate like in South Africa while you were growing up?

TR: The rewarding thing for me was, first of all you got the Western bands, particularly English bands at the time when I was growing up, from Zeppelin to Cream and that kind of stuff.

And I was fortunate that in doing sessions I would work with black musicians a lot, and really got into the jive thing, which I found so incredibly inspiring and so different from the Western kind of stuff. It was an intriguing time for me, and it really led me to be able to claim to be an African player. That whole black music side of things was very prevalent in my playing in the early days. I don't get to use it much in Yes, it being an incredibly white band! *(Laughs)*.

SW: This was all when apartheid was still going on in a big way.

TR: Oh, boy. It's kind of passé now, but I come from a family that was very involved in anti-apartheid activity. Donald Woods is my cousin. I don't know if you saw the movie *Cry Freedom*.

SW: Yeah, I did.

TR: He wrote the book. He was really the guy behind that whole thing. And I found it a little weird, going for lunch in the middle of a session and finding that I had to go to a different restaurant. I didn't enjoy that much. But you know, I recently went back, and it's all changed. It's fine now. It's really great.

SW: All in a fairly short time.

TR: I mean, there's a lot of work to be done, but there's faith, because obviously with Mandela being in charge, there's a lot of faith in the guy. He's an amazing human being.

SW: Did you ever think you'd live to see the day when those kinds of changes would go on over there?

TR: To be honest, no, I didn't think I'd see it. I was kind of amazed when it all came down. Everyone was. Well, not everyone. Some people were saying, "Oh, fuck!" *(Laughs)*. But I was just totally blown away. I was just knocked out by it.

SW: As you pointed out, you were in Rabbit while you were still a teenager. While the group never really made it to America, it was extremely successful over there, wasn't it?

TR: To this day it's still the most successful band that's ever come out of South Africa. It was kind of a teenybopper thing, which was a little bit unfortunate, because musically the players were phenomenal, particularly the drummer and the bass player. Just incredible players, solid as a rock, and it doesn't really come across so much on the record.

SW: How did that all come about?

TR: I was involved in sessions, and I started getting into production and engineering, which I obviously enjoy very much. Actually, there's an interesting guitar reason for me doing that; when I was doing sessions I used to come into the control room and listen back, and I'd say, "God, that's not what it sounded like in the studio." So I thought, 'I've really got to start engineering myself, so I'm not at the mercy of an engineer who might not hear things the way I hear them.'

But I was doing a lot of production, and it was unheard of to sign a white rock and roll band. And although I was very involved in the African thing, producing a lot of artists and having big records, I really wanted to get involved in doing a rock and roll record. And due to my success as a producer with a singer I was producing, I was fortunate enough to be able to convince the record company, along with the guy who I was producing with, to sign the band. They didn't think it would sell any records.

We ended up like the Beatles or something; we couldn't leave our rooms without bodyguards and stuff, which was crazy. So it worked, and it was very much a Western rock and roll kind of thing.

SW: How long did Rabbit last?

TR: It blew in so quickly that it blew out pretty quickly as well. And politics were involved; I wanted to leave the country, while the rest of the band were having such a great time bathing in the success of what we were doing that they didn't want to leave the country. And I was desperate to leave the country, so I just basically left, and they stayed, which is what broke the band up. *(Laughs)*.

There were tours that were organized to come to America. We were signed to Capricorn Records. That's when I first got to learn about Dixie Dregs, and have since become very good friends with Steve Morse. But because of the apartheid thing, it was impossible to get work permits. That was just one of the things we just didn't get around to doing.

SW: Did it bother you to be perceived as a teen idol?

TR: Oh, yeah, it was weird. I mean, I would go and play a gig in front of five thousand people and would be very warmly received by the fans, and then I would sneak off to the jazz club to play with all of these great fifty year old session musicians. So it was kind of strange to me that the only credibility we got was that our pictures looked good! *(Laughs)*.

That's not fair, actually. The press were very supportive in that this band was going to happen internationally, but we never really stood a chance because of the apartheid thing. The sanctions were such that we couldn't get permits to do anything. It was pretty difficult.

SW: After that, did you go back to playing sessions, or is that when you embarked on your solo career?

TR: I packed up and moved to London almost immediately. I actually started a record company in London and opened up some offices. You know, I was young and naive, thought I could do anything. I just thought I'd go and do my job in London, the same job I did before, which is be incredibly successful making records! I had a rude awakening. *(Laughs)*. Success is not something that's just part of the job. You can work as hard as you like, and sometimes that just doesn't come.

But I went to London and had a really great time there, and worked with a lot of great people. I produced Manfred Mann, and ended up working with Jack

Bruce and Simon Phillips on my third solo album, which was very enjoyable. I stayed there for a while, and did three solo albums and a tour.

SW: Interestingly enough, I saw your name one time in the weirdest place, on a Rick Springfield album.

TR: Oh my goodness! That wasn't my fault! *(Laughs)*. Funny enough, I learned about it in the same fashion as you. I just saw it. He recorded one of the songs that I'd written for Rabbit. That's really all it is. Of course, he's allowed to do that. Actually, I think he did the song better than Rabbit did it.

SW: I saw that and thought, 'Hmm, that's something not too many Yes fans would get into!' *(Laughs)*.

TR: Well, it took a while to get any kind of recognition from them, anyway. To this day! *(Laughs)*.

SW: I guess it always will be an awkward situation, with such a long history.

TR: *(Ruefully)*. Yeah.

SW: Having done so much session work, does any of it stand out as a particular favorite?

TR: I did a session for Bob Dylan once, which was very, very strange. *(Laughs)*. I walked in there and he explained what he wanted, and I started tuning my guitar, and I kind of played along while I was tuning it. And he kept some of the parts I played while I was just tuning the guitar. He has a very organic manner in what he keeps. It's quite interesting.

SW: I understand that he just doesn't like to do any more takes than are absolutely necessary.

TR: That's very true. *(Laughs)*. Very recently I've worked with Michael Jackson, which was actually far more fun than I could have imagined.

SW: You worked with him on material for a forthcoming album?

TR: Yeah. He's a highly talented guy. I was quite amazed at the depth of his talent.

SW: How did you wind up hooked up with that?

TR: I just got a call when the band was playing in New York saying, "Michael Jackson wants to know if you'll come play on his record." So it was quite interesting, actually.

SW: That is very interesting. I remember seeing him on television in some interview, and he started singing a song, and he was sort of keeping the beat with his hands against his legs. And it was amazing; I mean, it sounded like a percussion orchestra or something! And all just from him.

TR: The way he explains what he wants is amazingly vivid when you consider that he's not playing it, he's just mouthing the rhythmic elements.

SW: After living in London, how did you wind up in LA?

TR: I was producing Manfred Mann, and Manfred's catalog was available for America, and John Kalodner from Geffen Records came over to see if he wanted Manfred's stuff. And I met him there, and he actually ended up not doing anything with Manfred, but he talked to me. The idea was that I join this supergroup that he was putting together, which ended up being Asia. Which I didn't do.

SW: Oddly enough. Who was in the band at that point?

TR: Rick Wakeman, John Wetton, Carl Palmer and myself.

SW: Obviously, it turned out rather different from that.

TR: The whole thing kind of fizzled out, as these things sometimes do.

SW: Did you meet Rick during that whole process?

TR: Oh yes. Rick and I get on famously. In fact, we're talking right now with regard to a new Yes album. I'm very keen to have him involved. Because with the Yes records since I've been involved, Tony Kaye does a great job live, but when it comes to the records I get stuck with doing all the keyboards. Which I don't mind, but it would be nice to be able to reciprocate with someone. And so we're now seriously considering Rick. In fact, we've spoken to him; it's just looking at whether we do it or not.

SW: That would be very interesting. How did you come to be involved in Cinema?

TR: When I came to America, things with John Kalodner didn't quite work out. Like I said, he wanted me to join Asia, which I ended up not really wanting to do, because Rick was gone at that point, and then Steve Howe was involved, and I really didn't see the point of having two guitar players. I actually had some rehearsals with them due to contractual necessity, and it was just one of those things; I mean, it was very good, and they had a lot of success, but it just wasn't my cup of tea.

And so I parted with Geffen Records where Kalodner was, and just started writing, which is basically what I'm doing now. And I basically wrote *90125*, which was the first Yes album I was on, and then sent tapes out. At the time I was free, which was a great feeling, having not been that way for years. *(Laughs)*.

Atlantic Records got the tape, and they happened to be playing it for Chris Squire one day, and he said, "God, who is this? I'd like to get in touch with him, because I'm putting a band together." So Chris called me and said, "Look, I'm putting a band together; if you're interested, come over." So I said, "What kind of a band?" And he said, "Well, I'm looking for a singer and a songwriter and a guitarist, primarily." And I said, "Well, that's my job!" *(Laughs)*.

I went to London, and he'd been working on some stuff with Alan White and Jimmy Page which they hadn't finished, and I just re-did some of the guitars on that stuff. And he liked what was going on, so we just took off from there.

SW: At what point did Jon Anderson become involved?

TR: The album was totally finished, and Chris played it for Jon somewhere, and he enjoyed it very much. So Chris told me, and we decided to invite him to sing on it. I mean, Chris and Alan had been in Yes for some time, so getting Jon involved might be fun.

So he came in and sang on one of the tracks, which I thought sounded tremendous, so we asked him to sing on more. That's why some of the tracks my voice is still on, but not all of it. It wasn't some sort of contrived idea, it's just the way things turned out. Some of the songs didn't really suit Jon's voice, so we just left my voice on.

SW: Jon's name is in the songwriting credits in various ways. Did he contribute to the songs after the fact?

TR: What happened is, lyrically some of the stuff just didn't sit well with him, and didn't sound right with him singing it, and he said, "Look, why don't I just kind of do some re-writes on the lyrics so it's more in keeping with me?" And at this point it was obvious that it was going to work with him, so I had no problem saying to go ahead. So he ended up writing bits and pieces on it.

There was a great vibe in the band; on "Owner Of A Lonely Heart", I mean, Chris had something to do with bits and pieces, but the basic riff and the basic song didn't change from my demo. But I just felt that, given the vibe in the band, I should credit other people.

SW: When the decision was made to change the name to Yes, was that a cause for trepidation on your part?

TR: I was very much against it at first. Everyone was saying, "It will give us an opportunity to put on a big show, because there will be money," and so on. It really didn't sit well with me. I still don't know if it was a good idea or not.

SW: Because you're re-opening a can of worms that has a good deal of baggage attached to it from the past name association.

TR: Exactly. And it's not really because Steve Howe was the previous guitarist; it's just that it was a very different thing from what Yes had been, and I didn't want it to be judged on that level. But the album came out and it got favorable reviews, so everyone was happy. But I still don't know if it wouldn't have been better just to keep it as Cinema. We'll never know.

SW: Actually, the resulting album was the biggest hit of the band's career.

TR: To this day, I think it's two or three times bigger than any of the other albums.

SW: In some ways, with you being perceived as the new kid in an old band, that must have been pretty validating.

TR: Yeah. I did get very tired of when people would say, "What does it feel like to fill Steve Howe's shoes?"

SW: You should have said, "Hey, look, man, I created this band. I wrote these songs. These guys would be nothing without me." (*Laughs*).

TR: I brought my own shoes, thanks.

SW: When it came time to tour, how did you decide which of the older songs to play?

TR: They were very good about that. They said, "Look, these are the songs that always go down well with the Yes audiences from the old stuff. We'll give you a list of those, and you choose." I mean, there were certain things where I'd say, "I don't really want to do this one," and they'd say, "Well, that one we really have to do." So there was a bit of that involved. There's an old Yes song called "Sweet Dreams" that I really like, and we did that for a while, but we stopped doing that because not many people knew what it was.

It's been difficult, because it's such a traumatic kind of band. Every time something new is done, it's like, oh God, we've got to get together and do this, and this one lives here, and that one lives there…it's not an easy environment.

SW: The follow-up to *90125*, the *Big Generator* album, seemed to take forever, and it went through changes in locations and producers and so on and so forth. What was the story behind that?

TR: Basically, *90125* was based on material that I had written for a solo album. All the material was written and ready to go, whereas with *Big Generator* it was really a learning process of how do we work together as writers and creators? That was the hard part.

We ultimately managed to do it, but most Yes fans don't really consider that album one of Yes' highlights. The band does. The band is very into the album. But it was very difficult in that creatively we weren't sure how we were going to gel together on that level.

And Trevor Horn, who was the producer, got to the point where he didn't think he could help us any longer, and so we parted. And then it was really a starting again process. So we decided to go back to LA, and this after four months in England and three months in Italy. It was really tough, and a bit ridiculous a lot of the time. Ultimately we landed up back here, and I just went into Sunset Sound and mixed it once it was finished. But it was a very traumatic, difficult one.

SW: After that album, Jon Anderson left the band…

TR: What happened was, he wanted certain things to happen, and everyone was really looking at different things to do. I was determined to go and do a solo album, which I'd been planning for ages, and also had a commitment to do, business-wise. So he went and did his ABWH thing, and I did a solo album.

And once that was finished, they were doing a second ABWH album, and at some point Jon called me and said, "Things are going really good, but we need some songs." And I read into that that the record company was saying, "Come on, guys, we need singles." So that became the *Union* album.

SW: That surprised the world when the announcement was made. It was like, "What?! All those guys together?" How did that work out?

TR: The most favorable thing I can say…I think the album didn't work at all, because basically it was some ABWH stuff kind of fused together with some demos I had done in my studio. It was a bit ridiculous on that level.

SW: It seemed like there were about a hundred keyboard players on that album.

TR: Only on the ABWH stuff, because with our stuff, we just handed it in. I heard that Rick was unhappy. He mentioned that during that project he spent a lot of time and effort doing what he thought was very good, creative stuff, and next thing you know, Rick goes back and he hears all these new keyboards on the stuff. So I don't think he was very happy about that, nor should he have been.

We just handed songs in. I had these demos, "Lift Me Up" and a bunch of stuff. I guess some of the managers thought that by getting all these past and present Yes members together, it would be great. *(Laughs)*. It certainly wasn't that at all.

SW: How did the whole concept even evolve? In retrospect, it seems so absurd.

TR: The funny thing is, when it started off that's exactly how we thought of it, like "This is kind of ridiculous." Some of us did, anyway. For me, the most positive thing is that Rick and I got on really well, and we had some great musical experiences together on it. Hence the reason for wanting to get back together again.

SW: A lot of people wondered how it would go down with you and Steve Howe together.

TR: Well, it didn't, basically. He's very much into his style, and I tried for a while to get some kind of thing going. Jon recommended that when we do a guitar solo, that we do it together, and I thought that was a pretty good idea. But Steve point-blank said, "No, no, no, I don't want to do that." He wanted to do his thing, which is fair enough.

As people, though, Steve and I didn't have a problem. I mean, I spoke to him about a month ago. But musically, it's not something that really worked. There was no time to even try and get it to work. It was fortunate that with Rick and I, it just gelled immediately. With Steve, you know, our styles are so incredibly different…

SW: Almost polar opposites.

TR: Yeah. And one thing was, we were rehearsing the song "Miracle Of Life", and there was a part I was suggesting Steve play on it, and we were going through it. It was relatively difficult, and we were just trying to work the easiest way around the problem. And so I said, "Rather than sit here doing this, I'll just write it out for you, and you can take it home."

And he said to me, "I don't read," which kind of surprised me. It didn't amaze me or anything, it just surprised me, because he's a good player and I assumed he could read music. I don't know how well that went down with him. But I didn't say anything. I was just kind of surprised.

SW: People used to say of Yes that it was a band of musicians who sounded like they knew what they were doing, but they really didn't.

TR: That's *very* true. To this day, that's true! *(Laughs)*.

SW: When it came time to go on tour with all of you, it must have been a logistical mess.

TR: Oh boy, that's an understatement. *(Laughs)*. But it's amazing how quickly it just gelled in and worked. Everyone was surprised at how it finally kind of made sense. It definitely took a while before it got to that point.

SW: After that, the band returned to the *Big Generator* lineup for *Talk*. That one also seemed to take a while to come out.

TR: Part of the reason for that is that I was given the ominous responsibility of producing it, and the technology I used in the process was all Mac-based.

SW: It's all brand-new technology.

TR: It was pretty traumatic in that we'd get takes down and the Mac would crash or something. But there was a great company involved, Mark Of The Unicorn, a software company, and Macintosh Computers were very interested in the project, so we landed up actually not having too much of a problem with it, other than the fact that it would crash, and there's nothing you can do about that. It's all BETA stuff, and it's all new. There was also a learning curve where I had to learn the technology pretty comprehensively.

SW: Is that the only album that's ever been recorded with that technology?

TR: It was at the time. I'm sure there's now something else that's been done.

SW: How does the technology work, in layman's terms?

TR: You basically record onto hard drive, and you can manipulate and look at sound waves and do everything on screen. Obviously I had a huge learning curve there. But the ability to record your guitar onto the hard drive and then manipulate it afterward is fascinating. I'd never go back. I mean, right now I'm updating that, even. That's the way of the future. The days of tape recorders are fast drawing to a close, with any luck. *(Laughs)*.

SW: Does that make it more difficult when you go to mix down?

TR: Oh, much easier. Because everything's so completely controllable, and you can watch what you're doing. It's incredible. Incredible new developments in the last ten years.

SW: Did that affect the way you wrote and arranged the songs?

TR: Yes, because you can write as you're going along. Things are so interchangeable, and nothing's engraved in stone, as it were. It actually made it a lot easier, and I enjoyed it thoroughly. I really did.

And the inspiring thing was, the whole band, but particularly Jon, was behind it being done this way, which made it much easier when the record company was saying, "What's going on? What's taking so long?" Jon would say, "Look, Trevor's doing something with this new technology, and you've just got to be patient and back off." Which obviously made it much easier for me to zone in and not have too much pressure.

Obviously they were thinking, 'Oh, God, a guy from the band is producing it.' Which was their suggestion, not mine! But ultimately there's always that paranoia, and it was alleviated by the band being totally behind it.

SW: Did writing the songs that way alter the way you approached arranging them for live performance, or did that remain more or less the same?

TR: Funny enough, we were very worried about how this stuff was going to sound live, because of it being such a different thing. The beginning was a nightmare, pretty much. But the last song on the album, "Endless Dream", by halfway through the tour was just kicking butt. It was exactly where we wanted it.

SW: It's funny, I was hanging around at the Atlanta date watching you guys do your soundcheck, and you did "Purple Haze", of all things.

TR: Oh yeah, we actually ended up doing that, ultimately.

SW: I never thought I'd live to see the day when I'd hear Jon Anderson's voice on that song.

TR: Nor did Jon! *(Laughs)*.

SW: Because you've done so much with cutting edge technology, you're regarded as a very high-tech player. Do you feel comfortable with that?

TR: It's funny, because as I said to you in the beginning of the conversation, the reason for me to do anything like that is really because I want my guitar or keyboards or whatever to sound as good as possible, and the only way to really do that is to make sure you're on top if what's going on. Because things are still very cumbersome, and there's really still a long way to go.

SW: When you look at all the jobs you do, as far as producer, songwriter, singer, guitarist, keyboardist and whatever else, which one of those best defines your role in the band?

TR: I'm definitely a guitar player first and foremost. All the rest is, I wouldn't say "peripheral", but it's certainly not what I pride myself on. When I'm singing, really I'm just singing to put a lyric across. I don't consider myself Stevie Wonder. If I do a guitar solo which I'm not happy with, I get really upset. But if I sing something out of tune, I just say, "Oh well, that's me." *(Laughs)*.

SW: You mentioned earlier that you're writing. Are you writing for an upcoming solo project, for the next Yes album, or what?

TR: The best way that I write is just to write and not worry about what it's for, and just let it land up where it's going to land up. Although I am doing a solo album, and that's going to be very specifically written. Although it's going to be songs, it's going to be very specific to the kind of style that I'm looking at, which I can't really explain. It's very different from anything I've done in the past. It's very, very guitar-oriented.

SW: You once mentioned the possibility of doing a predominately guitar-based record and possibly inviting some other guitarists to play with you.

TR: Right. At this point I don't think I'm going to bring in other guitar players, but I might get together with some singers, or maybe some bass players.

SW: What does the future hold for Yes at this point?

TR: Like I said, we're looking at doing another album, and we'll see where it leads to. We've just finished a long tour, and it's been pretty traumatic, and it's just getting that out of the way.

SW: What would the future hold for you personally if Yes never got back together?

TR: I think I'm definitely going to be doing a lot of solo records. It's something I really haven't done in too long, and a lot of fans actually write and say, "When are you going to do another solo record?" And it's something I really want to do, so I'm going to go ahead and do that pretty soon. And there's some interesting CD-ROM stuff I'm getting involved in, and some movie stuff.

A lot of movie music that's not guitar-oriented, they go and get a guitar player to do it. Eric Clapton, for example. But what I'd like to do is specifically write a guitar-oriented score. That's something that I'm looking at doing, and

I've got an agent who's come up with some ideas, some of which I have liked, and some of which I haven't liked. So we'll see where that leads.

For more information about Trevor Rabin, please visit www.nfte.org/Trevor.Rabin

JUST FOR THE RECORD

Stephen Rothery shot to fame as the guitarist in the British progressive rock band **Marillion**, one of the most popular bands worldwide in the Eighties and Nineties. Taking its initial cue from such Seventies bands as Yes, Pink Floyd and Van der Graaf Generator, **Marillion** emerged into the post-punk wasteland of the early Eighties. The band's grandiose music and theatrical live presentation were an instant hit with the fans while earning scathing reviews and constant, unfavorable comparisons to Genesis.

Growing up in the Seventies in England, **Rothery's** early interest in British progressive rock led him to join a band called **Silmarillion** in his teens, taking the name from the works of J.R.R. Tolkien. The name changed to **Marillion** to avoid legal conflicts, and vocalist/lyricist **Fish** soon completed the initial lineup, traveling from Scotland after hearing a tape of an instrumental called "The Web", to which he added his own unique lyrical perspective.

By 1982 **Marillion** developed an enormous following on the strength of its well-received live shows, headlining prestigious venues such as the Marquee and the Friars, Aylesbury, without benefit of a recording contract. On the strength of word-of-mouth, the band signed a worldwide deal with EMI and released a three-song EP late in the year, touring the UK extensively and headlining three sold-out nights at the Marquee as the debut single "Market Square Heroes" hit #60 in the British charts.

In early 1983 **Marillion** released its first full-length album 'Script For a Jester's Tear', which peaked at #7 in the British charts mere weeks after the readers of **Sounds** voted **Marillion** the best new band of the year. The album was the first in a string of top ten smashes for the band which would include 'Fugazi', 'Real To Reel' and 'Misplaced Childhood', which entered the UK charts at #1 to cement the group's position as one of the most popular bands in Europe, spawning **Marillion's** sole US hit single, "Kayleigh".

1987 saw the release of the masterful 'Clutching At Straws', which proved to be the group's final album with **Fish**. Unable to reconcile musical, personal and professional differences, the singer announced his departure from **Marillion** in 1988 upon the release of the double live album 'The Thieving Magpie', which chronicled the final world tour with that lineup. **Fish** would go on to a successful solo career in Europe, while **Marillion** would record a string of albums with singer **Steve Hogarth**.

Guitarist **Rothery's** musical contributions dominated the band more than ever on its first post-**Fish** release, 'Season's End', which featured a heavier edge to the group's music and landed at #7 in the UK charts, giving the group the hit single "Hooks In You" and a new image. Subsequent album 'Holidays In Eden' continued to explore a more streamlined musical style which did not necessarily please the group's hardcore fans, but the next album, 'Brave', was embraced as a musical redemption as the musicians returned to their progressive rock roots in longer, more orchestrated pieces.

I spoke with **Stephen Rothery** on September 12, 1995 by phone from a rehearsal hall in

*England, where he was completing rehearsals for a forthcoming **Marillion** tour in support of the band's most recent album, 'Afraid Of Sunlight', which features **Rothery's** trademark soaring, melodic guitar playing and compositional sense as its centerpiece. **Rothery** has a great sense of humor about the ups and downs of the rock and roll roller coaster which has been his career with **Marillion**, a band which has certainly seen more than its fair share of acrimonious member changes and problems with record companies. (As a side note to this interview, I should add that when I approached El Dorado Records for a photo to accompany this text, they sent me a cover shot of the 'Afraid of Sunlight' record. When I approached the band's management, they in turn sent me a picture of singer Steve Hogarth). Amidst all these changes, **Rothery** has remained the rock upon which **Marillion's** music is anchored.*

SW: Do you remember your first guitar?

SR: The very first must have been a really horrible acoustic guitar for about ten dollars, that was unplayable. *(Laughs).* And my first electric guitar was from a company called Kay. I think it was Korean. It was a very cheap electric guitar, again unplayable.

Then when I was about fifteen, I got a sunburst Strat copy, which was the first thing that you could actually get any sort of sense out of. I had one of those for about a year and a bit, and then when I was about seventeen and a half I got a Strat. That was my first serious guitar.

SW: You've been identified with Strats for a good bit of your career.

SR: Yeah. Actually, after the Strat I went on to a Yamaha SG 2000, because I was really into Santana at the time. I used those for quite a long time, I mean for the first album, *Script For A Jester's Tear*, and for "Market Square Heroes". All that stuff was an SG 2000, and then I had an SG 3000 as well.

I only really started getting into the Strat again on the second album, *Fugazi*. I had a Roland guitar synth that was like a Strat configuration, and I just kind of fell in love with the combination of that and the Roland JC for the clean sound. I suppose I was trying to find a sound that I could work on and develop into something really special.

SW: What kind of music influenced you growing up?

SR: Some of the bands from the early and mid-Seventies, I suppose. Pink Floyd, Genesis, Camel, Yes, King Crimson, Caravan, Led Zeppelin, Hendrix, Santana, Jeff Beck…quite a few people, really. Not one more than any other, I suppose. I think Pink Floyd was probably one of the biggest influences.

SW: When you were in your first few bands, did you play lots of covers by those bands?

SR: *(Laughs).* I was in a band with a guy who was a Beatles nut, so we did lots of Beatles songs, and a few by Hendrix and Santana, just a few of the rock songs of the time. It was just school friends, really. We did small pubs and stuff around the area that I lived in the northeast of England.

We didn't play that much, and then I was only nineteen when I joined Marillion, really, so I just moved down two hundred and fifty miles and started playing some of the pub and club gigs around the area where I still now live, actually.

SW: How did you wind up getting hooked up with Marillion?

SR: There was a band called Silmarillion that at the time were advertising for a guitarist—I think it was in *Melody Maker*—and I came down to audition from where I lived, down to this little cottage in the country, and they weren't expecting me, so they were all still in bed. *(Laughs)*. So I rolled them out and made them rouse themselves. I'd just driven two hundred and fifty miles to do this audition, so for them to get out of bed seemed fair enough! *(Laughter)*.

They didn't seem very keen at the first, but they eventually managed to rouse themselves enough to set some equipment up, and then they were really impressed by what I did, and so I came down about a week later and played again, and it really clicked. I moved down, and really, that was it.

There were about thirty guitarists that they auditioned, but it wasn't so much…well, I really don't know what it was, but it was obvious that I was into the same kind of music, which was quite a specialized thing for that sort of band. It worked very well.

SW: Who was in the band at that point besides yourself?

SR: That was Mick Pointer, who was the drummer on the first album, and a bass player named Doug Irving.

SW: Then as time went on, how did the lineup evolve into the more familiar members who played on the first album?

SR: Well, this was in 1979, and we then got a local keyboard player named Brian Jelliman in, and some of the stuff from the first album, the basis of it was written around this time. The bass player then left, because he had promised himself that if he didn't make it by the time he was twenty-five, he would give up music. *(Laughs)*. So he had his birthday and he gave up music.

So we were looking for a bass player that could sing, and in the end we finished up with a singer and a bass player. We got a tape from Fish in reply to an ad we'd put in one of the music magazines, and a friend of his, a bass player called Diz Minnitt. So they both moved down and joined the band, and again, that's when a lot of the material really originated, with that lineup.

And then as things progressed, we got a bit dissatisfied with the keyboard player; really his attitude more than anything else. So we basically got rid of him, and approached Mark, from a band that we'd supported called Chemical Alice. And then…*(Laughs)*. This all sounds very ruthless, kind of like *Dallas* or something! *(Laughter)*. We then got rid of the bass player, Diz Minnitt, who's not a very good bass player, really. Kind of a weird chap, as well. *(Laughter)*.

Anyway, we got rid of him and got Pete in, who was playing in some local bands at the time. And that was the lineup that made the first EP that had "Market Square Heroes" on it, and the first album, after which Mick left the band, and Ian Mosley joined for the second album, *Fugazi*. And that carried on until the time that Fish left, which was *Clutching At Straws*, which is seven years ago now. And then Steve Hogarth joined. And so far, that's all that's happened! (*Laughs*).

SW: (*Laughing*). Sort of a whirlwind of members.

SR: Well, it's a bit like that, really. I mean, we had loads of drummers as well, in the meantime after Mick Pointer left, before we settled on Ian Mosley. Jonathon Mover, who went on to play with GTR and Alice Cooper and Joe Satriani, was in the band for about a week. Andy Ward, who used to play drums in Camel, we actually did our first US tour with him, as well as a few festivals in Europe. That didn't work out, so a guy called John Marter played drums just on a session basis for a while. We had a few! (*Laughs*). Like Spinal Tap, you know.

SW: What were the circumstances of Mick Pointer deciding to leave, just as the band had gotten successful?

SR: It was various things, really. It was partly a clash of personalities between Mick and Fish. I think because Mick had been in it from the beginning, he felt it was his band, and Fish sort of felt the same, so they never really saw eye to eye.

At the same time, it was Mick's attitude at that point. It sort of all went to his head. And there was definitely a lot of room for improvement in his playing. So it was a combination of bad attitude and bad playing, really. (*Laughter*).

SW: (*Laughing*). That's quite a combination.

SR: Not a wise thing, really. (*Laughs*).

SW: Once the lineup solidified, the band became successful fairly quickly.

SR: We were relatively fortunate. I mean, we did do a lot of work. We played all these pubs and clubs all around within a fifty or sixty mile radius of London, so when we started playing the London venues, which is where all these A&R guys from the record labels come to see you, we already had an audience.

I think that's really what got us a deal. We were playing at the Marquee in London and selling out for two or three nights in a row, without any kind of a deal. And you really had to do that to make an impression. We really had to show them there was an audience for this, because this was right after punk.

SW: So it's not as if the record companies were out actively seeking progressive rock bands to sign.

SR: Hardly! I mean, there were a few other bands playing that kind of music around at the time, but I'd like to think we had something that set us apart. We had a very dedicated following, and we're fortunate that we got the deal with EMI.

SW: Marillion has always had an almost fanatical following, even in the very early days. How do you account for that?

SR: I think it's really the kind of music we play. People tend to be very passionate about this kind of music. It's not just something they put on in the background while they're cleaning the house. It's the sort of music where people will really sit down and analyze and lose themselves in it. So people just tend to be very passionate about it.

Everywhere in the world we play, it's the same. It means an awful lot to people. It's a rather strange thing to go to a country for the first time and have five or six thousand people sing along, when it's not even their language. *(Laughs).* It's quite strange.

SW: It must have been very exciting for you to headline all those top venues before you were even signed.

SR: It was, really, looking back. When you're in the middle of doing it, it seems like the natural course of events. I suppose maybe you're naive. You're not really looking so far into the future. You're just trying to make things work as you go along.

SW: What led to doing the first album?

SR: We got the deal with EMI and made the first EP, with "Market Square Heroes" and "Three Boats Down From The Candy", and "Grendel" on the other side. That was the first thing we did, and then we were looking for producers for the first album and settled on Nick Tauber, and went to Marquee Studios in London and spent about three months making the first album, *Script.*

SW: How do you regard that album now?

SR: It's okay. It's the album I'm least satisfied with, listening to it, although I think a lot of the material is some of our strongest material in some ways. You know, the first album you make, you don't really know what you're doing. It's only after you get some perspective and experience that you get control over what you're trying to do.

SW: Do you record your parts separately, or does the band all play together live on the ground track?

SR: Yeah, that's how we've always recorded, really. We just set up and play.

SW: That's a lot different than some bands approach things these days.

SR: Well, not many bands can play, maybe! *(Laughs).* Or maybe not many bands can stand to be in the same room with one another. Maybe that's more the truth. *(Laughs).* For this kind of music, it makes the most sense.

SW: Maybe that's partially why Marillion has always been able to play very well together live.

SR: Maybe. We tend to do very well in a festival situation, where you don't have all the luxuries. You just have to go on and perform for an audience. It sort of separates the men from the boys! *(Laughs).* We tend to have a good reception live, on the whole.

SW: Most of the songs over the years are credited to the band collectively. How does the writing and arranging process work?

SR: It varies track by track. Quite a lot of the ideas come from the guitar, depending on which track it is. It changes album by album. The largest proportion of the music, I've written through the years. But sometimes it's a keyboard idea, or sometimes we're jamming in the studio and something comes that way. There's no one set way of working, really.

It's a very political situation, the whole thing with writing and writing credits. We had a few arguments about that while Fish was in the band.

SW: What were the arguments about?

SR: I fought for the recognition of being the main musical writer, and managed to argue the case successfully. But then, of course, I went on holiday, and when I came back, I found that it had been changed back again. *(Laughs).* Mysteriously, my credit was no longer there. It was just "Music by Marillion" again. That was on *Clutching At Straws*, the last album with Fish. That's just sometimes how things are. *(Laughs).* You make the mistake of going away…

SW: You mentioned Jonathon Mover briefly. I read an interview with him at one point in which he claimed to have written part of the second album, but said he had not been credited.

SR: *(Laughing).* The guy was only in the band a week! He was in the room while we were writing, put it that way. *(Laughs).* He still needed to develop as a musician…well, maybe that's not fair. He was very young, as well, while he was in that situation, and maybe he was a little bit naive to think that what his contribution was really constitutes writing. It's all very debatable, but I would certainly not look at it that way.

SW: When you guys went on your first tour of England, you were supported by Peter Hammill. How did that come about?

SR: That happened because Fish was a big Peter Hammill fan. He was very influenced by him, so when we did the *Script* tour, Fish asked him to do it. I think it was a good experience; I think he got some of the audience on his side. Unfortunately, not that much of the audience. He's quite an intense singer/ performer. It was him and a guitarist. It went okay for him. It wasn't the worst we've had a support band go down, but it wasn't an amazing reception he had, really.

SW: To be fair, he does have a very individualistic style of music that people tend to either love or absolutely despise. I guess you can't really expect an unfamiliar audience to get into it.

SR: I think the worst reception a support band ever had with us was when we had a band called the Cardiacs support us, and the audience tried to set fire to them! *(Laughter).* I think that's probably the worst reception of anybody. I think that was on the *Fugazi* tour. They were quite a weird band, kind of like a cross between King Crimson and Devo or something. *(Laughter).* Slightly punk, as well.

SW: That does seem like a strange combination. What about some of your own worst experiences as an opening act? Do any gigs stand out as particularly bad ones?

SR: Not really. We've opened for Rush a few times. The first time was five nights at Radio City in New York, and that was hard work. I think the audience really didn't know what to make of us at all.

But then we came back and supported them again a while later, all around the country, and it was really good, on the whole. There was one show where somebody was throwing coins or something like that; I think it was in Detroit. On the whole, we got a really good reception. That was their *Power Windows* tour.

SW: And then *Brief Encounter* was released as a document of that tour?

SR: Kind of, yeah.

SW: Oddly enough, in America you have never quite gotten the same reception for your albums as you have in the rest of the world. Do you have a theory as to why not?

SR: I think it's really just down to exposure. We just don't get the radio exposure we need. We had an opportunity to break in the States with "Kayleigh". It was starting to happen over there, and then the big payola scandal broke with Capitol, which we were on at the time. The head of promotion at Capitol, on the evening news, was filmed handing this big suitcase of money over to some mafia guy or something. *(Laughs)*.

That was the week that "Kayleigh" was breaking at American radio, and all Capitol acts suddenly got pulled. And there went our chance, really. *(Laughter)*. It proved not to be.

But we have a very dedicated following there. On this last tour we did there, people were coming from all over the States to see the shows. It's amazing.

SW: One bit of criticism that has plagued Marillion virtually since the moment you first appeared in public is that critics seem to always tag you as a Genesis rip-off. What are your thoughts on that?

SR: I'd say they need to take the cotton wool out of their ears, really. *(Laughs)*. Not since the first EP would I say that was a viable criticism. Maybe in part on the first album, if you want to be picky, but after that I think people just aren't giving it a chance. I think we're more guitar-based than Genesis, anyway, and I think the way we write music is very different. It's just a completely different thing, really.

People are always eager to compare things, because it makes it easier to describe to people. They don't have to think about what it actually is. It's people who haven't really taken the time to listen to us.

SW: It's ironic that the fans seem to understand the music so well, while the critics just don't get it at all.

SR: In the States I think Capitol were guilty of, when the first album came out, that's pretty much how they marketed us.

SW: You mean they went out and said, "These guys are just like Genesis"?

SR: Yeah, basically. *(Laughter)*. That was it. From what I remember of the first tour we did there, it was like, "…heavily influenced by Genesis, blah, blah, blah." It was like, "Hang on, I think you're missing the point here, guys." And obviously by then, it's too late. But we had some unfortunate experiences when we were with Capitol, to say the least.

SW: I take it you didn't have a great relationship with Capitol.

SR: Not really, no. When Fish left and Steve joined, we did a tour of the States, and maybe it wasn't anybody at the head of the company's fault, but we were playing areas we hadn't played before, and they were still sending out photos of Fish in the band! *(Laughs).*

SW: You're kidding! *(Laughs).*

SR: This was on the *Season's End* tour, so it's really not a good thing when you've just driven a day and a half to go somewhere you haven't played before, to find there's been no advance publicity, and that they've sent out the wrong photo. It's like, why do you bother?

SW: Over the years as you've done various albums, how has your approach to playing and recording the guitar changed?

SR: I suppose you know more and more what you want to do, and how it can sound, so you're less likely to be dictated to by a recording engineer who says, "Oh, you can't do that," or "Oh, I just want to compress you a bit, because you're a bit hot here." You learn to say, "No, don't do that." *(Laughs).* You get an idea how to get the different sounds.

You're always trying to find new variations or new approaches to stuff. On the last album we did, I've been using a Steinberger double-neck that they made for me a few years ago for the first time, and that's been interesting. The twelve-string part has been really nice to use. It's like a Strat configuration with three single-coils that they custom built for me, and it's a really nice guitar. That's all over the last album, *Afraid Of Sunlight.* That's probably the most radical departure for me, in terms of equipment, for a while.

SW: You've always used fairly simple effects set-ups.

SR: There's certain sounds that I like; chorus and echo and JC 120s, and Strats in the out of phase position is probably one of my favorites. A Boss DSI for distortion. But my rack is very advanced. It's a Sound Sculpture 16-way MIDI patch bay, PC 2290, Boss DSI, rack-mounted Boss chorus, quadreverb Rockman modules, a PC M5000 mainframe reverb-cum-effects processor, which I used a lot on *Afraid Of Sunlight.* That's a great unit, as well.

I use a Crybaby wah, two Marshalls, two JCs, and little bits and pieces. I've got a Boogie V-Twin pedal…I've got guitar multi-effects coming out of my ears! *(Laughs).* Just about anything you can think of, I've had, or I've got.

SW: With all the touring the band does, how many guitars do you wind up taking out on the road to recreate all the sounds from the albums?

SR: Two Strats, the Steinberger double-neck, and either two or three acoustics; a twelve-string, a six-string, and a classical.

SW: At this point in your career, you've done as many studio albums with Steve Hogarth as you did with Fish. When you're rehearsing for a new tour, as you've been doing, how do you balance out the material in terms of what you're going to play from the older records and what you're going to play from the newer records?

SR: It depends on the tour. You always want to play as much as you can of your most recent album, but you've got to try and balance it with a few of the older songs. You try to make it work dynamically through the course of a set. We try a combination, and then we'll probably change it two or three times, and then quite often during the tour you swap and change things about. Quite often we have almost a different set at the end of the tour than the beginning of the tour.

SW: When you switched singers, it was a fairly radical change in the sense that there's really nothing at all similar about their voices. What kind of a reception did Steve Hogarth get from the fans when he first toured with you?

SR: Brilliant, actually. We didn't have any problems anywhere in the world. It was really good. You had a few people in the audience who were kind of checking you out for the first three or four songs, but usually that's all it took, and then they were convinced. The only people that didn't like it were the people that didn't come! *(Laughter)*. Obviously. Everybody that gave it a chance was definitely convinced.

SW: I'm surprised you didn't have any problems with hardcore, radical Fish fans showing up to heckle the new guy.

SR: We didn't, actually. It's surprising. We expected more than we got, really.

SW: Will you be touring for most of the next year to promote *Afraid Of Sunlight?*

SR: We've already done a month in the States. We've got a month in Europe coming up, and then a break, and then possibly some shows in South America and Mexico, and possibly again in America on the West Coast. We don't know just yet. It just depends on how things go. *(Editor's Note: The West Coast tour never materialized.)*

SW: And what then? How much of a break do you usually take between records before you get back to work?

SR: We don't tend to take a break for very long. We usually go straight back into writing again, although we're not doing that this time. We have a little bit of a break. Various people are doing solo projects; I'm in the middle of doing an album at the moment, a project called The Wishing Tree. Pete from the band is playing with me, and an American drummer called Paul Craddick, who plays with a band called Enchant, and a female singer called Hannah Stobart. It's really interesting. It's a bit different from Marillion, but very interesting.

SW: It seems like at some of these record shows where you can find some of these rarities, I've seen some solo stuff of yours before. Had you done some solo work prior to Marillion?

SR: The only thing that's out there is a B-side called "Winter Trees" that was on one of the singles from *Brave*, and that wasn't really done as anything. We were desperate for B-sides, and I said, "Why don't we all do a track by ourselves and release them for B-sides?"

I already had a very rough sketch of an idea that I'd done at home, and it finished up being used. It's okay. It wasn't even a demo; it was just when I got my Proto system on my Mac, and I was just messing about trying to figure out how it worked! It ended up as a B-side, so it goes to show you can't be too careful. *(Laughs)*.

SW: You've always had lots of extra tracks that don't wind up on albums.

SR: Quite a few, which we do try to release as various B-sides.

SW: And you had the entire *B-Sides Themselves* compilation. Do you deliberately record more material than you'll need for each album, or does it just happen that way?

SR: Not really. There's only one track that we started recording on this album that didn't get used. It depends on how much time you've got, really. This time we didn't have much extra time.

SW: After you'd done two studio albums, you released *Real To Reel*, in some ways as a response to the burgeoning market for Marillion bootlegs.

SR: To a certain extent. And also, things were starting to happen in a lot of Europe, and we wanted an excuse to go out and tour again. *(Laughs)*. It was a mini-album, a live combination of the first two albums, sort of like U2 had done at Red Rocks. It really helped us in Europe, and set things up for when we released *Misplaced Childhood* in '85.

SW: Still, you guys are a very heavily bootlegged band all over the world. What is the band's attitude towards that? Some bands love it and encourage it, and others can't stand it.

SR: It's a compliment. The thing is, if people are going to buy a bootleg, they've almost always got everything else, anyway. The only shame is that it's your music that these people are selling, usually at extortionate prices. You can't help but be upset by that.

We try and control it a little bit. We have our own live CDs released, usually just for the fan club members, so if people do want a live recording, at least we can give them something of a reasonable quality, instead of paying through the nose for something that's recorded on a cassette player at the back of the hall. *(Laughs)*.

SW: Now for the old controversy. *(Laughs)*. When Fish decided to leave in 1988, what were the circumstances behind that?

SR: What happened was, we were writing music, and he was writing lyrics. He didn't like our music, and we didn't like his lyrics. It just really wasn't happening. He seemed to want to do something other than what the band had been about, and he seemed to be frustrated by the kind of music the band made, and he was writing lyrics that we felt weren't his strongest work, to say the least. We didn't really like them.

SW: Were any of those lyrics part of the material that ended up going on his solo records?

SR: Probably a couple of the lyrics, yeah. Anyway, it just really wasn't happening. At the same time, he was trying to get more and more control of the band. He delivered an ultimatum to the band saying that he wanted complete control of the band and half of the publishing money, otherwise he'd leave. So we just sort of said goodbye.

SW: See ya! *(Laughs).*

SR: *(Laughs).* Right. And that was it, really. He'd been working with Mickey Simmonds a little bit on some material, so maybe that gave him some incentive to do this, but for whatever reason, anyway, it was the best thing to happen for everyone.

SW: Living in America as I do, you really don't get as much information about Marillion over here. You hear a lot of crazy second and third-hand rumors, and I remember at one point there was a rumor that things were so bitter between you and Fish that the band wound up owning his clothes and refused to give them back! *(Laughs).* Care to comment?

SR: *(Laughs).* Well, actually, he did leave behind some stage clothes, which we auctioned off at a charity thing! *(Laughter).* It was nothing that he'd want to wear again. But it's quite funny!

There's all sorts of rumors that fly about. We're going to get an official web site on the Internet so that people can get the latest information on the band.

SW: That's great, even though that has a tendency to turn into a lot of rumormongering as well.

SR: Oh, absolutely. But at least if we have our own web site, then people will know where to go to get the latest truth.

SW: Several of the musicians I've spoken to for this book like to get on the Internet anonymously and pick up on what people are saying about them.

SR: Mark gets on the Freaks thing sometimes, and I've looked at the Alternative Marillion News Group on the NewsNet as well, occasionally.

SW: It's funny, because still to this day there are lots of rumors about the band in America. It's always this guy's getting ready to quit the band, or that guy stormed out of rehearsal, or whatever.

SR: Well, it makes for an interesting read for some people.

SW: What are the relationships in the band like now? Are there strong, friendly relationships between the band members now?

SR: Oh, yes. We get on very well. Occasionally you have little tensions, but on the whole, yes. That's why we're still together after all this time, because we really do get on.

SW: And the musical unit of Marillion has remained constant for a long time now.

SR: Until we sack somebody else! *(Laughter).* No, we have a good relationship, both musically and personally. Hopefully that will continue for a while.

SW: How long do you plan for the band to go on? Do you have any idea, or will you just keep on until someone gets sick of it?

SR: Until the audience gets sick of it, really. I think ultimately, if given the opportunity, we'll carry on making records for the next thirty years, until we reach retirement age. It's the only thing I want to do in life. Really, it's the only thing I'm good at, so I'd like to think it's the only thing I'll have to do. But who knows what's around the corner! *(Laughs)*.

For more information on Steve Rothery, please visit www.Marillion.com

HE IS BECOMING WHO HE IS

Ty Tabor is best known as one-third of the progressive, harmony-laden, not-quite-metal band **King's X**. *The spirit of exploration and innovation which is an important part of his playing is in evidence on such albums as 'Out Of The Silent Planet' and 'Faith Hope Love'. Though* **King's X** *has never quite infiltrated the mainstream, the band did make inroads to video and radio with "Over My Head" and "Black Flag".*

I spoke with **Ty Tabor** *during the recording of the album which was to become 'Ear Candy'. Though he didn't know it then, it would prove to be the group's final major label release; following its relative commercial failure,* **King's X** *was dropped from Atlantic Records. The band then faced several years of struggle, both professional and personal. Signed to the independent Metal Blade Records, the members of* **King's X** *strove to get out of the debt incurred by a previous management deal, while facing a backlash from some of its more conservative Christian audience after lead singer/ bassist* **Doug Pinnick** *came out and admitted he was homosexual. Two of the band members divorced, including* **Tabor**, *and the changes provided grist for the lyrics of several subsequent albums.*

I'm happy to be able to say that **King's X** *did not succumb to the pressures and disappear, like so many bands before it. By 2000 it seemed that the group had turned the corner, and while still not a mainstream act by any means,* **King's X** *was actually making more profit for its members than at any previous time, based largely on the strong word-of-mouth for the band's live performances.*

I was impressed with **Ty Tabor**. *He seemed to me a humble, quiet man, yet there is a core of strength in him which comes across in his music. I liked his quiet certainty about the rightness of his musical path, even though he knew that path was destined to limit him in terms of industry and public acceptance. I admired the fact that he didn't seem bothered by that knowledge. There are far too few musicians with that kind of integrity in today's rock and roll world.*

SW: Tell me about your new album. What's it like?

TT: It's hard for me to describe. *(Laughs).* I've been trying to tell people, but I don't think I have successfully done so. It's sort of more traditional-sounding, as far as tones and sounds and everything, more like early Seventies guitar albums used to sound. It's in that vein of things.

Of course, technology has progressed quite a bit, so it's more Nineties, but based on more of a traditional sound. It's real different for us, the most different music and sound we've done yet on an album. We're having a blast doing it. We weren't sure what it was going to sound like when we started. Now that it's coming together, it's like a neat little surprise.

SW: Who's producing this time?

TT: We're co-producing with a guy named Arnold Lanni. He did the recent Our Lady Peace album. He's from Toronto, and we just met him recently, so we're still trying to learn how to communicate, but it's turning out to be a cool thing.

SW: You said this album won't be out until the new year?

TT: I don't realistically see it coming out before Christmas, but it could, if everything goes absolutely perfect. *(Laughs).* But you know how that is. We don't even know what to call the thing yet. No idea about art yet or anything.

SW: How far along are you?

TT: We've got all of the tracks done. I guess we're probably about sixty percent done with it.

SW: Do you write the songs, then go in to record them, or do you go in with only a vague idea of what you're going to do?

TT: Usually we write everything and then go into pre-production about a month or two before we actually record. During pre-production we pretty much at least narrow it to a general idea that we know we want to do. Then we get into the studio, get sounds up, and change it entirely. *(Laughs).* We spent the first two weeks of the studio here not even recording, but just re-arranging songs and stuff based on the sounds we were getting.

SW: When you guys do a ground track, do you play live together and leave that as the track, or do you go back and extensively overdub?

TT: On the last album we did a lot of that, where we just kept everything, but this time, due to the facilities, whenever we live track together I've had to play at a very low volume on the guitar to keep from getting some room bleed through the drum tracks, and by doing that I'm getting some drum bleed in the guitar tracks. So all of the tracking is mainly dummy tracking to help Jerry get a drum track, and then I go back and replace it.

SW: How do you record your vocals? With all three of you singing, do you record them separate and then blend them together through mixing, or do you record together on a blend mic?

TT: Both, actually. A lot of times we'll do separate vocals, and then all three singing together also and have a blend track.

SW: Let's go back in time a little bit. Do you remember your first guitar?

TT: My first guitar? I remember my first *electric* guitar. It was called a Telstar. I think that you could buy those at Sears back then. I got it and an amp for twenty-five bucks, a Telstar amp. It was really a cool guitar. I remember every kid that played electric guitar back in the early Sixties had a Telstar. *(Laughs).* In Mississippi, anyway. It was blue. I still have the amp, as a matter of fact. What was cool about it was that you could turn it wide open and get a real cool distortion. This was around '65 or so, and it wasn't common to buy a cheap amp and have it have a real cool distortion. This one, you could turn it wide open and still talk over the volume, but it had a great distortion. It was like a little three-inch speaker or something like that. *(Laughs)*.

SW: That's funny. Do you ever play through it anymore?

TT: No, I think it's at my parents' house, but I do remember seeing it lately.

SW: How did you first become interested in playing guitar?

TT: The Beatles did it for me, man. My very first memory of music is, I was at a friend's birthday—it was his third birthday, that's how young we were—and his folks gave him one of those cheap little-kid turntables and a single, and the single was "I Wanna Hold Your Hand" by The Beatles, which was brand-new. I still have memories of being there at his house, and after we finished eating cake and all of that stuff, just going to his room and just playing that single over and over and over. And from that point on, on every holiday, birthday or anything, I would beg my parents for Beatles records.

SW: Why did you gravitate toward the guitar in particular?

TT: My dad played guitar. He used to sing to me all the time when I was a kid. At one point I remember, he would get up and go to work before I had to go to school, and I remember around six years old, when he left I started getting on his guitar, which was a Stella, and I'd start trying to figure out chords on it that I had seen him play.

The first thing I figured out was a G chord, and I remember sitting before school, just strumming G forever, until my mom made me leave and get on the bus. I couldn't believe that what I was doing was making a sound that sounded good. *(Laughs)*. That was my first introduction to the guitar, and from there I started figuring out things from watching him.

SW: Did he teach you after that?

TT: No, I never actually took lessons or anything like that. I'm sure he gave me pointers here and there, but I never really remember sitting down and saying, "Let's have some lessons," or anything like that.

SW: So how did you develop musically?

TT: Just by ear. I listened very carefully to everything I was listening to, and I'd try to figure it out. I started slowing down turntables and that whole thing, trying to figure it out. By the time I was eight years old, I have a tape of myself at eight years old singing and playing guitar, something, a song that my dad taught me. So I know that by eight I was well into it.

SW: Who were some of your other early influences?

TT: Originally, the Beatles were the only thing that mattered in the world, to me, for years. By the time I was about eleven or twelve, there was a major change in music. All of a sudden we had the very early Aerosmith, a real cool era of David Bowie, and Alice Cooper early stuff. All of those had a big impact on me. There's a lot of early Seventies stuff, it probably was my favorite time ever, listening to music growing up, was early-to-mid Seventies. There was just so much stuff out then that was just so unique.

I remember there was an FM station in Jackson, Mississippi...I was growing up in Pearl, Mississippi, which is a town right outside of Jackson, and there was station called WZZQ back then, that was the classic example of the FM station that was in the movie *FM*. It really was an institution in Jackson for the kids. Before school you would hear it blaring from people's cars, during high school. It was part of growing up there. It was a true album rock station. They would play a twenty-minute song if they felt like it. It didn't have the appearance of being governed by commercial reasons. It was people playing music that they loved, and it really didn't matter what the format was. So I was introduced to a lot of really off-the-wall music on this station, a lot of album cuts that normally don't get on the radio by people like Alice Cooper, David Bowie and whoever.

And every single person that would come on the radio in those days, you could tell instantly who they were. Everything was very unique. There weren't a lot of similar-sounding things. Think about it—early Aerosmith, early Alice Cooper, early David Bowie, and any other number of things that were out were radically different from one another, with a trademark of their own. I was just totally enthralled by all of the music that was coming out, and trying to learn how to play all of it. Early KISS, Johnny Winter, Queen, whatever.

SW: Growing up in Mississippi, what kind of a musical climate was there for a young person who aspired to play?

TT: Not really that bad, considering where we were. Jackson sort of has a feeling of being secluded from the rest of the musical world, in a strange way. You get the feeling that you could be a genius in Jackson and never get noticed when you live there, which I've learned isn't true. But that's kind of the feeling I had there. I always had the feeling that I'd have to get out of Mississippi to do anything musical.

But when I look back at it, the truth of the matter is that there were some very talented guitar players and musicians in Jackson, a lot of which have been successful. I mean, shoot, I was in Missouri when we put King's X together, and we got noticed from Springfield, Missouri, which is even smaller than Jackson. It kind of blew my theory that you had to be in a major city to make some noise. *(Laughs).* It doesn't really matter where you're from. But growing up there I had that feeling. One of the reasons being because there were several really, really talented guitar players that I knew of that I had the feeling would never get noticed, never do anything. Which turned out to be absolutely true. I thought I should move, and eventually I did.

SW: What kinds of early bands were you in?

TT: I started out playing bluegrass with my dad and my brother and another family. There were some friends of ours, a guy named Sam Pace who was very good friends with my dad and worked with him. He and his son Tim

Pace were really musical, so my dad and I and my brother joined with them and had a bluegrass thing going for a few years. We used to go hunting every year in Mississippi. Around Christmas you'd get a couple of weeks off from school, and we spent one of those weeks in the woods with no electricity or anything. We'd pull a Starcraft camper, one of those fold-out campers. We had this place where we'd literally hacked with our own hands a trail into the woods, and we'd pull our camper into there and be there for a week, no outside life for a week.

The only thing we'd bring along with us was a banjo and a couple of acoustic guitars. We would sit around the campfire after hunting all day, with our dog laying there or whatever, and start playing some bluegrass music. It was really a wild experience, because you'd be playing, and then a couple of guys would come straggling up through the woods with their dogs. Who knows where they came from, but they just followed the music, you know? (Laughs). Before long you'd have a bunch of true Mississippi woods people sitting around making music with a campfire, literally in the middle of nowhere. (Laughs). So that was originally what I was playing, as far as a band or whatever.

Of course, I was going home every day and putting on Beatles, and putting on Alice Cooper or KISS or whoever and playing electric guitar was the only thing I was even interested in, as far as sitting around by myself, what I was trying to learn. But I had a lot of fun playing bluegrass, and I learned a lot about blues playing bluegrass, I realized a few years later.

From there I went to different garage bands, doing this and that. I played in a Christian rock band called Matthew when I was seventeen, right before I left home, which was a very good band. I still look back at that band and think it was a very, very good band that I was really proud and happy to be a part of. It had excellent musicians and wrote really melodic, good music. It was just a good band.

SW: What happened to that band?

TT: Basically just marriage and girlfriends and everything. (Laughs). It just started falling apart. I wasn't married yet, but several of the members were, and they didn't want to tour anymore and that sort of thing. Around that time I moved to Missouri and met Doug and Jerry, and we became friends and played together in different things before we played together in this band. Eventually Doug called us up and said, "Hey, why don't we play together in our own band?" And we all just said, "Hey, sounds good." (Laughs). We've been playing ever since. That was nearly fifteen years ago.

SW: How did you actually meet those guys?

TT: It's a strange story. I used to play in this band called the Tracy Zinn Band. This was when I was in college in Springfield. Actually I wasn't a full-blown member of the band at the time. I had sort of filled in for them on a couple of occasions. One time the bass player had to go out of town and they asked me if I would play bass for them at this show and I did.

Shortly after that they had another show, and it was kind of a big show, in a large auditorium in front of several thousand people, opening up for a guy named Phil Keaggy. Their drummer quit right before the show, so they called me up and said, "Can you play drums?" And I said, "Yeah, I can do it." So they asked if I would mind playing drums on this gig. I said, "Oh, that'll be great." Of course, I didn't even have a drum set. *(Laughs).* So I didn't get to practice with them or anything. I don't remember practicing. So we get to the show, and Jerry is playing drums for Phil Keaggy. So my introduction to Jerry was to ask if I could use his drums *(laughs),* playing before Phil Keaggy. So that's how I met Jerry. And Doug was playing for Keaggy also, but I didn't meet him that night.

Shortly after that, Tracy asked me to join her band as a guitarist and become a full-fledged member. They used to have this talent thing at the college...boy, am I just rambling a lot of boring material here! *(Laughter).* Anyway, they had this talent show...like I said, it's a long story how we all met. I played at this talent show, I just did one song with one girl, and I did a small, very brief, blink-your-eyes-and-it's-gone solo. And Doug happened to be in the audience, and there was something about the solo he just really liked, I guess the vibrato or something. He just started asking people who that guy was playing guitar, until he found somebody that knew me and knew my name. Then he just looked up my number in the phone book and called me and said, "Hey, this is Doug, I play for Phil Keaggy." And I said, "Yeah, I know who you are. I know Jerry."

So we got together and started jamming, and like I said, we played in different things. Eventually Jerry ended up joining the Tracy Zinn Band and was our drummer. I got to know him real well. At the same time, Jerry was playing with Doug, doing gigs with Phil Keaggy and stuff. So in a roundabout way we had a connection through Jerry, and then started jamming together, and ended up playing together.

SW: At what point did you wind up as a trio?

TT: The first two years we were together, all during '81 and '82, we were a four piece band. Originally we had another guitarist. The original guitarist in the band with me was a guy named Dan McCullom. Dan quit about four months into it, and I had a good friend in Mississippi, a guy named Kirk Henderson, who was an exceptionally talented player. So I told the guys, "I know this guy who's just a killer player, and we ought to get him to replace Dan." So Kirk joined the band and played until the very beginning of 1983, and then he quit.

And we had been called The Edge up to that point, and U2 was beginning to get known, and they had the Edge, and there were several other bands called The Edge in different sates, so we started realizing this would be as good a time as any to change the name, because we're going three-piece at this point. So we changed our name to one of the stupidest names I've ever heard a band use. We were called Sneak Preview. *(Laughs).*

We just couldn't think of anything. But I can remember this, The Edge had a big following, I man we were doing some gigs that were large gigs for a bar band or a band with a label. We played some nights to over a couple of thousand people, massively packed out places. That didn't happen every night we played, but we did have some gigs like that. We were pretty excited, this nobody band really drawing massive crowds. So during this time that Kirk quit, we quit gigging for a short period of time and started working up some different types of music. We were all inspired, like, "Okay, we're a three-piece now, so let's just change everything now." So we started learning some obscure, ridiculous stuff that I have no idea why we thought anybody would like it. *(Laughs)*.

So our first gig back, we're playing this place called The Hangar, and we're three-piece, and bombing terribly. We're doing these songs we've never done out live before, and Doug's forgetting the words, and it's just an embarrassing experience. We're looking out and seeing the faces of these people who were die-hard fans of the band, usually out there with smiles, and they all had the look on their faces like, "I'm so sorry." *(Laughter)*. I remember Doug saying, "Well, we've changed our name now." And Jerry does a little drum roll, and he says, "We're called Sneak Preview now." And it's like in a bad movie, you hear two or three faint claps and the room is silent. And we're thinking, 'Somebody shoot me now, and end this horrible nightmare.' *(Laughter)*.

That was the beginning of King's X as a three-piece, the three of us doing what we're doing. We even did an album in 1983, which was a local album under the name Sneak Preview. I've still got five or six unopened copies. Someday, if they ever become collector's items and for some reason I need to pay the bills, I'll sell them. *(Laughs)*.

It eventually got better. It eventually got to where Sneak Preview was also packing out, drawing massive crowds. It just took a while to adjust to three pieces. I was used to playing my whole life with another guitarist, where you play different parts together and it all covers a big landscape of music. When we went to three piece, I just never realized there was such a radical difference in how you have to approach guitar playing when you're the only guitarist. It was a real shock for me to adjust to. After about a year of it, I was having so much fun in the three-piece situation covering up that ground all with one guitar, it really stretched out my idea of rhythm playing in a real healthy way, and after that I felt like, "I wanna play three piece." And we just stayed that way, since the very beginning of 1983.

SW: You talked about playing some obscure material. Were you playing mainly covers at the time?

TT: Yeah, we always got away with as many originals as we could without getting the club owners really mad at us. Usually that was about fifty percent. We were doing stuff like Pet Shop Boys…if I'm remembering correctly…I'm not positive, but we were doing real obscure stuff. We were doing stuff like "Climbing Up The Ladder" by the Isley Brothers, that in Springfield was unheard of. We were doing some Danny Kortchmar, off of an album that was immediately in a cutout bin when it came out, but we liked it. *(Laughs)*. And were doing stuff by a band called The Producers, that people in Springfield really loved, and was one of our favorite bands, but in most places we played nobody had ever heard of them.

SW: They're a local band, from here in Atlanta.

TT: Right, exactly! We did our last album in Atlanta, and they did a reunion gig of all the original members while we were there, including Kyle Henderson, the original bass player, and we went out to see them and ended up getting onstage doing the encore with them, doing a couple of Beatles tunes. And for us, for me and Jerry in particular, that was a supreme highlight of our musical careers, was getting to play in a small club with the original Producers. We're huge, huge fans of those guys.

I mean, we've played with all kinds of hugely popular people onstage .. as a matter of fact, while we were in Atlanta, Doug and Jerry played with Pearl Jam live. But doing this Producers thing was an even higher moment than that for me and Jerry. We were in the car yelling and giving each other high fives, acting like kids, like, "Man, we played with The Producers!" It was awesome.

SW: What's the origin of the name King's X?

TT: It's a phrase used, I guess, back in the early Fifties or Sixties, because the only people I've ever met who've heard the phrase are a little bit older, in their forties and fifties. It was basically something like a time out or a safety type of thing, where you cross your fingers and say, "King's X." I've heard different stories of what it means, and to this day I'm not conclusive to what it originally was. *(Laughs)*. But the way it came to us was, we were tired of being called Sneak Preview, which we knew from day one was the most lame name that a band had ever gone out and publicly played under. Especially doing heavy stuff. Here we were cranking out, and the name of the band was *Sneak Preview!* It was goofy as could be.

So around '85 we moved to Houston for different reasons, financial reasons and stuff. It was one of the towns we were playing on a circuit, and we moved there. Our manager kinda threw that name flippantly out to us one day, when we just couldn't think of any names. We were really wanting to change the name of the band. Over the next few weeks the name kept coming back up, and none of us were really flipped on the name. We didn't think it was that great either, but we couldn't think of anything else. But one thing about the name was it didn't make us immediately think of any one particular type of music, and that was good to us, because we wanted a name that didn't just sound totally metal, or totally this or that. Who knows what it sounded like to other people, but to us, it didn't sound, back in 1986, like a metal name.

So after a while I remember literally sitting around working on some music, and looking up and asking everybody, "So, are we King's X now, or what? Is that the name of the band?" And everybody's just sorta nodding their head, like, well, okay, whatever. *(Laughs)*. That's the way it happened.

SW: *(Laughing)*. So it wasn't any big dramatic decision...

TT: Right. We just kinda slowly became it. We kinda got used to the name in our heads for a couple of weeks, and then we just said okay.

SW: When you changed the name, did you change musically again at that point?

TT: Well, we were changing musically again at that point before the name changed. Basically during 1985 is when we started going through some serious changes. I started writing music apart from the band, and not even playing the music for the band. I was getting very bored with what we were doing as a band. I knew the potential was there for all of us, but we hadn't tapped into or learned what to do to be different. We kept *trying* to be different, which in my opinion is always a big mistake. People that are different are normally people who are doing what they naturally feel, and people who try to be different come off as fakes. And we were major fakes, trying to be different.

We knew we didn't want to be the same old same old, but we didn't have the concept of just be yourself...truly be yourself, and it will be something unique and different. We didn't fully understand that. We just felt like we had to figure out ways to be different, which was always a miserable mistake. So I was just getting very frustrated with the band, and I had a very good friend of mine from childhood, a guy named Marty Warren, who had moved to Houston and was my roommate at the time. This was just before I got married. We started writing music together apart from the band. And we probably wrote, during a year, about seventy or eighty songs. In my mind that was the beginning of the whole realization of I just need to write what makes me happy, and not even care about what anyone else thinks, not even worry about these people telling me you need a chorus here, and this and that kind of thing.

During that time another good friend of mine from childhood, a guy named Dell Richardson, was visiting me and Marty, and I started writing this song called "Pleiades." I kept throwing out ideas, like what do you think of this, and he'd say, "Yeah, I like it," so I'd just keep it. I was just bouncing things off of him, and he was just suggesting things here and there, and we came up with the song. It was the most different thing I had written, that didn't follow any kind of structural hit format or anything like that. I was real happy with it. When I listened to it, it was making me happy as being something I wanted to hear personally, that I had been missing in our music. I was afraid to really play it for the guys. In my mind I was thinking, 'They're not gonna like this at all.' All I knew is that it was fulfilling something in me that I was missing.

So I started writing like that, just writing freely, whatever I felt. I didn't care about format or sounds or anything. Just put it down. And after a while, we were on a plane flight to somewhere, and I passed the cassette across the aisle to Doug and I said, "Give this a listen." It was the song "Pleiades." He and Jerry listened to it at the same time. I was almost embarrassed to play it for them. Like I said, I had no idea what their reaction was going to be. And Doug completely flipped out and was just like, "Man, this is what we've been waiting for! This is exactly what I've been wanting to hear in my head, that I didn't know how to do it, what to do."

And that was the catalyst for us to just write what we feel, and just throw away all this garbage that we've been told for so many years, and not worry about trying to write hit music for anybody. Write what we want to write and enjoy our own music. That's why we got into this. And is was perfect timing, because this was right at the same time when we met Sam Taylor, and he was pounding that same message over our heads in a major way, trying to help de-program us from all of the things we had been taught about music, telling us, "Look, just be yourselves and play what it is you want to play." This was a major step for us, and the true beginning of what King's X became musically. That was around late 1985, early '86.

And shortly after that we were playing extremely small, hardly anybody showing up kinda gigs, and doing this really different music. Our manager at the time was Sam, he became our manager, and he sent out tapes to every record company in the industry, including some we had never even heard of. (Laughs). Every major and minor company that existed, and were turned down by everybody, including Atlantic. And then Megaforce, a small label in northern Jersey, called us up and said, "Look, we want to book a showcase gig for you in New York and hear what you sound like live." So we said okay. And actually we had done our own video of the song "Sometimes", off the first album. We had demoed four songs…oh, there's so much more story here, but you'd have to write the whole book on King's X history, so I'll try to leave it out. (Laughs).

We did this video and sent it to these guys. It wasn't even edited yet, but we sent it to them just so they could see what we looked like, because they were the only ones who showed any interest. So they booked this show for us at the Kat Club in New York City. We went and did this show, and felt like we did one of the worst shows we've ever done, to the point where Doug was just pissed off because the mic was shocking him, because we weren't grounded properly. I think eventually he kicked the monitors over and kicked the mic over and we left the stage totally disgusted, feeling like, 'Well, we blew that once and final chance for a record deal.' (Laughs). But people kept coming back to the backstage room we were in with this dazed look on their faces, like they had just been in some spiritual experience that had changed their lives or something. We kept looking at each other like, "This is really weird." Everybody was just coming up just jaws gaping open, just flipping, and we were thinking, 'Something's wrong. Something beyond us has happened here, because we sucked and that's all there is to it.' These people were acting like it's the greatest thing they've ever seen in their life. The guy that owned Megaforce Records, Johnny Z, came in and said, "You're not leaving town until you sign a contract."

And Atlantic was there also, who had turned us down, and what's so ironic is that three albums later, Atlantic was buying us from Megaforce to get us on the label! They bought us out right after the third album. We've been on Atlantic ever since, very happily. That was one of the labels we had always dreamed of being on, was Atlantic Records, and when they bought us out we were like, "Can you believe it, man...the same band that was Sneak Preview, dying in front of a club." And here we are on Atlantic Records getting ready to do our third album on Atlantic Records, our sixth album overall.

SW: As you pointed out, you were together for a long time before you signed a recording contract.

TT: Yeah, seven years.

SW: Were you making your sole living from the band that entire time?

TT: Oh yeah. From 1980 until now, really, playing in the band is all I've done. There was one brief period after I had gotten married where finances were pretty tough, and I decided to try this telemarketing job on the side.

SW: Oh, those are horrible!

TT: I went in for one day, and I left there going, "No, I play music for a living. This is what I do. I'm not a telemarketer." *(Laughs)*. Boy that was a hellish nightmare. I couldn't imagine going back there every day. I never even took a paycheck from them. I was just glad to be out of the room.

SW: *(Laughing)*. I know what you mean, I've actually done that too. It's just such total rejection, day in, day out.

TT: And feeling like total slime, reading this bull crap for them that you know is a bald-faced lie. I couldn't do it, man. I could not make myself do that kind of job. If it was credible, then I might have done it. I had no idea what I was getting myself into. It was definitely wading through slime to do that job. I left that place happily and with no money and said, "That's fine."

SW: The first King's X album takes its title from C.S. Lewis. What's his influence on the band, and how did you arrive at that title?

TT: Basically I'm a huge fan and respecter of C.S. Lewis, and so is Jerry, and also Sam Taylor, who was our manager at that time. We were recording the album, and it was the same old thing...we're the worst at trying to come up with titles for anything, even songs. We write songs, and I'll say, "The so-and-so song", and everybody will say, "Well, is that what it's called?" And I say, "I have no idea what it's called, I'm just letting you know what it is we need to practice." *(Laughs)*. So naming things has been a nightmare.

And Sam just threw it out sort of whimsically one time. He said, "How about let's call it *Out Of The Silent Planet*?" Because me and Jerry were huge fans of especially that Space Trilogy, that *Out Of The Silent Planet* is the first book of. We just looked at each other and said, "Can we do that?" Me and Jerry were very into it, and we convinced Doug of its coolness. We ended up calling it that. Because the silent planet is Earth, you know, and *Out Of The Silent Planet* was sort of like, here we are making our noise for the first time, so it's an appropriate name.

SW: You guys, when you came out, got pushed into the heavy metal envelope, as far as how the press perceived you. Was that more or less what you expected?

TT: It was what we expected, although we hoped it wouldn't happen. We expected it just because we were on Megaforce Records, and at the time, Megaforce was one of the most hardcore metal labels in the world. We were the first thing they signed that wasn't hardcore metal, and they were trying to get out of that stereotype themselves, and sign different types of music. But being the first thing that was different on the label, the industry would look at the label and just deem us heavy metal without even hearing a note. It was a drag. It still is.

There are people out there in the press who still think we're heavy metal, just because that's what we originally were called mistakenly. *(Laughs)*. I don't know, if they took the time to hear the music, I think they'd agree we're not really metal.

SW: With such unusual music, and a real different lyrical perspective, did it take a lot of convincing in order to break King's X on the radio?

TT: The truth of the matter is, radio is one of the places on a couple of occasions that we were given the most support and help. We've had several songs be Top Ten in airplay nationwide, and we've had two songs be Top Five in nationwide airplay. We've had several songs at Number One in metal radio nationwide. So we've had good radio support at times, but the thing is it's brief, usually.

They would originally come out and support us and play us, and we'd be way up the charts. I remember one time looking at the charts, and here we are over Bon Jovi, and over U2, all these mega-platinum albums on the charts, getting more airplay or at least showing up on the charts higher, and thinking, 'Wow, can you believe that's us right there at Number Three, above all these mega albums? Surely we'll sell records.' *(Laughs)*. The difference between us and them is they stay on the charts, and we didn't. We would be up there, and the radio people would give us the chance and be fans of the band, supporting us really beyond anything we deserved. Then when the album sales didn't follow, they would have to drop it, naturally.

So we got great radio support initially, but nobody's going to keep playing something that's not selling. So we would pop up on the charts, be there for two or three weeks, and then we'd be gone. But we got fair shots from people. We got more than fair shots from people. Even MTV gave us more than one very fair shot, where they played videos heavily. They played the "Over My Head" video heavily in prime time every day for weeks, almost ten weeks, without album sales following, and then they had to drop it.

And then the next album, with the "It's Love" video, they did the same thing. They gave us real good, serious support, and were really behind the band, and expressed the desire, hoping that we would break. And we did sell some albums with that video and that album. We were on tour with AC/DC, and we were selling a decent amount at that time. But it just didn't catch on in the way that everybody expected, and eventually it was dropped. Plus we left the country to go to Europe for a couple of months during the height of our career in America, which I've always felt was a terrible mistake. And of course the album died instantly when we went to Europe, because we weren't here still playing cities, getting radio support, doing interviews, just pushing the album and being in front of people. The album was coming down off the peak of sales, and nowhere near dead yet. You know, you make excuses…going to Europe may have had nothing to do with it, but I always felt it was a terrible mistake.

After that, radio as we knew it changed. There no longer is AOR radio like we once had. The few stations that are left are dividing their time slots with about half classic, half AOR. So nowadays getting on the radio for a band like King's X is much, much more difficult than back in those days, when we were getting a lot of help from AOR radio.

SW: In many ways, just because you don't fit into any particular trend that's come along.

TT: Right.

SW: It's hard to say, "Here's Soundgarden, and here's King's X!"

TT: Right. And alternative radio, which plays a number of bands that are King's X-influenced…I won't name any, but bands that never used drop-D tuning before King's X, and then made a sound out of drop-D tuning themselves, you hear that all day on alternative radio, but alternative won't touch King's X because it was originally called metal. And bands that are doing the same type of music, but didn't have that stigma originally, are getting played constantly.

SW: That puts you between a rock and a hard place.

TT: Yeah, but that the entire nature of King's X and we three guys. We've never fit in, any music we've done, anywhere we've been, we've never fit in with the norm. And that's just something we accepted a long time ago as just the way it's going to be for us.

SW: Although you do have a very strong following. The people who do support the band are somewhat fanatical.

TT: The fans that we do have are the kind of fans that you read about in magazines and think it's just an awesome fairy tale story. We have the most die-hard, dedicated, true music-appreciating crowd of fans that a band could ever hope to have. Just tremendous fans. They're the best. And there's enough of them to keep this thing going in some strange way. *(Laughs).* So we're very appreciative of them.

SW: You're a secular band on a secular label, but you do have a strong Christian following. Did you ever give any thought to recording on an exclusively Christian label, back in the beginning of your career?

TT: No. That's something that we all had personally never wanted to be a part of. Especially when the band first got together. When we first got together we were the type of guys...by the time we had become King's X, I guess is a better way of putting it, we all had had experiences in the Christian industry. We knew a lot of people, we had played on records and this and that. And although some of the people we had been involved in were good people, and I certainly don't want to discredit them or put them down in any way...they were very good people with honest hearts and good intentions. The industry itself was just sickening. It was something that repulsed us and that we wished to have no contact with, or be a part of and support in any way.

Like I said, that's not to be confused with the fact that we believe there are some sincere, good people in the industry. But the industry itself, and the way it operates, the Christian industry, is something that is just so...well, I guess the best way to say it is just, it's something that repulsed us that we did not want to be a part of in any way. And regardless of whatever our beliefs were, we didn't want to be a Christian band. We never wanted to be seen as a Christian band. Because the definition in America of a Christian band is a band that plays preachy music to Christians on a Christian label. And that's nothing that we ever cared to be a part of.

SW: It also causes the artists themselves a lot of problems, or so it seems to me. You see these people struggling with just trying to be ordinary, every day people, while carrying this extra burden of trying to live up to this ridiculous standard that's not human.

TT: Right. And we certainly weren't the definition of a Christian band, at least what people think of as a Christian band. We just wanted to be artists. We just wanted to be people who could freely express whatever it is we feel, just like anybody else does, and make records freely, out of the constraints of any industry rules. We wanted to make music that we were happy with, and that is true, from the heart music, whatever it is. Even if it's a song about taking the garbage out, we didn't care, as long as it's an honest feeling, which is what art is. That was our only desire all along, was to do music with that philosophy.

That's really the only way you can make true art, is just to be honest with yourself and say whatever you have to say, right or wrong, and be a human. People tap into human things, and they get different things from it. We didn't want to define our music to people. We didn't even want to say things in a way that boxed in what we were saying. We just wanted to throw out our ideas, whatever they may be, and see what people got from it.

Once we got the Christian stigma, I think a lot of doors started to shut all over the place. Just because people were deeming us "that Christian band" without ever hearing us. It spread like wildfire, and everybody automatically equated us with things like Stryper, which we certainly aren't. We're not only not that, we don't even know if we believe in that. And it's dangerous to say things like that and name people, because I don't want to judge the guys in Stryper. If they've done what they truly believe was the right thing to do, then they've done all they can do, and I'm not gonna put them down for that. I'm just saying as far as we were concerned, that was certainly not anything that we felt to do. If we were to do that, we would have been liars.

SW: Does it place you in a somewhat uncomfortable spot, given the fact that you do have a fairly strong Christian following, but you are in fact a secular band and playing to a predominately secular audience?

TT: No, not really. That gives us freedom. The only place we would be boxed in is if we were playing in the Christian industry to Christians. Only because they do have definite rules they have to follow. I mean, if Doug one night feels something on his heart, he can say whatever he wants to, whether it be cursing or whatever, if it's true to what's on his heart. He has the freedom to do so in our situation, and certainly would not have the freedom to do so in the other situation.

SW: It might be hard for you to have any kind of association with some of the tours you've done as well, like AC/DC for instance.

TT: We're happy to do any band like that. AC/DC asked for us specifically, and we were honored to do it. Anybody out there that truly would like us to open for them, we're always honored. We've done some gigs with some of the wildest match-ups you can imagine musically, and we did it just because we were asked to do it, and we were happy to.

SW: What are some the bands you've opened for that you remember as being very memorable musically?

TT: Touring with Pearl Jam was awesome. That was really an eye-opener, and a kick in the butt at the same time for me. It awakened something in me that used to drive me that had sort of laid dormant for a while. Going out with those guys and seeing the reaction of the crowd, and the impact of the music without hype, awoke this thing deep inside me that made me believe that you can make music that has an impact. That was a very encouraging thing, to be on that tour.

We've toured with AC/DC, Cheap Trick. In the early days we toured with people like Billy Squier, Blue Oyster Cult, Anthrax…we even did a short tour with Iron Maiden in Germany. We've done some one-off gigs with Robert Plant. I really can't think of all the bands we've toured with, there's been so many. We toured with The Scorpions.

SW: You have played some unusual instruments on King's X records. Are those things that you're interested in and bring into the record because of that interest, or do you bring them in just to provide a different element for the recordings?

TT: It's both, actually. I've always been drawn to strange instruments for some reason. I really like the Japanese koto. It's such a cool sounding instrument when it's played right. What a bizarre instrument, I love the way it sounds. Sitar is the same way. I wasn't sure if I could use that kind of stuff with our music or not. I really just wanted to play around with the stuff with no pressure, and see what happened. So I asked our manager to help find a sitar somewhere, and he located one in St. Louis, and the band bought it for me.

I'm not really a player by any means, but I started tampering around with it and getting some sounds I was really liking, and ended up using it on the record. That, and the dulcimer and whatever else. I've brought in a lot of stuff, I just play with it and see if it works. If it doesn't then we just scrap it, and if it does then good. I'm interested in different sounds being thrown in there for different flavors.

SW: You get some pretty unusual guitar sounds. What kinds of guitars and amps do you gravitate toward?

TT: For many years I only used this one guitar as my main guitar on just about everything, a Fender Strat Elite, which is a rare Strat that they made for a two-year period. It was way overpriced, and nobody bought them. But it was a great guitar that used very unique Fender active electronics that are very different sounding than any other active electronic pickups I'd ever heard before, and had its own unique pre-amp inside the guitar that had its own mid boost and all that kind of stuff. Really a great sounding guitar with great pickups, but very, very noisy. Amplified single-coil noisy. So if you got in a noisy room you couldn't even use the guitar. That was my favorite guitar, and it really had a lot to do with the tone on some of the early stuff that people used to write me and say they liked. It had a lot to do with the guitar and some old Lab Series amps I was using through Marshall cabinets. I used Pierce amps on some of the early stuff, and I also used a hopped-up Fender amp on the first album along with some Labs. I've used a combination of tube and solid state stuff all along.

Right now I'm using strictly Marshalls in the studio, and I've never used Marshalls on anything we've ever done. I used them growing up, and loved them, but I hadn't used Marshalls in a long time. Right now I'm getting a strange, different tone out of the Marshalls than I've ever gotten before, so I'm using those. My main sound is mainly that Strat Elite through old Gibson stuff, but right now I'm using a Zion guitar that I've been using for about three years now, that I really like. It's replaced my Strat Elites, I never play those anymore. It's not noisy, but has a very similar tone and great feel and sound, but without the noise. So I started using those through the Marshalls.

SW: What kind of set up do you take on the road to re-create those sounds?

TT: Basically I take on the road exactly what I'm using in the studio, just with some added power amp power and a lot more cabinets. I'll just have Marshalls out this time.

SW: What are some of your favorite solos of yours from the King's X catalog?

TT: Favorite solos? Hmm, I don't know about that. *(Laughs)*. Every solo I've ever done, I listen back to and think, 'Man, I wish could have done that better.' I'm very rarely satisfied with what I record, because we record usually when we've had several months off from touring, and it's usually when my chops are at their absolute worst that we make records. Usually when we get out on the road touring and playing every night, I finally, by the end of the tour, feel like I can play guitar again. And then we'll take nine months off and do an album. *(Laughs)*. Have no calluses, no...just be totally out of practice. Because I don't touch the guitar when we're not touring, except for to write music, I don't touch a guitar at all. I mean, my guitars literally rust up.

I don't know what it is; during my time off anymore, I just want to do other things. So my solos always sound to me like what I sound like after I haven't played for nine months and then pick up a guitar and am so completely out of practice that it's embarrassing. And all of my guitar work on the albums is done that way. So there's not much I've done on an album that I can say I'm happy with. There's a lot of live tapes that I listen to and I go, 'Oh man, I wish I could have put that on an album.' But it's just not destined to be. We don't come off the road and make albums. But there is one solo that I can listen to without cringing, and that's the solo for the song "Flies And Blue Skies" on the last album, *Dogman*. And there's probably a couple of solos on some of the earlier stuff that I remember liking, but off the top of my head I can't think of them, because I don't really listen to our stuff at all.

SW: You're obviously a lot happier with the way you play live.

TT: Much happier, just because the hands do what the head is thinking after a few months of playing. And in the studio it's so frustrating, because the head is still thinking, but the hands are no longer doing. *(Laughs)*.

SW: So do you think you'll do a live album?

TT: We've been threatening to do so since the Dawn of Man. *(Laughs)*. We've been fighting the label and management and everybody to let us do a live album forever, with them always trying to talk us out of it. I still maintain that it would be a good thing for King's X to do a live album, and would have been a good thing five albums ago! *(Laughs)*. But nobody else seems to believe us, so until that day...we'll do one eventually, and either it'll be great, or it'll totally flop. We'll find out. *(Laughs)*.

SW: You obviously have a great reputation as a live band.

TT: Well, we *are* a live band. That's what we are. We are a live band, and to not have live stuff put out seems ludicrous to me.

SW: That would be like Peter Frampton not having done his live album.

TT: Right. That was a live experience. It feels that way on the album, regardless of however it was recorded, I have no idea. There's a live excitement, a feel to it that doesn't sound like a studio album. It may be one, but it doesn't sound like it.

SW: A lot of so-called live albums are largely re-worked in the studio.

TT: Yeah. When we do a live album it's gonna be live, no overdubs, no repairing. It'll be the real deal, the way live albums should be, mistakes and all.

SW: The songs in King's X are generally credited to the three of you. How does the collaboration between you work when you're writing?

TT: The majority of everything is written by Doug or myself, and we make demos at home, at least an outline idea of where the song is going and what the intent is. Then we come together in pre-production and sometimes the songs don't change very much. But sometimes we completely tear them apart and almost re-write the song entirely, which we've done with some songs on this album. And usually that's really cool. Because everybody has their input, and everybody's playing things the way they feel to play, and it makes something different than what the original intent was. This certainly isn't a solo artist band. It is a band where we want everybody to have their input and be happy. We have to detach ourselves from the songs and just see what the band does to them. We treat it like that with each other.

SW: With your last album, you broke away from Sam Taylor and got a different manager. He had been perceived as a mentor figure for the band. What prompted that decision?

TT: Really nothing worth putting in the press. There were just some differences that were not going to be resolved, and probably never will be, really. We've resolved it to the point of both sides trying to come to an agreement we can both live with, but I think both sides will always have different views of things, and I think neither side will have the truth. The truth is somewhere between the two. It was time for both of us to go different directions.

SW: Who are some of the newer bands that you like?

TT: The truth is, there's a lot of stuff out there where I like one or two songs by somebody, but there aren't any bands out right now that I find myself being a massive fan of the band. As a matter of fact, it's been a long time since I've been a massive fan of any band. I just don't listen to music like I used to. I don't listen as often. It's like, once you start making albums and see how things are done, when I hear things, I hear them differently now. I hear how they made the record, instead of just loving the music like I used to and being unaffected by that. Some of the magic is gone, because some of the mystery has been unfolded to me by doing albums. That's sort of taken away from my listening pleasure with a lot of stuff.

But I like several tunes on the new Soundgarden album, I thought there was some good music on that. I like some of the Stone Temple Pilots. But like I said, it's a song here or there. The only thing that I find myself listening to consistently are some totally unknown albums. There's an album by a couple of guys that went under the name Toy Matinee, and I find myself listening to that album a lot still. I really think that's a good album, with good writing. There's some real artistry on that album, and I can really appreciate the record, so I still play it.

SW: It's bizarre that you should say that, because that happens to be one of my favorite records in the world. There is just not a bad cut on there. And you know, I find that although the album was not a huge hit, it's a big cult record. It seems like a lot of people who are really in the know about music gravitate toward that album.

TT: Same thing with a band called Human Radio. I listen to that album on a regular basis. And I have to say, I like some Pearl Jam. I was listening to a lot of Eric Johnson for a while, when the first album *Tones* came out. I really love that record, and of course I like the second one too. I'll forget something probably really important, because it's hard to name stuff.

I listen more to things from that period in the early Seventies that I told you about, that I really loved. I listen to things from that era more than I do new stuff. The music is still more interesting to me, and the sounds are more interesting to me, and the individual mark on things is more interesting to me from a lot of stuff back then still, than now. Now, bands like Pearl Jam, they definitely have their own mark and their own sound, and it's refreshing that there's still a band like them now. But the industry as a whole...I turn on alternative radio, and I hear the same band, one after another.

SW: Yeah, what's so alternative about that?

TT: It makes me want to vomit. And originally, when it first started to happen, bands like Nirvana or whatever that were the beginning of that sort of thing, it was really encouraging. It was different, and there were a few new things happening. And then suddenly everybody was sounding like them. Sort of like the U2 thing, when U2 first started catching on they were so incredibly different, and two or three years later everybody was playing like the Edge.

SW: Yeah, I lived here when REM really broke, and for years every single local band looked and sounded exactly like REM. It's only been in the last couple of years that you can go out to a club here and see anything even remotely different from that.

You recently produced the new Rez Band album. How did that come about?

TT: The truth of the matter is, I had been seriously considering doing some producing shortly before hearing about their new album. I'd been talking to my wife about the fact that in King's X, we're sort of in a pattern where we'll make an album, we'll have to or three months off, the album will come out and we'll tour, we'll come off the road and take another several months off. I just realized that there are several-month periods of life, just big chunks of open space that go by that I don't really do anything. I just ride motorcycles and hang with my family, which is totally awesome. I love that part of this, that I do have large areas of time to just be with my family and not have to go in to work. We're just together every day. And that's great. But I found myself feeling like I'm not really using myself, not really getting the most out of what I want to do musically in all areas. And I've got plenty of time to do some other things.

So I'd been talking with my wife about doing some producing, and I'd been asked by different people to do this and that. A guy named Mark Hollingsworth from REX Records contacted me, who was a friend of mine I'd known for years, telling me REZ Band was getting ready to do a new album. Originally he just asked, "How would you like to be an Executive Producer and have some input on the album?" And I said, "Man, that would be awesome." Because REZ Band, to me, even though they are a Christian band, they are a Christian band well outside the Christian industry. They've always been on their own, they've always been uncompromising, they've always had integrity, they've always been true to themselves and their hearts and to what they believe. They don't succumb to industry pressure because they have their own record label, their own publishing company, their own everything. so that they are self-contained and can do what they feel right about doing.

The truth is I was a huge fan of those guys years before they ever even had an album out. They came through Mississippi when I was young, in the Seventies, and I remember driving to see them in Yuteca, Mississippi, a really small town in the middle of nowhere. They played on a flat-bed trailer. Somebody in Jackson had told me, "You've got to check out this band, they're gonna be here." So I went, and I was completely floored. I'd never seen, especially back then, people who called themselves Christians who looked like Molly Hatchet or Lynyrd Skynyrd, who played through massive Marshall stacks, and played loud, massive rock and roll. I mean, just totally unapologetic, on-their-own thing. I was floored by it. I thought, 'Man, this is one of the most different things I've ever seen in my life.' So when they finally did start making records, the first two records I was a big fan of, and really liked the music on especially the second record, which had some music on it that I just thought was super. And all through the years I always thought, 'Man, I wish I could produce something for them.' Because I always had a different idea.

I mean, everybody does. People listen to the Beatles and have suggestions, which is ludicrous, because it's perfect, and it did what it did. But you can listen to anything, no matter how great it is, and have your own angle on it. So I always had those kind of things, too. There's nothing wrong with what REZ Band has done, but I always thought, 'Man, I'd love to be twisting the knobs for them and get this out of them.' So when Mark contacted me about it, I said, "Oh sure, I'd love to be a part of it." And at that point it was just going to be throwing in suggestions.

And the more I thought about it, the more I thought, 'Man, I've got this period of time, I might could actually produce this thing.' It started bothering me, I wanted to do it so bad. So I called him up and said, "I've got this big window of time; if we can record it during this window, then I could actually produce, so see if they're interested." And they were interested and called me up, and were like, "Why in the world do you want to produce us?" *(Laughs)*. So I went through the story with them. I have no problem with being a part of something like that, that has integrity, and I can really get behind and say, "This is good." So it was a real honor, a real privilege. It's kinda one of those musical things like playing with The Producers live onstage, that to the public would not seem like any big deal, but to me is something personally important, so I was very happy to do it.

SW: How long do you think King's X will last?

TT: I don't know. We've all quit the band so many times, I don't think anybody believes it even when somebody does. It just keeps going, even against our will. *(Laughs)*. I have no idea how long King's X will last. This could be our last album, or we might have twenty more and be eighty years old, doing an entirely different type of thing. Who knows? There's just no telling. We take things one day at a time.

Right now King's X is still making music that we feel at least is still making us happy, and we don't feel tapped out yet. We still feel like we have things to do. This album is a great example of it. This album has been very inspirational to all of us, because it's still fresh, different and new to us. I don't know what it will sound like to anybody else, but to us it's that. As long as we can feel that way, we'll keep doing it.

SW: If King's X ended after this album, what would you do?

TT: Probably do a solo album. I've had a couple of people make suggestions that they would be interested in me doing that. So I'd probably do some solo work, and I would most likely start taking some of these producer jobs that I've been invited to do. I really enjoy producing. I love studio work. That's one of my favorite parts of all of the music thing that we do, is studio work. It was such a cool experience producing the REZ album, that I realized I really would like to do some more. So I'd probably just do some of my own stuff and do some producing.

For more information, please visit www.tytabor.net

HOPE ONCE AGAIN

Richard Williams was a founding member of the Midwestern rock group *Kansas*, and bears a singular distinction in the band's history: throughout the group's twenty year career, *Williams* is the only member to consistently appear on every album and at every concert *Kansas* has ever performed.

In that time, *Williams* has served as the group's lead guitarist and self-described "Wall of Meat". His distinctive playing has graced such hits as "Carry On Wayward Son", "Dust In The Wind", "Fight Fire With Fire" and "Song For America".

Kansas formed in Topeka in 1972 out of the ashes of two previous bands, *White Clover* and another band named *Kansas* that had included guitarist/keyboard player *Kerry Livgren*. Recording a cheap demo of "Can I Tell You", the band worked the club circuit all through the Midwest, developing a style that was an improbable fusion of British progressive rock and Midwestern boogie.

Due to its rather unorthodox style, *Kansas* had trouble getting Midwestern audiences to accept its original music; the musicians would fool audiences into giving their music a chance by announcing their original songs as covers of Led Zeppelin or Yes. Shortly after *Livgren* rejoined in 1973, *Kansas* was signed to a recording contract by *Don Kirshner*, ironically the man who had previously brought the world the Monkees.

The band's self-titled debut album received a slow reception, eventually selling 100,000 copies as the band toured continuously. Subsequent releases like 'Song For America' and 'Masque' did little to improve the band's commercial fortunes, but by constant touring, *Kansas* built a solid relationship with a growing cult of devoted fans.

It was 1977's 'Leftoverture' that proved the band's breakthrough. Featuring the hit single "Carry On Wayward Son", the album became the band's first platinum seller, followed by 'Point Of Know Return', which proved an even bigger success as "Dust In The Wind" reached #6 in the charts. To document the band's celebrated concert performances, *Kansas* then released 'Two For The Show', a double live album.

That era proved to be the band's commercial peak as the next two albums, 'Monolith' and 'Audio-Visions', were marked by dissent among the musicians and dwindling sales. In 1980 vocalist *Steve Walsh* quit the band and was replaced by *John Elefante*, who recorded two albums with *Kansas*. Despite the success of such songs as "Play The Game Tonight" and "Fight Fire With Fire", neither 'Vinyl Confessions' nor 'Drastic Measures' lived up to expectations, and *Kansas* disbanded in 1983.

Livgren and bassist *Dave Hope* would go on to form the Christian band *A.D.*, while *Walsh*, *Williams*, and drummer *Phil Ehart* reunited in 1987 for 'Power', featuring new members *Billy Greer* and *Dixie Dregs* guitarist *Steve Morse*, who covered the violin lines and split the guitar *duties with **Williams**. The reunion proved a fair success, but the subsequent album 'In The Spirit Of Things' was sunk by problems at MCA Records, driving the band off the label.*

*   **Kansas** spent the next seven years working the club circuit in various permutations, trying to regroup enough to score another record deal. In 1992 the band released the live album 'Live At The Whiskey' independently, which began its relationship with Intersound Records.*

*   I spoke with **Richard Williams** on July 26th, 1995 from a tour stop in Phoenix. He was tremendously excited about the band's recent fortunes; **Kansas** had just released its first studio effort in eight years, 'Freaks Of Nature', and had returned to the road with **Alan Parsons**, back in the arenas the band had once called home. **Williams** was full of fire and fiercely proud of the new album, easily the best the band had recorded in fifteen years.*

SW: The new album really brings to mind some of Kansas' best work. What prompted the band to record a new studio album after eight years?

RW: Well, we've been *wanting to. (Laughs).* See, the second MCA album with Steve Morse, *In The Spirit Of Things*, that was a such a bitter experience of the record business. I can't remember the heads of the companies at the time, but they contacted Bob Ezrin to produce. He'd never done a record for us. And so we went off on this two-year endeavor to make the record, and everybody was all behind it. It was a lot of work.

And just as the album was released, they have Bloody Friday and fire everybody at MCA. And a whole new team came in, and everything that was from CBS they automatically just dropped. So that album was just barely even released. I don't think we did more than thirty-five shows.

That really broke our backs. Steve Morse had his own career, anyway, with the Steve Morse Project, and so we just kinda disintegrated. But we knew we had another record in us, and we wanted to do one bad. We took a little hiatus. Me and Phil just kind of kept all the ping pong balls in the air for a while, and we got a call from a German promoter, finally, about four years ago, to see if Kansas wanted to come over to Germany for a couple of weeks. And we thought that would be fun, so we got everybody back together.

This was with Kerry Livgren, and Dave Hope went, but it was also the other members; Greg Robert and Billy Greer went with us. And it was a lot of fun, so we thought, 'Gee, what if, this summer, an opportunity comes up where we could do a couple of weeks in the States? Would anybody be interested?' After that *In The Spirit Of Things* fiasco, our booking agency, our manager, everybody told us, "You guys are dead. There's not an outhouse for you to play in. Nobody cares. Start looking for work."

SW: Oh, that's the kind of encouragement you need! *(Laughs).*

RW: Well, when you hear that from your management, you believe it. So I don't think we knew why we were keeping the entity alive, but we didn't want to let it die, either. So here comes the summer, let's do a few dates. And, oh, good grief, about seven hundred dates later, here we are! *(Laughs).*

SW: You've spent the bulk of the past three or four years on the road.

RW: Yeah, we've been working real solid. We've been purposely avoiding major markets, because we wanted to make a record, and we didn't want to play some bar in Los Angeles, and then have an album out and play the Greek Theatre when we were just at a bar three months earlier. So we stayed out in the boonies. But what it did was it really built up a strong...you know, I had no idea we had such a strong fan base.

SW: It's almost like the way you did it in the beginning, really, touring around in order to break your new album.

RW: Oh, yeah, it's real familiar! *(Laughs)*. The only trouble is now, where radio is has really got us stuck.

SW: It's hard to program a new Kansas record in between the new Soundgarden and the new Alice In Chains.

RW: Well, that doesn't bother me; that type of station have their own format. What I'm having trouble with is the rock-oriented classic stations. We were the third most-played band last year. In fact, we're being inducted into the Rock Walk in two days. But they won't play the new material. They play classic rock only. We should have lied and said that this album was a composite of stuff that we had written ten years ago or something. *(Laughs)*. Because everybody that hears it loves it. It's very reminiscent of the *Leftoverture* era.

We approached the whole project that way, from producer to recording method, trying to get away from technology. Things started relying way too much on MIDI and computers, and this was a lot more just set up and play. We learned a lesson when we did *Live At The Whisky*, and that's that you're not building a watch. *(Laughs)*. It's really not that difficult. You just put mics in front of things and just start pounding them and whacking them.

SW: That was a great-sounding performance record, too.

RW: Yeah, and what we heard was *us*. We heard us playing, instead of just the whole homogenized process of being in the studio for three months and the sound of the producer producing. And on *Freaks Of Nature*, all of a sudden you can hear the band's personality again. You can hear the individual expression of each member.

SW: What strikes me immediately about the album is how completely different it is from the last two studio albums, the MCA albums. It sounds like a different band.

RW: I liked those records, but they're so technical and so smooth and homogenized. They're very well-produced, but I guess that's just not what we need to be.

Jeff Glixman, who did our first few albums, up to the *Point Of Know Return* album, has been a friend. I was in a band with him before I was in Kansas. We were in a band called The Rain. He did the bookings and he was the keyboard player/singer. He sucked, a horrible voice. *(Laughs)*. He picked the better career.

But he's a good diplomat, and since we've been friends for such a long time, it's easy for him to jump in the middle of things if we're stuck somewhere. If there was something he didn't like, it wasn't hard for him to just come out and say, "This isn't working for me." But once we got rolling, he was very good at staying out of the way, letting us do what we do.

Any song will come up, and it has to be filtered through. You can have any song you can imagine, and hand it to us, and it's going to go through the Kansas filter, and it's gonna come out our way.

SW: Somebody remarked that you were a terrible cover band.

RW: We weren't very good at it at all. We just wanted to do it our way. And that's what we're best at. Just leave us alone and let us do it our way. And Jeff understood that. What he did so well, I think, was to not put too much of a personal stamp on it. It sounds like the band. You hear the band playing, not the producer producing.

SW: Whereas someone like Bob Ezrin has a signature sound.

RW: Yeah, but what a great guy to work with. Wow, what an idea man! But it was such a technical endeavor, you know, sitting there for what seems like hours on end, linking the machines up, all that MIDI crap.

This album was done with no click tracks and no MIDI anything. All live performances. We all played together on the original tracks, and then would go back in and repair what needed repairing. In recent history it had gotten to where we'd have a click track and then get a drum track and then start layering it. And then just stacks of keyboards, multiple keyboard sounds that stood alone by themselves. You didn't even need the rest of the band to play. And then try to fit us in there.

Our early stuff, you would take a violin line and a guitar line and a single synth line, and that would create a symphonic element of its own. And then all of a sudden we have thirty keyboards playing on all the parts. Technology just took hold and kinda bit the balls right off of us.

SW: Did you try out any of this material live before you recorded the album?

RW: We went to Germany this last October, and we did four songs. Trying new material on people live is kind of a little nerve-wracking, but it went over so well. That gave us a lot of confidence going into the album.

SW: What songs from the album are you playing in your set now?

RW: With the Alan Parsons tour, we're stuck with such a short set, we're playing just two: "Hope Once Again" and "Desperate Times".

SW: Your guitar playing really returns to a more dominant role on this album. It's got a real presence in the mix.

RW: Well, I didn't have to fight through the keyboard sludge. (*Laughs*).

SW: Phil Ehart pointed out that you, in particular, are really the unsung hero of Kansas in the sense that in the early years, Kerry Livgren used to get most of the spotlight, and then in the Eighties the guitar magazines focused on Steve Morse. A lot of people might not realize that you're the guy that's been there the whole time and did a lot of the playing that they might have attributed to someone else.

RW: Well, if I had an ego problem it would bother me. I'm just glad to be here. I don't really care. I know what I've done. If somebody thinks that I've played second fiddle this whole career, whatever. I was there and they weren't. I know what happened and they don't.

SW: You and Phil are the only ones who have been on every album, is that right?

RW: Yup. Well, Phil's missed…he took last year off to get this album deal together. Since no majors would touch us, he dedicated the year to hunting down a deal. So Brian Holmes from the Producers played drums with us. And right before that Van Romaine, who plays with Steve Morse in the Steve Morse Project, also played with us in Phil's absence. So I'm the only person that's played every Kansas concert ever.

SW: There's been an awful lot of changes here and there. How long has the current line-up been together?

RW: This is the same line-up as *Live At The Whisky*, and that line-up had been together maybe six months to a year before that. Billy Greer and Greg Robert have been with us for ten years now, which is as long as the old members were with us! And David Ragsdale, the violinist, has been with us since just before *Live At The Whisky*, probably about five years.

SW: Where did you guys find him?

RW: He had been in contact with Phil. He had sent a few tapes and stuff. When you're a violinist that wants to play in a rock band, who do you call? *(Laughs).* And since Robby had been out of the picture since 1981, he had been sending tapes and stuff. But then Morse was in the band, and Morse was covering most of the violin lines, so at that point there wasn't much need for him.

Finally Kerry had him come in to do something on a track, and it just kinda gelled from there. He lived real close to us anyway. After Morse had left for good and we were going on the road—see, this two weeks on the road thing was gonna happen, and Kerry agreed to go out with us, so he went out for about two weeks. Then we booked about two more, so we talked Kerry into that, and then we talked Morse into going out for a couple more.

All of a sudden we had all these offers for the whole summer, and we needed that slot filled. And we said, "Let's get that darn violin back." Adding the violin, Dave's such a good player, that really put the stamp back on us, too.

SW: That returns it to that easily recognizable Kansas sound.

RW: Yeah.

SW: Your career with Kansas has taken you from clubs to halls to giant coliseums, and then back to halls and back to clubs and back to halls again.

RW: Yeah, the full gamut! *(Laughs).*

SW: After all the years on the road, do you still continue to learn about performing, and how to adapt to various situations?

RW: *(Laughs)*. Yeah. Last night was beyond adapting.

SW: How so?

RW: We played at this Indian college in Santa Fe, New Mexico. There's an outdoor amphitheater, and to say we were crammed is an understatement. Me and Steve were on top of each other.

I play an acoustic on a stand, so that's right in front of me. Then there's me and Steve, and we were just slammed together. My acoustic was on my blind side, and I spun around to get over to my amplifier. My guitar necks hit together. We don't have long breaks; I don't even get a chance to take a drink of water. My guitar just went completely out of tune, so I've got a six second hole to try to tune. "The Wall" was coming up.

I hit that tuner and it was so far out of whack, I started the solo and it wasn't even close, so I had to just stop. In my earlier days I might have hung my head in shame, but it was just like, 'Aw, fuck it.' *(Laughs)*. You know, shit's gonna happen sometimes. You've just got to kind of go with the flow and grin, anymore. If you let the little things bother you all the time, you'd get the itch in the top of your mouth that only a .38 could scratch.

SW: Let's go back to the very beginning. Do you remember the first guitar you ever owned?

RW: Absolutely. It was a Sears model Danelectro with the lipstick pickup. The pickup looked like an old Fifties lady's lipstick; it's tubular, silver, rounded on each end. It's in the bridge position, not down at the neck position. Still, they play great. I bought another one just like it about fifteen years ago. I had to have another one. They play great.

SW: Do you still have that one?

RW: Yeah.

SW: Who were some of the guitarists that influenced you growing up?

RW: Growing up, the first band I was ever in was with Phil, back in high school, and back then it was so easy. I took six weeks of guitar lessons and I was in a band. *(Laughs)*. And all you really had to do was know some chords.

When I started getting more serious about guitar playing, I think the album that really woke me up to guitar playing was the John Mayall, Eric Clapton and the Bluesbreakers album. That was Guitar Playing 101. That was like, whoa! That and *Truth*, the first Jeff Beck album. Those two albums showed me the expression that a guitar could have besides just whacking on it.

SW: What was the band you were in with Phil?

RW: *(Laughs)*. That was called The Pets. Phil even sang in that. Oh, write this; Phil will hate it! *(Laughter)*. Phil sang "California Sun"; remember that song?

SW: No, I honestly don't.

RW: *(Sings)* "I'm a-going out West where I belong..." *(hums the guitar line)*. He sang some Animals song, what was that...*(sings)* "The joint was rockin', going 'round and 'round." Phil sang that, and "Hey Little Girl". *(Laughs)*. "Hey little girl, you ain't got nothin' to hide no more!"

We did that type of stuff, Rolling Stones, just all sorts of stuff. We'd do "When A Man Loves A Woman" by Percy Sledge. We played rec centers and proms, that type of stuff, and then they kicked me out of the band because my parents wouldn't let me travel. I couldn't leave town.

SW: But you eventually hooked up with Phil again.

RW: Well, Topeka's not that big of a town, but at that point in time with the British Invasion, there was literally a garage band on every block. Somebody did some kind of survey, and at that time there were more bands per capita in Topeka than anywhere.

Everybody you knew was a bass player, drummer, guitar player or keyboard player. There was a friend of mine that lived behind me that was in the Axemen. Down the street was The Noblemen. You'd go out on a summer night and you'd hear bands everywhere, practicing out on their parents' patios.

What happens is that you have your people that just want to do it for fad or whatever. It's a weeding out process. To be in a band for a long time, it takes a certain personality. It takes a certain level of commitment. Not too many people really have that; they don't stick it out, or they're assholes and nobody can play with them. They can't be counted on; they say they'll be there and all of a sudden, boom, they're in another band.

I met Dave, our bass player; I was in several bands with him. Then I was back with Phil and Dave right after high school in a band called White Clover, and then out of that band again. Then I started my college career, but I'd do one semester of college, and then I'd join a band again and flunk out that semester, and go back for another semester and then join a band.

And meanwhile, the different versions of White Clover were going on, and they'd lose a guitar player, and then I'd join back up with them again. It was kind of a weeding out process. Finally you had the five most dedicated musicians in town; we just kind of slowly melted together.

Steve Walsh had become part of one of the White Clovers. Phil, meanwhile, was sick of the whole mess and went to England, where he learned how great it was to be in Kansas. *(Laughs)*. So he came back and wanted to know if we wanted to start a band, and we'd heard about this violin player, Robby Steinhardt, who was from Lawrence, Kansas. So we got the five of us; Dave Hope, Robby, me, Steve and Phil, and started up White Clover again.

We worked the bars and started working up material, and we got a recording deal with Don Kirshner. But we wanted more songwriting. And meanwhile there was another band called Kansas that Kerry was in, and Phil and Dave were in the original version of that. And they were folding up, and we had a recording deal, so we called Kerry up and said, "Hey, do you want to come over with us now?" And he said, "Sure!" *(Laughter)*. So that was the original Kansas.

SW: As one of two guitarists in the band, when you were working up new material, how did you decide who would play which guitar parts between you and Kerry?

RW: It would just naturally fall into place a lot of times. So much of the stuff that he wrote was really heavily keyboard-based, so he'd be stuck with keyboards and I'd be playing guitar. Then he might jump from keyboards to guitar to solo, and then there'd usually be the B section and another solo, and I'd take that solo.

There also might be a doubled part or a harmony thing. And I'd be on acoustic while he was on keyboards, or I'd be on acoustic while he was on electric. It was never, "I want that part!" "No, *I* want that part!" It never was that way.

SW: When the band went in to record the first album, I understand it was under a lot of time pressures and that you were later dissatisfied with the quality of the recording.

RW: Well, we were as green as an apple. We'd never been in a studio in our lives except for out in the middle of Liberal, Kansas, this little four track pseudo-studio where we did our demo.

SW: Was that the demo of "Can I Tell You" that was on the boxed set?

RW: Yeah. We'd never been in a studio, and all of a sudden we're in New York at the Record Plant, and Rick Derringer was working right next to us on a Johnny Winter album, and Alice Cooper was in there, and that guy, what's his name, he went country…he sang "Raindrops Keep Falling On My Head"…

SW: B.J. Thomas?

RW: B.J. Thomas. He was in there, all these people, and here we are, we know nothing. Wally Gold was our producer; he worked for Don Kirshner, and he had come out to Kansas to see us and told Don to sign us. He looked a lot like Paladin; do you remember that show *Have Gun, Will Travel?* He looked a lot like Paladin. He wrote "It's My Party". That was his claim to fame. *(Laughs).* The last album he'd had anything to do with the production of was a Barbara Streisand album.

So Jeff Glixman was with us, and a guy named Jimmy Shoes, who turned out to be a very big producer, was the second engineer. *(Editor's Note: Jimmy "Shoes" is Jimmy Iovine.)* We only had two weeks, and of course I was used to playing through Marshall amps, and they said, "Oh, no, that's not how you do it in the studio. People don't use those noisy amps."

So they had us play through these little Fender amps, and we'd set up and play and they'd say, "Okay, that's good enough." And we'd say, "What?!" It was just, boom! It was finished. And we didn't understand anything when it was mixed, and we didn't understand anything about mastering or anything. And then it was out and done.

There's a few things I'd love to go back and re-record. Me and Kerry have talked about that a lot of times, how neat it would be, now that Kerry's got a studio at his house, to do something like "The Pinnacle". You know, just go back and do all new performances. I'd love to do that, if only for our own listening enjoyment.

SW: What are some of your favorite bits as far as guitar playing in the early Kansas?

RW: My solo on "The Wall" was one of my favorites. It's such a signature. "A Glimpse Of Home", the solo there. There was a solo I really liked on *Vinyl Confessions*; there's a real obscure song on there that's got a real hustling beat that's got a solo I love on it. One day I was listening to the weather channel, and you know how they play musical excerpts on there all the time, and that was on there. So that was really neat. I've always liked that part in "Wayward Son" in the middle, that herky-jerky thing.

SW: Where you're playing to offset the rhythm guitar?

RW: Yeah. And oh, what is that song…first album…we actually do part of it live now…I'm horrible at song titles, as you can tell! *(Laughs)*. It's "Journey From Mariabronn". But the solo on the first album is painful for me to listen to. It was a difficult pattern to play over, anyway. There's a lot better solo on the live album *Two For The Show*.

SW: You guys had a very strong reputation as a live band, and in fact pretty much broke the band that way, just by touring a lot. You developed a reputation as a band that was capable of playing better than the headliner a lot of the time.

RW: We started running into trouble with bands that would not let us play with them anymore, and we had some bands sort of making us finish. They'd go on, then we'd go on.

It's not like we're all a bunch of virtuosos or anything; we're all adequate players, but we play real well together. We've always just had this…Phil's always been a pounder, and I've always just been the Wall of Meat. *(Laughter)*. We sound big, powerful, and it's a little hard to follow sometimes.

There's a lot of loud bands, there's a lot of bands with big guitars, but you add that classical twist to it, the chord progressions and violin and all that, and you become capable of creating some incredibly powerful symphony moods. I wouldn't want to follow us! And that's not really bragging, because it's not a talent show. If it was, we'd all be listening to the symphony.

I know my limitations. I have no aspirations of ever being close to the best guitarist in the city, let alone the world. But I know how to play with this band.

SW: Who were some of the bands that you played with that you felt could give you a run for the money, so to speak. Do any bands stick out as being particularly good live?

RW: Well, you get the right combination. Like now, with Alan Parsons, it's such a contrast. They're very techno, kind of Pink Floyd-like. They have long grooves and slow mood changes. It's apples and oranges; it's not like having two bands of exactly the same ilk playing. We're similar in ways, but different in approach, I think. So neither one of us is going to blow the other off the stage, but the crowd will like both of us.

We played with Mott The Hoople, and that was just a straight rock and roll band, but boy, talk about entertaining. There was no way we were going to blow them off the stage. No way. They were far too fun.

I don't know why everybody's got such a thing about music; it's almost like what brand of cigarettes you smoke or what kind of beer you like. You know, "I drink Bud. I'm a Bud man. If you drink Miller, Miller's a pussy beer!" You know? "I smoke Marlboros. What are you doing smoking those Carltons?" People choose up sides for some reason. "What do you mean, you like Kansas?"

It's ridiculous. Why can't you just kind of like it all? Just take the parts you like and let the rest go. There's something that happened—maybe it's always been that way, but it seems like from at least my sister's generation, who's six years older than me, that runs even stronger today is peer pressure. "Do you like this?" "Yeah." "Oh, okay, I like it too."

SW: Particularly in music, MTV has made it so much worse. The kids all go out and get their hair chopped to look like the MTV hero of the month, and then as soon as his video gets taken out of full rotation, they're on to the next one.

RW: That's where rap left me behind a long time ago. Everybody looks the same, dresses the same, and the songs are all the same, about the same thing. "I do this to express my individuality." *(Laughs)*. What are you talking about? You look like two hundred other clones!

SW: Not unlike the LA hair metal bands of a few years back. Poison? Ratt? Motley Crue? I used to get some of those guys confused with each other.

RW: Oh, who didn't? What we've done best is just be ourselves and weather the storm, and not try to be like anybody else. We never were good at it, anyway.

SW: Once the band became very successful, did you experience much in the way of pressure from record companies to become more commercially acceptable?

RW: Absolutely. There's so many things that come into play. Record company people are strange. If they had their finger on the pulse of what was going on, if there was any person that did, he'd be the richest man on Earth. Nobody knows. Most of them are all shoe salesmen anyway, basically. They're just selling product.

We'd get pressure from our management. "Hey, guys, things are changing. There's this guy, Tommy Tutone, and he's really hot right now." *(Laughter)*. We were like, "Tommy Tutone?! You want us to do shit like that?"

SW: *(Laughing)*. The thought of Kansas even attempting that style kind of boggles the mind. Although I must say, I'd love to hear you guys try to play "8-6-7-5-3-0-9". (*Laughter*).

RW: The record companies and management always want to make you bend with the times, but why shoot the horse you rode in on?

SW: Like all the bands that attempted a disco record and wound up making fools of themselves. Even the Grateful Dead had a disco record.

RW: It doesn't make any sense. Look at the country business. Somebody gets a style, and they have a hit, and they're made for life. When you're forty years old, you're still a young pup, instead of dead in the water.

I don't know, there's something that you did that made people like you, so why not stick with that? Instead of going, "Well, let's do something completely different now. Here's what's happening in Seattle now, let's try that." By the time you try to do that, it's two years down the road, and six hundred other people are trying to do it. It doesn't make any sense.

This new album's going to be hard to get out to the public. We're having a hard time getting it heard, just to let people know it exists, because if radio won't play it, what are your alternatives? But this Alan Parsons tour is going to get us in front of a lot more of a record buying audience than the corn dog circuit was. And we're hooking up with Bad Company for probably about twenty-five dates in the States, and then we'll take it to Europe next year, and probably Japan, and maybe down into Australia.

SW: That should work out well, because it seems like there would be quite a bit of crossover in the audience demographics.

RW: Well, one of our first tours was with Bad Company. That will be fun. Billy, our bass player, is a neighbor of Mick Ralphs. They both live down in Sarasota. Back when we played together in the early Seventies, there was a lot of competition; we did about forty shows together, and it was two young bands with an attitude. Things are different now. Everybody's a lot older, wiser, mellower. It's just another day, another gig.

SW: At this point, neither one of you has to go out and slay the other one in order to do well.

RW: Yeah. There won't be any upstaging. I can remember when we and Aerosmith were coming up at the same time, we were doing a lot of co-headlining small halls and stuff, and it was a real friendly atmosphere. Everything was just great. And then we played in Kansas City one night, and we were flip-flopping on the headlining slot, and it got fucked up; this was our neck of the woods, but we were going on first.

Well, we were going over too well, so Steven Tyler got pissed off and unplugged us. I mean, me and Glixman and Tyler used to sit around in the dressing room or hotel room and party after the gigs and stuff. Great guy, but all of a sudden, talk about a bunch of guys getting a big head.

When they got big, their heads got big, and then their drug problems got big. And it took those guys a long time to come back. I'm happy for them. They're back and straightened out and have got themselves together again. But we've had our run-ins.

We did a bunch of shows with Queen, and that was great. What a bunch of gentlemen. Brian May is probably about the nicest man you'll ever meet in your life. Roger Taylor sang backup on, oh, what was that song...

SW: That's right, I read somewhere that he had sung with you guys.

RW: It's not listed on the record. He couldn't work, because he didn't have a work permit. He was over in the States, but he didn't have a work permit. That was "Fire With Fire". He's one of the high voices in the background. And David Pack helped us with that record, too, from Ambrosia.

SW: You toured with them as well, didn't you?

RW: We did some shows together. They have an album called *Somewhere I Never Traveled*, their second album, that I can't find anywhere, and I want that album so bad. Alan Parsons produced it, and I asked him the other night if that was available anywhere on CD, and he said no, it probably never will be. But I'm wondering if he's still got the master tapes. If we get friendly enough, if he's got a half-inch master, maybe he could run me off a DAT. I loved that record.

SW: You never know, some of that stuff might wind up coming out somewhere. Some of the more obscure bands are finally coming out on CD. I waited forever for some of Gentle Giant's stuff, and some of it still isn't available, but most of it is.

RW: That's one of my all-time favorite bands.

SW: They were great, weren't they? Now, during the initial successful phase of Kansas, it seems like Steve quit the band several times and came back several times before he finally left for good. What was behind that?

RW: Steve and Kerry were oil and water, yin and yang all the way. Lennon and McCartney. They both wanted to write all the songs, they both wanted all the credit, they both couldn't stand to be edited by the other. Meanwhile, the rest of the band would edit the shit out of both of them. They didn't have a choice. But there was a real battle between them. And what I don't think they will ever admit is that what they've done together far surpasses what they do without each other.

We got Kerry to write a song for this new record, and we're on real friendly terms with Kerry, but he has no aspirations of going back out on the road again. But once in a while you'll mention to Steve, "Why don't you go up and try to write a few songs together?" And Phil has to kind of go up and mediate. It's just like, come on, guys, we're forty-five years old. This isn't eighth grade. Let's drop this crap. But that's just the way it is.

It's not like they don't get along. They bump heads musically, and what they don't realize is, creating great songs, most of the time it's not like a soft summer breeze. It's more like a hot jalapeno shit. It's a painful process. There's a lot of bloodletting and a whole lot of battling, and then when you've got the final product, it's great. There's a lot of fighting in between.

SW: I wanted to talk about the live album *Two For The Show*. The liner notes to the boxed set said there were no overdubs on that. Is that truly the case?

RW: No, I don't think there are any. There might a few spots where there was a quick moment where you just drop out real fast.

Live At The Whisky , too, for me and Phil, that was the night. That was the performance. Billy had one note that he had to go in and go "Bonk!" Dave had a problem with his rig that night, so he had to do a little overdubbing, but not much. There was very little patchwork involved. It's about ninety-eight percent pure.

SW: That's amazing, because those aren't easy pop songs. It showcases the fact that you guys play very tightly. Do you have to rehearse unusually long to achieve that tightness?

RW: Not really, no. We just rehearse about two weeks. This time we took a little longer, but we wound up taking more days off. *(Laughs)*. A lot of the songs that you've played long enough, it just takes a couple of times to do it and you're back. And what it really takes is a crowd in front of you.

SW: So no matter how much you prepare, you won't know how well you're going to play until you get there?

RW: Well, when you're practicing, it's like, okay, "Wayward Son"—ready? No! *(Laughs)*. Talk about a dredge to go through. We don't even do it in rehearsals. It's *painful*. But all of a sudden, live, it's a completely different animal. Because the crowd loves it so much. Anybody really feeds from the crowd. But it doesn't have to be a crowd that's jumping up and down screaming, per se.

We played a real obscure place recently, a real nice performing arts center, and it was an older crowd, and they didn't get out of their chairs. There was no whooping and screaming. You could hear a pin drop. On "Dust In The Wind", we fade it out manually; we just start playing the acoustics softer and softer, and Dave plays softer, until it just goes away. Usually the crowd sound creates enough of a murmur that you can get out easily, but you could hear a pin drop that night.

Afterwards we were talking, and it was like they were a bunch of *us*. That's how I would react to the concert. When I go to a concert, I'm not jumping up and down on my chair screaming; I'm sitting in my seat wishing those fuckers in front of me would sit down! We were playing for a crowd of people that were just like us, and when you realize that, it's a different intensity, because you know they're really listening. And that's even more intense. It's not a bunch of people having a good time no matter what you play, which is fun. These people know the material, they're there to see it, they're watching every move. So it keeps you on your toes.

SW: I wanted to talk a little about the John Elefante years. When Steve quit the band, how did you find John Elefante?

RW: Well, that was tough, because Steve quit on the last day of rehearsals. We were leaving the next day to go record. Of course we had a producer, Ken Scott, already on advance, and the studio booked.

SW: There was no prior indication that he was going to leave?

RW: No. He just stormed out. And it was all over philosophical differences. So we had no choice but to go start recording. We just started recording the material we had, and started auditioning some vocalists in the interim. We did some at the studio, and management was doing some in another studio. Quite a few people came in. Sammy Hagar is one of the people who came in. Ted Neeley, the original guy in *Jesus Christ Superstar*...

SW: You're kidding!

RW: They're back out on the road again with him now.

SW: Him and Dennis DeYoung, of all people.

RW: Oh, yeah, I forgot about Dennis. That's a perfect place for Dennis; he's always had that Broadway style voice.

SW: He sounds amazing in that show. Just astonishing. Better than anything else he has ever done.

RW: Yeah. He's got a great voice, but for rock and roll, I hated it! But it's a tremendous voice. But anyway, John heard about the auditions, and he sent a tape with him singing a bunch of Kansas songs, and also on it was some original material. And we brought him down for the audition, and he looked kinda similar; he was like a cross between Steve Walsh and O.J. Simpson. *(Laughter)*. Very talented kid. He was a good writer and a good singer, and plus we needed to fill the gap and get rolling.

So we did that for a few records, but it didn't really work out. He was too young. He thought we were a bunch of old dinosaurs and we were holding him back.

SW: That seems a little strange, since nobody had ever heard of him prior to his Kansas association.

RW: He had a little demo studio, him and his brother Dino, and they would make their demos with their friends, and then John would take our tapes back and he'd come back to us and say, "Well, I was playing this stuff for Mom, and Mom just doesn't think it's happening." How do you handle that? *(Laughs)*. Me and Phil had to control ourselves from strangling him for three or four years. It was a job, but there were a lot of times when it crossed my mind and crossed Phil's mind, "Why am I still here? Why do I keep putting my face into the fire?" *(Laughter)*.

Just like in the last few years, playing the corn dog circuit, we wondered that sometimes. The purpose was to get where we are now. We're the underdogs, we're back, we're strong, we've finally got a new record out and a damn good one. We're a solid band with unity again; it's all for one and one for all. We don't have that petty junior high bickering anymore. We wanted to at least give it one good last shot, instead of going out suffocating. We wanted to go down swinging.

SW: Do you think this will be the last record, or do you plan to do more?

RW: If we can recoup. That's all we have to do, and then we've got another record deal. And we had a pretty low budget, but still, the problem is if nobody knows it's there…it's really tough to get the buying public. If people come to the show and really like it, that doesn't mean that they're going to run out the next day and buy it.

But these twenty-five dates with Alan Parsons, and then off with Bad Company, that puts us in front of an audience that, instead of being in a bar in front of two thousand drunks that would be there no matter who's playing, it gets us in front of a lot more of a record buying public that is really interested. That's the only way we can sell records; we have to go out there and show them what we've got, because we've sure never been darlings of the press.

SW: Why do you think that is?

RW: When we first started, we kinda were, but it didn't take long before we were the mutt dog that the press just liked to kick. I don't really understand why that is to this very day. We've sold twenty-five or thirty million records, and it's not like we're Barry Manilow or something. I mean, I could understand that!

SW: Well, they hated almost all of the progressive rock bands, so it's not like you're alone.

RW: The only thing I can blame it on, if I try to find a reason, would be the Don Kirshner connection; you know, the Monkee man. From there, and then some of the CBS pressure making us go back in and put one more song on for some sappy love song single or something, because all of a sudden we started getting comparisons to Air Supply.

SW: That has to hurt. *(Laughs).*

RW: You know how some people just don't like asparagus, because when they were eight years old, Mom opened a can of it and it was all squishy and nasty, so they hate it to this day. But they've never gone to a great restaurant where it was picked in Brazil and stalks the size of big pencils, and it's real crunchy with a hollandaise sauce. They just don't like it, and they don't even know why.

There's people that just don't like Kansas, and they won't ever like us. Here's a perfect analogy: a friend of mine, his wife cooked him a carrot cake. She had to work late, and I was over at his house, and he had eaten about half the cake. He thought it was a spice cake. Then she said, "Boy, I didn't know you liked carrot cake so much." And he said, "I *hate* carrot cake." And he wouldn't eat any more of it.

You could play a song for someone, something off the new album, and they might love it. Then you tell them it's a Kansas album and they say, "Oh, God, I *hate* Kansas!" It's a pre-determined bias. It's like, well, I've just decided that I hate brown shoes. It's very close-minded.

SW: Do you think that one reason the press didn't take to Kansas was maybe because the band was very much a unit of musical equals; because there wasn't one person in the band like David Lee Roth or Mick Jagger that they could hang all the publicity on?

RW: But then look at the Eagles. Look at the Doobie Brothers. There's a lot of analogies the other way. So who really knows? Look at *Rolling Stone*. They've always hated us.

SW: Well, it's easy to see their bias. I think they hate everything good.

RW: Fuck them and their magazine. I wouldn't wipe my ass with that rag. I don't want to be liked by that magazine.

SW: It's funny, because *Rolling Stone* has always portrayed themselves as the arbiter of what's good and bad, and so much of the time they're so horribly wrong. I mean, we're talking about a magazine that put Fine Young Cannibals on the cover! It's laughable.

RW: The thing that bugs me is that people consider that as kind of the *Wall Street Journal* of rock and roll. The most prestigious, most informative, closest to the cutting edge, and you couldn't be further from the truth.

SW: As a matter of fact, some of the cheesy rock magazines actually do a better job of reaching the average person...

RW: A *much* better job.

SW: Although with magazines like *Circus* and *Hit Parader*, people don't even want to admit they read it. *(Laughter).* But at least they write the articles for the reader, as opposed to *Rolling Stone*, who write the articles for their own self-gratification and to force their own point of view onto the reader.

RW: On the other side of the coin, we've had some newspaper things, some reviews that were just so embarrassingly good that it was like, whoa, back it down a hair! You know, John Lennon didn't come back from the dead. The Beatles weren't onstage last night. *(Laughs).*

But we've had some that were so scalding! And it's like, what is news? What is a reporter and what is he supposed to do? He reports the news. There's an event; you go to this event, you observe, and you report what happens.

But then you read the review; you know, you've just played for three thousand people that had a ball, to thundering applause, and then stood outside for an hour signing autographs, and then the review the next day is like, "It was the worst concert of the year. These guys suck!"

SW: It's like, "Did you attend this show?"

RW: Well, we did catch one guy. He hated us, and that was his beat, the concert review beat. He didn't want to come to the show, but his roommate had seen us six or eight months earlier, because he was a fan. So his roommate gave him the song list, and then the guy went down the list and butchered us.

And as it turned out, it was a different tour with a different song list. He was bringing up songs that we didn't even play. We got hold of the paper and they had to write a retraction.

SW: How embarrassing. I'm surprised they didn't just get rid of him.

RW: They probably did after that! It doesn't make sense to get so personal. Although I have seen a few reviewers say, "Kansas is not my cup of tea; in fact, I've never liked them. But the crowd seemed to have a great time." I can appreciate that. That's just honesty. Not everybody likes everything.

Still, though, you would never hear Walter Cronkite say, "I don't really care for the French, but in France today…" *(Laughter)*. Why do you have to add your own personal quip? You're a news reporter, not a personality like Johnny Carson. Just tell the fucking news.

SW: You were talking about the John Elefante years and how you didn't feel those albums worked out too well. Was part of the problem with those albums the fact that the band was divided over the lyrical content of the songs?

RW: After *Point Of Know Return*, a lot of things changed. Instead of being a unified band, all of a sudden people were living in different states, and some people had made a whole lot more money than others from songwriting royalties. They started not wanting to play live that much. It was like, "This is my ball; I'll take the ball and go home now."

There were problems ranging from people wanting more time off, to Dave was going deep, deep, deep into drugs. Kerry had become a born-again Christian, and then Dave did. I don't know if you've ever had any friends that were suddenly born-again Christians, but they suddenly want to change everyone around them, too.

That was rough. All of a sudden they wanted us to be this platform for a ministry. Well, that's what we've never wanted to do. That's not what we're about. Inspirational, yes; "Wayward Son" is a very inspirational song.

SW: And even after Kerry and Dave had left the band, you continued to do songs like "The Preacher". *(Sings)* "We've all gotta come to the light together…"

RW: Steve was going to have to sing this stuff, deliver this sermon from the pulpit, and he just couldn't hack it anymore. That really got to be a problem. That's finally when Dave and Kerry wanted to go off and do their own thing. That's when they started the band A.D., and they thought that's what the world was waiting for, was for them to come along and tell them all about Jesus, but you can flip the channel any time of the day or night and hear all about it without paying.

I'm a Christian, but I don't walk around with a sign. Now they've had fifteen years to mellow; see, my sister's always been that way, and when I talked to her about it, she said, "Just give them a few years." You know, it's a personal thing. The unity of the band was gone.

SW: When John Elefante joined the band, was he also a born-again Christian at that point?

RW: Well, Dave and Kerry were still there, and that was one of the main reasons they let him in. But they still had me and Phil and Robby. I mean, Phil Ehart is the straightest guy you will ever meet. He's never drank, smoked, done drugs or anything; he has attended church since he was born. So it's not like they were wanting to sing about things we didn't believe in.

It's just that the messages of certain songs like "Wayward Son" or certain other songs just address the common man questions. People don't want to hear the answer, they want to figure out the answer for themselves. It's one thing to sing a song that makes people say, "You know, I've wondered about that, too, " or "Wow, what a thought." But it's a lot different when all of a sudden someone is saying, "Here's the way it is, you must follow exactly what I'm saying."

SW: In a sense, you're separating yourself from your audience, saying, "I know what's right and wrong, and you don't."

RW: Yes. At that moment was when Kerry lost his touch with lyrics. He was no longer searching. When Kerry was searching, he could really write lyrics. But once he found it, all he could write about was what he had found.

SW: It's not like all the lyrics were no good; I still thought some things like "No One Together" and "Mask Of The Great Deceiver" were great. But too often the songs would address the same points over and over and over. In trying to turn Kansas into Petra, it destroyed the essence of what people related to about Kansas in the first place.

RW: Exactly. Look at "Cold Grey Morning", the song that Kerry wrote for the new album. That's very reminiscent of an old Kansas song. It's very spiritual, bit it's not a diatribe, an "Oh Happy Day" kind of thing. *(Quotes lyrics)* "Reaching upward, sliding downward." It's about the situation of the world. It's very spiritual, but it's commentary. It's not like, "Heed me now ye brothers."

SW: When Kerry and Dave went off to form A.D., I was kind of surprised that John Elefante didn't take part in that.

RW: I don't think he was invited. They had had the same problems with him that we did. He was a young LA kid that wanted to be more hip. He's got a new album out now that I haven't heard, but I've heard it's really good. He's a very talented guy.

SW: I heard part of it and thought it was pretty good. I mean, he started recording it several years ago, and it's very much locked into that glossy Eighties anthemic sound, not unlike a lot of the other artists he has produced along those lines. The single called "No One Ever Died For Me Before" reminds me a little bit of Michael Bolton!

Interestingly enough, though, I read that that Jill Sobule song "I Kissed A Girl" was recorded at the studio he owns, and that since he is primarily associated with Christian music, some people were pretty upset about the whole thing.

RW: Why does everybody have to take everything so damn seriously? Things don't have to be that black and white. Everybody doesn't have to choose up sides. It's like Rodney King, "Why can't we all just get along?" *(Laughter)*.

Coming from a guy that just got the shit kicked out of him, that made a lot of sense. Everybody lighten up a little bit.

I heard on the bus last night that somebody saw this black woman walking around with a Casper T-shirt on with black ghosts, and underneath it said "Not All Ghosts Are White". I mean, lighten up! It's a cartoon! Ragsdale's analogy was, okay, let's get a dog turd and let it sit there and petrify until it was white, and then let's say not all dog shit is black. *(Laughs)*.

I mean, just waking up in the morning and getting through your day is hard enough without having to battle all these points of view. It doesn't have to be that complicated. The politics of everything drives me crazy. I live on a street that's a long block, a dead end. You could blow up the whole world and this would be all that was left, and in a hundred years we'd multiply and there'd be battles and bickering and ten different sides. Put ten people in a room, and you can't get ten people to get along.

Hey, we're not all the same. We're not all alike. We're all created equal, but what you do with it from there is completely different. I'm glad everybody in the world isn't like me. I'd be bored to death. I like the differences.

SW: After everybody in Kansas went their separate ways, it wasn't too long, just three or four years before you got back together.

RW: Well, Steve's band Streets was still going on. The first Streets album got them rolling, did pretty well, but the second one came out and nothing happened, and we had to wait for them to milk the last drop out of it.

Meanwhile we'd been talking with Morse, and the Dregs were breaking up, and he'd always been a fan, and we'd always been fans of him, and he lived in the neighborhood. Plus, we had a record deal, so we called Steve and he said sure. Kerry wasn't there for Walsh to worry about, and me and Steve always worked real well together. We needed a bass player, and Billy was available from Streets, and off we went with that project and made the two albums on MCA.

SW: I was surprised that you didn't have a violin player in the band at that point.

RW: With Morse in the band, he's such a player, God, I don't know where we would have fit it. With two keyboards—and this is when we got into the technology with six keyboards all MIDI'd together—with this mountain of sound, and two guitars, bass, drums...where is a violin going to fit?

And it was an image change, too. Kansas was *that*, and it is now *this*. We thought adding Steve Morse would have more of an impact than it did. I thought the last album we did, *In The Spirit Of Things*, was a great record, but it just never got a chance to be heard. They just shelved that one after Bloody Friday, where they fired everyone at MCA.

SW: How did you come to do *Live At The Whisky*?

RW: After we had done the reunion tour with Kerry and Dave in Germany, we started doing the summer dates. We did some with Kerry and some with

Morse, and then neither one of them were going out, and we had all these offers. Then we had Ragsdale.

Phil is always scheming to do something, and rock videos at the time were a pretty sellable item. So we set that gig up for doing that. That was all done by ourselves, and it was very expensive to do a five or six camera shoot, and to have Le Mobile, which is the best mobile truck in the world, come in and record it.

And all of a sudden the market on rock videos just dumped. It just didn't exist anymore. Nobody picked it up, nobody would sell it for us. So we had this huge overhead, there was debt to pay. Luckily we had also formatted it for selling CDs with it, too.

They printed about five thousand copies of the video, and we wound up just selling it out of the T-shirt booth. And one by one we got rid of them. The CD and cassette were available in record stores, and we finally, as of about now, have cleared the debt. But if it wasn't for the CD, we would have had to dig deep.

If there's not a company that wants to put money in it, it might be a pretty good idea to don't do it. When you put your own neck on the chopping block, it's a scary proposition. That hurt Steve with Streets. He hired everybody and put them on payroll, and it just didn't work; he had to move a family from England, and house everybody, and it didn't take Steve long to lose everything he had made in Kansas. So if nobody's interested in it, it's best not to do it.

SW: I thought it was interesting that the song list on both *Live At The Whisky* and the boxed set focused exclusively on material from the original line-up. You didn't touch on either the John Elefante years or the Steve Morse period.

RW: That was intentional. We were looking forward to this record. We wanted to put old Kansas to bed as far as having people ask me all the time, "Is Kerry gonna be here tonight?" What is this, have you been fuckin' freeze dried? He hasn't been here since 1982! It's been thirteen years! Or "Is Robby coming back?" All that type of thing. That was Kansas then; let's put it to bed. If we added the Elefante era in there, then what about the Steve Morse era? We just wanted to leave it right there, the original Kansas.

SW: And in so doing, you kind of come full circle.

RW: Yeah. We're still struggling; every day is a struggle for people to identify us, this band, as Kansas. It's always like, "Why isn't Robby here?"

I get angry, anymore. Hey, listen, David's here because he *wants* to be. Robby's not here because he *doesn't* want to be here to play for you tonight. He doesn't care if you're here. David cares. He's here. Call Robby and bitch at him for not being here. Don't fucking gripe at me. I'm here because I want to be. Don't get mad at me because some other original members that don't care about playing anymore aren't here. Take it up with them. (*Note: shortly after this interview, Ragsdale departed from Kansas, and Robby Steinhardt returned to his former band*).

SW: What do you think the future will hold for Kansas? Do you have any real idea?

RW: It's like the AA system, one day at a time. Pieces of the puzzle are filling in daily. With this Rock Walk thing and the Greek Theatre, there's going to be a lot of advertisement around that, a big media blitz. Hopefully it will generate interest. You can go gold in Los Angeles alone.

Intersound is going to do some major promotions in major markets. We're playing the Beacon Theatre in New York. We'll just try to recoup so we can get to another record. It's a slow, struggling process, but we're about where we thought we'd be. We're rebuilding again.

It's like a baseball team that won the pennant fifteen years ago, and all of a sudden in the last five years has got a new, young line-up, and is starting to get into contention again. We're ready for it. *(Laughs)*. We're just waiting for everybody else to hear it.

Plus there's the South American market that we've never tapped, and we've never aggressively worked Europe. Intersound has sold us to a label over there now. This last trip in Germany was so successful, there's such a good fan base in Europe. We're very cult over there, because we've hardly ever been there. If we could get a real good blitz, if the distributor over there gets off their butt and makes an event out of the new record, I think we could be like Toto. They're huge in Europe. When's the last time you heard a Toto record here?

SW: I knew there was one out a couple of years ago, but I didn't get to hear it, because it didn't get played here.

RW: Exactly. They are giants in Europe. *Giants*. We've always been narrow sighted, like a horse with blinders, like our boundaries were the Atlantic and the Pacific. The musical atmosphere over there right now is really ripe for what we're doing. That's what I'm hoping, that we can bust Europe wide open. If the press doesn't like us here, fuck them. I'll gladly tour six months a year in Europe.

SW: You know, it's not impossible that the press here might still change their minds. Sometimes if an older band is willing to prove that it can come back and do the hard work and not just expect instant success because of the name recognition, the press will turn around and give them some respect, even if it's somewhat grudgingly.

RW: They think, 'We kicked them and kicked them, and they wouldn't die.' *(Laughs)*. 'Look at the stamina these guys have.' Who knows? When I was approaching thirty, I never thought I'd be thirty and still doing this. Forty, no way! Now I'm forty-five, and I'm pretty sure I'll be doing it when I'm fifty. It's the first time I've ever been sure of anything! *(Laughs)*.

If we work this album through April, take a little time off and start on a new record, by the time the tour for that is over it will be 1999, and I've *gotta* play a Kansas show at the turn of the century! *(Laughs)*.

For more information about Richard Williams, please visit
www.kansasband.com

ABOUT THE AUTHOR

Sterling C. Whitaker is a Nashville-based writer and musician. Born in Texas in 1969, he lived in Minnesota before moving to Atlanta in 1983, where he remained for thirteen years. He has called Music City home since 1996.

Whitaker wrote his first full-length novel at the age of thirteen. *The Warlord* was a swords-and-sorcery fantasy novel in the vein of Tolkien, one of the author's earliest influences. "I found the handwritten manuscript last time I moved," he states. "It was terrible!"

Starting on trumpet in the sixth grade, Whitaker switched to guitar three years later. Taking an interest in the British progressive rock of bands like Yes and King Crimson, he performed with the Atlanta-based prog band Roots of Consciousness before switching gears to write about music. Whitaker has interviewed such luminaries as Yes guitarist Steve Howe, Styx' Tommy Shaw, and Candlebox singer Kevin Martin. His work as a freelance writer has appeared in magazines such as *Southern Vibes, Creative Loafing* and *Billboard.* He also served as Director of Publicity for Michael Malott Films in Atlanta.

Currently Whitaker performs as one-half of the acoustic rock duo Beggarz Opera, which released its debut album, *The Hits Just Keep On Coming,* through MP3.com in 2002 (www.mp3.com/beggarzopera). In addition to performing with Beggarz Opera, Whitaker lends his voice and guitar skills to various sessions in Nashville's busy studio scene.

With the release of *Unsung Heroes of Rock Guitar,* Whitaker has realized his ambition to fuse his two main passions; music and writing. He is hard at work on his second book, a biography of the rock group Styx tentatively titled *The Grand Delusion.* He also plans a sequel to *Unsung Heroes of Rock Guitar.* His long-range plans include developing and producing a screenplay, writing a Top Ten hit for another artist, and scoring a hit record with Beggarz Opera. "And from there," he says, "world domination!"

Sterling Whitaker lives in Nashville with his longtime girlfriend, two dogs, and four cats, as well as three grandchildren on certain weekends. A self-confessed "total nerd", his main hobby is collecting Casper memorabilia.

For more information please visit
www.sterlingwhitaker.com

CPSIA information can be obtained at www.ICGtesting.com
Printed in the USA
BVOW11s0643050915

416575BV00016B/383/P